THINGS COOKS LOVE

Dedicated to the Sur La Table staff who embody the art and soul of cooking, and have created a 35-year legacy of knowledgeable and passionate service.

THINGS
COOKS LOVE

Sur La Table with Marie Simmons

PHOTOGRAPHY BY Ben Fink

Andrews McMeel
Publishing, LLC

Kansas City

08 09 10 11 12 SDB 10 9 8 7 6 5 4 3 2 1

Library of Congress Cataloging-in-Publication Data
Things cooks love : implements, ingredients, and recipes / Sur La Table,
with Marie Simmons.
     p. cm.
  ISBN-13: 978-0-7407-6976-4
  ISBN-10: 0-7407-6976-6
 1. Kitchen utensils. 2. Cookware. 3. Cookery, International. I.
Simmons, Marie. II. Sur La Table (Firm)
  TX656.T44 2008
  683'.82—dc22

2007036246

The Things Cooks Love brand books are brought to you by Sur La Table, Inc., and Things Cooks Love
is a trademark belonging to Sur La Table, Inc., of Seattle.

www.andrewsmcmeel.com
www.surlatable.com

Design: Vertigo Design NYC
Food Stylists: Jaime Kimm, Alison Attenborough
Prop Stylist: Sharon Ryan

ATTENTION: SCHOOLS AND BUSINESSES
Andrews McMeel books are available at quantity discounts with bulk purchase for educational,
business, or sales promotional use. For information, please write to: Special Sales Department,
Andrews McMeel Publishing, LLC, 4520 Main Street, Kansas City, Missouri 64111.

Contents

Foreword

A wonderful if quiet culinary revolution began on the West Coast in the 1970s: Alice Waters founded the acclaimed Chez Panisse restaurant in Berkeley; Ruth Reichl, currently editor in chief of *Gourmet* magazine, began her food writing career in California; and in Seattle, Shirley Collins followed her dream and opened a store called Sur La Table in the Pike Place Farmers' Market.

Nestled in a tiny space that once held a speakeasy and barbershop, Sur La Table was packed to the rafters with tools for every cooking task imaginable. News about the store quickly spread and it soon became a gathering place for local chefs and foodies, with customers traveling from as far away as Florida and Mexico to visit the little store with the big reputation. Shirley introduced customers to Julia Child, a regular visitor to the store, who was just one of the many chefs and authors who came to the store for cooking demonstrations and book signings; the *New York Times* called Sur La Table "the closest thing we have to a culinary salon."

Although Shirley sold the company in 1995, her lifelong passion for quality tools and fresh seasonal foods set the standard for excellence that continues today. We see her heritage in our dedicated employees, many of them serious cooks themselves, who share their enormous knowledge about a wealth of products and foods; in our buyers who travel the world seeking innovative and authentic tools from small artisanal businesses; and in our chefs who share their expertise and their love of cooking in our well-respected cooking class program.

"Educate and inspire." That was the vision of Renée Behnke, one of Sur La Table's owners, when she created the company's first cooking class program in 1996. Renée felt that the company should provide a place for all ages and all skill levels to learn professional tips and techniques in a relaxed and fun environment. The program has continued to grow and is now one of the largest avocational cooking programs in the United States. We've shown our customers, from young children to retirees, how to chop, dice, julienne, sauté, braise, deglaze, fold, and even hone and sharpen their own knives.

To walk into a Sur La Table store is to enter a haven for cooks, where questions can be answered about unusual and everyday products and recipes can be discussed with kindred spirits. Stop and listen to the lively conversations: Do you have fish tweezers? A *mezzaluna*? A tapered icing spatula? A cake comb? I don't know how to use my mandoline, can you show me? Who could have imagined this forty years ago?

For more than three decades, Sur La Table's culinary expertise has been called upon on a daily basis, and it's from this rich heritage that we, along with writer Marie Simmons, have created *Things Cooks Love: Implements, Ingredients, Recipes*, this wonderful book packed full of essential information. Not only will it show you how to properly use your kitchen tools but also how to maximize their use with an enticing collection of simple yet delicious international recipes. *Things Cooks Love* is the first in a series of cookbooks we'll be introducing in the coming years, sharing our expertise and passion for cooking to all the cooks—and future cooks—who inspire us every day. At Sur La Table, too many cooks in the kitchen only make the broth better.

May your days be filled with seasonal fresh foods and your kitchen stocked with the essentials to prepare the foods you love for the people you cherish.

KATHY TIERNEY
CEO, Sur La Table

Introduction

No matter how grand or how humble, the kitchen is where everyone gathers, and where countless memories are made. The room itself and the variety of essential equipment it holds have changed dramatically in the past several decades. Since 1972, the Sur La Table product selection has been responding to these evolving kitchen needs, inspiring passion and curiosity in its loyal clientele every step of the way. During this time, our customers have asked questions about how to use both our basic and our more exotic utensils and have encouraged us to stock products they have encountered on their culinary journeys. This book is the culmination of years of responding to those needs. We know that to feed both body and soul you must cook surrounded by your favorite tools and ingredients. *Things Cooks Love: Implements, Ingredients, Recipes* was inspired by that knowledge and by the ever-expanding enthusiasm for the pleasures of cooking and eating, the increasing popularity of global cuisines, and the growing ease with which home cooks can add new foods, cookware, tools, and recipes to their kitchen repertoire.

Having the right ingredients and tools for a specific job makes cooking easier and more fun, and the results often taste better. You can, of course, slice potatoes with a knife for a gratin or *pommes Anna*, but only a razor-sharp mandoline can achieve those perfect, paper-thin slices that make the dish a pleasure to prepare and to eat. Or, you can buy dried pasta of every kind at most grocery stores, but none compares in taste or texture to the fresh pasta you can make at home with a pasta machine. Because the tools you love are the foundation of good cooking, *Things Cooks Love* begins with "Essential Cookware and Tools." In this first part, we take you on a journey through the heart of your kitchen and then into the global kitchen beyond.

Chapter 1, "The Basic Kitchen," lists all of the essential implements for everyday cooking. It is both an easy reference for setting up a new kitchen and a convenient checklist for when it's time to add new items. The chapter is divided into four categories: cookware, knives, tools, and small appliances, with over one hundred pieces of cookware listed in easy-to-reference alphabetical order. Here you'll find answers to many of your most frequently asked questions: How many skillets do I need? Does a food mill do more than puree tomatoes? Should I buy stainless steel or copper? What is a rasp grater? From braisers to saucepans, paring knives to peelers, colanders to whisks, blenders to toasters, each item is described in just enough detail to assist you in making an informed decision when you shop for basic cookware.

"The Well-Stocked Global Kitchen" is the ultimate wish list for the avid cook who wants to go beyond the basic kitchen. The description of each implement includes answers to more of your questions: Will my metal fondue pot work for meat, cheese, or chocolate fondue? Is there a substitute for a Moroccan *bisteeya* pan? How do I use a raclette grill to serve the foods that traditionally accompany this alpine dish? Here you will find many ethnic cookware classics, such as the small, woklike Indian *karahi*; the giant, clamshell–shaped Portuguese *cataplana*; and the tepee-lidded Moroccan *tagine*.

Once you've explored the essentials, it's time to put them to use in part II, "Cooking with Kitchen Essentials," which showcases more than twenty-five items described in chapters 1 and 2. You'll learn more about how to select them, tips for their use, how to care for them, and what you can substitute if you don't have them. The recipes are categorized by cookware or tool within each chapter and are also referenced by type in the index. In other words, if you've just purchased a mandoline and are wondering what you can make with it, you can search for recipes in the mandoline section or look them up in the traditional way, under such subheads as "salads" or "pasta."

Chapter 3, "On the Stove and in the Oven," focuses on the "big stuff" in your kitchen: baking dishes, roasting pans, skillets, sauté pans, Dutch ovens, and stockpots are among the seventeen pieces profiled. Each includes notes on dimensions, capacities, materials, features, colors, and styles. Did you know that two sturdy, looped handles on a roasting pan are a must for moving it safely in and out of a hot oven? Or that when purchasing a large, heavy pot or skillet, you should look for one with an opposing helper handle to lessen the strain of lifting it? All of the information you need to confidently select the best, most durable cookware for your kitchen is right here.

Because every piece of cookware has multiple uses, there are "Tips for Using" that detail the cookware's versatility and practicality. For instance, the braiser used to cook foods slowly on the stove top and in the oven can double as a sauté pan or a baking dish. The Dutch oven, perfect for cooking beans and stews slowly, is just as handy for boiling vegetables or simmering a soup. The double boiler used for making delicate egg-based sauces works equally well for cooking polenta without having to stir it constantly, or for heating up leftovers without fear of them sticking to the pan bottom. The handsome fish poacher is also practical for cooking corn on the cob or asparagus spears. A wealth of handy tips such as these will guarantee that you use all of your cookware often.

To help you ensure that your cookware lasts a lifetime and always produces first-rate results, each equipment description covers "Care in Using," with helpful advice on everything from how to season a pan and dishwasher safety to how to loosen stubborn baked-on particles.

Because you won't have on hand every type of specialized cookware, each entry also includes "Alternatives" that allow you to cook the accompanying recipes using a different vessel.

The appealing recipes paired with each piece of cookware showcase its versatility and practicality. For example, the traditional Creamy Polenta with Two Cheeses and the contemporary Orange–Chipotle Chile Hollandaise, recipes that initially appear to be worlds apart, are both made in a double boiler. Or, a baked dish of corn bread with mozarella and sun-dried tomatoes and a classic hamburger gussied up with Stilton cheese and caramelized onions illustrate how a cast-iron skillet works well for two very different recipes.

The recipes are designed to accommodate every skill level and to incorporate a variety of cookware. To make them particularly reader friendly, they include preparation times, step-by-step instructions, and an Implement section that lists not only the featured cookware, but also items from "The Basic Kitchen" and "The Well-Stocked Global Kitchen" used in preparing the dish (though not the tools needed for prepping the recipe ingredients). However, don't think you can't make a specific recipe if you don't have one of the tools listed, as alternatives are included for almost every piece of equipment.

Chapter 4 is dedicated to the cook's best friends, "Handheld Tools." These are the implements you use to stir, puree, whisk, slice, pound, grate, and beat. You'll be amazed by the many creative ways these simple tools can be put to use in your kitchen. As in the previous chapter, each one is profiled in detail, including function, size, and variations in design, material, and color. The "Tips for Using" reveal their remarkable versatility. For example, the chef's torch is more than just a tool for caramelizing sugar on top of a crème brûlée. It will also heat slices of goat cheese for a beautiful beet salad or melt and brown cheese on top of roasted tomatoes and asparagus. The potato ricer makes featherlight pureed potatoes and does a stellar job of pressing excess moisture from cooked spinach. The utilitarian meat pounder is indispensable for flattening chicken breasts into thin cutlets and for crushing a handful of walnuts.

The description of each handheld tool is followed by two recipes illustrating its versatility. Once you've made— and tasted—Green Bean, Tomato, and Potato Salad with Almond and Basil Pesto, Panko-Crusted Chicken Cutlets with Arugula Salad, and Zucchini and Crescenza Gratin with Mint, you'll regard the time-honored mortar and pestle, meat pounder, mandoline, and grater with newfound respect.

Part III, "Globe-Trotting Kitchen Essentials," serves up some of the world's most intriguing tables. Its seven chapters take you into the kitchens of China, Japan, Mexico, France, India, Italy, Spain, Portugal, and Morocco, all of which have prompted many questions from Sur La Table customers. Why does a Moroccan *tagine* have a pointed lid? Should I use a round- or flat-bottomed wok? What's the difference between a Mexican *molcajete*, a French mortar, and a Japanese *suribachi*? When should I use a French *chinois*? How do Indian cooks use the *karahi* and the *tawa*? The answers to these and other global cooking questions fill the final chapters of the book.

Much of the cookware in these chapters reflects the longstanding resourcefulness of the countries' cooks, with many of the entries documenting the historical origin of the items. Keeping with the earlier format, each piece of equipment is described in detail, followed by "Tips for Using," "Care in Using," and "Alternatives." Recipes that bring the flavors of the world into your home accompany every entry.

The recipes, a mix of authentic and innovative, illustrate the versatility of the featured cookware. Classic Chinese Shrimp and Pork Dumplings are cooked traditionally, in a bamboo steamer, while a Japanese *suribachi* is used to make the dressing for a contemporary Avocado, Persimmon, and Butter Lettuce Salad. A stove-top pepper roaster is used to char chiles for *rajas* in one recipe, and to melt the cheese and heat the fruit in a modern quesadilla in another. A French crepe pan is ideal for making both buckwheat crepes from Brittany and *crespelle* (thin semolina pancakes) from Italy.

In addition, each global chapter includes a "Pantry," a glossary of ingredients—once hard to find but now widely available in supermarkets and specialty shops—specific to the country. Are you curious about Japanese wasabi or Mexican epazote? Do you want to learn more about Moroccan couscous or the various types of Asian soy sauce? The "Pantry" pages make the exotic more accessible, with information on buying, storing, substitutions, and uses.

Throughout *Things Cooks Love*, you'll find other helpful features to make cooking easier, including boxed information on such kitchen essentials as herbs, vinegars, rice, and nuts. And to help you locate any ingredients you need that are unavailable in your local stores, there is a convenient "Shopping Sources" section with all the necessary contact information. To make your time in the kitchen more efficient and more pleasurable, helpful "Tips and Techniques" accompany many recipes. This is where you'll discover how to quickly peel tomatoes or peaches or the most convenient way to make fresh bread crumbs and clarify butter. You'll also find inspiring quotes from your favorite cookbook authors and food experts sprinkled throughout the recipe chapters.

Things Cooks Love is for everyone who has not only a passion and enthusiasm for all things culinary, but also a healthy sense of adventure. And just as your kitchen equipment can last a lifetime, this book will serve you well time and again as you continue to expand both your recipe repertoire and your cookware collection.

PART I

ESSENTIAL COOKWARE and TOOLS

1 | The BASIC KITCHEN

The consensus among cooks is that the dividing line between having fun and not having fun in the kitchen is whether you have the most suitable tool for the job. *Things Cooks Love: Implements, Ingredients, Recipes* begins with a comprehensive list of basic cookware and tools.

For easy use, the list is divided into four subcategories: cookware, knives, tools, and small appliances. Entries are arranged alphabetically within each subcategory, and each comes with a brief yet informative description, including colors, materials, sizes, and uses. Not a checklist of must-haves, it is a list of suggestions that can make cooking easier.

Use the list in one of two ways: as an easy reference for setting up and equipping your kitchen or as a checklist of the latest cookware when it's time to add a few new tools to your repertoire. With this information at your fingertips, you can make well-informed decisions as you select new items for your kitchen—or simply learn more about what you already have at home.

Once you're familiar with the cookware and tools, you can put them to good use with the delicious recipes that follow in parts II and III.

Cookware

Baking Dish

For maximum flexibility in your cooking, every kitchen needs an assortment of baking dishes in a wide range of materials, styles, shapes, and designs. The classic is the shallow, rectangular glass baking dish, which comes in standard inch sizes and volumes. Other materials include beautifully crafted earthenware, stoneware, glazed terra cotta, sturdy enameled cast iron, and brightly colored and stark white porcelain. Highly versatile, the baking dish can be used for a wide variety of recipes, from roasted fish to baked macaroni. The more handsome designs perform double duty as serving dishes. (See page 37 for more details.)

Braiser

This multiuse round, shallow, two-handled stovetop-to-oven pan has a domed lid that keeps braised foods moist throughout cooking. Without the lid, it can be used in the oven as a baker or as a sauté pan. It is made from a variety of materials, some attractive enough to use for serving. (See page 41 for more details.)

Double Boiler

A double boiler is made up of two separate parts: the bottom is a standard saucepan and the top is an insert with a base that nests in the top of the lower pan. Water kept hot in the lower pan will warm and/or slowly cook food in the insert. Double boilers are used for making custards and other easily curdled egg-based sauces, and for gently cooking foods or reheating leftovers without fear of scorching. (See page 55 for more details.)

Dutch Oven or 5- to 8-quart stove-top to oven casserole

Traditionally, a Dutch oven is a heavy cast-iron pot with a flat bottom, high sides, opposing looped handles, and a tight-fitting lid. Other pots with this shape but made from other materials are also called Dutch ovens, and like the original cast-iron version, can be used on the stove top, in the oven, or a combination of the two. The Dutch oven is prized for its ability to retain heat, and thus keep food warm, after it has been removed from the oven. Every kitchen needs at least two Dutch ovens, a smaller 5- to 6-quart pot and a larger 7- to 8-quart size. (See page 59 for more details.)

Rimmed Sheet Pan

These large, rectangular rimmed metal pans are also called jelly-roll pans or half sheet pans and come in a variety of sizes. Select heavyweight pans suitable for everything from baking cookies to roasting potatoes, with dozens of uses in between. (See page 72 for more details.)

Roasting Pan

Select one of two basic sizes, medium or large, depending on your needs. Roasting pans come with and without a nonstick finish, and many are sold with a matching rack. For easy cleanup, opt for the pan with the rack that has a nonstick finish. Make sure the pan has sturdy, rigid handles that are roomy enough to accommodate mitted hands. (See page 75 for more details.)

Saucepan and Saucier

Two saucepans, one small (1½ to 2½ quarts) and one larger (3 to 4 quarts), are kitchen essentials, used for boiling potatoes, making soups, and more. The shallower, broader saucier is also a versatile pan to have hand. Both come with a tight-fitting lid and should have a comfortable, sturdy handle. (See page 79 for more details.)

Skillet

Skillets, also known as frying pans, are shallow, with gently flared sides, and come in a variety of sizes and materials. Those with aluminum or copper cores conduct heat faster and more evenly than those without. A small nonstick skillet (8 inches), also called an omelet pan, and a medium nonstick skillet (10 inches) are handy for cooking eggs any style or sautéing vegetables over moderate heat. A large skillet (12 inches), made from stainless steel or anodized aluminum, is useful for cooking fish, steaks, and chops. For cooking over high heat, select a 10-inch cast-iron skillet. (See page 47 for more details.) A skillet is sometimes mistakenly called a sauté pan, though the latter is traditionally deeper and has straight sides. (See page 83 for more details.)

Stockpot

The tall, narrow stockpot, most commonly available in stainless steel and aluminum, can be used for more than making the occasional stock or broth. For example, the 8-quart size is convenient for cooking soups, pasta, or chili for a crowd. Make sure any stockpot you choose is light enough for you to lift when it is full. The matching lid is typically flat and tight fitting. (See page 95 for more details.) There are also stainless-steel steamer inserts and pasta inserts sold separately that will fit an 8-quart stockpot.

A Guide to Popular Metals Used for Cookware

Copper

DESCRIPTION

Copper is an excellent heat conductor, transferring it rapidly and evenly throughout any pan, and it cools rapidly once it is off the heat. It is a reactive metal, which means that most foods (exceptions are high-sugar foods and egg whites; see "Use" below) should not come in direct contact with it. Copper pans are typically lined with tin or stainless steel. Tin is soft and scratches easily, whereas stainless steel is highly durable, making it the choice of many chefs.

CARE

Some copper pans are treated with a clear lacquer finish to protect them during shipping and display. To remove it, rub the pan with a soft cloth dipped in acetone (available in beauty-supply stores). Or, immerse the pan in a large pot of boiling water to which a tablespoon of baking soda has been added. The coating will loosen and peel away easily.

Tin-lined copper cookware must be handled carefully because it is subject to scratching, plus it will wear away over time. The tin lining can be replaced professionally, or you can do it yourself with a home kit. Tin melts at temperatures above 450°F, so never use tin-lined copper over high heat. In contrast, stainless steel–lined copperware is scratch resistant, nonreactive, can handle high temperatures, and is relatively easy to maintain.

CLEANING

Copper may discolor or oxidize in moist air, forming a green patina called verdigris. Clean copper by rubbing it with a mixture of equal parts salt and flour to which enough lemon juice or white vinegar has been added to make a paste, or by dipping the cut side of a lemon in coarse salt and rubbing it into the copper. Dry immediately to prevent streaking. Decorative or delicate pieces should be cleaned with a soft cloth and commercial copper polish to avoid scratching. Stainless-steel or tin-lined copper and unlined copper can be similarly cleaned.

USE

Use unlined copper pans and bowls with nonreactive foods such as egg whites or high-sugar mixtures such as jams and jelly. Stainless steel-lined copper is a good choice for sauté pans, baking dishes, gratins, saucepans, fondue pots, and fish poachers.

Cast Iron

DESCRIPTION

Cast iron heats more slowly than many materials, but it heats evenly to a high temperature and stays hot for a long time. Cast-iron cookware can be used on the stove top, in the oven, on a grill, or under a broiler. A porous metal that will absorb fats and flavors, it is often coated with enamel (enameled cast iron is a favorite material for Dutch ovens), which makes it both nonreactive and easier to maintain.

CARE

Because new cast iron is dry and brittle, it must be seasoned. To season, coat the entire pan lightly with canola oil, peanut oil, or another vegetable oil with a high smoking point. Invert the pan on foil or a baking sheet to catch any oil drips and bake in a 350°F oven for 1 hour. Let cool in the oven, and then rub off the excess oil. Repeat the seasoning often between uses to maintain the seasoned patina. Cast-iron pans that are seasoned frequently develop a natural nonstick coating that keeps food from sticking.

Cast iron is heavy but brittle, which means it can break if dropped on a hard surface. And although it can be heated to high temperatures, it may crack if subjected to rapid changes in temperature. For example, avoid pouring cold water into a hot pan.

Store cast-iron cookware in a dry place. If stacking pans for long storage, slip paper towels between them to combat moisture. Also, moisture in the iron may rise naturally to the surface and form rust. To prevent rusting, place cast-iron cookware on a low burner or in a warm oven for a few minutes after washing and drying.

CLEANING

To clean a seasoned cast-iron pan without removing the seasoning, sprinkle it generously with coarse salt and rub clean with wadded-up paper towels. The use of soap and water is not recommended, but if you must use them, make sure to immediately reseason the pan. Rubbing with scouring pads or cleaning compounds will also damage the seasoning. Cast iron should never be placed in a dishwasher.

USE

Cast iron can be used for high-temperature cooking, such as frying hamburgers, searing shrimp or meat, or deep-frying. Because cast iron holds and maintains temperatures evenly it is popular for stove-top baking and broiling. It will also keep food hot until serving time. Cast iron reacts with acidic ingredients, such as tomatoes, wine, or vinegar, which can sometimes change the color of food or give it an off flavor.

Blue Steel and Carbon Steel

DESCRIPTION

Steel is a favorite material for woks and skillets because it is thin, light, quickly heats to a high temperature, and cools down quickly when removed from direct heat. Blue steel is carbon steel that has been heat treated. The blue color is a result of this treatment and helps the pan resist oxidation.

CARE

Some steel pans come with a lacquer finish that must be eliminated before the pan can be used. To remove it, rub it with soft cloth dipped in acetone (available in beauty-supply stores). Pans without a lacquer coating have probably been oiled to prevent rusting before sale. Wash them with soap and warm water, and dry thoroughly.

Both blue or carbon steel should be seasoned. Follow the directions for seasoning cast iron (left).

Steel is prone to rusting. To prevent this, dry thoroughly after washing, then place on a low burner or in a warm (300°F) oven for a few minutes. Finally, rub lightly with a paper towel dampened with canola oil, peanut oil, or other vegetable oil before storing in a dry place.

CLEANING

Do not place steel cookware in a dishwasher. Hand wash blue or carbon steel pans in warm, soapy water. Avoid abrasive cleaning solutions and pads. Wipe the pan with a dry paper towel to remove all traces of surface oil. If soap and water are used, the pan will need to be reseasoned.

USE

Avoid cooking acidic foods in steel pans (see cast iron, page 7). However, with enameled steel this isn't a problem. Because steel is light, thin, and heats quickly, some chefs prefer it for sautéing and for making omelets and crepes. Tarts and other baked goods cooked in blue steel brown more than when baked in shinier metals.

Stainless Steel and Variations

DESCRIPTION

Stainless steel is a poor conductor of heat, which is why it is almost always paired with good conductors, such as copper or aluminum. Either combination is widely used for saucepans, skillets, and Dutch ovens.

CARE

Stainless steel is nonporous, generally won't pit, is nonreactive, is durable, won't dent or crack, is scratch resistant, and is dishwasher safe.

Overheating will cause blue blotches to appear on the surface of the pan. Once a stainless-steel pan is heat damaged, it is almost impossible to remove the discoloration. However, such blotches do not effect the performance of the pan, only its appearance.

CLEANING

Although stainless steel is dishwasher safe, warm, soapy water will often do the job. If necessary, stainless-steel pots and pans can be scrubbed with a stiff brush, fine-mesh scrubber, and/or mild scouring powder.

USE

Pure stainless steel can be used for roasting pans, steamer inserts, colanders, bowls, handheld tools, and flatware. Heavy-gauge stainless-steel roasting pans are preferable for use over direct heat, such as when making gravy.

Anodized or Treated Aluminum with Variations

DESCRIPTION

Aluminum is an excellent conductor of heat, but it reacts less negatively to common cooking ingredients such as salt, all acids, and eggs, and has a tendency to impart a metallic taste. For this reason, pure aluminum pans are not recommended. But aluminum combined with other nonreactive metals (see "Stainless Steel and Variations," left) or anodized produces an excellent cookware material.

Anodized aluminum is aluminum that has been treated to an electrolytic process that makes the surface dark gray, smooth, hard, resistant to corrosion, and nonreactive.

CARE

Anodized aluminum or aluminum combined with other metals is durable and requires no special care.

CLEANING

Putting anodized aluminum pans in the dishwasher will ruin their surface. Wash with warm, soapy water and scrub with a stiff brush or scouring pad. Mild abrasives can be used on baked-on particles without fear of scratching.

USE

Everything from sauté pans and Dutch ovens to roasting pans, stockpots, and more are made of aluminum. Just be sure to avoid cooking reactive foods in pure aluminum pans.

Nonstick

DESCRIPTION

There are a number of excellent nonstick coatings on the market, used on a variety of cookware materials. Nonstick aluminum cookware is a good, inexpensive choice for two reasons: aluminum is a good heat conductor and the nonstick surface solves the problem of aluminum's being a reactive metal. A nonstick finish on stainless steel–clad copper and/or aluminum is another excellent option.

CARE

Nonstick is more durable now than it was when it was first introduced, but using only wooden, silicone, or other nonmetal utensils with it will lengthen the life of your cookware. In time, however, the nonstick surface may scratch or become thin and you'll need to replace the pan.

Do not place nonstick cookware in a dishwasher because the strong detergents can damage the finish. Instead, scrub it with a stiff brush and warm, soapy water.

Use nonstick cookware for sautéing over medium or medium-low heat. Nonstick surfaces are particularly good for cooking eggs, omelets, and pancakes, and for general low-fat cooking. They won't leave browned bits in the pan as cast iron or stainless steel will, however, which makes them less desirable when pan sauces and gravies are on the menu.

Knives

Knives are among the most important tools in your kitchen. Knife blades are made from a wide range of metals. Pure carbon steel blades keep the sharpest edge, but because carbon steel will discolor and rust without special care, most of the knives available today are made from high-carbon stainless steel alloys that will keep a sharp edge well and will not discolor or rust. The exact blend of metals in these alloys will vary from manufacturer to manufacturer.

When well cared for, knives will last a lifetime. Here are some important rules for knife care:

- Never wash knives in a dishwasher.

- Never allow knives to sit in a sink where the blade may get damaged by other utensils.

- Promptly after use, rinse knives with warm water, wipe with a soapy sponge or stiff brush, dry, and put safely away.

- Keep knife blades sharp by running them along a sharpening steel (page 10) often, preferably before or after each use.

Bread Knife

A bread knife has a long, rectangular blade with a serrated or scalloped edge. The edge ensures a clean cut down through the crust and into the soft center without crushing the slice. Look for a knife 8 inches long that feels neither too heavy nor too light in your hand.

Chef's Knife

A chef's knife is one of the most frequently used knives in the kitchen. There are two broad categories, French style and Japanese santuko style. The French knife has an 8- to 10-inch-long, broad blade that narrows to a fine edge along the bottom and gently curves to a point. This profile accommodates the rocking motion of chopping. The Japanese santuko knife has a straighter, slightly shorter blade that rounds down from the top and comes to a fine point nearer the cutting surface. The blade, which is more delicate than the French blade, best accommodates an up-and-down chopping motion.

The handle design of any knife is important, but this is especially true for the chef's knife, which is most commonly used for chopping, a highly repetitive and often extended motion. Try out a knife before you decide to buy it. Hold it in your hand to judge its weight and comfort. How does it feel when you simulate chopping? Do your knuckles clear the surface of the cutting board? Is it too heavy or too light? The variables are extensive, and not every knife fits comfortably in every hand. A good chef's knife will last a lifetime.

Kitchen Scissors

Heavy-duty stainless-steel scissors that are comfortable to use and fully washable are invaluable in the kitchen. Use them to snip herbs, open a bag of chips, cut up a chicken, or simply clip a recipe. There are specially designed scissors (or shears) for dismembering poultry, but a pair of well-made, sharp, sturdy all-purpose scissors can also be used.

Paring Knife

The paring knife is the most commonly used knife in the kitchen. The two most popular choices are the 3- to 4-inch straight-bladed paring knife and the shorter (2 to 3 inches) curved blade model, called the bird's beak paring knife. Owning one of each is ideal but, if you have to make a choice, choose the straight-bladed knife and always keep it sharp. It is handy for trimming vegetables and cutting up fruit, and can also be used to cut down on a cutting board. The bird's beak blade is good for digging out the stems from strawberries, peeling an apple, or coring a tomato.

Utility Knife

Similar to a paring knife, a utility knife has a longer curved blade (usually 5 to 6 inches) that comes in handy for cutting a sandwich in half, slicing a pear or apple, cutting up a small onion, or cutting off chunks of carrot. In other words, it is the ideal knife for the medium-sized job in your kitchen, and like the chef's knife, it will get lots of use.

Knife Block, Magnet, and Guard

Knives crowded into a drawer can result in cut fingers or nicked or dulled blades. There are a number of choices for sound storage. A vertical wooden block that sits on the countertop and accommodates a dozen or more knives, plus kitchen scissors and a sharpening steel, is one option. Wall-mounted magnetic holders are convenient for a few paring knives and, if strong enough, a small chef's knife. (Test the magnet's strength in the store.) In-drawer magnetic strips anchor knives, prevent-

ing them from hitting one another when the drawer is opened and closed. A shallow in-drawer wooden block is another good way to hold knives out of harm's way. Finally, individual knife guards are sturdy plastic sleeves that slip over the blade to protect the edge.

Sharpening Steel

Because dull knives are both inefficient to use and more likely to produce a painful cut finger, keeping your knives razor sharp is highly recommended. A sharpening steel made of high-carbon steel is the classic sharpening tool. Steels are round, oval, or flat metal rods, and a countertop or drawer knife-storage unit sometimes has a slot to accommodate one. To use the steel, hold it in one hand (a good steel has a handle designed for comfort), hold the knife at a 20 to 30 percent angle to the steel in the other hand, and then sweep the edge of the knife across and along the length of the steel two or three times. To keep a knife sharp, make it a habit to sharpen it briefly before each use.

Other types of sharpeners include a sharpening stone, which is used like a steel but sits flat on a countertop, rather than being handheld. Another model mounts the steel inside a top-slotted plastic casing that sits on a countertop. The knife blade is pulled through the slot, where it makes contact with the blade. Both manual and electric models of this type are available. The stationary countertop sharpening devices are especially convenient if you are not adept at using a handheld steel.

Tools

Brush

Brushes with natural boar or soft nylon bristles are ideal for coating pans with softened or melted butter or with oil, for adding egg wash to unbaked goods, and for applying glazes on sweets and savories. They come in a wide range of sizes, usually with wood or wire handles. Avoid using nylon brushes on hot surfaces, as the bristles will melt. Also, these are dishwasher proof.

Silicone brushes have thicker bristles. They work well for buttering or oiling pans and are heat resistant to temperatures between 500° and 800°F (their degree of resistance varies with the manufacturer), which makes them great for basting hot foods in the oven or on the grill. Practically indestructible (dishwasher sturdy), they come in a variety of brush sizes, handle lengths, handle angles, and fun, eye-popping colors.

Can Opener

Can openers come in two types, handheld or manual, and electric. When needing to open a large volume of cans, electric openers are quick and easy. Handheld openers with padded, easy-to-grasp handles and smooth running gears are dishwasher proof, which simplifies thorough cleaning. If counter space is an issue, a handheld opener that slips into a drawer is probably best.

Citrus Juicer

You can choose from four different types of citrus juicers, depending on your needs. If you consume large amounts of fresh juice every day, the fast and highly efficient electric juicer is the best choice. For small quantities of juice, the choices are the handheld, two-part, or reamer style.

Many handheld juicers come in sizes and colors to match the fruit: green for limes, yellow for lemons, and orange for oranges. They are a leverage press with a hinged handle that compresses the fruit fully and forces out the juice. Place the halved fruit cut side down in the curved well, so that the ridged cone presses against the skin, and squeeze firmly, turning the citrus half inside out. Some of the flavorful citrus oils in the skin are released into the juice, adding a welcome spritz of citrus essence to the juice. Perforations on one side ensure the juice comes out, leaving the seeds behind. Made from enamel-coated metal, they are dishwasher safe.

The two-part juicer consists of a ridged cone (the reamer) molded into a dish or tray with perforations. The tray sits on top of a bowl or cup that captures the juice. As the juice is extracted, it flows down the reamer, into the tray, through the perforations, and into the bowl underneath, leaving the pits and solids behind in the tray. Some bowls or cups are clear and graduated, so the juice can be measured, and have a lip for easy pouring. Two-part juicers are made of durable plastic, glass, ceramic, or stainless steel.

Reamers are juicers without a bowl or strainer. The reamer is held in one hand and the halved citrus in the other hand. As the cut surface of the fruit is pressed against the ridged cone, the juices are released directly into a strainer set over a bowl or measuring cup. Reamers are made of all wood, stainless steel, or plastic with a comfortable cushioned handle.

Colander

Bowl shaped and covered with perforations or slits for draining water or other liquids from cooked or raw foods, colanders come in a range of useful sizes. A large one is handy for draining cooked pasta or potatoes, rinsing fruit, or washing greens, and a smaller one is good for rinsing or draining small quantities of cooked or fresh foods. Make sure your largest colander fits comfortably in your sink and has either a ring base or sturdy, well-balanced legs so it doesn't tip over. Colanders come in a rainbow of colors and can be made of sturdy stainless steel or silicone. Some of the silicone colanders are also collapsible, making them easy to store.

Cutting Board

A wooden board used for chopping should be thick (1 to 2 inches) and heavy. These are typically made from sturdy maple or bamboo. A carving board with a moat for capturing precious jus makes carving a turkey or a roast a snap. All wooden boards should be hand washed with soap and water.

Boards are also available in plastic, rubber composites, and laminates. The advantage of nonwood cutting boards is that they are dishwasher safe. Some have a moat for catching juices, so they can double as a carving board.

Flexible plastic cutting boards (11 by 15 inches) come in handy for small jobs. They lift, bend, and funnel easily and clean up quickly. Nonskid backing prevents slippage during use. A color-coded variety pack keeps vegetables, meat, poultry, and fish separated, avoiding risk of cross contamination. Use them on a countertop or as a "liner" for wooden boards. They are also easy to store because they are thinner than the wood or silicone types.

Fat Separator

Made from heat-resistant plastic with a sturdy, padded handle, a fat separator looks like a measuring cup with a long spout rising from the base. It is a great tool for skimming fat from gravies, soups, and stocks. The clever design allows the slimmed-down liquid to flow into the spout and out of the cup when you tip the cup for pouring. The fat, which settles on top of the liquid, works its way down to the bottom of the cup, where it remains. The separator, which is available in 2- and 4-cup sizes, comes with a strainer insert to catch solids that could clog the spout.

Food Mill

The food mill is a tool that produces purees to rival those made in a food processor. A hand-operated crank moves a blade through soft or cooked food, forcing the soft solids through a perforated disk (this is the puree) while leaving the hard solids (such as skins and seeds) behind. (See page 109 for more details.)

Funnel

A nesting set of two sizes—one small and one large—is easy to store and will accommodate a multitude of kitchen jobs, from filling bottles with liquids to transferring spices to storage jars. Some come with a handy detachable strainer. A funnel with a wide opening, also called a wide-mouthed canning funnel, is handy for transferring thicker liquids or solids without spills. They are made of durable, heat-resistant plastic or stainless steel, and have soft handles that provide a firm grip. Collapsible silicone funnels are easy to store.

Garlic Press

The garlic press is a hinged device with a small, perforated cup for the garlic in the top of one section and a plunger in the other. When the handles are compressed, the garlic is forced through the perforations. Look for sturdy construction and comfortable handles that allow maximum leverage with a minimum of muscle. Some come with extra-large padded handles for a more comfortable grip. Various devices to simplify cleaning are sometimes included, such as a plastic disk with hard pins that, when pressed into the perforations, remove the garlic skin. Others come with a removable press plate with a nonstick coating. All are dishwasher safe for easy cleanup.

Grater

The three most common types of grater are the box grater, the rotary grater, and the rasp grater. The box grater has at least four different grating surfaces— coarse shred, fine shred, basic grate, and fine grate— and can handle almost any grating or shredding task. The rotary grater, also called a hand-cranked grater, often comes with removable cylinders with various-sized grating surfaces (usually one fine and one coarse) and is especially handy for nuts, chocolate, and hard cheeses. The rasp grater, a narrow piece of curved stainless steel with razor-sharp perforations, does a fabulous job on almost anything you need finely grated, from citrus zest and fresh ginger to garlic, chocolate, and cheese. (See page 113 for more details.)

Ice Cream Scoop

Made from stainless steel or cast aluminum with a handle that includes self-defrosting fluid, the ice cream scoop comes in two primary styles: a smooth-ball type and a spring-loaded type. Both are good for ice cream, but the latter, which "ejects" the contents, is also handy for portioning uniformly sized meatballs or cookies. Look for a scoop with a comfortable handle.

Instant-Read Thermometer

Small, lightweight, and easy to read, the instant-read thermometer takes its name from its action: you insert it into the food and it registers the temperature quickly and accurately. It takes the guesswork out of knowing when a roast chicken, a baked fish, a grilled steak, or a prime rib is done. Instant-read thermometers can be analog or digital and register temperatures up to 220°F.

Ladle

A ladle is a cup with a long handle attached. It is an essential tool, one that you will reach for repeatedly for dipping into soups, stocks, sauces, and other liquids. The best ladles are made from a continuous sheet of metal, preferably stainless steel, or sturdy nylon. A hook or hole at the tip of the long handle is convenient for hanging. Ladles come in various capacities; a 4-ounce and an 8-ounce ladle are especially handy sizes.

Measuring Cups

There are two types of measuring cups, one for dry measures and one for liquid measures. Distinguishing between them as you cook will help to ensure that recipes turn out successfully.

Dry measuring cups are sold in nested stacks in sizes from ⅛ cup up to 2 cups, though the typical stack includes only ¼ cup, ⅓ cup, ½ cup, and 1 cup measures. They have even rims, so they can be leveled off with a straight edge for accurate measuring. The cups are available in a variety of designs and materials. Oval cups are great for scooping sugar or rice from a canister. Collapsible silicone cups, in bright colors,

are attractive, and can be easily tucked into a drawer. Heavy-gauge stainless-steel cups are nicely sleek and wash up easily, but check on how securely the handle is attached for long life. The sturdiest handles are a continuous sheet of metal or well riveted to the cup portion. Most dry measuring cups are dishwasher safe.

Liquid measuring cups made of glass, with the calibrations (both standard and metric measures) brightly printed vertically on the side, are classic. Made of thick, durable glass, with a rounded rim, handy pouring spout, and easy-to-grasp molded glass handle, they are available in convenient graduated sizes (1 cup, 2 cups, 4 cups, and 8 cups)—so you'll have the right size for the job at hand— that stack one inside the other. A calibrated 8-cup (2-quart) liquid glass measuring cup with a pour spout and sturdy handle is useful for measuring large quantities of liquid and can double as a mixing bowl or storage container. (Some come with snap-on plastic lids.) There is also a similar plastic version.

An innovative entry to the liquid measure market is a santoprene angled plastic cup that can be viewed for accuracy by looking down into the cup as well as from the side, ensuring an accurate measure if you are unable to view the contents at eye level. Calibrated in both metric and standard measures, it has a comfy cushioned, nonslip handle and is dishwasher safe. It is available in 1-cup, 2-cup, 4-cup, and 8-cup capacity.

Measuring Spoons

Every kitchen needs at least two sets of measuring spoons for use in measuring both liquid and dry ingredients. Typically sold in stacking sets of four (1 tablespoon, 1 teaspoon, ½ teaspoon, and ¼ teaspoon), measuring spoon sets also sometimes include ½ tablespoon and ⅛ teaspoon measures. Heavy-duty stainless-steel and silicone sets in splashy colors are equally durable. They won't bend, scratch, melt, or discolor, and they will last a lifetime. The shape selections range from narrow and rectangular, for an easy reach into spice bottles, to standard round or oval bowls. Some spoons have handles sheathed in easy-to-grasp rubber, and most are labeled in bold lettering for easy reading.

The set is usually held together by a removable ring or chain, or conveniently snap and unsnap at the far end of the handle. To take the guesswork out of measuring, you can buy nesting sets of odd sizes that cover all the possibilities, including a pinch, ⅛ teaspoon, 1½ teaspoons, and 2 teaspoons. There are also uniquely designed adjustable spoons that accurately measure ⅛ to 1 teaspoon and ½ teaspoon to 1 tablespoon.

Mixing Bowls

Stainless-steel bowls with 1- to 4-quart capacities are a must-have. An 8-quart bowl is also handy but not essential. Stainless-steel bowls are a good choice because they are lightweight, heatproof, and highly durable. Nesting bowls in graduated sizes are easy to store. For a second set, consider glass bowls in an attractive design that can double for serving. For liquids such as pancake batter, bowls with a pouring spout—and a handle—are useful.

Oven Mitt and Pot Holder

Every kitchen should be outfitted with at least 2 oven mitts and 2 pot holders. Oven mitts are either square or in the shape of a hand and will protect both sides of your hands as you reach into the oven to grasp a roasting pan or heavy Dutch oven. Flat, well-padded pot holders are for less fiery jobs, like sliding a saucepan off the stove or removing a hot lid from a sauté pan. They are designed primarily for protecting only one side of your hand. Some are also made of heat-resistant silicone.

Peeler

Peelers are remarkable for their comfort, durability, and, most importantly, their razor-sharp swivel blades. They are used not only for peeling the skins from fruits and vegetables, but also for making curls from a wedge of hard cheese, removing wide strips of orange and lemon zest, and creating chocolate shavings. You can choose from a handful of designs. Hold each one in your hand when deciding which is best for size and comfort.

The Y-shaped peeler, with the swivel blade perpendicular to the handle, peels off slightly thicker strips of skin. It's efficient for peeling winter squashes, celery root, or other thick-skinned vegetables. The vertical peeler, designed with the blade as an extension of the handle, removes slightly thinner strips. It's good for peeling potatoes, eggplant, cucumbers, and other thin-skinned vegetables and fruits.

The serrated-edged peeler is meant for tomatoes, but it also does a fabulous job of zipping the skins off potatoes, carrots, peaches, nectarines, and other thin-skinned vegetables and fruits.

The julienne peeler is designed like the vertical peeler, except that it has sharp blades set ⅛ inch apart. These blades yield julienne strips of orange zest, zucchini, carrot, and other firm vegetables.

Pepper Mill

To appreciate their distinctive pungency, peppercorns should be ground moments before use. For table-top use, the material and design are more important than the capacity or the range of different grinds. For kitchen use, look for a sturdy mill made from a light yet durable material that can withstand the rigors of kitchen use, such as greasy hands and the constant need to be wiped down. Adjustable grinds, large storage capacity, and a stainless-steel or other sturdy mechanism (stainless steel and ceramic are considered the best) that will deliver a generous shower of ground pepper and remain sharp throughout a lifetime are also important features. Make sure you test for comfort and ergonomics before purchase.

Potato Masher

There are several types of handheld potato mashers on the market. All have a base secured with narrow shafts that extend from a vertical handle. The base can be a flat disk with perforations or a grid pattern, or heavy, rigid steel coils looped into parallel rows. The advantage of a masher is that the cook can control the consistency of the mashed potatoes from rough to smooth. It can also be used for mashing avocados for guacamole, hard-cooked eggs for salad, roasted eggplant for baba ghanoush, or chickpeas for hummus.

Spatula

The term *spatula* is used for a broad category of tools, and every kitchen should be stocked with an equally broad array of spatulas.

Once limited to rubber, these are now also manufactured from heat-resistant silicone. Silicone can withstand heat from 500° to 800°F (check manufacturer's instructions), making these spatulas suitable for use with either cold foods or in hot pans. The handles are either wooden with removable heads for washing, or dishwasher-safe durable plastic or lightweight metal. The head shapes vary according to use: narrow heads reach down into tall, slim jars and measuring cups; heads with a pointed edge get into the corners of saucepans; concave heads double as spoons; and extra-long handles and broad heads are great for big jobs and reaching into deep pots. Some heads are perforated, which makes them safe for stirring without the fear of splashing. Available in a rainbow of colors, these spatulas are unquestionably the workhorses of the kitchen, and every kitchen needs a supply of different sizes and shapes.

A second type of spatula, sometimes called a pancake turner, is useful for a lot more than pancakes. The wide, solid square or rectangular blade is attached to a long, narrow heat-resistant handle set at the perfect angle for reaching down into a skillet. A nicely beveled edge ensures the blade slides easily under the food. The solid surface is handy for turning drippy burgers, grilled-cheese sandwiches, sunny-side-up eggs, French toast, and more. These spatulas are available in stainless steel, nonscratch nylon, and silicone, and come in a range of sizes and with a variety of different handles.

A third type of spatula is similar to the solid turner except the blade has wide slots. The spatulas are great for turning and lifting foods fried in oil—think potato pancakes or breaded veal cutlets—because they allow the oil to drain off the food as it is being turned or lifted.

Spoon

The spoon, like the spatula, comes in a variety of guises. First, every kitchen needs a couple of large, attractive serving spoons. They are sold separately, or in sets with a large serving fork, in brushed stainless steel, pewter, silver plate, or other materials. Other necessary spoon types include solid, slotted, and wooden, with plenty of variations in each category.

One or more solid stainless-steel spoons with a deep bowl are ideal for lifting meats from stews, or retrieving potatoes or vegetable chunks when you want to include some of the cooking liquid. A spoon with a shallow bowl is used for skimming fat (if using a fat separator is inconvenient) or slow stirring. The sturdiest spoons are made from a continuous sheet of stainless steel. Solid nylon spoons, which are lightweight, durable, and heat resistant, are another option. They often have a flat edge that ensures even contact with the bottom of a pan. Use these for lighter jobs, such as sautéing foods in a skillet, transferring vegetables to a serving dish, or gently stirring a sauce or creamy soup. They also won't scratch your nonstick pans, they withstand temperatures of up to 400°F, and they are dishwasher safe.

Whether the spoons are stainless steel or nylon, their handles should be at least 10 inches long, so you can reach deep into a pot without fear of burning your hand. The handles should be easy to grasp, comfortable, and preferably heat resistant. A cutout or curled tip that permits hanging from a hook or a rack is also a handy feature.

Long-handled slotted spoons, also commonly made from stainless steel or nylon, are great for stirring liquids without splattering and for removing solids from liquids. These indispensable spoons—you need at least one in your kitchen—typically have long slots, though some sport round perforations.

But many cooks turn to a wooden spoon before they reach for a metal or nylon one. Wooden spoons are popular with good reason. They come in a myriad of shapes and sizes, are invariably lightweight, and won't scratch nonstick surfaces. The bowls can be long and shallow (a good choice for gently stirring liquids and semiliquids), wide and shallow, flat edged for reaching into corners and scraping the bottom of a pan, or even slotted, and handles range from short to very long. Stand an assortment of wooden spoons in a decorative crock on the counter near the stove and you'll find yourself using them constantly.

Steamer Basket

This is an inexpensive collapsible basket, usually made of stainless steel. It has "leaves" that fold in and out from a central rod, allowing it to adjust its size to fit nearly every vessel, from a small saucepan to a wide sauté pan, and small feet that hold it above the water. Because of its adjustability, it's useful for steaming a variety of shapes and sizes of vegetables. It is also dishwasher safe. (See page 91 for more details.)

Strainer

Available in a variety of sizes from very fine to coarse, a strainer is usually made of stainless steel with a fine wire-mesh bowl used to separate solids from liquids. The finest mesh is useful for straining fine particles from sauces, and the coarse mesh is good for straining liquid from large pieces of cooked foods. Some are designed like colanders and are large enough to be used interchangeably with a colander. Others have a long handle with a hook opposite the handle for resting the strainer firmly on the rim of a pot or bowl. A nesting set (in three graduated sizes) takes up a minimum of storage space and has multiple uses. A large, easy-to-store, collapsible silicone strainer is yet another option.

Timer

Every kitchen needs a timer. In fact, every kitchen needs at least two timers. Digital timers are accurate, easy to read, and time seconds, minutes, and up to several hours. Some have extra-loud bells. Others come on a cord to wear around your neck, or with magnetic strips, so they can be mounted to the oven or refrig-

erator door. Some have multiple settings for as many as three or four tasks. Digital timers require batteries, whereas the mechanical-dial timers, powered by spring action, do not. In most cases, the extras that come with digital timers more than compensate for having to keep batteries on hand.

Tongs

At least one and possibly more spring-loaded metal tongs are a must for any kitchen. They come in handy for turning sautéed foods, lifting vegetables from boiling water or a steaming basket, and moving other hot foods. Try them out before buying, so you get a pair with action that is suitable for your hand strength. There are many styles to select from. The most durable and efficient are stainless steel with scalloped tips. A locking mechanism that keeps tongs closed for storage is an advantage. For use in nonstick pans, have a pair with plastic or silicone "mitts" at the end, or use wooden tongs. Two lengths, 9 and 12 inch, will come in handy.

Whisk

Whisks are made in various sizes and shapes depending on their uses, but the three primary types are the sauce or standard whisk, the flat or roux whisk, and the balloon whisk. In all cases, stainless-steel wires are considered the most durable. However, for use in nonstick pots and pans, select a whisk with silicone-coated wires or nylon wires. The sauce whisk, which comes in a range of lengths, has a relatively narrow head and stout wires. You need an 8-inch whisk for stirring small amounts in a shallow bowl or saucepan and a 10-inch whisk for deeper bowls or pans. The standard whisk is similar to the sauce whisk, but with thinner wires. The wires of the flat whisk are curved into flat loops that are ideal for combining fat and flour for making a pan sauce or gravy. The balloon whisk, which boasts many thin wires in a spherical shape, turns cream or egg whites into a fluffy mountain in no time flat. (See page 137 for more details.)

Appliances

Blender

A blender is an indispensable appliance, even if you already own a food processor. Admittedly, the latter is more versatile, but a blender, with its narrow canister that holds food close to its small but very sharp blade, performs some specific tasks better. For example, depending on the power level, it makes the smoothest iced drinks, perfectly emulsifies dressings, and creates velvety pureed soups.

Think about how you intend to use the blender before deciding what power, speeds, design, and material suits you. For example, not all blenders are powerful enough to crush ice or pulverize carrot chunks. The canister can be wider or narrower, and made of glass, plastic, or metal. Bases can also be plastic or metal. A plastic jar is lighter than a glass jar, but both have the advantage of letting you see what's going on inside. A metal container eliminates viewing, but it is the sturdiest of the three materials, with no chance of it cracking or chipping, plus its sleek look fits right into the equally sleek look of many contemporary kitchens.

Coffeemaker

The least-expensive electric coffeemaker requires a paper cone, a few scoops of ground coffee, a glass carafe, and a filled water reservoir. All you need to do is press a button and the canister fills with brewed coffee. At the other end of the spectrum is the brewer with a washable (paperless) coffee cone, a buzzer to alert you when the brewing is complete, automatic shutoff after a specific number of hours, a grinder, a water filter, an electronic clock and timer, a thermal carafe, and many more features. Choose the one that best suits your needs.

Hand Mixer

The electric handheld mixer is convenient for whipping cream to top a dessert, beating together butter and sugar for the occasional batch of cookies, or for transforming a pot of cooked Yukon Golds into velvety mashed potatoes. The beaters are easily detachable and the handheld part is small enough to stow snugly in a kitchen drawer. For heavy-duty jobs, such as creaming butter and sugar for cakes, mixing big batches of cookie dough, or kneading bread dough, a stand mixer (see page 31) is both more efficient and convenient.

Toaster

Toasters have become increasingly accomodating, with wider openings for bagels, waffles, and thick-sliced hearth breads and sensors that automatically lift the bread when fully toasted. Consider your counter space and the number of slices you'll need to toast at one time when selecting a toaster. If you have room for a larger appliance and you like toasted muffins and thick baguette slices, you might want the more versatile toaster oven.

2 | The WELL-STOCKED GLOBAL KITCHEN

The items listed in "The Well-Stocked Global Kitchen" will help you take your basic kitchen to a new level of sophistication. Here, you will find suggestions for the more specialized cookware that many adventurous cooks dream of owning. Like "The Basic Kitchen," "The Well-Stocked Global Kitchen" is divided into four categories: cookware, knives, tools, and appliances. For easy use, the equipment is listed alphabetically within each category.

Much of the equipment is put to use in the chapters in part III that cover cooking in the global kitchen. Others items are not specifically global, but appear here because they sit a few rungs above what's needed in a basic kitchen. Think of this inventory as the ultimate wish list for the super-passionate cook.

Cookware

Bamboo Steamer

The bamboo steamer, a handsomely crafted tray with a lid, is designed to sit over boiling water in a wok or other wide pan, and is used to cook Asian specialties, such as dumplings, vegetables, and fish. These are available in multiple sizes. They can also be conveniently stacked. (See page 149 for more details.)

Bisteeya Pan

In Moroccan kitchens, a special large, round, shallow copper pan called a *tobsil dial bestial* is used to make *bisteeya,* a flat pie of chicken, eggs, and sugared almonds encased in layers of flaky pastry (see recipe on page 321). A large (12-inch) cake pan, 10-inch spring-form pan, paella pan, or pizza pan can be substituted.

Cataplana

A *cataplana* is an oval metal pan unique to the southern Portuguese region of Algarve. Its rounded top and bottom are attached by a hinge, giving it the appearance of a giant clam shell. Traditionally made of hammered copper and available in different sizes, the *cataplana* is used to cook dishes made from seafood, poultry, meats, and sausages. (See page 297 for more details.)

Clay Cooker

The term *clay cooker* embraces a broad category of earthenware vessels called both clay cookers and clay pots. Some have glazed and unglazed tops and bottoms. Both the glazed and unglazed portions need to be soaked in water before using. Clay pots are appreciated for their ability to cook without added fat, and for retaining the natural flavors of the food in a moist atmosphere. (See page 51 for more details.)

Cocotte

Cocotte, a French pot similar to a Dutch oven, has a heavy, tight-fitting flat lid. The weight and design of the lid helps trap moisture inside the pot, to produce particularly moist and tender slow-cooked braises and stews. (See page 201 for more details.)

Couscoussière

A large, two-tiered typically stainless-steel pot used to steam couscous, pellet-sized semolina pasta. The top section, which holds the couscous, has perforations in the base. Water or stew in the bottom section simmers, releasing rising steam that cooks the couscous. (See page 315 for more details.)

Crepe Pan

Similar in shape to a skillet, this pan has extra-low sides to ease lifting, turning, and sliding crepes from it. It is ideally made of a metal, such as nonstick aluminum or blue steel, that conducts heat well and is relatively lightweight, so the cook is able to easily lift and rotate the pan to distribute the batter evenly. It is available in a range of sizes. (See page 207 for more details.)

Fish Poacher

Long, deep, and oblong, this pan simplifies poaching a whole fish. It is fitted with an easy-to-lift rack for removing the fish from the poaching liquid. Several sizes are available, but are all designed to fit on two stove-top burners. (See page 63 for more details.)

Fondue Pot

There are three basic types of fondue: cheese fondue; *fondue bourguignonne,* in which meat is cooked in hot oil (or sometimes butter); and chocolate fondue. Some pots are sturdy enough to be used both on the stove top for making the fondue and for keeping it hot at the table, and others are not. Typically, ceramic pots are used only for cheese and chocolate, but metal pots can be used for all three types. In addition, the metal type can be sued for Asian-style hot-pot dishes. Fondue pots come with steel bases that hold fuel for keeping the contents hot. Some pots come in sets with long-handled forks for dipping into the pot. (See page 213 for more details.)

Garlic Roaster

Made of ceramic or terra-cotta, a garlic roaster, also known as a garlic baker, is a round tray with a domed cover. Two sizes are available: small, which holds up to three heads of garlic, and large, which holds up to six heads. When the heads are roasted, the flesh turns soft, succulent, and jamlike and can be squeezed free of the skins and spread on crostini, whisked into dressings, whipped into mashed potatoes, stirred into soup, or dolloped on top of pizza. The roaster is microwave safe and should be hand washed.

Gratin

This traditionally oval baking dish is shallow and wide, which encourages cheese and/or bread-crumb toppings to turn golden and crunchy during baking. Gratins are typically made of copper, known for its beauty and ability to distribute heat evenly, or of durable, heat-resistant white porcelain. (See page 216 for more details.)

Griddle

A griddle is a flat cooking surface used for cooking pancakes, burgers, eggs, and other foods. It can be round, rectangular, or square and comes in a range of sizes that will fit on one or two burners. Larger griddles have a pair of looped handles or have lips on two sides that are used as handles. Smaller griddles have a single long handle. They can be made from cast iron or a range of steel and aluminum blends.

Grill Pan

Grill pans, available round, rectangular, or square, have a raised grid or ridges that leave dark grill marks on the surface of steaks, vegetables, sausages, or other foods. Made from heavy cast iron or from a range of steel and aluminum blends, some also have a nonstick surface. Like griddles, they are designed to sit on one or two burners. Some are reversible, with a flat (griddle) side and grill (raised grid) side. Smaller models have detachable handles, whereas others have short, stubby grips on either side, or a single long, sturdy handle. (See page 69 for more details.)

Grilling and Roasting Planks

Foods cooked on wooden planks are infused with the flavor of the wood. Planks are good for cooking steaks, salmon or other fish, shrimp, vegetables, even fruit. There are two basic types: thin planks, which are designed for use on charcoal or gas grills and have a limited life, and thicker planks, which can only be used in an oven and have a long life.

Karahi

This classic wok-shaped, flat-bottomed pan of the Indian kitchen comes in two sizes and can be used for both stir-frying and deep-frying. Also spelled *kadhai, kadai,* and other ways, it has opposing looped handles and is typically made of steel or cast iron, two materials that hold and distribute heat well. (See page 243 for more details.)

Mattone

This two-part terra-cotta press can be used on a gas or electric stove top with a heat diffuser or in an oven up to 350°F. The *mattone* is used to cook the classic Italian *pollo al mattone,* or "chicken under a brick," and also works for *panini,* or grilled Italian sandwiches. (See page 267 for more details.) A modern version is called a panini pan. This is a heavy, square skillet with a lid configured to sit down in the pan, weighing down the food being cooked.

Mussel Pot

Made of cast iron and shaped like a giant mussel shell, the mussel pot is used for cooking mussels or clams. It has a stainless-steel strainer at its narrow end, making it easy to dip bread into the deep pool of flavorful juices. The pot comes in two sizes, with the smaller one suitable for two servings and the larger one for four servings. (See page 221 for more details.)

Omelet Pan

An omelet pan is a small skillet (about 8 inches) just big enough for a two- or three-egg omelet. A nonstick surface, while not necessary, will help the omelet slide smoothly out the flared sides of the pan. Omelet pans are available in a range of materials, all of which ideally heat evenly and quickly. The handle is especially important, since the art of omelet making calls for lifting and turning the pan with one fluid twist of the wrist, so the omelet smoothly folds and then slides free of the pan.

Paella Pan

If you like paella, this classic pan is a must. It is sold in a range of sizes, from 13 to 22 inches in diameter, and comes in a wide variety of materials and designs. The traditional Spanish pan has red looped handles and a dimpled bottom for even heat distribution. Also available is a burner and adjustable tripod stand for cooking paella outdoors. (See page 307 for more details.)

Pommes Anna Pan

This round, two-piece copper pan has a flat lid that cuffs over the sides of the pan. The bottom is typically 9½ inches wide and 5 inches deep, and the slightly wider lid is only 1½ inches deep. Layers of thinly sliced, well-buttered potatoes—*pommes Anna*—are cooked in the bottom section until crisp and well browned, and then the covered pan is inverted, so the cooked potato cake is served with its browned bottom on the top. Copper is the best material because it conducts heat quickly and evenly to brown the potatoes. The sections can be used separately as handsome serving or baking dishes. (See page 229 for more details.)

Pressure Cooker

This specially designed pot has an airtight lid that builds up pressure inside when liquid is brought to a boil, which raises the internal temperature beyond what is possible in a regular covered pot on the stove top. That means foods cook more quickly. Outfitted with fail-safe locking devices and pressure gauges, the pressure cooker is convenient for cooking more quickly (usually in about one-third the time) foods that would normally require long cooking times, such as pot roasts, dried beans, and whole grains. They are available primarily in stainless steel; look for a model with a thick, heavy encapsulated aluminum base that improves heat distribution and promotes even cooking.

Risotto Pan

The traditional copper risotto pan has a tin lining and a removable steel bale handle that in the past was used to suspend the pan over a cooking fire. The straight sides and broad cooking surface provide ample room for stirring and even heat distribution. (See page 287 for more details.)

Sauté Pan

A sauté pan has straight, high sides (2 to 3 inches) and comes with a tight-fitting lid. This versatile pan is designed primarily for sautéing but is also suitable for preparing many dishes, from cooking rice to braising meats or greens. Typical sizes range from 2 to 6 quarts. (See page 83 for more details.)

Steamer and Steamer Insert

The large, versatile steamer insert is shaped like a pot but has perforations along the sides and bottom and a handle on either side. It fits into a large pot, comes with a tight-fitting lid, and is available in several sizes. These are also available in sets that include the pot, the lid, and the steamer insert. (See page 91 for more details.)

Stockpot

The basic kitchen can get by with an 8-quart stockpot (page 6), but the global kitchen benefits from having a larger stockpot (12 to 16 quarts) on hand for big batches of chicken, meat, or vegetable stock or broth. Its large size contributes to its versatility for noncooking uses, too, such as keeping drinks iced for a party. (See page 95 for more details.)

Stove-top Pepper Roaster and Tortilla Grill

If you like the flavor of roasted peppers and find yourself regularly heating up tortillas, this combination pepper roaster and tortilla grill is handy to have. It is about 10 inches in diameter, has two sturdy wooden, heat-resistant handles that detach for washing, and the top is heavy mesh with a baked-on finish. It works on either a gas or electric burner, and can also be used for making quesadillas, charring tomatoes and onions for salsa, and more. (See page 179 for more details.)

Stove-top Smoker

This typically rectangular pan has a sturdy handle and either a sliding lid or one that lifts off and can double as a roasting pan. Inside the pan, the food sits on a rack above a small amount of wood chips. The smoker can be used for ribs, pork tenderloins, shrimp, fish, chicken, and a variety of other foods. (See page 99 for more details.)

Tagine

Tagine is both the name of a pot used in North African kitchens (especially Moroccan) and of the stewlike dish cooked in it. It is traditionally made of terra-cotta, but now is also available in a combination of materials, including stainless steel with an aluminum core or cast iron. The clay conical lid, which is topped with a round knob, rests on a shallow base. (See page 325 for more details.)

Tawa

Available round or oval, this traditional Indian pan usually has a pair of opposing rounded handles. It is used for roasting spices or for cooking chapatis or other breads, but can also be used as a stove-top griddle for searing kebabs and cutlets. (See page 251 for more details.)

Teakettle

Because it is commonly kept on the stove top, the teakettle can be as much a fashion item to coordinate with the color scheme of your kitchen as it is a practical vessel for boiling water. Before selecting the color or shape, try out the handle to make sure it's comfortable. Look for a kettle with a whistle, to remind you that the water is boiling.

Terra-cotta Bakeware

Rustic and homey, these baking dishes (also called *cazuelas*) are made of red clay and come in a variety of shapes and sizes. They can be used on the stovetop and in the oven, and are attractive enough for serving, especially if you're enjoying the sunny flavors of Mexico, Spain, and Portugal. (See pages 183 and 301 for more details.)

Wok

This indispensable pan of the Chinese kitchen, with its high, gradually sloping sides and curved base, is ideal for cooking food quickly over high heat, but is also used for steaming and deep-frying. The traditional wok has two metal handles to facilitate lifting and tilting, but now woks with a single long handle are sold as well. Buy a round-bottomed wok only if you have a gas range with burner grates that will hold it stationary (a wok ring helps keep it steady, as well). A more recent design is the flat-bottomed wok, also known as a stir-fry pan, which works on both gas and electric stoves. (See page 167 for more details.)

Knives

Boning Knife

A boning knife has a thin, narrow, curvaceous blade about 6 inches long and ½ to 1 inch wide. Because boning requires considerable dexterity, the handle should fit and feel comfortable in your hand.

Carving Knife and Fork

Also called a slicing knife, this knife has an 8- to 12-inch-long, narrow, slightly tapered blade and an easy-to-grip handle. Knives designed to cut through cooked meat and poultry are tapered to a point at the end. Knives for slicing smoked fish or ham are a bit longer, with a straight edge and a squared-off end. A meat and poultry carving knife is often sold in a set with a two-pronged fork, for holding the meat steady while it is being carved.

Cheese Knife

A number of distinctive cheese knives are available, each suitable for different types of cheese. One popular design has an offset blade, which angles down from the handle before straightening out to a length of about 5 inches. This knife works with soft, semisoft, and semi-firm cheeses. Another model, also for soft cheeses, has large perforations in the blade that prevent the cheese from clinging to it and a sharp scalloped edge that ensures a tidy cut. Another useful knife is the Parmesan knife, which has a stubby, spade-shaped blade and a sturdy, oval wooden handle. It efficiently cuts such hard cheeses as Parmesan and aged Gouda, Asiago, and provolone into jagged chunks.

Chef's Knife

The chef's knife is covered on page 9 in "The Basic Kitchen," but here you'll have a chance to think about adding more chef's knives to your knife block. For a novice cook, a small chef's knife (8 inches) is usually perfect. But if you are a more adept cook with greater knife skills, you might find a chef's knife with a longer blade more practical. Chef's knives can be as long as 14 inches, but a 10-inch knife is more than adequate for home use. You might also consider adding a smaller (6-inch) chef's knife for your kitchen as well. Before buying, always hold the knife in your hand so you can judge the weight, balance, and comfort of the handle. Simulate the rocking motion of chopping before buying to decide what feels most comfortable.

Cleaver

The extra-strong, wedge-shaped, sharp-edged blade of a meat cleaver is designed for cutting through bones, but this large knife can also be used for many other tasks, such as halving acorn squash, cutting apart a slab of ribs, or smashing a garlic clove. There are also vegetable cleavers shaped like wide squares available that are designed primarily for cutting vegetables. These are not durable enough for cutting through meat bones. Whichever one you choose, make sure to buy a cleaver with good heft for both efficiency and versatility.

Paring Knife

Owning paring knives in a variety of sizes and styles eases tasks in any kitchen. Two styles, the straight 3-inch blade and the bird's beak blade, are described on page 10. Among other types is one designed specifically for vegetables, called a standard parer, which has a curvaceous blade and sharp upward tip and looks a little like a miniature boning knife. Yet another type has a narrow, triangular 3-inch blade that is useful for such small jobs as slicing handheld strawberries or mushrooms.

Poultry Shears

Heavy-duty kitchen scissors are a versatile and indispensable kitchen tool (page 10), and some of them are sturdy enough to cut through poultry bones. However, true poultry shears are always stronger. There are several models on the market, so be sure to look for some or all of the following features: a curved blade for getting around and into chicken joints, a cushioned handle that permits a firm grasp, a notch at the back of the blade for keeping the bones in place while you cut down, a serrated bottom blade for extra cutting power, a strong lock for keeping the spring-loaded blades safely closed during storage, and made of stainless steel that is dishwasher safe.

Tools

Bulb Baster

Sometimes called a turkey baster, the bulb baster looks like a giant eyedropper. The bulb and tubular shaft are made from heat-resistant materials. The tube is typically plastic, stainless steel, or Lexan, a brand of thermoplastic; although stainless steel is appreciated for its durability, the Lexan and plastic are transparent, making it easy to see how much liquid has been siphoned. A bulb baster is handy for sucking up pan juices, marinades, glazes, melted butter, or syrups, and then pouring them back on top of all types of foods.

Cheesecloth

A versatile kitchen accessory, cheesecloth is a loosely woven, lightweight natural cotton cloth (fine and coarse weaves are available). Keep some on hand for trapping minute particles when straining liquids (stocks and broths, cheese making, draining rehydrated dried mushrooms), for bundling herbs for a bouquet garni, for "capping" lemon or orange halves to catch seeds, for lining molds, and for wrapping fish for poaching.

Chef's Torch

The chef's torch is lightweight and easy to hold in the average hand, making it perfect for the home cook. Most commonly fired up for caramelizing sugar on a crème brûlée, it has countless other uses, from browning disks of goat cheese for a salad to adding golden highlights to a meringue. The small butane canister that powers it is easily purchased at hardware stores. (See page 105 for more details.)

Cheese Plane

A stubby, V-shaped spatula with a sharp-edged horizontal opening in the middle, the cheese plane is used for shaving firm and semifirm cheeses into slivers on a cheese tray, or for making curls of cheese for garnishing salads, pastas, or other dishes. It is also useful for making chocolate shavings.

Chinois

This cone-shaped, all-stainless-steel ultrathin mesh strainer is primarily used for straining broths, custards, sauces, and jelly. Some models come with a matching tripod; others include an opposing handle that hooks over the rim of a pot or bowl. A long, narrow wooden pestle is sold to rub the mixture through the mesh. In professional kitchens, the *chinois* is sometimes referred to as a China cap. (See page 197 for more details.)

Chitarra

This traditional tool, typical of the Abruzzo region of Italy, is used to cut fresh pasta sheets into thin ribbons. The rectangular wooden frame, fitted with fine wire strings pulled lengthwise, is reversible, with wires positioned for the wider cut on one side and for the narrower cut on the opposite side. (See page 261 for more details.)

Cooking String and Reusable Silicone Ties

For years, 100 percent cotton string has been used for trussing poultry, securing a bouquet garni, or tying a rolled roast. New to the market, and a good substitute for cotton string, are reusable silicone ties available in bright colors and sold with a mesh bag for holding them as they run through the dishwasher. They are heat resistant up to 675°F, and their length can be adjusted by linking several loops together.

Custard Cup, Pudding Cup, and Ramekin

Custard cups, pudding cups, and ramekins come in a variety of materials but are typically made of clear oven-proof glass, stoneware, or porcelain. Custard cups have slightly flared sides. The classic ramekin, sometimes called a custard cup, has straight sides that help souf-flés to rise. The pudding cup, a variation on the custard cup, is slightly deeper than the custard cup or ramekin and has a rounded cup-shaped bottom. Ramekins are available in a range of shapes; the most traditional are round or oval. All come in a range of sizes; the most commonly used are 4 to 8 ounces.

Fish Bone Tweezers or Fish Bone Pliers

Made from stainless steel, fish bone tweezers have a wide, smooth easy-to-grasp surface and tapered flat tip designed to grab pin bones and extract them without tearing the delicate fish flesh. The pliers (similar to needle-nose pliers), also made of stainless steel, have long, slender tips and a comfortable handle. They can be used interchangeably for removing fish bones and are dishwasher safe.

Garlic Peeler

This is a crushable tube about 5 inches long that looks like a rubber cannoli shell. To use it, place a garlic clove in the tube and simultaneously and briskly press and roll the tube back and forth. The friction loosens the skin, releasing the clove whole.

Heat Diffuser

A heat diffuser is a round, heavy, flat disk typically made of enameled cast iron that sits on a stove-top burner. It modifies the intensity of the heat, thus pro-tecting the contents of a pot from cooking too fast. It also protects terra-cotta or other heat-sensitive cooking vessels from exposure to direct heat. Some diffusers come with convenient detachable handles.

Mandoline

A mandoline is a hand-operated vegetable and fruit slicer. Depending on the sophistication of the design, it will have one or two sets of folding legs or it will be completely flat, so it can rest on the rim of a bowl. The fanciest slicers are made of stainless steel or a combination of stainless steel and durable plastic, and can be fitted with a variety of blades to slice, julienne, make crinkle cuts, and more. Many slicers come with guards to protect fingers and hands from the razor-sharp blades. One popular model encases its blades in a V shape. (See page 121 for more details.)

Meat Pounder

The meat pounder comes in two designs: a round, smooth disk with a sturdy handle welded into its center, and a hammerlike tool. Both are made of heavy metal and are used to flatten meat into cutlets. The hammer design often includes a waffle pattern on one side, to use for tenderizing meat.(See page 125 for more details.)

Melon Baller

A melon baller looks like a simplified version of an ice cream scoop. On one or both ends is a hollowed-out half bowl ¾ to 1 inch in diameter. It is used to scoop out rounds from ripe melons or other fruit, make small scoops of ice cream, portion cookie dough, or make potatoes Parisienne (small potato balls sautéed in butter until browned and sprinkled with parsley). Some melon ballers have a small serrated half bowl, called the tomato shark, for coring tomatoes or hulling strawberries.

Mezzaluna

In Italian, *mezzaluna* means "half-moon," which is the shape of the blade on this classic doubled-handled knife. The cook uses a rocking motion, which quickly yields finely chopped herbs and vegetables with a mini-mum of hand pressure. (See page 273 for more details.)

Molcajete

Crafted from volcanic rock, this is the Mexican version of the mortar. Traditionally, a *molcajete,* in concert with a *tejolote* (pestle), is used to grind corn, crush chiles, and make salsa and guacamole. Be aware that not all imported Mexican mortars and pestles have been sufficiently seasoned to use without adding grit or residue to the food. Some are purely decorative, so read the manufacturer's instructions carefully. (See page 175 for more details.)

Mortar and Pestle

The mortar is the bowl and the pestle is the thick, bat-shaped wand used to pound the food into a paste. It is used to grind spices, make seasoning pastes, or, in larger sizes, to make sauces, dips, and spreads. Mortars come in a wide range of sizes, so select one or more models based on your needs. (See page 129 for more details.)

Nutmeg Grater

Two types of nutmeg grater are available. One is a simple rasp-type grater and the other is similar to a pepper mill. Whichever style you choose, grating whole nutmeg as needed ensures the flavor of the spice will be at its peak.

Parchment Paper and Nonstick Baking Liner

Parchment paper is paper infused with silicone to make it nonstick and fireproof up to 450°F. Cut your cleanup time by using parchment for cooking *en papillote* and for lining a sheet pan for oven-frying chicken, toasting bread for crostini, or roasting vegetables or other foods with a sticky glaze. Because it is taste free, there is no need to worry about transferring any unwanted flavors to food. It is available in rolls or in packets of a variety of precut sizes and is discarded after a single use. Nonstick baking liners, made of sturdy food-grade silicone reinforced with a glass weave, are as effective as parchment paper but can be washed and used again and again. They are made to fit rimmed sheet pans in a variety of sizes.

Pasta Machine

This heavyweight steel, hand-cranked machine is used for rolling out fresh pasta. It comes with a table clamp, adjusts to a range of thicknesses, and includes attachments for cutting two widths, fettuccine and tagliatelle. There are additional attachments available for cutting varying sizes, and some have an attachment for making filled pasta shapes. (See page 277 for more details.)

Pizza Peel

A pizza peel is a wide, flat, thin hardwood or metal shovel-shaped surface with a long handle. It is used for sliding a pizza or a loaf of bread into or out of a hot oven. One ingenious model has a fold-down handle for easy storage. (See page 283 for more details.)

Pizza Stone

This large, round (14 to 16 inches in diameter) or rectangular (14 by 16 inches) stone slab is placed directly on an oven rack for baking bread or pizza. Typically made of unglazed terra-cotta or stoneware, the stone produces crisp, well-browned crusts because the heat directly in contact with the dough is constant and high, rather than subject to the normal temperature fluctuations of an oven. (See page 283 for more details.)

Potato Ricer

Designed for mashing potatoes, the potato ricer consists of a can-shaped canister with perforations on the bottom. The cooked potatoes go into the can and, with a squeeze of your hand, a flat disk forces them through the holes in fine strands. (See page 133 for more details.)

Salad Spinner

The salad spinner is useful for rinsing, drying, and storing any type of greens. Centrifugal force pushes the washed greens to the sides of the interior basket, forcing any moisture into the bowl below while minimally bruising the greens. The outside bowl can be used to wash the greens before spinning, and the basket can double as a strainer or colander. The spinner—bowl, colander, and lid—will keep washed and dried salad greens crisp and fresh in the refrigerator for several days. A one-handed model has a nonskid base, a knob to start the basket spinning, and a pushbutton brake for stopping it. Another model has a pull cord, which requires one hand for holding the basket and the other for pulling. Salad spinners are plastic, dishwasher safe, and come large and small (the latter for small jobs like parsley and watercress) and in a variety of colors.

Salt Mill

Cooks generally prefer loose salt measured with a spoon or between the thumb and forefinger when cooking, but the salt mill is perfect for table service. Handsomely designed, salt mills are often sold in matched sets with a pepper mill. The mechanisms, which are similar, should be made of durable stainless steel or ceramic. The exteriors are made of attractive acrylics, woods, or stainless steel or other metals. The growing popularity of unrefined coarse salts from around the world has made the salt mill for table use more common. Wet or moist salt requires a mill with a corrosive-resistant ceramic mechanism to handle the higher humidity content.

Scale

Kitchen scales can be electronic or digital, spring, or balance. The balance scale, similar to the type used in doctors' offices, is the most accurate. The next most accurate, and the most popular for home kitchens, is the electronic scale. It is typically easy to read, compact and thus convenient to store, and gives both metric and standard weights. The spring scale, which is the least expensive, uses tiny lines similar to those on a ruler to display weights. Its disadvantage is that its spring can lose its elasticity with long use. Whichever type you choose, make sure it covers a wide range of weights (up to 5 pounds), can be automatically adjusted to zero to factor in the weight of a bowl or other container, is undemanding to clean and store, does standard to metric conversion, and is easy to read.

Skimmer

A mesh or perforated metal skimmer with a long handle is essential for removing froth from simmering stock or for reaching down into hot liquid to retrieve cooked vegetables or other foods. It is also handy for scooping up and discarding bay leaves or large herbs, pieces of ginger, garlic cloves, large whole spices, or the like.

Suribachi

The *suribachi* is a Japanese mortar used for mashing all kinds of foods, from sesame seeds to tofu, to a paste. The exterior surface is glazed earthenware, while the interior is ridged, unglazed clay. A wooden pestle (*surikogi*) is used to work the food against the rough interior, pulverizing it. These are usually sold as a set. (See page 157 for more details.)

Sushi Tools

The rice paddle and straw mat are the two tools necessary for making sushi rolls. The rice paddle, which is about 8 inches long and has a 2½–inch broad, flat paddle at one end, is traditionally made of wood, although plastic paddles are also available. The flexible straw mat, or *makisu,* is made of thin, parallel bamboo rods. A sheet of nori (dried seaweed) is laid on the mat, the sushi rice is spread on the nori, the rice is topped with one or more fillings, and the mat is rolled into a tube, creating a cylinder of nori-wrapped rice with the filling at its heart. (See page 161 for more details.)

Thermometer

Ideally, you can add three additional thermometers to the instant-read thermometer (page 13) of "The Basic Kitchen." The combination candy and deep-frying thermometer does double duty. It measures the temperature of a sugar syrup when making candy, and it helps keep hot oil at the correct temperature when deep-frying. Look for one with an easy-to-read dial, preferably color coded for specific temperature needs, a stainless-steel frame, and a metal clasp for mounting on the rim of the pot.

A probe-type thermometer includes a probe with a thin wire connected to a transmitting unit that sits on the countertop next to the oven. You insert the probe into the item being roasted and program the unit with the desired doneness temperature, and the unit alerts you with a tone when the exact internal temperature has been reached.

The classic oven thermometer ensures your oven temperature is accurate. Its horizontal shape means it sits firmly on a rack without tipping, or you can use its sturdy hook to suspend it from a rack. To test your oven's accuracy, turn the oven dial to a desired temperature, allow the oven to preheat, and then check the thermometer, preferably through the oven window. If the temperature on the thermometer differs from the oven dial temperature, adjust the dial to accommodate the difference.

Tortilla Press

Made of heavyweight cast aluminum or iron, the tortilla press is used for flattening a ball of *masa* dough into a thin cake. It has two round plates, each about 7 inches in diameter, connected by a hinge. Directly across from the hinge is a long handle that, when pulled down, forces the top plate against the bottom plate to flatten the dough. (See page 187 for more details.)

Wok Tools

PLATE LIFTER With this nifty tool, you can lift a plate from a bamboo steamer without fear of burning your fingertips. It has three arms that meet at the top with a double handle. You hook the tips of the arms under the lip of the plate and the arms contract and hold the plate firmly as you lift it from the steamer.

WIRE SKIMMER OR MESH SPOON This versatile utensil has a large (3 inches in diameter), round, spoon-shaped steel-mesh bowl with a long, split-bamboo handle. It can be used to lift fried foods from hot oil or to retrieve solid food from simmering liquid.

COOKING CHOPSTICKS More than a foot long, these chopsticks come in handy for lifting pieces of food from a hot wok, for mixing stir-fries, and for cooking fried rice.

WOK RING This circular metal ring, also called a collar, fits around a single burner. Its rim prevents a round-bottomed wok from tipping.

WOK SPATULA Shaped like a shovel, this long-handled metal utensil has a rounded end that matches the contours of the wok, making it easy to clear the rounded sides and bottom.

Appliances

Bread Machine

This amazing countertop machine will mix, knead, proof, and bake a loaf of bread in only a couple of hours. Machines come with a recipe booklet for handy reference, plus entire cookbooks devoted to the subject are available and many supermarkets sell convenient mixes.

Citrus Juicer and Juice Extractor

An electric citrus juicer is a must-have if you like to drink freshly squeezed citrus juice every day. Favorable features are reamers in different sizes for small or large fruits, ease of disassembly for washing, and a quiet motor. A more powerful machine that pulverizes vegetables or fruits and extracts all their essence in liquid form is called a juice extractor. Important features are again ease of cleaning and a quiet motor, plus a relatively large receptacle for capturing the extracted juice.

Coffee and Spice Grinder

The small, efficient electric coffee grinder is ideal for both grinding your morning coffee beans and for grinding spices for your cooking. The coarseness of the grind can be adjusted by how long you grind it. Two grinders are recommended, one for spices and one for coffee. (See page 247 for more details.)

Food Processor

The food processor has revolutionized the way we chop, slice, grate, puree, whip, and shred foods. Some models even have sufficiently powerful motors and large enough work bowls to knead dough. Now, instead of spending hours doing these tasks by hand, there is a machine that does them all in seconds. Many types of food processors are on the market. Some are basic and others have all sorts of bells and whistles. Select one to suit your level of expertise and cooking needs.

Immersion Blender

Also called wand hand blender, the immersion blender is a long, narrow rod with rotary blades that yield perfectly smooth purees. Its portability and heat resistance means that it can be used directly in a cooking pot or bowl. (See page 117 for more details.)

Panini Grill

In bars and cafés all over Italy, *panini,* or grilled sandwiches, are toasted on a specialized electric grill. The home model is smaller and has a hinged lid that can adjust to the thickness of the sandwich you are grilling. Look for a grill with a nonstick finish to reduce cleanup time, an outer casing that doesn't get hot when in use, and a grilling surface large enough to accommodate the number of sandwiches you anticipate making at one time. There is also a stove-top version called a panini pan.

Raclette Grill

This electric tabletop cooking hearth is used for making the classic Swiss dish of the same name. The reversible grill top (flat surface or with raised grids) cooks food served with the cheese as well as keeps food warm. Small individual trays that slide beneath the grill are used for melting cheese. Traditionally, the melted cheese is spread on warm potatoes and served with pickles, but many other delicious cheese, vegetable, and meat combinations are possible. (See page 232 for more details.)

Rice Cooker

The rice cooker does its job well, turning out perfectly cooked rice every time. Some models are quite sophis-ticated, with fancy timers, multiple settings, and even additional uses, such as steaming vegetables. Others are simple and straightforward, but still typically hold cooked rice at an even temperature for hours. (See page 153 for more details.)

Slow Cooker

The slow cooker takes the concept of the oven casserole and applies it to an electric countertop unit that cooks a dish at a very low temperature over a period of several hours. It is perfect for making soups, stews, and braised meat dishes, requiring virtually no further attention once you push the button. It also eliminates the overheated kitchen that often results when you use your oven. Many models have a timer that turns off the cooker when the cooking time is up and keeps the dish warm until serving time. Cookware shops stock a variety of sizes and styles at every price level.

Stand Mixer

While a hand mixer (page 17) can handle many kitchen tasks, a stand mixer is particularly good for heavy batters and large quantities. Before you purchase a stand mixer, consider both your baking ability and how frequently you will use the mixer. If you make bread, cakes, or cookies fairly often, your best bet is a model with a powerful motor and good capacity. The standard attachments are a wire whisk or whip for whipping cream, egg whites, and the like; a paddle for beating batters or creaming butter and sugar; and a dough hook for kneading bread dough. A variety of optional attachments are available that add different functions, such as pasta making, sausage stuffing, ice-cream making, and more.

Waffle Iron

Modern electric waffle irons cook the top and bottom of the waffle simultaneously. A nonstick coating covers the grid, so the waffles lift right off without tearing. Some models have reversible plates that transform the waffle iron into a smooth grill that could be used for pancakes or sandwiches.

PART

II

COOKING with KITCHEN ESSENTIALS

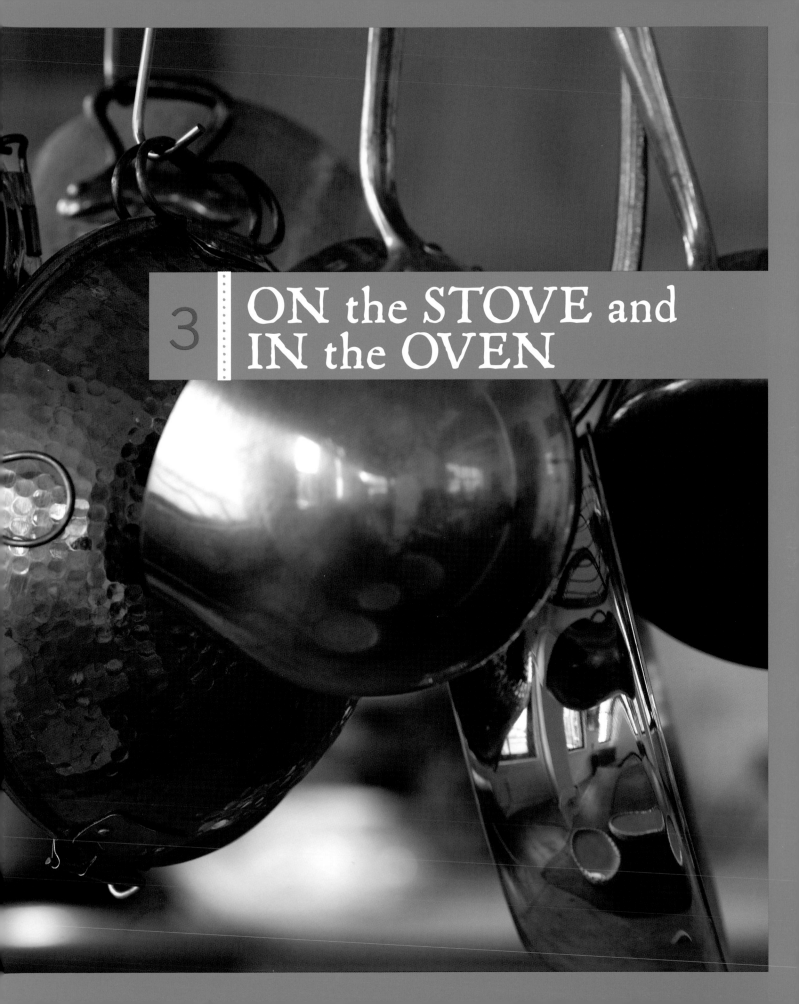

3 | ON the STOVE and IN the OVEN

Sausage-Stuffed Roasted
Artichokes with Tomato Sauce

*Roasting is one of the oldest and most spectacular
forms of cooking. Originally, roasting was done on a
spit in front of the fire. What we call roasting—food
cooked by dry heat in the oven—was known until the
end of the nineteenth century as baking.*

James Beard, AUTHOR, *JAMES BEARD'S THEORY & PRACTICE OF GOOD COOKING*

Baking Dish

For many cooks, the baking dish is the most popular piece of cookware in their kitchen. At one end of the spectrum is the tempered-glass baking dish, known for its durability and practicality. It is the dish our mothers and grandmothers kept in their cupboards and used daily for comforting casseroles of scalloped potatoes, macaroni and cheese, and rice pudding. At the opposite end of the spectrum are the handcrafted clay and the colorful enameled cast-iron baking dishes. In some cases, these dishes are more durable than basic glass and are typically admired for their beauty and design. Some are so beautiful you'll display them on a sideboard, instead of tucking them into a cabinet.

Baking dishes should be least 2 inches deep. The sides are either straight or slanted, and the shapes are round, oval, rectangular, or square. Many are microwave safe, and some can even go from the freezer to the oven. Every kitchen ideally has a selection of sizes, materials, and shapes.

Tips for Using

Baking dishes with easy-to-grip sculpted handles are more practical than dishes designed without handles, especially if the dish is large. Deep baking dishes are good for layered casseroles and lasagna.

Large, shallow dishes work well for roasting potatoes or other vegetables.

Oval dishes are good for roasts or poultry.

Baking dishes with an enamel coating or a heavy glaze are easier to scrub clean and have high heat retention.

Brightly colored clay dishes make handsome servers.

Care in Using

Soak with a bit of detergent or baking soda to help loosen baked-on particles.

Many are dishwasher safe.

Always consult the manufacturer's instructions.

Alternatives

Metal baking pans can be substituted but are not as attractive for serving; and gratins, which are usually shallower, can be used for some recipes.

recipes
Sausage-Stuffed Roasted Artichokes with Tomato Sauce | Roasted Potatoes with Mushrooms and Red Bell Peppers

SAUSAGE-STUFFED ROASTED ARTICHOKES with TOMATO SAUCE

PREP 30 min | COOK TIME (tomato sauce) 25 min |
COOK TIME (artichokes) 20 to 25 min |
COOK TIME (finished dish) 35 to 40 min | SERVES 6

Artichokes, those outrageous-looking giant thistles, are often available throughout the year, although the high seasons are in early spring and again in the fall. For the first-time eater—not to mention the first-time cook—artichokes can be intimidating. But once you get the hang of it, the preparation is not difficult. They are festive and perfect for cooking ahead, which makes them a good menu item when you are entertaining. The hearty stuffing of Italian sausage and bread crumbs makes this artichoke recipe substantial enough for a main dish.

Implements Chef's Knife, Kitchen Scissors, Dutch Oven, Slotted Spoon, 9 by 13-inch Baking Dish, Tongs, Medium Skillet, Wooden Spoon

Ingredients

2½ cups Oven-Roasted Tomato Sauce (page 73)

6 large globe artichokes

Juice of ½ lemon

Coarse salt

About 2 tablespoons extra-virgin olive oil

Freshly ground black pepper

STUFFING

2 cups coarse dried Italian bread crumbs
(¼-inch pieces) (page 219)

½ cup low-sodium chicken broth

1 tablespoon extra-virgin olive oil

1¼ pounds sweet Italian sausage, preferably with fennel, casings removed

½ cup chopped yellow onion

1 clove garlic, minced or grated

⅓ cup plus ½ cup grated Parmigiano-Reggiano cheese

¼ cup pine nuts, toasted (see page 85)

1 tablespoon finely chopped fresh Italian parsley

2 teaspoons finely chopped fresh oregano

Coarse salt and freshly ground black pepper

1. Make the tomato sauce.

2. Trim the artichokes: Fill a large bowl half full with water and add the lemon juice. Working with 1 artichoke at a time, cut the stem flush with the bottom with a chef's knife. Pull away and discard any tough or blemished outer leaves. Turn the artichoke on its side and, using a chef's knife, cut off about ½ inch from the top, removing the thorny leaf tops. Then, using kitchen scissors, snip off the prickly tips from the remaining leaves. Wash under cold running water, then drop into the bowl of lemon water. Repeat with the remaining artichokes.

3. Add water to a depth of about 2 inches to a large, wide, deep pan—a Dutch oven with or without a steamer insert works great. Add 2 teaspoons of salt and bring to a boil over high heat. Add the artichokes stem side down, cover, and cook over medium heat for 20 to 25 minutes, or until the artichokes are tender when pierced with the tip of a knife. Remove with a slotted spoon and tongs or lift the steamer insert from the pan. Invert the cooked artichokes onto a folded kitchen towel to cool.

4. Turn the artichokes upright. Working with 1 artichoke at a time, pull the leaves open at the center, reach into the artichoke, and pull out and discard the sharp pointed leaves. Then, using the tip of a teaspoon, scoop out the fuzzy choke. This little "pocket" you have created will hold some of the stuffing. Repeat with the remaining artichokes.

5. Spread the tomato sauce in the bottom of a 9 by 13-inch baking dish. Stand the artichokes upright in the dish. Add about 1 teaspoon of olive oil, a pinch of salt, and a grinding of pepper to each pocket.

6. MAKE THE STUFFING: In a medium bowl, combine the bread crumbs and chicken broth and toss to mix; set aside. Heat a medium skillet over low heat. Add the olive

oil and sausage and cook, stirring and breaking up the sausage with the side of a wooden spoon, for about 5 minutes, or until no longer pink. Add the onion and cook, stirring, for about 5 minutes, or until the onion is golden and the sausage is browned. Add the garlic and cook for 30 seconds, or until softened. Remove from the heat.

7. Add the bread-crumb mixture, 1/3 cup of the cheese, and the pine nuts, parsley, and oregano to the sausage mixture and mix well. Season to taste with salt and pepper.

8. Preheat the oven to 350°F. Stuff the sausage mixture into the artichoke pockets, dividing it evenly and mounding it on top. Sprinkle the remaining 1/2 cup cheese over the top of the artichokes, dividing it evenly.

9. Cover the baking dish with aluminum foil and bake for 25 to 30 minutes, until heated through. Uncover and bake for 10 minutes, or until the cheese is golden.

10. Serve each artichoke with some of the tomato sauce from the bottom of the baking dish spooned over the top.

ROASTED POTATOES with MUSHROOMS and RED BELL PEPPERS

PREP 20 min | COOK TIME 45 to 55 min | SERVES 4

Almost any trio of vegetables well seasoned with salt and pepper, liberally sprinkled with fresh herbs, drizzled with olive oil, and roasted in a hot oven will make a delicious side dish. Cook the vegetables for about an hour, stirring them occasionally so the pieces that have caramelized along the edges of the dish change places with the slower-cooking vegetables in the center. Here is a simple combination to get you started. Serve with grilled meats, baked polenta, or roasted chicken.

Implements 9 by 13-inch Baking Dish, Wide, Slotted Spatula

Ingredients

1 pound Yukon Gold potatoes, unpeeled,
cut into 3/4-inch chunks

2 large (about 1 pound total) red bell peppers,
seeded and cut into 3/4-inch squares

8 ounces mushrooms, any variety,
halved or quartered if large

1/2 yellow onion, cut into 1/8-inch wedges

2 cloves garlic, finely chopped

3 tablespoons extra-virgin olive oil

2 tablespoon chopped fresh oregano,
or 1/2 teaspoon dried

1 teaspoon coarse salt

Freshly ground black pepper

1. Preheat the oven to 400°F.

2. Spread the potatoes, bell peppers, mushrooms, onion, and garlic in a 9 by 13-inch rectangular or oval baking dish. Drizzle with the olive oil. Sprinkle with 1 tablespoon of the fresh oregano or all of the dried oregano, the salt, and a generous grinding of black pepper. Toss with your hands to coat evenly.

3. Roast for 45 to 55 minutes, turning the vegetables with a wide, slotted spatula every 15 minutes, or until the vegetables are caramelized and tender. Sprinkle with the remaining 1 tablespoon fresh oregano. Serve hot.

*Succulence. This is the true goal of braising:
it is the aim toward which one strives from
the very beginning, and it is the direction in
which all the techniques and methods lead.*

LA BONNE CUISINE DE MADAME E. SAINT-ANGE

**Beef Braciole Stuffed
with Sausage, Two Cheeses,
and Dried Currants**

Braiser

The braiser, also known as the bistro or buffet casserole, is handsome enough to go directly from the oven or stove top to the table. It is relatively shallow (2½ to 3 inches deep) and has a large cooking surface, making it suitable for sautéing, browning, and braising compact foods such as chicken, fish, chops, and vegetables. The snug-fitting domed lid locks in the juices and allows the condensation to drip back onto the food, keeping it moist while it slowly cooks.

The pan, which has two looped opposing handles, is available in relatively lightweight, polished stainless steel–clad aluminum that heats up quickly and cleans easily. The other choice is a matte-finished enameled cast iron, which is a much heavier pan and heats more slowly but holds the heat longer, making it perfect for keeping foods warm on a buffet.

Tips for Using

Not just for braising, the pan—sans the lid—works as a baking dish and as a skillet on the stove top.

Because it is flameproof, the braiser can be used under the broiler.

Its broad, shallow profile means the brasier is good for cooking rice, and rice dishes like pilaf, perfectly.

The braiser is handsome enough to use as a serving dish.

Care in Using

Both stainless steel and enameled cast iron wash like a dream. Warm, soapy water and a stiff brush or scouring pad are all you need.

Always consult the manufacturer's instructions.

Alternatives

Dutch oven, *cocotte,* sauté pan, or broad skillet with a lid

recipes

Beef Braciole Stuffed with Sausage, Two Cheeses, and Dried Currants | Chuck Steak with Braised Onions and Pan-Browned Potatoes

BEEF BRACIOLE STUFFED with SAUSAGE, TWO CHEESES, and DRIED CURRANTS

PREP 45 min | COOK TIME 1 to 1½ hr | SERVES 4

Braciole is a favorite Italian dish of meat slices pounded flat, spread with a filling, rolled into little bundles, and then slowly braised. For this recipe, you can use beef round, flank, or chuck, but pork cutlets, cut from the leg, will also work. As with so many slow-cooked dishes, the flavors improve if the recipe is made ahead and then reheated just before serving. Serve with mashed potatoes, polenta, or a small pasta shape, such as orzo. Serve with Creamy Polenta with Two Cheeses (page 57) or Fluffy Yukon Gold Potatoes with Goat Cheese and Green Onions (page 111).

Implements
Meat Pounder, Cooking String or Silicone Ties, Braiser, Tongs, Flat-Edged Wooden Spoon or Flat Whisk, Food Mill, Cutting Board

Ingredients

STUFFING

8 ounces sweet Italian sausages, preferably with fennel, casings removed

1 large egg, lightly beaten

½ cup fine dried bread crumbs

½ cup (2 ounces) diced aged provolone cheese

½ cup grated pecorino romano or Asiago cheese

2 tablespoons chopped fresh Italian parsley

2 tablespoons dried currants or dark raisins

1 clove garlic, minced

8 thin slices (¼ to ⅓ inch thick) boneless beef top round, flank, or chuck (about 1¼ pounds total)

Coarse salt and freshly ground black pepper

2 tablespoons extra-virgin olive oil, plus additional as needed

SAUCE

½ cup finely chopped yellow onion

½ cup finely chopped carrot

1 clove garlic, minced

½ cup full-bodied red wine

1 (28-ounce) can Italian plum tomatoes with juices

1 bay leaf

1 tablespoon finely chopped fresh Italian parsley, for garnish

1. **MAKE THE STUFFING:** In a large bowl, combine the sausage meat, egg, bread crumbs, provolone cheese, pecorino romano cheese, parsley, currants, and garlic, and stir until well blended.

2. Lay a large piece of plastic wrap on a flat surface and place a slice of beef on top. Place a second piece of plastic wrap on top of the beef. Using a meat pounder, gently but firmly pound the meat, beginning in the center and working your way to the edges, until the meat is an even ⅛ inch thick. Repeat with the remaining beef slices. Depending on the weight of the pounder and the thickness of the meat, each slice can take 10 to 20 firm, purposeful whacks to achieve the correct thickness.

3. Cut 16 pieces of cooking string each 10 inches long, or have ready silicone ties. Sprinkle each meat slice with a pinch of salt and a grinding of pepper.

4. Divide the stuffing into 8 equal portions (each one will be a heaping ¼ cup). Place a portion in the center of a meat slice and spread to within ½ inch of the edges. Press the stuffing evenly into the meat. Beginning with the narrow end, roll up the meat around the stuffing to make a neat bundle. Using the string or ties, tie each roll crosswise and lengthwise, like a package, securely but not too tightly. Repeat with the remaining meat slices and stuffing.

5. Heat the braiser over medium heat until hot enough for a drop of water to sizzle on contact, then add the olive oil. Arrange the meat rolls in the pan (they fit best if arranged like wheel spokes) and brown on all 4 sides, turning the rolls with tongs, for about 5 minutes total, or until evenly colored. Using the tongs, transfer the meat to a plate.

6. MAKE THE SAUCE: If the pan is dry, add an additional drizzle of oil. Add the onion and carrot, and cook, over medium-low heat, stirring occasionally, for 5 minutes, or until softened. Add the garlic and cook for 1 minute, or until softened. Add the red wine and bring to a boil. Using the flat edge of a wooden spoon or a flat whisk, scrape the browned bits from the bottom of the pan. Boil the wine for 5 minutes, or until reduced by half. Remove from the heat.

7. Set a food mill fitted with the fine disk on the rim of a medium bowl, add the tomatoes with their juices, and puree. Or, puree the tomatoes in a food processor and then press though a fine-mesh strainer to remove the seeds.

8. Add the tomatoes and bay leaf to the braiser and bring to a boil. Return the beef rolls to the sauce, turning with the tongs to coat well, and reduce the heat to low. Cover and cook for 1 to 1½ hours, until the meat is tender when pierced with a fork. Turn the rolls occasionally and check to make sure the sauce isn't boiling too hard.

9. Transfer the rolls to a cutting board and let rest for 5 minutes. Meanwhile, boil the sauce over high heat for 2 to 3 minutes, until slightly thickened.

10. Snip the strings from the beef rolls and discard, or untie the silicone ties. Cut the rolls on the diagonal into slices ½ inch thick, and arrange the slices on a warmed deep platter. Remove and discard the bay leaf from the sauce. Spoon the sauce on top of the rolls and sprinkle with the parsley. Serve hot.

tip BRINGING DRIED HERBS BACK TO LIFE

If a fresh herb called for in a recipe isn't available, you can substitute its dried equivalent, using one-third of the amount. For example, you can substitute 1 teaspoon dried oregano for 1 tablespoon chopped fresh oregano. To reconstitute dried herbs and bring out their flavor, finely chop with moist parsley leaves, pound in a mortar with a garlic clove and coarse salt, or rub between your fingertips. The friction will release the aromatic oils and helps replace some of the moisture—and flavor—lost when the herb was dried.

CHUCK STEAK with BRAISED ONIONS and PAN-BROWNED POTATOES

PREP 35 min | COOK TIME 1¼ hr | SERVES 4

A thick-cut boneless chuck steak is the best choice here. It's ideal for when you want a pot roast but don't want to cook a big roast with lots of leftovers. Chuck is generally well marbled and will cook up soft and tender.

Implements
Braiser, Tongs, Wide Spatula, Flat-Edged Wooden Spoon or Flat Whisk, Food Mill, Cutting Board

Ingredients

2 tablespoons extra-virgin olive oil, plus more as needed

1 (2-pound) boneless chuck roast, about 1¾ inches thick

Coarse salt and freshly ground black pepper

2 large (about 8 ounces each) yellow onions, cut into ½-inch wedges, plus ⅓ cup finely chopped

1 tablespoon fresh oregano leaves, chopped, or 1 teaspoon dried

8 small red potatoes (about 1 pound total), unpeeled, halved, or equal weight larger red potatoes, cut into 1-inch chunks

⅓ cup finely chopped carrot

⅓ cup finely chopped celery

½ cup full-bodied red wine

2 cups low-sodium beef broth

2 tablespoons tomato paste

2 tablespoons finely chopped fresh oregano leaves, for garnish

1. Heat the braiser over medium heat and pour in 1 table-spoon of the olive oil. Tilt the pan to coat. Sprinkle the meat well on both sides with salt and pepper. Add to the pan and cook, adjusting the heat between medium and medium-high as needed, for about 5 minutes per side, or until well browned. Use tongs and a wide spatula to transfer the roast to a plate.

2. Add the onion wedges to the pan and cook over medium to medium-high heat, stirring, for 10 minutes, or until well browned. Season with the oregano and some salt and pepper. Transfer to a large bowl.

3. Add the remaining 1 tablespoon of oil to the hot pan and place the potatoes, cut side down, in the pan. Cook, without turning, for 10 minutes, or until well browned on the cut side. Use a spatula to transfer the potatoes to the bowl with the onions.

4. Add the chopped onion, the carrot, and the celery to the hot pan along with a drizzle of oil if the pan is dry. Cook over medium heat, stirring, for 3 minutes, or until tender. Pour in the wine, bring to a boil, and stir with the flat edge of a wooden spoon or a flat whisk to scrape the browned bits from the bottom of the pan. Boil for 2 min-utes, or until the wine is reduced by half. Add the beef broth and tomato paste and bring to a boil, stirring until blended.

5. Return to the pan the meat and any juices that have ac-cumulated on the plate. Spoon the broth over the meat. Cover and cook over low heat for about 1 hour, or until the meat is very tender.

6. With the tongs and wide spatula, gently lift the meat from the pan and place on a plate. Set a food mill fitted with the fine disk on the rim of a medium bowl, add the juices and solids from the pan, and puree to make a sauce. Alternatively, use an immersion blender, a stand blender, or a food processor. Add the puree to the re-served onions and potatoes, and stir to combine. Slide the meat and juices back into the pan. Spoon the veg-etable mixture on top of the meat. Cover and cook over low heat for 10 to 15 minutes, until the potatoes and onions are tender. Season to taste with salt and pepper.

7. Transfer the meat to a cutting board and cut crosswise into thick slices. Arrange the slices on a warmed platter and top with the vegetables and sauce. Sprinkle with the fresh oregano.

tip BRUISING GARLIC

Bruised garlic is often the precursor to chopped garlic. Once bruised, the garlic will cook to a soft and silken consistency, gently flavoring any dish. Trim the hard, dried stem end from the garlic clove. Rest the broad side of a large, heavy knife against the clove and press down hard with your hand until the garlic gives. Alternatively, use a long rubber tube called a garlic peeler (page 27) to loosen the skin. Once loosened, the papery skin slips off and the garlic is slightly flattened or "bruised."

Olive Oil

Buying Olive Oil A solid wall of olive oil bottles can be overwhelming at the market, even for the most experienced cook. Many types are available from a slew of countries, and the prices vary widely. How do you know which one to buy?

Reading the Labels Most olive oils sold today are labeled either "olive oil" or "extra-virgin olive oil."

If the label says simply olive oil or pure olive oil, it means the original oil was treated with chemicals and heat to remove odors or impurities. The "cleaned" oil was then blended with some flavorful olive oil to bring it back. Although it is inferior to extra-virgin olive oil, it is economical, and many cooks use these lesser oils for roasting, sautéing, and other preparations where the flavor of an extra-virgin olive oil would be lost.

Extra-virgin olive oil has not been subjected to heat or treated with chemicals. The olives were picked at their height of ripeness and stored under tightly controlled conditions to avoid bruising and spoilage, and to protect the natural taste of the fruit. The taste can be fruity and rustic, light and buttery, or fall anywhere in between. Extra-virgin olive oil can be used for cooking, except for the very expensive oils, which should only be used as finishing oils.

Making a Selection Olive oil is an agricultural product, so its character is defined by the soil and the variations in climate. In general, oil pressed from olives grown in hot climates, such as those of Sicily and Morocco, is a bit more rustic and fruity. (In this case, fruity means tastes strongly of the olive.) Oil pressed from olives harvested in cooler climates, such as Tuscany and Umbria, in central Italy, are usually smooth, buttery, and a bit more elegant. The age of the trees, the olive variety, and the style of the region also affect the final product, so look for information on the labels.

Extra-virgin olive oils come in a dizzying range of prices due to various factors, including quality and supply and demand. Also, larger producers will often sell oil at a reduced price, whereas small producers can't afford to discount their limited stock.

A sensible way to approach buying olive oil is to purchase several types. Keep a small bottle of expensive oil on hand as a finishing oil to use sparingly for coating salad greens, drizzling on bread, or sprinkling over cooked vegetables. Use less-expensive extra-virgin olive oil for roasting, sautéing, or frying.

i own a few hundred pots and pans, but the one i use most frequently is a cast-iron skillet left behind by a college roommate back in the '60s. Nothing beats this skillet for cooking thick steaks or pork chops to juicy perfection.

Bruce Aidells, COAUTHOR, *THE COMPLETE MEAT COOKBOOK*

**Double Corn Bread with Smoked
Mozzarella and Sun-Dried Tomatoes**

Cast-Iron Skillet

If you're looking for a piece of cookware that will last a lifetime, look no further. The cast-iron skillet is legendary. In fact, your great grandmother and her mother's mother probably cooked in one. Quite possibly, your family heirloom is still in use today. Solid as a rock and with a sensible design, it's amazingly durable. The secret to the iron skillet's longevity is the extra-thick cast iron used to make it and its versatility in the kitchen. Cast iron isn't a fast conductor of heat, but once it gets hot, it distributes the heat evenly and steadily, holding its temperature like an oven (see Dutch Oven, page 5). You can choose from a variety of sizes, from small (6½ inches) to huge (15¼ inches), but the 10-inch model is the most convenient, perfect for searing hamburgers or for baking corn bread.

Tips for Using

This is the skillet to use for techniques that require a sustained medium to high temperature: pan frying, stir-frying, searing meat, browning onions, cooking bacon, and even baking corn bread.

A cast-iron skillet can be moved from the stove top to a hot oven or broiler to finish cooking.

When shopping for a skillet, test its weight to make sure you can lift it comfortably. Some of the larger models have a useful smaller handle directly opposite the longer handle, making it possible to get a grip with both hands.

The long handle gets very hot during use. A silicone or heatproof handle cover is useful for protecting your hand.

Acidic foods—wine, lemon juice, tomatoes—can react with the iron and develop an off flavor. Otherwise, a cast-iron skillet is perfect for braising and stewing.

Cast iron doesn't respond quickly to temperature change, so it is less useful for making sauces or any dish that needs to cool down quickly when it's taken off the heat.

Care in Using

The cast iron will rust if it's not properly seasoned. Seasoning occasionally will keep its surfaces smooth and practically nonstick.

Season a cast-iron skillet prior to its use. With a paper towel or clean cloth, rub the entire skillet—inside, outside, and the handle—with a thin film of vegetable oil. Don't use too much oil or the pan will be sticky. Put both oven racks in the lowest positions in the oven, and place a sheet of aluminum foil on the lower rack to catch any dripping oil. Preheat the oven to 350°F. Invert the skillet on the rack above the foil and bake for 1 hour. Turn off the oven and let the skillet cool in the oven. Repeat as needed.

Clean a seasoned cast-iron pan by sprinkling it generously with coarse salt and rubbing with clean paper towels. If you must use a mild deterent and warm water, make sure to immediately reseason the pan.

Wipe a just-washed skillet dry with a paper towel or dish cloth, and set it over low heat to dry thoroughly. While still warm, use a paper towel to rub in a small amount of vegetable oil. Store in a dry place.

Always consult the manufacturer's instructions.

Alternatives

An enameled cast-iron skillet that has a baked-on matte black enamel interior also works well for high-temperature cooking.

recipes

Double Corn Bread with Smoked Mozzarella and Sun-Dried Tomatoes | Stilton-Stuffed Burgers with Caramelized Red Onions and Balsamic Vinegar

DOUBLE CORN BREAD with SMOKED MOZZARELLA and SUN-DRIED TOMATOES

PREP 20 min | COOK TIME 25 min | SERVES 8

There are many tempting flavor possibilities when it comes to corn bread. For this version, smoked mozzarella or Gouda is substituted for the more traditional Cheddar or Monterey Jack. The addition of buttermilk gives the bread a tender crumb and a slight tang, the dried tomatoes add a salty edge, and the corn kernels reinforce the taste of the yellow cornmeal. Fresh corn is preferred, although canned or thawed frozen kernels can be used.

Implements 10-inch Cast-Iron Skillet, Two Large Bowls, Standard Whisk, Rubber Spatula

Ingredients

1¼ cups yellow cornmeal

¾ cup all-purpose flour

4 teaspoons baking powder

1 tablespoon sugar

1 teaspoon coarse salt

⅛ teaspoon coarsely ground black pepper

2 large eggs

1 cup buttermilk

¼ cup plus 2 tablespoons flavorless vegetable oil

1 cup fresh corn kernels (from 2 ears)

½ cup plus 2 tablespoons coarsely shredded smoked mozzarella or Gouda cheese

¼ cup minced smoked ham (optional)

2 tablespoons finely chopped olive oil–packed sun-dried tomatoes, rinsed and drained

1 tablespoon finely chopped fresh Italian parsley

1. Preheat the oven to 400°F. Place a 10-inch cast-iron skillet over low heat on the stove top and leave it to heat while preparing the batter for the corn bread.

2. In a large bowl, combine the cornmeal, flour, baking powder, sugar, salt, and black pepper, and stir with a standard whisk to mix. In a second large bowl, whisk together the eggs, buttermilk, and ¼ cup of the oil until blended. Stir into this second bowl the corn, ½ cup of the cheese, the ham, the tomatoes, and the parsley.

3. Make a well in the center of the dry ingredients. Add the buttermilk mixture and fold together with a rubber spatula just until blended.

4. Drizzle the heated skillet with the remaining 2 tablespoons of oil, tilting the pan to coat evenly. Immediately add the batter (the oil will sizzle and bubble up around the edges to coat the sides of the skillet), and spread it to the edges of the skillet, using a rubber spatula. Sprinkle the top with the remaining 2 tablespoons cheese.

5. Bake for 25 minutes, or until the top is golden and the edges have pulled away from the sides of the skillet. Serve hot or at room temperature, cut into wedges.

tip STORING FRESH HERBS

To keep fresh herbs perky, stand them in a cup or glass of water and cover loosly with an inverted plastic bag. They will keep for at least 5 days (basil) or up to 2 weeks (parsley and thyme).

STILTON-STUFFED BURGERS with CARAMELIZED RED ONIONS and BALSAMIC VINEGAR

PREP 25 min | COOK TIME 35 min | SERVES 4

Rather then melting a slice a cheese on top, like the classic cheeseburger, these burgers hide it in the center. If you like blue cheese, there's no greater treat than biting into a nugget of warm, runny blue cheese. Serve the red onions as a side dish or as a topping for the burger. This new twist on the revered hamburger is so successful that you may decide to skip the usual toasted bun and squirt of ketchup. A mandoline or other slicer will make quick work of slicing the onions.

Implements
10-inch Cast-Iron Skillet, Large Spoon, Large Bowl, Digital Scale, Silicone Brush, Silicone Spatula, Wooden Spoon

Ingredients

2 tablespoons extra-virgin olive oil, plus more as needed

1½ pounds red onions, thinly sliced (about 4 cups)

2 tablespoons balsamic vinegar

1 teaspoon coarse salt

⅛ teaspoon freshly ground black pepper

3 ounces firm blue-veined cheese (such as Stilton, Cashel blue, or Cabrales), crumbled

1½ pounds ground beef

1 tablespoon finely chopped Italian parsley

1. Heat a 10-inch cast-iron skillet over medium heat. Add the oil and heat until hot enough to sizzle an onion ring. Add the onions, adjust the heat to medium-low, and sauté, stirring, for 2 minutes, or until evenly coated with the oil. Cover and cook for 3 minutes, or until wilted. Uncover and cook, stirring occasionally and adjusting the heat between medium and medium-low, for about 20 minutes, or until the onions are a dark golden brown. Add the salt and pepper. Remove the skillet from the heat. With a large spoon, transfer the onions to a large bowl. Add the vinegar, salt, and pepper to the onions and set aside. Rinse and dry the pan.

2. Divide the ground beef into eight 3-ounce portions, and shape each portion into a patty about 4 inches in diameter. Divide 2 ounces (about ½ cup crumbled) of the cheese evenly among 4 of the patties, sprinkling it on the surface and lightly pressing it into the meat. Top with the remaining 4 patties, to make 4 cheese-stuffed burgers. Press around the edge of each burger to seal the top and bottom patties together, to prevent the cheese from oozing out during cooking. Brush both sides of the burgers lightly with olive oil.

3. Heat the skillet over medium heat until hot enough for a drop of water to sizzle on contact. Place the burgers in the pan, increase the heat to high, and cook, flipping them at the midpoint with a spatula, for 4 minutes per side for medium-rare and 5 minutes per side for well done. Transfer the burgers to a platter.

4. Add the onions to the hot skillet and reheat briefly over low heat for about 1 minute, or until hot. Spoon the onions over the burgers. Sprinkle with the remaining 1 ounce of cheese and the parsley, and serve.

Earthenware cooking pots speak to us of soothing and nurturing 'grandmother-style' dishes. They speak, too, of the potter's skill, and of gastronomical moments frozen in time. They speak of the mysterious process by which raw products are transformed into magnificent food.

Paula Wolfert, COOKBOOK AUTHOR AND EXPERT ON CLAY COOKWARE

**Winter Vegetable Stew
with Moroccan Flavors**

Clay Cooker

The design of a clay cooker, also known as a clay pot, imitates the ancient practice of covering food with wet clay, roasting it in an open fire until the clay forms a hard shell, and then cracking the shell to expose the cooked food, likely losing most of the tasty juices at the same time. Today, clay cookers are far easier to use and are especially appreciated because foods cooked in them require little or no added fat.

Some clay cookers are unglazed on the inside but all need to be soaked in cold water for about 30 minutes before using for the first time. As the heat of the oven permeates the pot, the wetness in the clay is drawn out, adding moisture to the cooker's interior.

Tips for Using

Read the instructions that accompany your clay cooker before use. All clay cookers—even glazed ones—must be soaked—typically 30 minutes—before they are used the first time.

All clay cookers should also be soaked each time they are used, but for a shorter length of time, typically 15 minutes.

To soak, slip the cooker into a sink filled with cool water.

Some clay pots must be placed in a cold oven, which is then turned to the desired temperature, usually 400° to 450°F. Make sure to read carefully the instructions that accompany your clay cooker.

Because the soaked pot adds so much moisture to the food, it's the perfect vessel for making soup.

Care in Using

Don't take a clay cooker from a hot oven and place it on cold granite, tile, stainless steel, or another cold surface. Instead, place it on a folded kitchen towel to buffer it from extreme temperature changes.

Wash with warm, soapy water and gently scrub with a stiff plastic brush. Use only mild dishwashing liquid, never strong cleaners.

To remove stubborn burnt-on food or residual odors from the interior, fill the clay pot with warm water, add a spoonful of baking soda, and let stand overnight. It should then scrub clean.

Always consult the manufacturer's instructions.

Alternatives

Dutch oven, *cocotte,* or braiser

recipes
Winter Vegetable Stew with Moroccan Flavors |
Roasted Boneless Leg of Lamb with Orange Gremolata

WINTER VEGETABLE STEW with MOROCCAN FLAVORS

POT SOAK 15 to 30 min | PREP 25 min |

COOK TIME 1¾ hr | SERVES 6–8

Eight different vegetables and such heady spices as cinnamon, cumin, and paprika all contribute to the wonderful flavor of this hearty stew. Feel free to add other vegetables, but avoid adding any strongly flavored ones, such as cabbage, broccoli, or cauliflower, or any vegetable that won't benefit from the long cooking time. If you have preserved lemons on hand, mince them and sprinkle on top of the stew just before serving.

Implements 3-Quart Clay Cooker, Rubber Spatula

Ingredients

2 large carrots, peeled and cut into ¾-inch pieces

2 stalks celery, cut into ¾-inch pieces

2 tablespoons golden or dark raisins

2 cloves garlic, bruised with knife

1 leek, trimmed and cut into ¾-inch pieces

8 ounces winter squash (such as butternut or acorn), peeled, seeded, and cut into ¾-inch cubes

8 ounces Yukon Gold or other potatoes, unpeeled, cut into ¾-inch cubes

8 ounces rutabagas, peeled and cut into ¾-inch cubes

8 ounces turnips, peeled and cut into ¾-inch cubes

2 tablespoons extra-virgin olive oil

1 (28-ounce) can Italian plum tomatoes with juices

1 teaspoon ground cumin

1 teaspoon Hungarian sweet paprika

1 teaspoon coarse salt

1 cinnamon stick

1 bay leaf

2 tablespoons chopped fresh cilantro, for garnish

2 tablespoons minced Preserved Lemons (page 328), optional

1. If new, soak both portions of a 3-quart clay cooker for 30 minutes in cold water. If the pot has been used before, soak both parts for only 15 minutes. Drain and pat dry before using.

2. Combine the carrots, celery, raisins, garlic, leek, winter squash, potatoes, rutabagas, turnips, and olive oil in the bottom portion of the clay cooker. Add the tomatoes, cumin, paprika, and salt. Fold together until blended. Tuck in the cinnamon stick and bay leaf.

3. Cover and place in a cold oven. Turn the oven to 450°F. Bake without disturbing for 1¾ hours. Remove from oven and let stand, covered, for 10 minutes. Sprinkle with the cilantro and preserved lemons. Serve hot from the oven or at room temperature.

ROASTED BONELESS LEG of LAMB with ORANGE GREMOLATA

POT SOAK 15 to 30 min | SOAK TIME (beans) 1 hr, 4 hr, or overnight | PREP 20 min | COOK TIME 2 hr 10 min | SERVES 6–8

Typically, foods aren't browned before they go into a clay cooker, but browning the meat and cooking the aromatic vegetables (onion, carrot, and garlic) until golden add extra flavor to the mild-tasting beans that cook along with the lamb. The *gremolata,* which is sprinkled on top of the finished dish, is traditionally a finely chopped mixture of lemon zest, garlic, and parsley. For this dish, orange zest is substituted for the lemon.

Implements 3-Quart Clay Cooker, Paring or Boning Knife, Mortar and Pestle, Cooking String or Silicone Ties, Large Heavy Skillet, Tongs, Wide Spatula, Oven Mitts, Cutting Board, Slotted Spoon

Ingredients

1 pound (about 2½ cups) dried small white beans

1 (4-pound) boneless leg of lamb

10 cloves garlic

1 tablespoon coarse salt

1 tablespoon chopped fresh rosemary

¼ teaspoon freshly ground coarse black pepper

2 tablespoons olive oil

1 large (8 ounces) yellow onion, chopped

1 large carrot, peeled and chopped (1 cup)

1 cup drained canned Italian plum tomatoes, cut up

2 bay leaves

1 (3 by ½-inch) strip orange zest

4 cups lamb, beef, or low-sodium chicken broth

ORANGE GREMOLATA

½ cup loosely packed fresh Italian parsley leaves

2 (3 by ½-inch) strips orange zest

2 cloves garlic, bruised with knife

1. Place the beans in a large bowl, add cold water to cover by at least 2 inches, and soak in the refrigerator for at least 4 hours or up to overnight. Drain well before using. Alternatively, place the beans in a saucepan, add cold water to cover by 2 inches, bring to a boil, cover, and boil for 3 minutes. Remove from the heat and let stand in the water, covered, for 1 hour. Drain well before using.

2. If new, soak both portions of a 3-quart clay cooker in cold water for 30 minutes. If the pot has been used before, soak both parts for only 15 minutes. Drain and pat dry before using.

3. Lay the lamb flat, fat side up, on a work surface. With a paring or boning knife, trim off any large clumps of fat the butcher might have missed. Turn the lamb, cut side up. Use a mortar and pestle to crush together the garlic, salt, rosemary, and pepper to a paste. Alternatively, use a garlic press to mash or a rasp grater to grate the garlic and then mash together the garlic, salt, rosemary, and pepper in a small bowl, using a fork. Measure out and reserve 2 teaspoons of the garlic mixture. Spread the remaining garlic mixture on the cut surface of the lamb.

4. Cut 8 lengths of cooking string each about 20 inches long, or use silicone ties. Position the lamb with a long side facing you, and roll it into a fat oval, tucking in the edges as you roll. Position the lamb horizontally on the work surface, and place 6 lengths of the string, at equally spaced intervals, under it. Tie each string firmly, but not too tightly, around the meat. Run the remaining 2 pieces of string lengthwise around the lamb, and tie them in place, tucking any protruding pieces of lamb under the strings.

5. Heat a large, heavy skillet over medium heat and add the olive oil. Add the lamb and brown, turning with tongs and a wide spatula, for about 20 minutes, or until well colored on all sides. Transfer the lamb to a plate. Add the onion and carrot, and cook over medium heat, stirring, for 10 minutes, or until golden. Add the reserved 2 teaspoons of the garlic mixture and cook for 30 seconds. Add the drained beans, tomatoes, bay leaves, and orange zest, and stir to blend.

6. Spoon the bean mixture into the bottom half of the soaked clay cooker. Place the lamb on top of the beans with any juices that accumulated on the plate. Add the broth.

7. Cover and place in a cold oven. Turn the oven to 450°F. Bake without disturbing for 2 hours. Remove from the oven and let stand, covered, for 20 minutes.

8. **MAKE THE *GREMOLATA:*** On a cutting board, finely chop the parsley, orange zest, and garlic together with a knife, or chop them together in a food processor. Set aside.

9. Using oven mitts, lift the lid from the clay cooker. Use a wide spatula and tongs to transfer the meat to a cutting board. Tent the meat with aluminum foil. Taste the beans and add salt and pepper, if needed. Remove the bay leaves. Use a slotted spoon to transfer the beans to a deep platter and tent with foil to keep warm. Transfer the excess juices in the clay cooker to a saucepan and boil for 3 minutes, until reduced slightly.

10. Remove the strings or ties from the meat. Carve the meat into ¼-inch-thick slices and arrange the slices on top of the beans. Spoon the reduced juices over the top. Sprinkle the *gremolata* evenly on top and serve.

Once a standard item in every kitchen, a double boiler is still enormously practical since it allows you to cook foods such as polenta and flour-based sauces without stirring.

Deborah Madison, AUTHOR, *VEGETARIAN COOKING FOR EVERYONE*

**Easy Blender Orange–Chipotle
Chile Hollandaise**

Double Boiler

The double boiler is designed for foods that call for gentle heat, or if you wish to cook food slowly without the risk of it burning or sticking to the bottom of the pot. It consists of two separate parts: the top part holds the food and the bottom holds the hot or gently simmering water that gently diffuses the heat. (A container placed in, rather than over, hot water to keep it warm is called a bain-marie, or water bath.) The steam that rises from the hot water heats the top part and in turn the food.

The most versatile double boiler is a 2-quart single stainless-steel insert that fits into any 4-quart saucepan. These also come in a range of other sizes. The lid of the saucepan fits the insert as well. There is also a double-boiler unit made up of a stainless-steel insert, a matching saucepan, and a lid that fits both the top and bottom. Yet another model combines a porcelain insert and a copper bottom pan that is preferable for delicate sauces and melting chocolate. However, the porcelain insert cannot be used by itself directly on a burner.

Tips for Using

Double-boiler tops or inserts are not designed to be used directly over the heat, although metal inserts can be used cautiously over very low heat for a short period of time.

The bottom pan can sometimes do double duty as an independent saucepan.

The double boiler is perfect for melting butter or chocolate, making custard or other egg-based sauces, and warming or cooking other heat-sensitive foods, such as cooked rice or mashed potatoes.

Add water to a depth of about 2 inches to the bottom pan, or just enough to avoid touching the bottom of the insert.

Keep the heat level low, because if too much steam is generated, the top part will get too hot and ruin the temperature-sensitive food you're cooking.

A double boiler is great for cooking polenta and other slow-cooked cornmeal-based dishes and for keeping food warm, such as mashed potatoes or soup, without fear of scorching.

Use for reheating leftovers without fear of scorching.

Care in Using

Stainless steel washes up easily by hand. Always consult the manufacturer's instructions.

Alternatives

You can use a stainless-steel bowl that fits snugly into the rim of a saucepan. Make sure the bottom of the bowl does not touch the simmering water in the saucepan. For polenta, use a heavy, enameled cast-iron Dutch oven on low heat.

recipes
Easy Blender Orange–Chipotle Chile Hollandaise | Creamy Polenta with Two Cheeses | Variation: Oven-Baked Polenta with Two Cheeses

EASY BLENDER ORANGE-CHIPOTLE CHILE HOLLANDAISE

PREP 10 min | **COOK TIME** 10 min | **MAKES** 2 cups
SERVES 8

Hollandaise made in a blender has a fluffier, lighter texture than hand-whisked hollandaise. Finishing the sauce in the double boiler has two advantages: it ensures the yolks are heated to a safe temperature and it keeps the sauce warm for up to an hour before serving. The sauce can also be made ahead, chilled, and then gently reheated in the double boiler. The orange and the chile play off the richness of this buttery classic with a touch of sweet and a hint of heat. Serve with poached eggs for a new twist on Eggs Benedict, or spoon over steamed or roasted asparagus, roasted and peeled red peppers, or thickly sliced cooked beets.

Implements Two Small Saucepans, Double Boiler, Blender, Standard Whisk

Ingredients

1 cup (2 sticks) unsalted butter

½ cup freshly squeezed orange juice

3 large egg yolks

2 tablespoons freshly squeezed lemon juice

2 teaspoons grated orange zest

1 teaspoon minced canned chipotle chile in adobo sauce

¾ teaspoon coarse salt

¼ teaspoon freshly ground white pepper

1. Heat the butter in a small saucepan over low heat until melted and hot. In a separate small saucepan, bring the orange juice to a boil and then keep it hot over low heat.

2. Combine the egg yolks and lemon juice in a blender. With the motor running, add the hot orange juice in a slow, steady stream.

3. With the motor still running, add the hot butter to the egg mixture in a slow, steady stream. Add the orange zest, chipotle chile, salt, and white pepper, and process until combined.

4. Add water to a depth of 1 inch to the bottom of a double boiler and bring to a simmer over medium heat. Place the top of the double boiler over the simmering water. Transfer the contents of the blender to the top of the double boiler. Alternatively, use a heatproof bowl that will sit snugly over simmering water in a saucepan. Over medium-low heat use a standard whisk to whisk the sauce over very hot water for 5 to 7 minutes, or until the sauce is thickened and hot to the touch.

5. Serve at once, or keep warm over hot water (not boiling) for up to 1 hour before serving.

CREAMY POLENTA with TWO CHEESES

PREP 15 min | COOK TIME 45 min | SERVES 4–6

Stirring polenta over low heat until the texture is soft and the flavor is sweet requires time, patience, and fortitude. Here, the double boiler comes to the rescue. Cook and stir the polenta in the top part over direct heat for a short period of time and then place it over simmering water in the bottom portion. The polenta will cook slowly without needing stirring and emerge soft and fluffy 45 labor-free minutes later.

Implements Large Metal Double Boiler, Sauce Whisk

Ingredients

3 tablespoons unsalted butter or extra-virgin olive oil

½ cup finely chopped yellow onion

4 cups water, or 2 cups each low-sodium chicken broth and water, plus more as needed

1 cup yellow cornmeal or polenta

1 teaspoon coarse salt

½ cup (2 ounces) grated Parmigiano-Reggiano cheese

1 cup (5 ounces) cubed mozzarella cheese

1. Heat the butter in the top of a large (3-quart) metal double boiler over low heat until melted. Stir in the onion and cook, stirring, for 5 minutes, or until softened. Add 2 cups of the water and bring to a boil.

2. In a bowl, use a sauce whisk to stir together the cornmeal, the remaining 2 cups water, and the salt until blended. Slowly whisk the wet cornmeal mixture into the boiling liquid until blended. Cook over low heat, stirring constantly, for 5 minutes, until the polenta begins to thicken.

3. Add water to a depth of 2 inches to the bottom of the double boiler and bring to a simmer over medium heat. Place the top of the double boiler with the precooked polenta over the simmering water. Make sure the bottom of the top part is not touching the water. Decrease the heat to medium-low, cover, and cook the polenta for 45 minutes, or until thick and fluffy. Stir in the Parmigiano-Reggiano and mozzarella until melted. Taste and adjust the seasoning with salt.

4. Serve at once or keep warm over hot water until ready to serve, up to 1 hour. If the polenta gets too thick, stir in a small amount of water, broth, or milk to thin to the desired consistency.

variation OVEN-BAKED POLENTA WITH TWO CHEESES

The polenta can be made ahead, poured into a lightly buttered shallow 1½-quart baking dish, covered, and refrigerated. When ready to serve, sprinkle the top with ¼ cup grated Parmigiano-Reggiano cheese and place in a cold oven. Turn the oven to 350°F and bake for about 45 minutes, or until the polenta is bubbly. For a bubbly cheese topping, broil for 5 minutes, or brown with a chef's torch (page 26).

tip BANISH THE LUMPS IN YOUR POLENTA

To avoid stubborn lumps that are difficult to dissolve in boiling liquid, first whisk the cornmeal with half of the cold liquid.

The Dutch oven is the quintessential braising pot. The round shape is generally more useful, but if you do a lot of braising, acquiring both a round and an oval Dutch oven makes good sense.

Molly Stevens, AUTHOR, *ALL ABOUT BRAISING*

Oven-Braised Short Ribs with Fennel

Dutch Oven

This popular pot was named for the Pennsylvania Dutch, who although immigrants from Germany were called Dutch, from the German *Deutsch*. The Pennsylvania Dutch popularized this sturdy pot in the eighteenth century, before they had ovens. On a stove top, the heavy cast iron held and diffused heat like an oven. Deep and with a heavy, tight-fitting lid and short handles on two sides, most Dutch ovens' size and weight make them perfect for braising stews and large cuts of meat, both on the stove top and in the oven.

Today, Dutch ovens come in a variety of materials, but the original cast iron lives on. If you're in the market for a Dutch oven, keep in mind that the cast iron reacts with acidic ingredients, such as tomatoes and wine. You may want to consider a model made of a nonreactive metal or cast iron coated with enamel. Brightly colored enameled Dutch ovens are especially popular for both their beauty and durability. Sometimes referred to as a casserole, the Dutch oven comes round or oval and in a variety of depths.

Tips for Using

An oval Dutch oven is a good choice for roasting a whole chicken or an oval roast, such as a leg of lamb or a pot roast.

Use a round Dutch oven for hearty soups, stews, beans, short ribs, and lamb or veal shanks.

Sizes range from small to quite large; the most practical size is 6 to 8 quarts.

When selecting a cast-iron Dutch oven, make sure you can comfortably lift it. The lid is one-third of the total weight of most heavy pots. If possible, lighten the load by removing the lid before lifting the pot.

Some Dutch ovens come with glass lids, making it possible for the curious cook to check on slow-cooked foods without lifting the lid and losing precious moisture and heat.

Many Dutch ovens are handsome enough for serving and will hold heat and keep food warm for an extended period of time.

Care in Using

Enameled cast iron takes all kinds of tough cleaning without damage. If possible, avoid strong detergents or hard scrubbing on regular cast iron. If you must use soap, dry the pot thoroughly over low heat and then rub dry with a paper towel dipped in vegetable oil.

Always consult the manufacturer's instructions.

Alternatives

Braiser, *Cocotte,* or Sauté Pan

recipes

Oven-Braised Short Ribs with Fennel | Oven-Baked Cannellini Beans | Variation: Cannellini Bean Salad with Red Wine Vinaigrette

OVEN-BRAISED SHORT RIBS with FENNEL

PREP 30 min | COOK TIME 2 to 2½ hr | SERVES 4–6

Buttery tender short ribs make a great company meal. It's best to cook short ribs, and other slow-cooked rich meat dishes, one day ahead so the juices can chill and the excess fat, which will solidify on the surface, can be lifted off. The recipe serves six, but to add more servings, simply increase the number of short ribs and the size of the cooking vessel. Serve with Roasted Potatoes with Mushrooms and Red Bell Peppers (page 39), polenta, or mashed potatoes.

Implements
Cooking String or Silicone Ties (Optional), Large Dutch Oven, Tongs, Mortar and Pestle, Large Metal Spoon, Slotted Spoon or Spatula, Strainer, Large Fat Separator with Strainer (Optional), Skimmer (Optional), Small Saucepan

Ingredients

3½ to 4 pounds meaty bone-in short ribs

Coarse salt and freshly ground black pepper

2 tablespoons extra-virgin olive oil

1 cup diced yellow onion

½ cup diced celery

½ cup diced carrot

2 cloves garlic, coarsely chopped

1 tablespoon fennel seeds

2 cups hearty red wine

2 bay leaves

1 (28-ounce) can Italian plum tomatoes with juices

1. If you want to keep the short ribs together, tie each one tightly across the bone with cooking string or silicone ties. Combine 1 tablespoon of salt and ½ teaspoon of black pepper. Rub over all the surfaces of the short ribs.

2. Heat a large (7- to 8-quart) enameled cast-iron or other nonreactive Dutch oven over medium heat. Add the olive oil. When hot, add the ribs, being careful not to crowd them or they won't brown properly. (If the ribs don't all fit in the Dutch oven, brown them in two batches, or use a heavy skillet to brown any remaining ribs at the same time.) Cook, adjusting the heat between medium and medium-high to maintain a steady sizzle without getting the pan too hot and turning with tongs as needed, for about 3 minutes per side, or until browned. As the ribs are browned, transfer them to a large bowl.

3. When all the ribs are browned, spoon off all but 1 tablespoon of the fat from the pot. Add the onion, celery, and carrot, and cook over medium-low heat, stirring, for about 8 minutes, or until golden. Meanwhile crush the garlic and fennel seeds together with a mortar and pestle or with a large chef's knife. Add to the vegetables and cook for about 30 seconds, or until fragrant.

4. If necessary, rearrange the oven racks to accommodate the large size of the pan. Preheat the oven to 325°F.

5. Add the wine and bay leaves to the Dutch oven and bring to a boil. Boil for 5 minutes, or until reduced by half. Stir in the tomatoes and again bring to a boil, breaking up the tomatoes with the side of a large metal spoon. Add the browned ribs and any juices that accumulated in the bowl. Turn the ribs to coat them evenly with the tomato mixture.

6. Cover and braise in the lower half of the oven for 2 to 2½ hours, until the meat is pulling away from the bones.

7. Use a slotted spoon or spatula and tongs to lift the ribs from the pan to a platter. Discard any loose bones. Snip off the strings and discard, or remove the silicone ties.

8. Pour the remaining contents of the Dutch oven through a strainer set over a large bowl. Discard the bay leaves and then spoon the strained vegetables onto the ribs. Cover the platter with aluminum foil and keep warm in the turned-off oven.

9. Use a large metal spoon to spoon off and discard the fat that comes to the top of the bowl and then pour the juices into a small saucepan, or pour the juices into a fat separator and then pour the defatted juices into a small saucepan. Alternatively, chill the strained juices for several hours or overnight and lift off the fat that solidifies on top with a skimmer. Refrigerate the ribs and vegetables, tightly covered, and then return them to the Dutch oven with the defatted juices and slowly reheat over low heat.

10. Reheat the juices to a simmer, taste, and adjust the seasoning with salt and pepper. Pour the juices over the short ribs and vegetables and serve hot.

OVEN-BAKED CANNELLINI BEANS

SOAK TIME (beans) 1 hr, 4 hr, or overnight | **PREP** 10 min | **COOK TIME** 1½ to 2 hr | **STAND TIME** 30 min | **SERVES** 8

Beans slowly baked in the oven tend to be more flavorful and have a smoother texture than beans boiled on top of the stove. These beans can be cooked up to 5 days in advance of serving. Store them tightly covered in the refrigerator, and then serve them cold in salads or as a warm side dish. Embellish the beans with sautéed cherry tomatoes, chopped fresh Italian parsley, and pitted Kalamata olives.

Implements 4- to 8-Quart Dutch Oven, Strainer

Ingredients

1 pound (about 2½ cups) dried cannellini or other dried white beans

4 cloves garlic, bruised with knife

2 tablespoons extra-virgin olive oil

1 small yellow onion, halved

1 bay leaf

2 to 3 cups water or unsalted chicken broth, or as needed

Coarse salt and freshly ground black pepper

1. Place the beans in a large bowl, add cold water to cover by at least 2 inches, and soak in the refrigerator for at least 4 hours or up to overnight. Drain well before using. Alternatively, place the beans in a saucepan, add cold water to cover by 2 inches, bring to a boil, cover, and boil for 3 minutes. Remove from the heat and let stand in the water, covered, for 1 hour. Drain well before using.

2. Preheat the oven to 325°F. Combine the beans, garlic, olive oil, onion, and bay leaf in a medium (4-quart) or large (7- to 8-quart) Dutch oven and stir to blend. Add water or broth to cover the beans.

3. Cover and bake for 1½ to 2 hours, until the beans are tender. Let stand for 30 minutes. As the beans cool, they will absorb most of the excess cooking liquid. Scoop out the onion halves and bay leaf, and discard. Drain the beans in a strainer to eliminate any liquid that isn't absorbed. Discard the liquid or reserve it for soup.

4. Season the beans with salt and pepper and use in recipes calling for cooked white beans, or season to taste and serve as a side dish.

variation CANNELLINI BEAN SALAD WITH RED WINE VINAIGRETTE

In a large serving bowl, whisk together 3 tablespoons extra-virgin olive oil, 2 tablespoons red wine vinegar, ½ teaspoon minced or grated garlic, ½ teaspoon coarse salt, and a generous grinding of freshly ground black pepper until blended. Add 2 to 3 cups drained cooked cannellini beans (above), chilled or at room temperature; 2 cups diced celery; ½ cup diced red onion; and ¼ cup finely chopped fresh Italian parsley. Use a rubber spatula to gently fold together all the ingredients until blended. Serve at room temperature as a side-dish salad, or add shrimp, tuna, or cooked diced chicken and serve as a main-dish salad on a bed of lettuce with tomato wedges. Serves 4.

*The fish poacher has a removable perforated rack,
which makes it easy to lift up the fish and slide it onto
a platter. But you can use a large turkey roaster,
set a rack in the bottom, and curve the fish to fit.*

Julia Child, AUTHOR, *THE WAY TO COOK*

Fish Poacher

A fish poacher is a long, oblong pan typically made from stainless steel and fitted with a rack that rests over two stove-top burners. The handles on the rack should lift or extend at right angles to the frame, so the fish can be easily lowered into and lifted from the poaching liquid. For the avid cook, this is a must-have piece of cookware. Handsome and sleek, with a tight-fitting lid and a sculpted handle (one model has an elegant fish handle on the lid), it comes in a variety of sizes. A model that measures 16 to 18 inches long is the most practical.

Tips for Using

Before buying a fish poacher, measure the top of your stove to make sure it can comfortably accommodate the poacher across two burners.

A 4- to 6-pound fish (without its head and tail) will fit in an 18-inch poacher. If you want to cook a fish with its head, you'll need a smaller fish.

Measure your poacher and bring a tape measure to the fish market and measure the fish.

If poaching a whole fillet, fold under the thin narrow tail end so it won't overcook.

Generally, it's best to keep the skin on the fillet, as it will help keep the fish in one piece.

Begin poaching in room-temperature liquid and then slowly heat the liquid almost to a boil. This method guarantees that the outer flesh won't cook more quickly than the interior flesh. Never let the liquid boil.

Basic timing for poached fish is 10 minutes (from when the poaching liquid begins to bubble) per inch of thickness.

The fish is done when the internal temperature registers 130° to 140°F on an instant-read thermometer.

Some cooks wrap whole fish in cheesecloth for poaching, but if the bottom of the rack is brushed liberally with olive oil, this shouldn't be necessary. A fish poacher can also be used for steaming fish fillets, fish steaks, asparagus, corn on the cob, and chunks of winter squash.

Care in Using

Stainless steel washes up easily by hand. Always consult the manufacturer's instructions.

Alternatives

You can improvise with a roasting pan and roasting rack covered with heavy-duty aluminum foil for a large fish. An oval Dutch oven, large sauté pan, or braiser can be used for smaller fish, fish steaks, or fish fillets.

recipes

Sea Bass Poached in Orange, Basil, and Wine with Citrus and Herb Sauce | Cold Salmon with Cucumber Veil and Avocado and Dill Sauce

SEA BASS POACHED in ORANGE, BASIL, and WINE with CITRUS and HERB SAUCE

PREP 30 min | COOK TIME (poaching liquid) 15 min |
COOK TIME (fish) 15 to 20 min | SERVES 6

The traditional liquid for poaching fish is called court bouillon. This is a broth made from cooking vegetables and herbs in water and wine. This recipe deviates from the classic by using orange juice, white wine, and basil. Prepare it ahead of time so it has time to cool to room temperature before you poach the fish. (Used poaching liquid can be strained and frozen for 1 to 2 months for a second use.) You'll need enough liquid to cover the fish. Remember the fish should be slowly cooked in simmering, never boiling, liquid. Sea bass, a fine-fleshed fish with a sweet, mild flavor, is a good choice for poaching, but almost any firm-fleshed fish can be used.

Implements
Large Saucepan, Fine-mesh Strainer or Chinois, Vegetable Peeler, Fish Bone Tweezers or Pliers, 18-inch-long Fish Poacher, Small Knife or Instant-Read Thermometer (or Probe Type), Small Saucepan, Medium Bowl, Sauce or Standard Whisk, Oven Mitts, Rimmed Sheet Pan (Optional), Two Long Flat Spatulas or One Long and One Shorter Spatula, Ladle

Ingredients

POACHING LIQUID

4 cups water

2 cups dry white wine

2 cups orange juice, preferably fresh

1 (3 by ½-inch) strip orange zest

1 large, leafy stem fresh basil

1 large, leafy stem fresh Italian parsley

1 yellow onion, thinly sliced

1 bay leaf

1 clove garlic, bruised with knife

1 teaspoon coarse salt

½ teaspoon black peppercorns

1 (3-pound) whole sea bass fillet with skin intact

SAUCE

1 cup orange juice, preferably fresh

1 cup extra-virgin olive oil

2 tablespoons freshly squeezed lemon juice

2 green onions, white and green parts, thinly sliced (about ¼ cups)

¼ cup chopped fresh basil

¼ cup chopped fresh Italian parsley

2 tablespoons chopped fresh oregano

½ teaspoon grated orange zest

1 teaspoon coarse salt

Freshly ground black pepper

8 thin slices navel orange, halved, for garnish

3 sprigs fresh basil, for garnish

1 cup tiny cherry tomatoes, for garnish

1. **MAKE THE POACHING LIQUID:** In a large saucepan, combine the water, wine, orange juice, orange zest, basil, parsley, onion, bay leaf, garlic, salt, and pepper, and bring to a boil over high heat. Adjust the heat to a gentle boil and cook, uncovered, for 15 minutes. Let cool to lukewarm. Strain through a fine-mesh strainer or chinois. Taste and adjust the seasoning with salt.

2. To ensure even cooking, the fish and poaching liquid should be almost the same temperature. To achieve this, remove the fish from the refrigerator about 1 hour prior to cooking.

3. Run your hand over the surface of the fish fillet to locate the pin bones and determine the direction of their growth. Use the tip of fish bone tweezers or pliers to pinch the top of the pin bone and slowly tug at the same angle as the bone. If the bone breaks off, you are pulling in the opposite direction of growth, so you must reverse direction.

4. Remove the rack from a fish poacher 18 inches long and 7 inches wide. Lightly oil the rack with the olive oil.

Place the fish, skin side down, on the rack. Lower the rack into the empty fish poacher. Gently pour the room-temperature poaching liquid into the pan.

5. Set the pan over two burners and turn them on to medium heat. Cover and heat the liquid, checking under the cover frequently, until a bubble or two comes to the surface. (This will take about 15 minutes.) Adjust the heat to medium-low, re-cover, and cook, without boiling, for 15 to 18 minutes, until the tip of a small knife inserted into the thickest part of the fillet finds no resistance, or the internal temperature registers 130° to 140°F on an instant-read thermometer.

6. WHILE THE FISH IS POACHING, MAKE THE SAUCE: Place the orange juice in a small saucepan and bring to a boil over high heat. Adjust the heat to medium and boil gently for 5 minutes, or until the juice is reduced by half. Pour into a bowl and let cool to lukewarm.

7. Gradually whisk the olive oil into the orange juice until blended. Add the lemon juice, green onions, basil, parsley, oregano, orange zest, salt, and a grinding of pepper. Stir to blend and set aside.

8. When the fish is cooked, turn off the heat. Place next to the stove a rimmed sheet pan large enough to accommodate the poaching rack. Remove the cover of the fish poacher. With your fingers protected with oven mitts, carefully lift the rack from the fish poacher and place it on the sheet pan. (Alternatively, you can place the poaching rack with the fish in the sink.) Let the fish sit on the rack for 10 minutes. Loosen the fish by running a large, flat spatula between the fish and the rack. Then, use 2 long, flat spatulas, or 1 long spatula and 1 shorter one, to carefully lift the fish off the rack and place it on an oval platter.

9. Stir the sauce and ladle half of it over the fish. Arrange the orange slices on the surface of the fish in a slightly overlapping pattern to simulate fish scales. Garnish the platter with the basil sprigs and cherry tomatoes. Serve the fish warm, and pass the remaining sauce at the table. Or, cover the fish with plastic wrap and chill until ready to serve.

COLD SALMON with CUCUMBER VEIL and AVOCADO and DILL SAUCE

PREP 30 min | COOK TIME (poaching liquid) 15 min | COOK TIME (fish) 15 to 20 min | SERVES 6

If preferred, salmon steaks or salmon fillets can be substituted for the whole fillet in this recipe. If using single portions of fish, follow the recipe as directed, but reduce the cooking time by half.

Implements
Large Saucepan, Fine-mesh Strainer or Chinois, Fish Poacher, Fish Bone Tweezers or Pliers, 18-inch-long Fish Poacher, Small Knife or Instant-Read Thermometer (or Probe Type), Rimmed Sheet Pan, Oven Mitts, Two Long Flat Spatulas or One Long and One Shorter Spatula, Chef's Knife or Mandoline, Tablespoon, Food Processor, Sauté Pan

Ingredients

POACHING LIQUID

6 cups water

2 cups white wine

4 large, leafy stems fresh dill

2 large, leafy stems fresh parsley

2 thick lemon slices

1 yellow onion, thinly sliced

1 bay leaf

1 clove garlic, bruised with knife

2 teaspoons coarse salt

½ teaspoon black peppercorns

1 (3-pound) whole salmon fillet with skin intact

1 large English (seedless) cucumber, trimmed

SAUCE

1 ripe avocado, halved and pitted

½ cup mayonnaise

½ cup plain thick whole-milk yogurt

½ cup coarsely chopped fresh dill, plus
3 tablespoons finely chopped

½ cup coarsely chopped seedless cucumber

3 tablespoons snipped fresh chives

1 tablespoon freshly squeezed lemon juice

1 teaspoon coarse salt

Pinch of cayenne pepper

1 firm, ripe avocado, halved, pitted, peeled,
and cut into ¼-inch wedges, for garnish

1 cup small yellow plum tomatoes, for garnish

Dill sprigs, for garnish

1. **MAKE THE POACHING LIQUID:** In a large saucepan, combine the water, wine, dill stems, parsley stems, lemon slices, onion, bay leaf, garlic, salt, and pepper, and bring to a boil over high heat. Adjust the heat to a gentle boil and boil, uncovered, for 15 minutes. Let cool to lukewarm. Strain through a fine-mesh strainer or chinois. Taste and adjust the seasoning with salt.

2. To ensure even cooking, the fish and poaching liquid should be almost the same temperature. To achieve this, remove the fish from the refrigerator about 1 hour prior to cooking.

3. Run your hand over the surface of the fish fillet to locate the pin bones and determine the direction of their growth. Use the tip of fish bone tweezers or pliers to pinch the top of the pin bone and slowly tug at the same angle as the bone. If the bone breaks off, you are pulling in the opposite direction of the growth, so you must reverse direction.

4. Remove the rack from a fish poacher 18 inches long and 7 inches wide. Lightly oil the rack with the olive oil. Place the fish, skin side down, on the rack. Lower the rack into the empty fish poacher. Gently pour the room-temperature poaching liquid into the pan.

5. Set the pan over two burners and turn them on to medium heat. Cover and heat the liquid, checking under the cover frequently, until a bubble or two comes to the surface. (This will take about 15 minutes). Adjust the heat to medium-low, re-cover, and cook, without boiling, for 15 to 18 minutes, or until the tip of a small knife inserted into the thickest part of the fillet finds no resistance, or the internal temperature registers 130° to 140°F on an instant-read thermometer.

6. When the fish is cooked, turn off the heat. Place next to the stove a rimmed sheet pan large enough to accommodate the poaching rack. Remove the cover of the fish poacher. With your fingers protected with oven mitts, carefully lift the rack from the fish poacher and place on the sheet pan. (Alternatively, you can place the poaching rack with the fish in the sink.) Let the fish sit on the rack for 10 minutes. Loosen the fish by running a large, flat spatula between the fish and the rack. Then, use 2 long, flat spatulas, or 1 long spatula and 1 shorter one, to carefully lift the fish off the rack and place it on an oval platter.

7. Thinly slice the cucumber with a chef's knife or mandoline. Arrange the cucumber slices on the surface of the fish in a slightly overlapping pattern to simulate fish scales. Cover with plastic wrap and refrigerate for 2 hours, or until chilled.

8. **MAKE THE SAUCE:** Scoop the avocado flesh from the skin with a tablespoon, dropping it into a food processor. Add the mayonnaise, yogurt, coarsely chopped dill, cucumber, chives, lemon juice, salt, and cayenne pepper to the processor and process until smooth. Taste and adjust the seasoning with more lemon juice, salt, and pepper. Transfer to a bowl. Add the finely chopped dill and stir to blend. Cover and refrigerate until ready to serve.

9. To serve, remove the plastic wrap covering the fish and garnish the platter with the avocado slices, tomatoes, and dill sprigs. Serve with the sauce spooned over each serving or pass the sauce at the table.

Salt

There are two types of salt: salt mined from underground deposits and salt collected from evaporated seawater. Although the salt in both cases is primarily made up of sodium chloride, the differences in flavor depend primarily on the minerals present in the earth or water from which the salt was taken. There are broad flavor and color distinctions between mined salt and sea salt, and more finite differences among the individual salts from different geographic areas and bodies of water.

Kosher Salt has coarse, irregular crystals and is typically additive free. It is traditionally used in the preparation of kosher meats, because of its ability to draw out a maximum of blood. Many cooks use kosher salt as their everyday salt. Its large crystals make it easy to grab a pinch between your fingers for sprinkling into a cooking pot or on a salad. It has a fresh, clean taste without any discernable mineral notes.

Sea Salt is harvested everywhere from Bali to Maine. Among the popular varieties are French *fleur de sel,* harvested from the surface of seawater; French *sel gris,* or gray salt, harvested from the bottom of salt ponds along the Atlantic coast; Maldon salt from England; Hawaiian red salt, which takes it distinctive color from a red clay; and Hawaiian black salt, which takes its color from lava deposits.

Some sea salts are cut into light flakes, some are fine or coarse crystals, and some are shaped into rounds. The bright, briny flavor of all of these salts adds zip to salad greens, bruschetta rubbed with ripe tomato and drizzled with olive oil, freshly made mozzarella cheese, meats and fish *before* they are roasted or grilled, and raw or cooked fresh vegetables. Because processing sea salt is more labor intensive than mining salt, the cost is much higher. The costliest sea salts are reserved for use as finishing salts.

Table Salt, which is mined from the earth, is very fine granular, pure white crystals. It is sometimes fortified with iodine for nutritional reasons and usually contains an additive to keep it free flowing in damp weather. When a recipe calls for salt, it usually means table salt, unless otherwise noted. Because table salt is fine, the grains take up more room when measured, so that 1 teaspoon of table salt will weigh more than 1 teaspoon of coarse salt. If you are substituting one for the other, remember that a teaspoon of table salt will add more salt flavor than will a teaspoon of coarse salt.

Table salt has a slightly saltier edge than kosher or sea salt. To decide which salt you prefer, dip a toothpick in water and then into one type of salt and taste. Use a clean toothpick to taste the second salt, and then the third.

**Marinated Grilled Zucchini with
Oregano and Dried-Tomato Vinaigrette**

*i use my skillet grill for chicken breasts, fish, and
vegetables. i prefer the 12-inch pan because it works as
well for two servings as it does for four or six. i place
the food in the center of the pan when cooking for two.
That way the spatters stay in the pan and keep the
stove top clean.* **Marge Poore,** AUTHOR, *THE BEST GRILL PAN COOKBOOK EVER*

Grill Pan

The grill pan, also called a skillet grill, comes in all sizes and shapes (round, square, and rectangular) and is made from a variety of materials, such as steel and aluminum blends, or cast iron. Designed for use on the stove top, it has raised grids that leave seared grill marks on the surface of the food, making it possible to pretend you're grilling even when it is snowing outdoors. The wells between the grids catch fat and juices, leaving the surface of the food dry—a boon for anyone interesting in low-fat cooking.

Tips for Using

Before adding the food to the grill pan, preheat it over medium heat for about 2 minutes, or until a drop of water sizzles and evaporates on contact.

Oil the grill pan or the food, just as you would when using an outdoor grill.

The grill pan is perfect for quickly heating up hot dogs or fully cooked sausages, and great for grilled sandwiches, thin cutlets, chicken breasts, and vegetables.

Food cooks more slowly on a grill pan than it does on a flat surface, because contact with the food is limited to the grids.

Hamburgers are only successful on a grill pan if the patties are less than ½ inch thick. This is true of most meats cooked on the grill pan.

Vegetables cook best when they are thinly cut, so all surfaces will come in contact with the hot grid.

Care in Using

Never scour a grill pan with abrasive cleaners. Instead, soak the pan in warm, soapy water, loosen cooked-on particles with a stiff brush, rinse, and dry.

Before storing a washed grill pan, rub all of its surfaces with flavorless cooking oil until they are dry, with no trace of oil remaining.

Always consult the manufacturer's instructions.

Alternatives

A *panini* grill can be substituted for a grill pan.

recipes

Tamari-Glazed Swordfish with Mango, Ginger, and Sweet Onion Salad | Marinated Grilled Zucchini with Oregano and Dried-Tomato Vinaigrette

TAMARI-GLAZED SWORDFISH with CHOPPED MANGO, GINGER, and SWEET ONION SALAD

PREP TIME 20 min **|** **COOK TIME** 6 min **|** **SERVES** 4

This versatile recipe can be used to prepare almost any variety of fish. Steaks work best because of their uniform thickness, so try tuna, mahi mahi, salmon, or escolar. The salad is just as versatile. Try papaya, peach, or nectarine in place of the mango; red onion or green onion for the sweet onion; or basil for the cilantro. Tamari is a bit thicker and has a milder taste than soy sauce, so it makes a better glaze. But in a pinch, soy sauce may be substituted. Accompany the swordfish with basmati, sushi, or other fragrant rice.

Implements Small Bowl, Flat or Sauce Whisk, Silicone Brush, Medium Bowl, Rubber Spatula, Grill Pan, Wide Flexible Spatula, Small Knife

Ingredients

GLAZE

2 tablespoons tamari

1 teaspoon toasted sesame oil

1 teaspoon peeled, grated fresh ginger

¼ teaspoon grated fresh garlic

4 (6-ounce) swordfish steaks, about ½ inch thick

CHOPPED MANGO, GINGER, AND SWEET ONION SALAD

1 tablespoon unseasoned rice vinegar

1 teaspoon tamari

½ teaspoon toasted sesame oil

½ teaspoon peeled, grated fresh ginger

¼ teaspoon grated fresh garlic

1 cup (¼-inch-dice) ripe mango

1 cup (¼-inch-dice) sweet onion

¼ cup (¼-inch-dice) red bell pepper

2 tablespoons finely chopped fresh cilantro

½ teaspoon minced jalapeño chile, or to taste (optional)

1. **MAKE THE GLAZE:** In a small bowl, whisk the tamari, sesame oil, ginger, and garlic until blended. Place the swordfish steaks in a single layer on a large plate and brush with half of the glaze. Turn the steaks and brush with the remaining glaze. Refrigerate for 20 minutes. Meanwhile, prepare the salad.

2. **MAKE THE SALAD:** In a medium bowl, combine the rice vinegar, tamari, sesame oil, ginger, and garlic, and stir until blended. Add the mango, onion, red bell pepper, cilantro, and chile. Using a rubber spatula, fold gently until well blended. Set aside until serving.

3. Heat the grill pan over medium heat until hot enough for a drop of water to sizzle on contact. Add the swordfish and immediately increase the heat to medium-high. Cook the fish for 3 minutes, adjusting the heat back to medium after 1 minute. Use a wide, flexible spatula to turn the fish over. Cook for 3 minutes more, or until the fish is almost firm to the touch, or until the center is opaque, rather than translucent, when tested with the tip of a small knife.

4. Transfer the steaks to a serving platter, top each steak with an equal amount of the salad, and serve.

MARINATED GRILLED ZUCCHINI with OREGANO and DRIED-TOMATO VINAIGRETTE

PREP 10 min | COOK TIME 8 min per batch | SERVES 4

Zucchini is mild flavored, so it is the perfect canvas for the bold tastes of fresh oregano and dried tomatoes. Use your best extra-virgin olive oil and aged red wine vinegar for the dressing.

Implements Small Bowl, Flat or Sauce Whisk, Mandoline or Chef's Knife, Grill Pan, Silicone Brush, Tongs

Ingredients

VINAIGRETTE

6 tablespoons extra-virgin olive oil

¼ cup red wine vinegar

1 clove garlic, grated or pressed

½ teaspoon coarse salt

Freshly ground black pepper

3 medium (about 5 ounces each) zucchini

Coarse salt

1 tablespoon minced fresh oregano

2 tablespoons finely slivered olive oil–packed sun-dried tomatoes, drained and patted dry, for garnish

1. MAKE THE VINAIGRETTE: In a small bowl, combine the olive oil, vinegar, garlic, salt, and a grinding of black pepper, and whisk until blended.

2. Trim the stem and blossom ends from the zucchini. With a mandoline or chef's knife, cut each zucchini lengthwise into 5 slices each about ¼ inch thick, and then spread the slices in a single layer on a platter.

3. Heat the grill pan over medium heat until hot enough for a drop of water to sizzle on contact.

4. While the pan is heating, brush the zucchini slices on both sides with a film of the vinaigrette. Working in batches, place the zucchini on the pan and grill for 4 minutes, or until grill marks appear. Turn with tongs and grill the other side for 4 minutes, or until tender. As each batch is cooked, return the slices to the platter.

5. Sprinkle the zucchini slices lightly with salt. Whisk the oregano into the remaining vinaigrette and drizzle on top of the zucchini. Sprinkle with the tomato slivers. Serve warm or at room temperature.

Rimmed Sheet Pan

This large rectangular pan, sometimes called a jelly-roll pan or half sheet pan, is an indispensable piece of cookware. They typically measure 17½ by 12¼ by 1 inch or 15½ by 10½ by 1 inch, and fits either lengthwise or crosswise in most ovens. Its uses are numerous, including roasting potatoes, asparagus, zucchini, red peppers, and dozens of other vegetables; browning chicken legs or fish fillets; and toasting bread slices for crostini or triangles of pita for chips.

These handy pans are primarily made from rolled aluminum, nonstick coated aluminum, and other materials. Aluminum is reactive and should not be used with acidic foods, such as tomatoes, but the nonstick coated aluminum is nonreactive. All of these materials are durable, have excellent heat conductivity, and are versatile. Be sure to choose a pan made of sturdy material that will not warp under the heat of a hot stove.

Tips for Using

Add a wire rack to a sheet pan and use to drain bacon, to catch drips from fried or honey-dipped foods, as a roasting rack for duck parts or chicken wings, or as a substitute for a broiler pan.

Use sheet pans for making soufflé roulades (soufflés that are filled and rolled like jelly rolls) and for baking cookies.

Slip a sheet pan under any baking dish that may bubble over in the oven.

Use the sheet pan as a tray for all sorts of tasks, including holding your *mise en place,* the French term for having all the ingredients for a recipe prepped and in bowls before you start to cook.

Care in Using

Wash in warm, soapy water. Use a stiff brush to remove cooked-on foods, but avoid harsh abrasives.

Always consult the manufacturer's instructions.

Alternatives

Although deeper, a large roasting pan and sometimes a baking dish can be substituted.

recipes with Provençal Herbs   Oven-Roasted Tomato Sauce | Roasted Vegetables

OVEN-ROASTED TOMATO SAUCE

PREP 15 min | COOK TIME 1 to 1¼ hr | MAKES 3 cups

Oven-roasted tomatoes make a flavorful chunky tomato sauce for tossing with pasta, couscous, rice, or other grains. Or, try stirring it into Oven-Baked Cannellini Beans (page 61) or using it as the sauce for Sausage-Stuffed Roasted Artichokes with Tomato Sauce (page 38). Because tomatoes are acidic, be sure to use a nonreactive rimmed sheet pan. The tomato sauce can be frozen for up to 3 months.

Implements Nonreactive Rimmed Sheet Pan, Spatula or Flat-Edged Wooden Spoon, Food Mill or Immersion Blender (Optional)

Ingredients

4 to 5 pounds ripe plum tomatoes, coarsely chopped (¼-inch pieces)

2 cloves garlic, finely chopped

1 teaspoon coarse salt

¼ teaspoon freshly ground black pepper

¼ cup extra-virgin olive oil

1 leafy stem basil, plus 2 tablespoons chopped fresh basil

1. Preheat the oven to 400°F.

2. Spread the tomatoes on a nonreactive rimmed sheet pan. Sprinkle the garlic, salt, and pepper evenly over the top. Drizzle with the oil. Add the basil.

3. Roast, stirring once after 30 minutes with a spatula or flat-edged wooden spoon, for 1 to 1¼ hours, until the tomatoes are bubbly and the sauce is beginning to caramelize around the edges of the pan. Remove from the oven and stir in the chopped basil.

4. Use while hot, or cool, cover, and refrigerate for up to 3 days. If the tomato skins are thick or if you prefer a smooth sauce, pass the sauce through a food mill or puree with an immersion blender.

ROASTED VEGETABLES with PROVENÇAL HERBS

PREP 20 min | COOK TIME 45 to 55 min | SERVES 4–6

The vegetables can be served hot or at room temperature. If serving cold as a salad, add a dash of good red wine or balsamic vinegar just before serving.

Implements Nonreactive Rimmed Sheet Pan, Flat-Edged Wooden Spoon or Spatula

Ingredients

4 large ripe plum tomatoes, cut into ½-inch wedges

2 zucchini (4 ounces each), trimmed, halved lengthwise, and cut into ½-inch pieces

1 yellow crookneck squash, trimmed, fat end quartered lengthwise, and cut into ½-inch pieces

1 yellow onion, cut into ⅛-inch wedges

1 red bell pepper, seeded and cut into ½-inch squares

3 tablespoons extra-virgin olive oil

1 teaspoon chopped fresh rosemary

1 teaspoon chopped fresh thyme

1 (3 by ½-inch) strip orange zest, finely slivered

1 clove garlic, chopped

½ teaspoon coarse salt

Freshly ground black pepper

8 to 12 Niçoise or other small black olives, pitted and coarsely chopped

1. Preheat the oven to 400°F.

2. Spread the tomatoes, zucchini, yellow squash, onion, and bell pepper on a nonreactive rimmed sheet pan. Drizzle with the olive oil. Sprinkle with the rosemary, thyme, orange zest, garlic, salt, and a generous grinding of pepper. Stir to blend.

3. Roast, stirring every 15 minutes with a flat-edged wooden spoon or spatula, for 50 to 60 minutes, until the vegetables are evenly caramelized and tender. Remove from the oven and sprinkle with the olives.

The small (roasting) pan has become a treasure in my kitchen. It is perfect for a small bird and for enough vegetables to feed four.

Barbara Kafka, AUTHOR, *ROASTING*

Walnut Pesto–Stuffed Pork Roast

Roasting Pan

Every kitchen needs a sturdy roasting pan. In fact, two pans—one smaller for pork tenderloins or a small chicken and one larger for a turkey, ham, or roast beef—are ideal. The smaller pan is approximately 9 by 13 inches, and the larger is approximately 14 by 16 inches. They are most often made of stainless steel or a mixture of metals, and they come with and without a nonstick finish. The nonstick finish makes cleanup a cinch, although you will get fewer browned bits for your gravy. Make sure that any pan you choose is sturdy enough to hold the weight of a good-sized bird or roast.

Also check the handles on the pan. A heavy roasting pan can be a handful even when it's empty. Make sure the pan has thick, sturdy handles riveted to either end and that they are roomy enough to accommodate the comfortable grip of mitted hands. Pans without handles or with hinged handles that fold flush to the pan are difficult—and dangerous—to lift when the pan contains sizzling-hot food. Many roasting pans come with a V-shaped rack, a real bonus. For easy cleanup, make sure the rack has a nonstick finish.

Tips for Using

Roasting isn't just for the holiday turkey. Leave the rack in the cupboard and use the roasting pan for roasting party-sized batches of potatoes, vegetables, macaroni and cheese, or any other recipe calling for a large, shallow baking pan.

The shallow, roomy interior of a roasting pan is perfect for use as a bain-marie (hot-water bath) for slowly cooking custards, cheesecakes, or bread puddings.

If the fish you're cooking is too long for your fish poacher, it may fit in your roasting pan. Just outfit the pan with a rack.

Care in Using

Pans with a nonstick or other baked-on finish require less elbow grease than those without. But usually a soak in soapy water followed by a scrub with a stiff brush will loosen any stubborn residue.

Always consult the manufacturer's instructions.

Alternatives

There really is no substitute for a sturdy roasting pan. Don't be tempted to use an aluminum foil pan. It will buckle under the weight of the food.

recipes
Walnut Pesto–Stuffed Pork Roast | Balsamic-Marinated Beef Tenderloin with Herb and Dried-Tomato Sauce

WALNUT PESTO-STUFFED PORK ROAST

BRINING 12–24 hr | PREP 15 min | COOK TIME 1¼ hr | SERVES 8

In summer, when big bunches of fresh basil are sold everywhere, take advantage of the bounty and make batches of pesto. Classic pesto is typically made with basil, pine nuts, and pecorino romano cheese, but this adaptation is made with walnuts and Parmesan cheese and is slathered in the center and on top of the pork roast. Because the loin is lean, brining is recommended for 12 to 24 hours before roasting.

Implements
Large Bowl, Rimmed Sheet Pan, Blender or Food Processor, Small Bowl, Spoon, Large Roasting Pan with Rack, Kitchen String or Silicone Ties, Kitchen Scissors, Cutting Board, Rubber Spatula, Instant-Read Thermometer (or Probe Type), Thin Flat Metal Spatula or Narrow Rubber Spatula, Two Sturdy Spatulas

Ingredients

BRINE
½ cup coarse salt

1 cup hot water

2 quarts very cold water

1 cup ice cubes

1 (3½- to 4-pound) boneless pork loin, untied

WALNUT PESTO
3 cups packed fresh basil leaves

1 cup extra-virgin olive oil

½ cup chopped walnuts

2 cloves garlic, chopped

1 teaspoon coarse salt

½ teaspoon freshly ground black pepper

⅔ cup grated Parmigiano-Reggiano cheese

1. **ONE DAY BEFORE ROASTING THE PORK, MAKE THE BRINE:** In a large bowl, dissolve the salt in the hot water. Add the cold water and the ice cubes. Place the pork in a large, heavy-duty resealable plastic bag. Add the brine and seal the bag closed. Seal it in a second plastic bag for reinforcement. (Or, use any large container and cover it tightly.) Place on a rimmed sheet pan and refrigerate for 12 to 24 hours. When ready to cook, drain the brining liquid and discard, and then wipe the roast dry with paper towels. Let stand at room temperature for 30 minutes before roasting.

2. **MEANWHILE, MAKE THE PESTO:** In blender or food processor, combine the basil, ½ cup of the oil, and the walnuts, garlic, salt, and pepper, and process until finely chopped. With the motor running, slowly add the remaining ½ cup of olive oil and process until the mixture is well blended. Be careful not to overprocess the pesto. You should be able to see small pieces of basil throughout. Transfer the pesto to a small bowl and stir in the cheese.

3. Preheat the oven to 400°F. Have ready a large roasting pan with a rack. Cut 8 pieces of cooking string each about 18 inches long, or have ready silicone ties. Place the pork loin on a cutting board and butterfly it by making a slit along the side from the top to the bottom, cutting just deep enough so that the loin opens up and lies flat like a book. Using a thin, flat metal spatula or a narrow rubber spatula, slather the cut surface with about ½ cup of the pesto. Fold it over and tie firmly, but not too tightly, at 1-inch intervals with the lengths of string or the ties.

4. Place the tied loin on the rack in the roasting pan. Roast for 45 minutes. Remove the pan from the oven and slather about ¼ cup of the remaining pesto on top of the roast. Continue roasting for 30 minutes longer, or until an instant-read thermometer registers 135°F. Remove from the oven and let rest for 10 minutes. As the pork rests, the internal temperature will rise to 145°F, or medium-rare.

5. Using 2 broad spatulas, lift the roast from the rack to a cutting board. Snip off the strings, or remove the silicone ties. Cut the pork into ½-inch-thick slices. Arrange the slices, overlapping them, on a large platter. Drizzle any juices from the cutting board over the meat. Serve warm or at room temperature. Pass the remaining pesto at the table.

BALSAMIC-MARINATED BEEF TENDERLOIN with HERB and DRIED-TOMATO SAUCE

PREP 25 min **|** **MARINATING** 2 to 24 hr **|** **COOK TIME** 20 to 35 min **|** **SERVES** 6

A beef tenderloin is meltingly tender, flavorful, and easy to prepare and serve. Because it can be expensive, it's often considered a celebratory dish. The balsamic marinade, made from carefully aged and highly flavored vinegar, contributes a nice dark brown crust to the meat. Serve the roast at room temperature or hot, with the herb and dried-tomato sauce on the side.

Implements Small Roasting Pan with Rack, Instant-Read Thermometer (or Probe Type), Food Processor, Small Bowl, Cutting Board, Tongs

Ingredients

1 (2-½ pound) trimmed, ready-to-cook beef tenderloin

2 teaspoons coarse salt

½ teaspoon freshly ground black pepper

2 tablespoons balsamic vinegar

2 tablespoons extra-virgin olive oil

HERB AND DRIED-TOMATO SAUCE

1½ cups lightly packed coarsely chopped fresh Italian parsley

2 tablespoon fresh oregano leaves

2 tablespoons chopped fresh chives

2 cloves garlic, chopped

3 tablespoons drained capers (if using salted capers, soak in water and pat dry)

1 cup extra-virgin olive oil

2 tablespoons finely minced oil-packed sun-dried tomatoes, drained

2 tablespoons oil-cured black olives, pitted

1 to 3 teaspoons aged red wine vinegar

½ teaspoon coarse salt

Freshly ground black pepper

1. At least 2 hours or up to 24 hours before serving, rub the beef evenly with the salt and pepper. Place on a large piece of plastic wrap or in a resealable plastic bag, drizzle with the balsamic vinegar, and turn to coat. Wrap in the plastic wrap or seal the bag and refrigerate.

2. One hour before roasting, remove the meat from the refrigerator. Remove it from its wrapping and place it on a rack in a small roasting pan. Drizzle the olive oil on the meat and rub it evenly over the surface. Let stand at room temperature until ready to roast.

3. Preheat the oven to 450°F. Roast the meat for 20 to 35 minutes, until an instant-read thermometer registers 120°F for rare, 125°F to 130°F for medium-rare, or 130° to 140°F for medium. Remove from the oven and let the meat rest on the rack in the pan for 5 minutes.

4. **WHILE THE MEAT IS ROASTING, MAKE THE SAUCE:** In a food processor, combine the parsley, oregano, chives, garlic, and 2 tablespoons of the capers, and process until finely chopped. With the motor running, add the olive oil in a slow, steady stream and process until well blended. Transfer to a small bowl and stir in the remaining 1 tablespoon of the capers, the tomatoes, and olives. Add 1 teaspoon of the vinegar, the salt, and a grinding of pepper. Taste and adjust the seasoning with more vinegar and pepper. Cover with plastic wrap and let stand at room temperature until ready to serve.

5. Use tongs to transfer the meat to a cutting board and cut into ¼-inch-thick slices. Arrange the slices, overlapping them, on a large platter. Drizzle any juices from the cutting board over the meat. Spoon a stream of the sauce down the center of the slices. Pass the remaining sauce at the table.

When it comes to saucepans, it's good to have a 1-quart for small jobs and at least one all-purpose 3- or 4-quart for cooking vegetables, soups, and the like. i particularly love the curved-bottom saucier, a shape ideal for sauces and puddings as there's no corner to trap food.

Linda Carucci, AUTHOR, *COOKING SCHOOL SECRETS FOR REAL WORLD COOKS*

Creamy Leek and Ginger
Soup with Carrot-Puree Swirl

Saucepan and Saucier

The classic saucepan for the home kitchen has always been a round pan with relatively high, straight sides and a long handle. The capacity is usually 1 to 4 quarts, sometimes with ½-quart variations. More recently, the saucier, a broad, bowl-shaped saucepan with gently curving sides, has been available to the home cook. Similar to a French pan known as a *fait-tout,* or "do everything" pan, the saucier lives up to its cousin's name. Even when the saucepan and saucier are the same volume, the latter is a bit more versatile because its broader surface area means that it can be used for sautéing and for soups, sauces, and risotto that require thorough stirring and even heating. Saucepans come in a range of metals and always with a tight-fitting lid. The larger pans sometimes have an opposing handle to help even the load when lifting. Hold a pan in your hand before purchasing, to be certain you are strong enough to lift it. The saucepan will be the most often-used pan in your kitchen, so you'll need a variety of sizes. Saucepans come in a variety of materials as well, including stainless steel, enameled cast iron, copper, anodized aluminum, and others.

Tips for Using

A collapsible steamer for cooking vegetables works well in a good-sized saucier or saucepan.

A sauce reduces faster in the broader saucier than it does in the straight-sided saucepan, so you may need to lower the heat to slow the reduction.

Larger sauciers and saucepans (4½ or 5 quarts) are ideal for gently simmering a tomato sauce or for making soups.

Because of it broad surface and shallow depth, a saucier is a better choice than a saucepan for cooking rice.

The bowl shape of the saucier matches the curved lines of a whisk and a rubber spatula for easy stirring.

Care in Using

Wash in warm, soapy water.

Use a stiff brush to remove cooked-on food, but avoid harsh abrasives.

Always consult the manufacturer's instructions.

Alternatives

There is no true substitute for the ubiquitous saucepan. In a pinch, however, vegetables can be steamed in a sauté pan with a lid and soups can be made in a stockpot or Dutch oven.

recipes

Warm Chopped Broccoli and Grape Tomato Salad with Mustard and Olive Oil | Creamy Leek and Ginger Soup with Carrot-Puree Swirl

WARM CHOPPED BROCCOLI and GRAPE TOMATO SALAD with MUSTARD and OLIVE OIL

PREP 20 min | **SOAK TIME** (broccoli) 15 min | **COOK TIME** 5 min | **SERVES** 4

Chopped broccoli, rather than the more typical stalks, can change your perception of this popular vegetable. Here, the florets are small and the stems and stalks are cut into ½-inch dice. Then they are cooked, cooled off quickly in an ice-water bath, tossed with a tangy mustard dressing, and served as a side-dish salad. You can also toss the salad into a pot of cooked short-grain brown rice for a tasty broccoli pilaf. Don't be tempted to add vinegar or lemon juice to the dressing, as the acid will quickly turn the broccoli a drab green. You can instead garnish the serving bowl with lemon wedges, so that each diner can add a squirt before eating.

Implements
Chef's Knife or Paring Knife, Steamer Insert with Matching Saucepan or Collapsible Steamer and Saucier or Saucepan, Large Bowl, Oven Mitt, Colander or Large Strainer, Sauce Whisk or Flat Whisk

Ingredients

1 bunch broccoli

6 tablespoons extra-virgin olive oil

2 teaspoons smooth Dijon mustard

2 teaspoons whole-grain Dijon mustard

Pinch of coarse salt

Freshly ground black pepper

½ cup thinly slivered sweet onion

1 cup grape or other tiny red or yellow tomatoes

Lemon wedges, for garnish

1. Cut the thick, woody stems from the broccoli and discard. Trim the florets from the stems, leaving about 1 inch of the stem attached. Cut florets into clusters about ½ inch wide. Cut the remaining stems into ½-inch pieces. Soak the cut-up broccoli in a bowl of cold water for 15 minutes, or until ready to cook.

2. Add water to a depth of 1 inch to a saucepan or saucier and add a matching steamer insert to the saucepan or a collapsible steaming basket to the saucier or saucepan. Heat the water to a boil. Drain the broccoli, add it to the steamer, cover, and cook for 5 minutes, or until a broccoli stem is crisp-tender.

3. Meanwhile, half fill a large bowl with water and ice cubes. Place the bowl in the sink. When the broccoli is cooked, remove the steamer with a mitted hand and plunge directly into the ice water to cool off the broccoli and stop the cooking. Let stand for 30 seconds, and then drain well in a colander. Spread out the broccoli on a large dish towel and pat dry.

4. In a serving bowl, whisk together the oil, both mustards, salt, and a grinding of pepper until well blended. Add the broccoli, onion, and tomatoes, and toss to coat evenly. Garnish the bowl with the lemon wedges and serve at once.

CREAMY LEEK and GINGER SOUP with CARROT-PUREE SWIRL

PREP 25 min | COOK TIME 25 min | SERVES 4

This light soup is made creamy by pureeing the leeks and potatoes, not by adding any dairy. The ginger is a surprise, adding a pleasant zing to the mix, while the bright orange swirl of pureed carrot atop each serving adds both color and flavor.

Implements
3- or 4-Quart Saucepan or Saucier, Slotted Spoon, Small Bowl, Immersion Blender (or Stand Blender or Food Processor), Small Saucepan, Ladle

Ingredients

5 to 6 cups low-sodium chicken broth

2 pounds leeks (about 3 large), white and pale green parts only, chopped (about 4 cups)

2 carrots, peeled and trimmed, cut into 2-inch lengths

1 cup potatoes, peeled and cubed (about 5 ounces)

1 tablespoon peeled, finely chopped fresh ginger

1 tablespoon tomato paste

1 clove garlic, chopped

Coarse salt and freshly ground black pepper

1 teaspoon curry powder

1 teaspoon finely chopped fresh cilantro leaves, for garnish

1. In a 3- or 4-quart saucepan or saucier, combine 4 cups of the broth, the leeks, carrots, potatoes, ginger, tomato paste, garlic, and ½ teaspoon salt, and bring to a boil over high heat. Adjust the heat to a simmer, cover, and cook for 25 minutes, or until the vegetables are very tender. Let cool slightly, then lift the carrots from the pan using a slotted spoon and set aside.

2. Process the soup directly in the pot until very smooth, with an immersion blender. Alternatively, working in batches, transfer to a stand blender or food processor and process until very smooth. Add a small amount of the remaining broth to thin the soup to preferred consistency, and then return to the saucepan.

3. Place the curry in a small saucepan over low heat for 1 minute. Add the reserved carrot pieces and ½ cup of the remaining chicken broth and simmer for 3 minutes. Remove form the heat. Puree the carrot mixture with an immersion blender. Or, puree the mixture in a stand blender or food processor. Taste and adjust the seasoning with salt.

4. Reheat the soup and season to taste with salt and pepper. Ladle the soup into bowls, and swirl a spoonful of the carrot puree in the center of each bowl. Garnish with the cilantro leaves and serve hot.

In many of my recipes I refer to a sauté pan. This is the workhorse of my kitchen. It is a broad pan with a flat bottom and low, straight sides. You should have it in two or three sizes, of the heaviest, most solid construction you can afford.

Marcella Hazan, AUTHOR, *MORE CLASSIC ITALIAN COOKING*

Toasted Bulgur Pilaf with Cinnamon, Dried Cherries, and Pistachios

Sauté Pan

Like the skillet, the sauté pan needs to be made of a heavy material that heats up quickly and evenly, but the similarity ends there. The sauté pan comes with a tight-fitting lid and high (2 to 3 inches), straight sides. The most popular models are made of stainless steel or anodized metal. Some come with slightly domed see-through lids and others have flat lids. There is usually a single long handle, though larger models often have a short handle on the opposite side to make lifting easier.

This is a particularly versatile pan, useful for sautéing as well as browning foods. Its generous depth also means that it can accommodate liquid for braising slow-cooked meats and other foods. Although it comes in sizes ranging from 2 to 6 quarts, the larger pan is probably the most useful. If you can afford to have two sauté pans in your arsenal, make your second choice a 3-quart pan, which can double as a shallow saucepan.

Tips for Using

Its shape and noncorrosive material make most sauté pans perfect for browning foods, deglazing the pan—scraping up the browned bits from the pan bottom—with wine, broth, or another liquid, and then reducing the liquid to make a pan sauce. In France, this same pan is called a *sauteuse*.

A large sauté pan is excellent for frying foods, like steaks, chops, or chicken, or for steaming clams or mussels.

The depth and broad interior of a sauté pan make it a good choice for cooking rice or other grains, especially if the grains are toasted in oil or butter before they are simmered in liquid.

The largest sauté pan is an excellent vessel for making risotto. There is plenty of room to stir, the heat distribution is good, and the broad surface helps the rice to cook and absorb the broth evenly.

Some sauté pans come with a nonstick surface.

During cooking, the sauté pan's flat, even bottom makes sliding the pan on and off the burner easy, handy for when you need to move quickly.

Care in Using

Wash with warm, soapy water. The tough interior, if it isn't nonstick, and exterior can take strong detergents. Some materials even stand up to the dishwasher.

Always consult the manufacturer's instructions.

Alternatives

Braiser

recipes

Braised Round-Bone Lamb Chops with Wilted Onions, Oregano, and Lemon | Toasted Bulgur Pilaf with Cinnamon, Dried Cherries, and Pistachios | Variation: Brown Jasmine Rice Pilaf

BRAISED ROUND-BONE LAMB CHOPS with WILTED ONIONS, OREGANO, and LEMON

MARINATING TIME 1 to 2 hr | **PREP** 15 min | **COOK TIME** 35 min | **SERVES** 4

Round-bone lamb chops are cut from the sirloin or top portion of the lamb leg. This is a great cut because you can eat the tasty meat of the lamb leg without having to cook a whole or half leg. In this recipe, the sauté pan shows off its versatility. First it is used to brown the meat and the onions, and then it is covered and the meat slowly cooks until tender. Use a mandoline or other slicer to make quick work of the onions.

Implements Large Sauté Pan with Lid, Wide Spatula or Tongs, Slotted Spoon

Ingredients

4 (8-ounce) round-bone lamb chops, about ¾ inch thick

Freshly ground black pepper

4 teaspoons plus 1 tablespoon finely chopped fresh oregano

4 teaspoons plus 1 tablespoon freshly squeezed lemon juice

4 teaspoons plus 2 tablespoons extra-virgin olive oil

1 pound sweet onions, cut into ⅛-inch wedges (about 4 cups)

4 ripe plum tomatoes, quartered

2 cloves garlic, minced

1. Place the chops on a tray or platter in a single layer and sprinkle lightly with salt and pepper. Sprinkle each chop with about ½ teaspoon of oregano and ½ teaspoon each of lemon juice and olive oil. Turn the chops over and repeat with the salt, pepper, oregano, lemon juice, and olive oil. Cover and marinate in the refrigerator for 1 to 2 hours.

2. Heat a large sauté pan over medium heat until hot. Add the remaining 2 tablespoons olive oil and tilt the pan to coat. Add the lamb chops, increase the heat to medium-high, and cook for 2 minutes, or until lightly browned. Use a wide spatula or tongs to turn the chops over. Spoon the onions over and around the lamb.

3. Cover, decrease the heat to medium-low, and cook, stirring the onions occasionally, for 25 minutes, or until the onions are wilted and golden brown and the chops are cooked through. Stir the tomatoes, garlic, and ½ tablespoon of the oregano into the onions and cook, uncovered, for 5 minutes, or until warmed.

4. Transfer the lamb chops to a platter. Using a slotted spoon, lift the onion mixture from the pan, leaving the drippings behind, and top the chops with it. Sprinkle the remaining 1 tablespoon of lemon juice and the remaining ½ tablespoon of oregano on top of the onions and serve.

TOASTED BULGUR PILAF with CINNAMON, DRIED CHERRIES, and PISTACHIOS

PREP 5 min | COOK TIME 30 min | SERVES 4

The broad surface of a sauté pan is perfect for slowly toasting the bulgur in oil before simmering it. The cinnamon stick makes the pilaf especially fragrant, and the nutty flavor of the bulgur is complemented by the toasted nuts sprinkled on the finished dish.

Implements Sauté Pan with Lid, Silicone Spatula or Flat-Edged Wooden Spoon, Small Skillet (for Toasting Nuts)

Ingredients

2 tablespoons extra-virgin olive oil

1½ cups chopped yellow onion

1½ cups coarse bulgur

2½ cups low-sodium chicken broth, or 1¼ cups each broth and water

⅓ cup dried cherries, golden raisins, or dark raisins

1 cinnamon stick

Coarse salt

⅓ cup pistachios or walnuts, toasted (see below)

1. Heat a 5-quart sauté pan over medium heat. Add the oil and tilt the pan to coat. Add the onion and cook, stirring, for 10 minutes, or until golden. Add the bulgur and stir to coat with the onion and oil. Cook, stirring, for 5 minutes, or until the bulgur is lightly toasted.

2. Add the broth, cherries, cinnamon stick, and ½ teaspoon of salt, and bring to a boil. Decrease the heat to low, cover, and cook for 15 minutes, or until the broth is absorbed and the bulgur is tender.

3. Transfer to a serving bowl and top with the toasted nuts.

variation BROWN JASMINE RICE PILAF

Proceed as directed for Toasted Bulgur Pilaf with Cinnamon, Dried Cherries, and Pistachios, but substitute 1½ cups of brown jasmine rice for the bulgur, increase the broth to 4½ cups, and cook for 45 minutes.

Toasting Nuts and Seeds

Preheat the oven to 350°F. Spread the nuts or seeds in a single layer on a rimmed sheet pan and place in the oven. Toast for 8 to 15 minutes, until the nuts are the desired color. If you are toasting unskinned nuts, cut a nut in half and check the darkness of the inside.

You can toast small quantities of nuts or seeds in a small, dry skillet set over medium-low heat, stirring almost constantly, for 2 to 5 minutes, or until the nuts or seeds are toasted or fragrant. Because nuts and seeds are high in fat, you don't need to add any fat to the skillet, unless you want the extra flavor of a drizzle of oil or a teaspoon of butter.

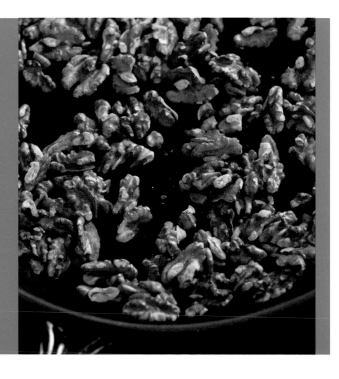

Skillet

The terms *skillet* and *frying pan* are frequently used interchangeably. Both refer to a shallow pan with a long handle and sloping sides in sizes that range from small (6 to 8 inches) to medium (10 to 11 inches) to large (12 to 14 inches). Skillets are typically used—and therefore sold—without a lid, and their sloping sides make it easy to stir and turn foods, or to catch foods tossed in the air as you sauté.

These indispensable pans come in an array of materials, from heavy, brightly colored enameled cast iron to lighter weight, handsome stainless-clad aluminum to beautiful, pricey stainless-lined copper to practical nonstick. Always look for two qualities in a skillet: good heat conduction and good heat distribution. Both depend on what the skillet is made of and how heavy it is (see "Tips for Using," following, for more on selecting skillets for specific uses). Ideally, every kitchen includes a nice selection of skillets in different sizes and materials.

Tips for Using

Use any metal skillet without a nonstick coating for sautéing poultry or meat. The bits of food—proteins and sugars—that stick to the bottom of the pan and form a browned crust on the food and the pan will add lots of flavor to the finished dish. Deglaze the pan with wine or broth to create a delicious pan sauce.

Many experienced cooks preheat a skillet over medium-low to medium heat until a drop of water sizzles on contact before adding any fat to it. Preheating ensures that the food is less likely to stick and burn.

Some skillets come with a baked-on black matte finish similar to a nonstick finish and an additional side handle to assist in lifting. Every kitchen should have at least one heavy, enameled cast-iron skillet with a satin black enamel interior finish.

Food cooked in a nonstick pan will not adhere to the surface, which means you need to add little or no fat.

Use pans with a nonstick coating for foods typically cooked over low to medium-low heat, such as eggs, toasted nuts, or gently sautéed vegetables.

Do not use metal utensils in a nonstick pan (they will scratch the finish). Nonstick skillets should not be used under the broiler but can be used in the oven up to 400°F.

Aluminum and also aluminum-core stainless-steel (without the nonstick finish) skillets are relatively lightweight and sturdy, making them good all-purpose pans for sautéing.

Care in Using

Most skillets are easily cleaned with soapy, warm water and a stiff plastic brush. Do not scrub nonstick skillets with wire scrubbers.

When cooking in a skillet, stir or turn foods with silicone, wooden, or other heat-resistant spatulas, whisks, or spoons that won't scratch the interior, whether it has a nonstick coating or not.

Always consult the manufacturer's instructions.

Alternatives

A sauté pan can be used as a substitute for a skillet.

recipes

Bubbling Shrimp in Tomato Sauce with Feta Cheese | **Scallops with Lime Butter, Snow Peas, and Black Sesame Seeds**

BUBBLING SHRIMP in TOMATO SAUCE with FETA CHEESE

PREP 15 min | COOK TIME 20 to 25 min | SERVES 4

Traditionally served in Greece's seaside tavernas, shrimp simmered in tomatoes and topped with melted feta is a classic Greek meze, or appetizer. Simmer, broil, and serve directly from the skillet, or simmer in a skillet, transfer to a large baking dish or four individual baking dishes, and broil until hot and bubbly. Serve the shrimp with lots of crusty bread to sop up the delicious juices.

Implements 10-inch Skillet, Silicone Spatula, Large Spoon

Ingredients

¼ cup extra-virgin olive oil

½ cup finely chopped yellow onion

2 cloves garlic, minced

Pinch of crushed red pepper

1 (28-ounce) can Italian plum tomatoes with juices

1 pound large uncooked shrimp, peeled and deveined, tails left on

2 tablespoons chopped fresh dill

1 teaspoon coarse salt

½ teaspoon sugar

Freshly ground black pepper

8 ounces feta cheese, patted dry and crumbled (about 1½ cups)

1. Position a rack in the top third of the oven. Preheat the broiler.

2. Heat a 10-inch skillet with a heat-resistant handle over low heat until warm. Add the oil and heat over medium-low heat until hot enough to sizzle a pinch of chopped onion. Add the onion and cook, stirring, for 5 minutes, or until softened. Stir in the garlic and red pepper, and cook, stirring, for about 1 minute, or until fragrant.

3. Add the tomatoes and bring to a boil. Adjust the heat so the mixture boils gently and cook, breaking up the tomatoes with the side of large spoon, for 10 to 15 minutes, until the sauce is very thick. Add the shrimp, 1 tablespoon of the dill, the salt, the sugar, and a grinding of pepper. Cook over medium-high heat, stirring, for 5 minutes, or until the shrimp are partially cooked. Remove from the heat.

4. Keep the mixture in the skillet, or spoon it into a large, shallow broiler-proof baking dish or 4 shallow, broiler-proof individual baking dishes, such as small, white porcelain gratins. Sprinkle the feta evenly over the top.

5. Broil for 5 minutes, or until the mixture is bubbly and the feta is browned.

6. Sprinkle with the remaining 1 tablespoon of dill and serve.

SCALLOPS with LIME BUTTER, SNOW PEAS, and BLACK SESAME SEEDS

PREP 15 min | **SOAK TIME** (snow peas) 10 min |
COOK TIME 8 to 10 min | **SERVES** 3–4

Virtually preparation free, scallops are one of nature's gifts to the world of quick cooking. The only task that may be required is pulling off the tiny muscle from the side of the scallop that is sometimes left attached when the scallop is shucked. Other than that, scallops are ready to go when you get them home. The two most common varieties are sea scallops (1 to 2 inches in diameter) and bay scallops (½ to ¾ inch in diameter). Scallops cook quickly—in a minute or two—so it's important to have all the ingredients prepped and the pan hot before you begin.

Implements
Medium Bowl, 10-inch Skillet, Silicone Spatula, Slotted Spoon, Tongs, Flat Whisk

Ingredients

8 ounces snow peas, trimmed and strings pulled off

1 tablespoon flavorless vegetable oil

1 teaspoon peeled, grated fresh ginger

1 teaspoon grated fresh garlic

1 pound small sea scallops or large bay scallops, about 1 inch in diameter

Coarse salt and freshly ground black pepper

¼ cup freshly squeezed lime juice

4 tablespoons cold unsalted butter, cut into small pieces

¾ teaspoon black sesame seeds, for garnish

1. Soak the snow peas in a medium bowl of ice water for 10 minutes, or until crisp. Drain well and set aside.

2. Heat a 10-inch skillet over medium heat until hot. Add the oil, add the snow peas and cook, stirring and adjusting the heat as necessary to prevent browning, for 3 minutes, or until crisp-tender. Add the ginger and garlic and cook, stirring, for 30 seconds, or until fragrant. Using a slotted spoon, transfer to a plate.

3. Add the scallops a few at a time to the hot skillet. Adjust the heat between high and medium-high to maintain a steady sizzle, so the outside of the scallops sear and the juices aren't released. Cook for 30 to 45 seconds, until golden. Turn with tongs and cook the other side for 30 to 60 seconds, until the scallops are just cooked through or their interior is opaque. Transfer to the side dish with the snow peas; sprinkle with salt and add a grinding of pepper.

4. Add the lime juice to the hot skillet and boil over high heat for 1 minute, or until reduced by half. Remove from the heat and use a flat whisk to whisk in the butter a piece at a time, fully incorporating each piece before adding the next one. Whisk the sauce until smooth.

5. Use the slotted spoon to transfer the snow peas and scallops to the skillet. Stir to blend into the sauce, and then transfer to a serving dish. Sprinkle with the sesame seeds and serve.

Herbs

Herbs add flavor and fragrance to your cooking. Here are some ideas for using your favorite herbs.

Basil Basil is pleasantly sharp, with notes of mint, thyme, and clove. The herb's mintlike taste goes well with tomatoes, seafood, chicken, pasta, and fresh fruits.

Bay Leaf This highly aromatic herb is used in broths, soups, and sauces. Most cooks prefer the taste and aroma of Mediterranean bay (or Turkish bay) to the more pungent California bay.

Chervil Chervil's mild parsley flavor with notes of licorice goes well with salmon, potatoes, peas, and carrots.

Chives The delicate onion flavor of chives goes well with eggs, potatoes, fish, shellfish, and many vegetables.

Cilantro Also called Chinese parsley and fresh coriander, cilantro has a distinctive taste. It is widely used in cooking all over the world.

Dill The flavor of fresh dill is reminiscent of lemon and celery. It's popular for salmon and other seafood, eggs, tomatoes, potatoes, and in salad dressings.

Marjoram Marjoram is in the same family as oregano, but has a sweeter flavor. Italians use it in frittatas, eggplant dishes, and with tomatoes.

Mint There are many varieties of mint, but the most common is the mild spearmint. It is a classic flavoring in iced tea, tomato salads, with green beans or braised carrots, and in tabbouleh.

Oregano Oregano's flavor notes of pepper and thyme pair well with chicken, red meats, pork, tomatoes, and most vegetables. Use it sparingly as too much can produce a bitter taste.

Parsley Parsley has a pinelike flavor. It's available as curly leaf and as Italian, or flat leaf, which has a more distinctive flavor. Use a finely chopped mixture of parsley and shallots or garlic, called *persillade* in French, to flavor sautéed mushrooms and other vegetables.

Rosemary The camphor notes in rosemary go well with hearty flavors such as roasted poultry and meats, or vegetables and legumes. It is a key flavor in the herb mixture herbes de Provence.

Sage Like rosemary, the camphor notes in sage define its flavor. It goes well with turkey and it is also used to season duck, pork, and breakfast sausage.

Tarragon The unique aniselike taste of tarragon marries well with eggs, and mild-flavored vegetables such as zucchini and other summer squashes.

Thyme A member of the mint family, thyme is often used with other herbs, and is always included in a bouquet garni and in herbes de Provence. It is also used on its own in soups, stews, vegetable dishes, and seafood and meats.

Beet Salad with Red Onion,
Oranges, and Orange Olive Oil

Steaming is one of the gentlest ways to cook, since it is only the even, moist heat of the vapors—not simmering water—that envelops the food, allowing it to retain most of its natural juices and nutrients.

Irma S. Rombauer, Marion Rombauer Becker, and Ethan Becker,

Steamer Insert

There are many pieces of equipment sold as steamers and steamer inserts. The most popular is the simple, inexpensive steaming basket designed with leaves that fold in and out around a central rod. Called a collapsible steamer, it fits in the smallest pan and is handy for steaming small amounts of vegetables or other foods. (For details on the bamboo steamer, see page 149.)

The most versatile and convenient steamer is a stainless-steel insert that fits snugly into a pot with a tight-fitting lid. Some companies make steamers that are sold separately but are designed to fit a specific pot such as a 3-quart saucepan, 6-quart Dutch oven, or an 8-quart stockpot. However, the same-sized insert sometimes fits both the 6-quart Dutch oven and the 8-quart stockpot and is spacious enough for most steaming jobs. You can also purchase a steamer set that typically includes a stainless-steel steamer insert, a clad stainless-steel pot with an aluminum base, and a lid.

Tips for Using

Steam is very hot and can cause painful burns, so protect your hands with an oven mitt when lifting the lid and removing the steamer insert from a pot of steaming water.

Beets, artichokes, broccoli, corn on the cob, carrots, and cauliflower are just a few of the many nutritious and flavorful vegetables that are good candidates for steaming.

Only steam young, tender, perfectly fresh green beans. Mature beans, which will turn out tough and chewy, should be cooked in a large pot of boiling water.

Steamers are good for cooking such shellfish as mussels, clams, and lobsters. Collapsible steamers work well for small steamed fish steaks or fillets.

A steamer is handy for reheating rice and some vegetables.

Some 8-quart stockpots come with a deep steamer insert. Although it is typically called a pasta insert, it can be used for steaming large batches of bigger foods, such as corn, tamales, lobsters, and pumpkin.

Care in Using

Use warm, soapy water. Stainless steel is dishwasher safe.

Always consult the manufacturer's instructions.

Alternatives

A cake rack set in a sauté pan or broad pot (such as a Dutch oven) and topped with a heatproof plate will work as a steamer. Add vegetables, fish steaks, cooked rice, or other foods to the plate. Make sure the pot has a tight-fitting lid to prevent steam from escaping.

recipes
Beet Salad with Red Onion, Oranges, and Orange Olive Oil | Corn on the Cob with Flavored Butters

BEET SALAD with RED ONION, ORANGES, and ORANGE OLIVE OIL

PREP 15 min | **SOAK TIME** (onions) 15 min |
COOK TIME 35 to 45 min | **SERVES** 4

Steaming preserves the firm texture and rich flavor of beets better than boiling does. Once the beets are cooked, their skins will slip right off. Of course, your fingers will turn pink, but the color washes off easily. You can also wear lightweight latex gloves to protect your hands. This pretty beet and orange salad is spooned onto a bed of greens lightly dressed with a drizzle of the same orange oil used to dress the beets.

Implements
8-Quart Steamer or Steamer Insert, 8-Quart Stockpot, Tongs, Large Bowl, Medium Bowl, Strainer, Vegetable Peeler, Rubber Spatula

Ingredients

2 pounds beets (about 6), tops trimmed to within ½ inch of crown, scrubbed

1 red onion, slivered lengthwise

Handful of ice cubes

2 oranges

4 tablespoons orange-infused olive oil or fruity extra-virgin olive oil

3 tablespoons finely chopped fresh mint leaves

1 tablespoon freshly squeezed lemon or lime juice

Coarse salt and freshly ground black pepper

2 romaine hearts

1. Place the beets in the 8-quart steamer insert. Add water to a depth of 2 inches to the stockpot, making certain that the bottom of the insert won't touch the water. Bring the water to a gentle boil. Place the steamer insert over the boiling water. Cover and cook over medium to medium-low heat for 35 to 45 minutes, until a fork pierces the beets easily. Use tongs to remove the beets to a plate. Let cool, then slip off the skins and cut the beets into ½-inch wedges. Transfer the beets to a large bowl.

2. Place the onion slivers in a medium bowl and add water to cover. Add the ice cubes and soak the onion slivers for 15 minutes. Drain the onions in a strainer, discarding the water and any unmelted ice. Blot the onion slivers on a paper towel and add to the beets.

3. Use a vegetable peeler to remove 2 strips, each about 1 inch wide and 3 inches long, from 1 of the oranges. Cut the strips into long, narrow, julienne strips and add to the beets. Use a sharp, thin knife to cut the peel and all of the white pith from both oranges. Working with 1 orange at a time, and holding it over the bowl containing the beets, cut along both sides of each segment to release it from the membrane, allowing the segments to drop into the bowl.

4. Add 2 tablespoons of the oil, the mint, the lemon juice, ½ teaspoon of salt, and a generous grinding of pepper to the beets. Using a rubber spatula, gently fold together all the ingredients until well blended.

5. Trim away the core and tough stem portion of each romaine heart, and then cut the hearts crosswise into ¼-inch-wide slices. There should be about 3 cups lightly packed. Place in a separate bowl. Drizzle with the remaining 2 tablespoons of oil, add a pinch of coarse salt, and toss to coat evenly.

6. Spread a layer of romaine on each of 4 salad plates. Spoon the beet salad in the center and serve.

CORN on the COB with FLAVORED BUTTERS

PREP 10 min | **COOK TIME** 8 to 10 min | **SERVES** 4

Corn on the cob, the classic American summer vegetable, can be boiled, grilled, or steamed. But steaming is the best way to preserve its pure corn flavor and toothsome texture. A shallow steamer, steamer insert, or pasta insert for an 8-quart stockpot will hold up to 8 ears of corn comfortably. For an added treat, set out one or two flavored butters along with the usual favorites: unsalted or salted butter and extra-virgin olive oil.

Implements 8-Quart Steamer or Steamer Insert, 8-Quart Stockpot, Tongs, Oven Mitts

Ingredients

8 ears of corn, husked
Unsalted or salted butter, softened
Extra-virgin olive oil
Asiago Cheese and Parsley Butter (page 94)
Chipotle Chile and Honey Butter (page 94)
Coarse salt

1. Place the corn in the 8-quart steamer insert. Add water to a depth of 2 inches to the matching pot, making certain that the bottom of the insert won't touch the water. Bring the water to a gentle boil. Place the steamer insert over the boiling water. Cover and cook over medium to medium-low heat for 8 to 10 minutes, until the corn is heated through.

2. Use tongs to transfer the corn to a platter. Serve hot with butter, olive oil, seasoned butters, and salt.

ASIAGO CHEESE and PARSLEY BUTTER

PREP 10 min | MAKES ½ cup or enough for 8 ears of corn

Asiago, a tangy, relatively inexpensive Italian cow's milk cheese, is widely available. If you like, you can substitute Parmigiano-Reggiano or pecorino romano.

Implements Small Bowl, Wooden Spoon (or Fork), Ramekin or Custard Cup

Ingredients

½ cup (1 stick) unsalted butter, softened

¼ cup grated Asiago cheese

2 teaspoons finely chopped fresh Italian parsley

1. Combine the butter, cheese, and parsley in a small bowl and mash with a wooden spoon or the back of a fork until blended.

2. Transfer to a custard cup or ramekin. Cover with plastic wrap and refrigerate. It will keep for up to 1 week. Remove from the refrigerator about 20 minutes before serving.

CHIPOTLE CHILE and HONEY BUTTER

PREP 5 min | MAKES ½ cup or enough for 8 cups of corn

The robust combination of spicy chipotle, sweet honey, and salty butter nicely complements the sweet crunch of just-steamed corn.

Implements Small Bowl, Wooden Spoon (or Fork), Ramekin or Custard Cup

Ingredients

½ cup (1 stick) butter, preferably salted, softened

2 teaspoons honey

½ teaspoon coarse salt

1 teaspoon chipotle chile in adobo sauce

½ teaspoon chili powder

1. Combine the butter, honey, salt, chipotle chile, and chili powder in a small bowl and mash with a wooden spoon or the back of a fork until blended. Taste and adjust the seasoning with more chile if you like a spicier butter.

2. Transfer to a ramekim or custard cup. Cover with plastic wrap and refrigerate. It will keep for up to 1 week. Remove from the refrigerator about 20 minutes before serving.

tips EASY-ACCESS CHIPOTLE CHILES

Most cooks use canned chipotle chiles packed in adobo sauce, a spicy vinegar and tomato mix. Because the chiles are fiery hot, only a small amount is needed. The best way to handle an opened can of chipotle chiles is to puree its contents in a food processor, spoon 1-teaspoon portions of the puree onto a sheet of aluminum foil, and slip the foil into the freezer. Once the spoonfuls are frozen, pull them off the foil and store them in a resealable plastic bag or other container in the freezer. They will keep for up to 6 months.

STICKY HONEY To prevent honey from sticking to a measuring spoon or cup, coat it with a thin layer of flavorless vegetable oil before you add the honey.

Stockpot

For broth to develop a full rich flavor, the water, vegetables, poultry, or meats must cook very slowly. The tall narrow profile of the traditional stockpot serves this purpose as it limits the rate of evaporation as the broth slowly simmers on the stove.

Stockpots range in size from 8 to 16 quarts. The 8-quart size is a good choice for the home cook as it is relatively easy to lift and is big enough for most uses.

Stockpots come with a flat lid in a variety of heavy-duty materials, from stainless clad to anodized aluminum. If you're shopping for a pot, make sure the handles fit your hand size, as you will want a good, comfortable grip when lifting 8 quarts of liquid.

Tips for Using

The 8- to 12-quart stockpot is convenient for making large batches of soup, chili, and tomato sauce or for cooking lobsters.

Many kitchens lack a pot large enough for boiling pasta. The 8-quart stockpot, will handle the task easily.

Invest in the pasta insert for an 8-quart stockpot, and you'll enjoy using your stockpot not only for cooking pasta, but also for steaming large batches of corn and other "big" vegetables, such as beets, celery root, or chunks of winter squash.

The larger stockpots (12 to 16 quarts) are useful for brining a small turkey or icing drink cans or bottles for a party.

Care in Using

Wash in warm, soapy water, scrub any stubborn spots with a stiff plastic brush and mild cleanser.

Always consult the manufacturer's instructions.

Alternatives

Any large, heavy pot (8 to 12 quarts) with two sturdy handles can stand in for a stockpot.

recipes
Chicken Broth with a Bonus | Pasta with Broccoli Rabe, and Cherry Tomatoes

CHICKEN BROTH with a BONUS

PREP 10 min | SOAK TIME (chicken) 1 hr | COOK TIME (chicken) 35 min | COOL TIME (chicken) 20 min | COOK TIME (broth) 2 hr | COOL TIME (broth) 1 to 2 hr | MAKES 2–2½ quarts, plus 3 cups cooked chicken meat

For this excellent chicken broth, select a whole chicken that gives you both the neck and giblets, to add flavor to your broth. Ask the butcher to cut up the chicken for you, or cut it up yourself with a poultry shears or sturdy kitchen scissors. If only cut-up chicken is available, buy extra chicken backs to add to the broth to make up for the absence of the neck and giblets. Plan to make the broth at least several hours before you need it, so it can be chilled and the fat, which will solidify on the surface, can be easily lifted off. The broth freezes well. Store it in 1- or 2-cup containers for convenience.

Implements
Peeler, Large Bowl, 8-Quart Stockpot, Fine-Mesh Skimmer, Perforated Spoon or Chinese Mesh Strainer, Fine-Mesh Strainer Lined with Cheesecloth or Chinois, Large Bowl

Ingredients

1 (4-pound) whole chicken with giblets, cut up

Coarse salt

1 large carrot, peeled and quartered crosswise

1 stalk celery with leafy top attached, quartered crosswise

1 yellow onion, quartered

2 whole cloves

6 cloves garlic, bruised with knife

2 leafy sprigs fresh Italian parsley

1 stem thyme

6 black peppercorns

1. Place the chicken in a large, deep bowl. Add the neck and all the giblets except the liver; reserve the liver for another use. Add ½ cup of coarse salt. Cover the chicken with cold water and refrigerate for 1 hour. Drain and rinse the chicken. Transfer the chicken to a stockpot and add water to barely cover (about 3 quarts).

2. Add the carrot, celery, onion, cloves garlic, parsley, thyme, and peppercorns to the stockpot. Set the pot over low heat, cover, and heat slowly until just barely simmering. Uncover and watch the pot. As foam rises to the top, skim it off with a fine-mesh skimmer or perforated spoon.

3. Cook the chicken in the barely simmering water over low heat for about 35 minutes. Use a Chinese mesh strainer or a perforated spoon to lift the legs, thighs, and breasts from the broth and place them on a deep platter, leaving the remaining pieces in the pot. Continue to cook the broth, uncovered, over low heat.

4. Let the chicken cool for about 20 minutes, or until it can be easily handled. Then pull the skin off the meat, reserving the skin. Pull or cut the cooked chicken from the bones in pieces and reserve separately. Add the bones, any gristle, and the reserved skin to the simmering broth. Continue to cook, uncovered, over low heat for 2 hours longer, or until the broth is reduced to about 2 quarts.

5. Remove the pot from the heat and let the broth stand for 1 to 2 hours, until lukewarm. Line a fine-mesh strainer with cheesecloth and place over a large bowl. Or, place a chinois over a large bowl. Strain the broth and discard the solids.

6. If there isn't room in the refrigerator for the bowl of broth, divide it among smaller bowls or other containers. Cover and refrigerate the broth for several hours or overnight or until is well chilled and the fat has solidified on the surface. Lift off the fat, using the fine-mesh sieve. The broth will keep, tightly covered, in the refrigerator for up to 3 days or in the freezer for up to 4 months.

7. Use the delicious cooked chicken meat in sandwiches, salads, soups, or as a filling for crepes.

PASTA with BROCCOLI RABE, and CHERRY TOMATOES

PREP 20 min | **COOK TIME** 20 minutes | **SERVES** 6–8

Broccoli rabe has a slightly bitter, pungent taste that is particularly good with pasta or beans. If *ricotta salata* is not available, substitute a mild feta, or lightly dust the pasta with grated Pecorino Romano.

Implements 8-Quart Stockpot with or without Pasta
Insert, Paring Knife, Large, Deep Skillet or Sauté Pan, Wooden Spoon, Slotted Spoon, Oven Mitts, Ladle, Large Metal Spoon

Ingredients

2 bunches (about 1½ pounds each) broccoli rabe

½ cup extra-virgin olive oil

2 cloves garlic, bruised with knife

¼ teaspoon crushed red pepper, or more to taste

2 cups tiny cherry or grape tomatoes

About 3 tablespoons coarse salt

1 pound dried orecchiette, cavatelli, or shell pasta

1 (6-ounce) wedge *ricotta salata* cheese, sliced into small pieces with a cheese plane

IF USING THE PASTA INSERT

1. Place a pasta insert in an 8-quart stockpot and fill three-fourths full with water. Cover and bring to a boil.

2. Wash the broccoli rabe thoroughly in cold water and drain. Trim off the thick, fibrous portion from the base of the stalks, usually about ½ inch. Cut the tender stalks and the thin tops with flowers attached into 1½-inch lengths. Set aside.

3. Heat the oil and garlic together in a large, deep skillet or sauté pan over low heat for 30 seconds, or just until the garlic begins to sizzle. Decrease the heat to very low and cook the garlic, stirring, for about 5 minutes, or until softened. Be careful that it does not brown. Stir in the red pepper and remove the skillet from the heat. Stir in the tomatoes and let stand until the pasta is ready.

4. Add the salt to the boiling water. Gradually add the pasta, stirring with a slotted spoon. Cook, uncovered, stirring gently until the water comes back to a boil. Cook the pasta for 8 minutes, or until almost tender. Add the broccoli rabe to the boiling pasta and cook for 3 to 5 minutes, until tender. The broccoli rabe and pasta should be quite soft.

5. Set a large, shallow pasta bowl or deep platter on the counter next to the pot on the stove. With mitted hands, slowly lift the pasta insert from the pot and hold it briefly over the pot to allow the water to drip out, then set it on the bowl. Ladle out ½ cup of the pasta cooking water from the pot and reserve.

6. Transfer the cooked pasta and the ½ cup cooking water to the tomato mixture in the skillet. Stir gently over medium-low heat for about 2 minutes, or until combined.

7. Pour out any water left in the serving bowl, dry the bowl, and spoon in the pasta, greens, garlic, oil and juices. Sprinkle with the cheese and serve at once.

IF NOT USING THE PASTA INSERT

1. Fill an 8-quart stockpot three-fourths full with water and bring to a boil. Proceed as directed through step 4.

2. When the pasta and broccoli rabe are cooked, place a large, shallow pasta bowl or deep platter in the sink with a colander set inside and drain the pasta in the colander. This method of draining the pasta in the serving bowl simultaneously warms the serving bowl and saves some of the pasta cooking water for adding flavor and moisture to the finished dish.

3. Proceed as directed in steps 6 and 7.

The newest rage in smoke cooking is doing it indoors. The result is not quite barbecue, but it's close enough to fool a foreigner and tasty enough to inspire yelps of joy in a Carolina pork lover.

Cheryl Alters Jamison and Bill Jamison AUTHORS, *SMOKE & SPICE*

Smoked Shrimp Wrapped with
Prosciutto

Stove-Top Smoker

The taste and aroma of smoked foods have a special allure. But if you have avoided smoking foods yourself because you thought it required hours of attention and a cumbersome piece of equipment meant only for use outdoors, it's time to take a look at the stove-top smoker. This plain, rather unassuming piece of equipment is amazingly efficient. It consists of a pan with a sturdy handle that stays surprisingly cool, a tray with a rack that sits on top of a small inside pan that holds the wood chips (usually less than 2 tablespoons), and either a sliding lid or, for some models, a removable lid that can double as a roasting pan. Some smokers include samples of wood chips in a variety of woods.

Stove-top smokers call for medium heat, so the cooking times are reasonably short. They come in several price ranges, with a lightweight stainless-steel smoker the least expensive, and a heftier cast-iron smoker a bit pricier.

Tips for Using

Most of the smoke is contained within the smoking pan, but an open window and/or turning on an exhaust fan are recommended.

Read the cooking guide carefully. Especially helpful are information on the different flavors delivered by the various types of wood chips and the list of suggested cooking times.

Easy does it on the wood chips. The wood chips sold for stove-top smokers are ground into small pieces, so very little is needed to produce the distinctive wood flavor that makes smoked foods so appealing. Because the area within the smoker is small, you'll need less rather than more. If you use too many chips of some woods, such as mesquite, the food will taste bitter.

Alder, hickory, and oak produce the most intense smoke flavors. Pecan, apple, maple, and cherry release more subtle flavors. Don't be afraid to experiment with mixing smoke flavors.

Smoking doesn't necessarily mean browning, so some foods need to be finished in the oven or in a preheated heavy skillet. For example, burgers, steaks, and brisket are smoked for only 20 to 30 minutes and then browned directly on a grill, under a broiler, or in a skillet or grill pan.

Care in Using

Before each use, spray the rack liberally with nonstick spray for easy cleanup.

For lighter-weight models, simplify cleanup by wrapping the inside tray completely with aluminum foil and lining the bottom and sides of the smoking pan with foil.

A stiff brush and warm, soapy water will clean off the drippings.

Always consult the manufacturer's instructions.

Alternatives

A stove-top smoker can be assembled using a heavy pot, lined with foil, and a wire rack.

recipes
Smoked Shrimp Wrapped with Prosciutto | Chinese Five Spice–Smoked Pork Tenderloins

SMOKED SHRIMP WRAPPED with PROSCIUTTO

PREP 15 min | **COOK-SMOKE TIME** 12 min | **SERVES** 6 as an appetizer or 4 as a main course

For convenience, look for frozen uncooked large shrimp, peeled and deveined but with the tail segments intact. Shrimp are always a popular finger food, and the tail works well as a little handle. These small, delicious bites are also excellent served as a garnish for a chef's salad. Suggested wood-chip flavors are cherry, mesquite, or apple.

Implements
Rimmed Sheet Pan, Paring Knife, Stovetop Smoker, Tongs, Pepper Mill, Timer, Oven Mitts

Ingredients

1 pound frozen peeled, deveined large shrimp with tail segments intact, thawed (20 to 24 shrimp)

Coarse salt and freshly ground black pepper

1 teaspoon chopped fresh rosemary

8 to 10 thin slices prosciutto

1. Pat the shrimp dry and lay them out on a rimmed sheet pan. Sprinkle each shrimp with a few grains of salt, a grinding of pepper, and a few bits of rosemary. Turn the shrimp over and season the other side the same way.

2. Separate the prosciutto slices and cut them lengthwise into ½- to ¾-inch-wide strips. You need as many strips as you have shrimp. Do not trim off the fat. Wrap each shrimp with a prosciutto strip, leaving the tail exposed.

3. Set up the smoker, following the manufacturer's instructions. Place 2 tablespoons of the desired wood chips in the center of the pan, or as directed in the manufacturer's instructions. Place the tray directly on top of the wood chips, and then place the rack on top of the tray.

4. Line up the shrimp in an orderly fashion (6 arranged across or lengthwise and 4 arranged down) on the rack.

5. Close the smoker and turn the heat to medium, or follow manufacturer's instructions. Set the timer for 12 minutes.

6. Turn off the heat when the timer goes off. With mitted hands, open the smoker, lift the shrimp from the smoker with tongs, and arrange on a platter. Serve at once.

tip WASHING HERBS

Do not wash herbs until just before using. Running water bruises the leaves and causes them to spoil quickly.

CHINESE FIVE SPICE-SMOKED PORK TENDERLOINS

PREP 15 min I BRINING 2 to 3 hr I COOK-SMOKE TIME
25 min I SERVES 4–6

A combination of Chinese five-spice rub and wood chip–generated smoke is the perfect antidote to the relatively mild flavor of pork tenderloin. Because it is so lean, brining it for 2 hours is recommended, but not essential. Suggested wood-chip flavors are cherry, pecan, or apple.

Implements
Paring or Utility Knife, Cutting Board, Large Bowl, Large Spoon, Stove-top Smoker, Small Bowl, Timer, Oven Mitts

Ingredients

2 (1-pound) pork tenderloins

BRINE

2 quarts water

½ cup coarse salt

3 star anise

1 cup ice cubes

2 tablespoons soy sauce

2 teaspoons five-spice powder

1 teaspoon coarse salt

½ teaspoon freshly ground black pepper

2 teaspoons honey

4 (3 by ½-inch) strips orange zest, finely slivered

1. First, remove and discard the silverskin from the pork tenderloins: Lay 1 pork tenderloin on a cutting board and with a sharp paring or utility knife trim any excess fat. Locate the silverskin, which is a long, narrow, shiny white membrane that runs along the surface of the meat. With the tip of a thin, sharp knife, make a small cut at the top of the silverskin long enough for you to hold onto the skin with the fingertips of one hand. With the other hand, pull the knife, its blade leaning toward the skin, along the skin and parallel to the meat to separate it from the meat. Discard the skin. Repeat with the remaining tenderloin.

2. MAKE THE BRINE: In a large bowl, combine the water, salt, and star anise, and stir to dissolve the salt. Add the tenderloins and the ice cubes, cover, and refrigerate for 2 to 3 hours. Do not brine longer or the texture of the meat may be altered. Remove the pork from the brine, discard the brine, and pat the pork dry with paper towels. (The pork can be brined a day ahead, drained, and reserved for smoking the next day.)

3. Set up the smoker, following the manufacturer's instructions. Place 2 tablespoons of the desired wood chips in the center of the pan, or as directed in the manufacturer's instructions. Place the tray directly on top of the wood chips, and then place the rack on top of the tray.

4. Rub each of the tenderloins with 1 tablespoon of the soy sauce. In a small bowl, mix together the five-spice powder, salt, and pepper. Using your fingers, rub half of the spice mixture into each of the tenderloins. Place the tenderloins on the grilling rack in the prepared smoker, folding under the narrow end of each tenderloin so it will fit. Lightly drizzle each tenderloin with 1 teaspoon of the honey. Sprinkle half of the orange slivers on top of each tenderloin.

5. Close the smoker and turn the heat to medium, or follow the manufacturer's instructions. Set the timer for 25 minutes.

6. Turn off the heat when the timer goes off, and let the pork rest in the smoker for 5 minutes. With mitted hands, open the smoker and transfer the meat to a cutting board. Cut on the diagonal into ¼- to ½-inch-thick slices and serve.

4 | HANDHELD TOOLS

Sometimes called a kitchen torch, this tool has only recently been available to the home cook. I find the intense heat from the torch offers a quick way to brown a dish without having to turn on the broiler.

Diane Rossen Worthington, AUTHOR, *SERIOUSLY SIMPLE*

Toasted Goat Cheese, Roasted Beet, and Pear Salad

Chef's Torch

This handy torch is the scaled-down home version of the industrial blowtorch. It is fired by butane, and the pointed flame is hot enough to caramelize sugar on a crème brûlée, turn on a cheese bubbly and golden, brown the tops of casseroles, melt herb butter on top of vegetables, and transform pale gold chicken skin to deep mahogany in a matter of seconds. Although many restaurant chefs use industrial-strength torches, the chef's torch, lightweight and just 6 inches long, is perfect for the home cook.

Tips for Using

The butane canisters are small and inexpensive. Buy two, so you'll always have one in reserve. One canister is good for about 1½ hours of use.

Carefully follow the manufacturer's instructions before using your chef's torch. For example, pay attention to the advice about the angle of the barrel. If the angle is too severe, the flame will extinguish itself.

The torch is not recommended for caramelizing brown sugar, but works well with turbinado and granulated white sugar.

Use the torch to toast marshmallows, to char chiles or bell peppers, and to melt jelly or jam glaze on fruit tarts, cheesecakes, and tortes.

Use the torch to heat the bottom of a custard cup or pan to ease the unmolding of *panna cotta,* a gelatin mold, a cheesecake, or other cold mixtures.

The torch is handy for warming up a knife blade before slicing cold, firm cheesecakes, ice-cream cakes, or pies.

Care in Using

Remove sticky fingerprints from the handle with a clean, damp cloth.

Always consult the manufacturer's instructions.

Alternatives

The chef's torch is difficult to replicate, but a preheated broiler will work for some tasks, such as browning the top of a casserole. Commercial chefs prefer the brawny hardware-store torch, but it's not recommended for the typical home cook.

recipes

Toasted Goat Cheese, Roasted Beet, and Pear Salad | Roasted Asparagus and Tomatoes with Bubbling Mozzarella

TOASTED GOAT CHEESE, ROASTED BEET, and PEAR SALAD

PREP 30 min | COOK TIME (beets) 1 hr | SERVES 4

The easy-to-use chef's torch will lightly toast the outside of a cold disk of fresh goat cheese while simultaneously warming and softening its heart. Placed in the center of a salad, the seared cheese holds its shape until it's broken with the side of a fork. The creamy center oozes into the salad, mingling with the dressing and creating a delicious second dressing for this mixture of roasted beets and bitter greens. The beets can be roasted and peeled up to 2 days before serving.

Implements
9-by-13-inch Baking Dish, Fork, Large Bowl, Two Small Bowls, Small or Spiral Whisk, Thin Blade Paring or Utility Knife, Chef's Torch, Rimmed Sheet Pan (Optional), Wide Spatula

Ingredients

1½ pounds beets, tops trimmed to within ½ inch of crown, scrubbed

¼ cup water

2 ripe Bartlett pears, quartered, cored, and cut into thin wedges

2 tablespoons freshly squeezed lemon juice

DRESSING

5 tablespoons extra-virgin olive oil

3 tablespoons sherry vinegar

1 teaspoon coarse salt

Freshly ground black pepper

2 cups packed torn pale green frisée leaves, arugula leaves, or a mixture of bitter salad greens

½ cup thin (⅛-inch) red onion wedges

1 (3½-ounce) log fresh goat cheese, or semi-aged Bucheron, well chilled

2 tablespoons coarsely chopped pistachios

1. Preheat the oven to 400°F. Spread the beets in a 9-by-13-inch baking dish. Add the water, cover the pan tightly with aluminum foil, and roast the beets for 1 hour, or until tender when pierced with a fork. The cooking time will vary depending on their size. When cool enough to handle, use a small paring knife to remove the skins. Cut the beets into ½-inch wedges and set aside in a large bowl.

2. In a small bowl, combine the pears and lemon juice and toss to coat evenly. Set aside.

3. MAKE THE DRESSING: In a small bowl, whisk together the oil, vinegar, salt, and a grinding of pepper until blended.

4. Add the greens and onion to the beets. Drizzle with the dressing and toss to coat evenly. Divide among 4 salad plates, distributing the beets evenly. Tuck the pear wedges into the salad, dividing them evenly.

5. Use a thin-bladed knife to carefully cut the goat cheese into 4 equal disks each about ¾ inch thick. To make a clean cut straight through the cheese, heat the blade with the chef's torch before each cut, or rinse the blade with hot water and wipe it dry before each cut. Place the cheese disks, with a cut side down, on a flameproof surface.

6. Turn on the chef's torch and, with the flame about 2 inches from a cheese disk, move it slowly back and forth for about 30 seconds, or until the surface is toasted to a golden brown. Repeat with the remaining disks. Alternatively, the goat cheese can be browned under the broiler: Position an oven rack so that the surface of the cheese will be about 3 inches from the heat source, and preheat the broiler. Place the cheese disks on a rimmed sheet pan and broil, watching carefully and turning the pan as needed to toast evenly, for 1 to 3 minutes, until the cheese is golden.

7. Carefully slide a wide spatula under each cheese disk and transfer it to the center of a salad. Sprinkle the cheese and salad with the pistachios and serve while the cheese is still warm.

tip BEET TOPS

If the green leafy tops on your beets are fresh and unblemished—as they should be—save them to serve as a cooked side dish. Remove the long, tough red stems and discard. Coarsely chop the leafy green tops, wash in a couple of changes of water, and shake dry in a colander. Transfer to a Dutch oven or other large, wide pot with only the moisture clinging to the leaves. Cover and cook over low heat for 8 to 10 minutes, or until the leaves are wilted and tender. Remove from the heat. Serve drizzled with 1 tablespoon extra virgin olive oil, 1 to 2 teaspoons red wine vinegar or sherry vinegar, and a pinch each of salt and freshly ground black pepper. Serve warm or at room temperature. Beet greens are also good stirred into soups or served as a garnish on a plate of sliced cooked beets.

ROASTED ASPARAGUS and TOMATOES with BUBBLING MOZZARELLA

PREP 20 min | COOK TIME 25 min | SERVES 4

Roasting asparagus retains their bright green color, intense green taste, and toothsome texture. In a hot oven, they're ready in only about 15 minutes. In this recipe, small tomatoes are roasted first and then the asparagus are added. The tomatoes need a head start so that they will have collapsed and caramelized at the same time the asparagus are ready. The dish is finished with slices of mozzarella cheese, which are turned bubbly and golden brown with a chef's torch.

Implements Serrated Peeler, Large Shallow Bowl, Nonreactive Rimmed Sheet Pan, Tongs, Flameproof Baking Dish

Ingredients

1 bunch asparagus (about 1¼ pounds)

1 pint tiny cherry or pear tomatoes, red or a mixture of colors

3 tablespoons extra-virgin olive oil

Coarse salt

Freshly ground black pepper

2 tablespoons torn fresh basil leaves

4 ounces mozzarella cheese, cut into thin slices

1. Break off the tough stem ends from the asparagus. Use a serrated peeler to remove the scales from the lower section of the stalks. Place the spears in a large, shallow bowl, add cold water to cover, and set aside until ready to roast.

2. Preheat the oven to 450°F. Place the tomatoes in the center of a nonreactive rimmed sheet pan and drizzle with 2 tablespoons of the olive oil. Add a pinch of salt and a grinding of black pepper. Toss the tomatoes with your hands to coat with the oil. Roast for 10 minutes and then remove the pan from the oven.

3. Drain the asparagus and place them back in the bowl. Add the remaining 1 tablespoon of oil, a pinch of salt, and a grinding of black pepper. Toss to coat. Spread on the sheet pan. Spoon the tomatoes on top of and around the asparagus. Return the pan to the oven and roast for 15 minutes, or until the asparagus are tender.

4. Use tongs to transfer the asparagus to a flameproof baking dish or serving dish. Spoon the cooked tomatoes and juices over the asparagus. Sprinkle with the basil and lay the slices of mozzarella over the top.

5. Turn on the chef's torch and, with the flame about 2 inches from a cheese slice, move it slowly back and forth for about 30 seconds, or until the cheese begins to bubble and brown. Repeat with the remaining slices until all the cheese is melted. Alternatively, the cheese can be browned under the broiler: Make sure the vegetables are in a broiler-proof baking dish. Position an oven rack so that the surface of the cheese is be about 3 inches from the heat source, and preheat the broiler. Broil, watching carefully and turning the baking dish as needed, for 1 to 3 minutes, until the cheese is bubbly and browned. Serve at once.

Using a food mill means you don't have to seed and peel apples and tomatoes before making a sauce since it separates them out for you.

Deborah Madison, AUTHOR, *VEGETARIAN COOKING FOR EVERYONE*

Old-Fashioned Tomato and
Meat Sauce for Pasta

Food Mill

Don't underestimate the usefulness of the food mill. It may be manually operated, but there is no better tool for turning out smooth purees. It is a classic, but is it better than the food processor? For some tasks, it is infinitely better than the food processor. For example, unlike a food processor, it won't introduce unwanted air and added volume to a puree. (If you've ever eaten a foamy gazpacho, you'll recognize the problem.)

The food mill design is masterful in its simplicity. It's a sturdy perforated disk, or sieve, with a hand-operated crank that moves a blade through the food, forcing soft solids through the perforations (this is the puree) and leaving the hard solids (like skins and seeds) behind. It will puree any soft food, cooked or uncooked. When shopping for a food mill, look for one made of rust- and acid-resistant stainless steel. Some models have removable disks in different sizes that give you a choice of puree textures and make cleanup easier.

Tips for Using

Set the food mill on top of a sturdy bowl or saucepan large enough to catch the puree. If necessary, place a folded dampened towel or a silicone mat under the bowl or saucepan to keep it from sliding on the work surface as you crank.

Turning the crank clockwise forces the food through the disk. Reverse the crank periodically to redistribute the food being pushed through. Also, occasionally lift the mill from the bowl or saucepan and scrape off the puree stuck to the underside with a rubber spatula.

The mill is perfect for pureeing canned tomatoes because it finely crushes the pulp while separating out the seeds. It separates the skins and seeds from the pulp when used for fresh tomatoes. Use the fine disk for tomatoes.

It is a must-have for quick applesauce because no peeling or coring is necessary. Cooked chunks of apple pass easily through the coarse disk, leaving skin and seeds behind.

Use the coarse disk to make terrific mashed potatoes.

The food mill is great for creating pureed vegetable combinations, such as potato and parsnip, acorn squash and celery root, and beets and carrots.

Use the fine disk for smooth pureed vegetable soups.

Care in Using

A brush might be needed to dislodge food or seeds stuck in the sieve. All parts are dishwasher safe.

Always consult the manufacturer's instructions.

Alternatives

A food processor or blender and a strainer work. However, you'll need two steps to do what a food mill can do in one.

recipes

Old-Fashioned Tomato and Meat Sauce for Pasta | Fluffy Yukon Gold Potatoes with Goat Cheese and Green Onions

OLD-FASHIONED TOMATO and MEAT SAUCE for PASTA

PREP 45 min | COOK TIME 3 hr | SERVES 6

This rich tomato sauce is excellent served with rigatoni or other sturdy dried pasta with ridges that will hold the sauce. The meat in this recipe—the pork ribs and beef chuck—adds to the rich flavor. However, meatballs, Italian sausage, veal stew meat, Italian fennel sausage, or even a browned pork chop or piece of beef sirloin can be substituted. Just make sure not to use more than 3 pounds of meat, which are served as a side dish with the pasta.

Implements
8-Quart Dutch Oven, Tongs, Food Mill, Rubber Spatula, 8-Quart Stock Pot with Matching Pasta Insert or Other 8-Quart Pot and Colander, Large Ladle, Two Large Spoons

Ingredients

SAUCE

1 to 1½ pounds meaty pork spareribs or country-style ribs

1 to 1½ pounds boneless beef chuck or stew meat, cut into 2-inch pieces

Coarse salt

Freshly ground black pepper

2 tablespoons extra-virgin olive oil

½ cup coarsely chopped yellow onion

3 cloves garlic, minced

3 (28-ounce) cans Italian plum tomatoes with juices

1 (16-ounce) can tomato sauce

1 (6-ounce) can tomato paste

1 teaspoon dried oregano

Pinch of crushed red pepper (optional)

1 pound rigatoni, *penne rigate,* or *conchiglie* (large shells)

Grated Parmigiano-Reggiano or Pecorino Romano cheese, for serving

1. **MAKE THE SAUCE:** Blot the meat dry with paper towels and sprinkle generously on all sides with salt and pepper. Heat the oil in an 8-quart Dutch oven or other large, wide pan over medium heat. Working in batches, add the meat to the oil and cook, turning with tongs, for 10 to 15 minutes, until browned on all sides. As each batch is done, transfer it to a large plate. When all of the meat has been browned, set it aside.

2. Spoon off all but about 2 tablespoons of the fat in the pan. Add the onion and cook over medium heat, stirring, for 5 minutes, or until golden. Add the garlic and cook for 1 minute, or until softened. Remove from the heat.

3. Fit a food mill with the medium disk, and set the mill on the rim of the Dutch oven. Put the tomatoes with their juices in the food mill and puree. Reverse the crank to extract every bit of flavor from the tomato pulp, and occasionally stop to clean the underside of the mill with a rubber spatula, so the puree falls freely. Add the tomato sauce, tomato paste, oregano, and red pepper to the pan and stir to blend.

4. Add the browned meats and any juices that accumulated on the plate to the pan and turn the heat to medium-low. Cook uncovered, stirring and adjusting the temperature to maintain a slow simmer, for 2 to 2½ hours, until the sauce is thickened and slightly reduced.

5. **COOK THE PASTA:** Fill a deep 8-quart pot, outfitted with a pasta insert if using, three-fourths full with water. Bring the water to a rolling boil. Add 3 tablespoons of coarse salt to the boiling water and then gradually add the pasta. Stir with a long-handled slotted spoon until the water returns to a boil. Boil the pasta for 10 minutes. Remove 1 piece of pasta with the slotted spoon and test for doneness. Pasta is cooked when it is only slightly resistant to the bite. If the pasta is too hard, cook for 2 minutes more and test again. Keep testing the pasta every 2 minutes, or until it is cooked to your liking.

6. Slowly lift out the pasta insert, allowing the water to drain back into the pot, or set a large colander in the sink and pour the pasta and water slowly into the colander. Do not shake all of the water off the pasta.

7. Ladle a pool of just the sauce—no meat—in the bottom of a large pasta serving bowl. Add half of the pasta. Top with another ladle or two of sauce, again without the meat. Top with the remaining pasta. Top with 2 more ladles of the sauce. Using 2 large spoons, gently mix the pasta with the sauce until evenly coated. Reserve the remaining sauce.

8. Use tongs to lift the meat from the sauce and either arrange it along the edges of the pasta or place it in a separate serving bowl. Pour the remaining tomato sauce into a gravy boat or a small bowl, and serve along with the pasta and meat. Pass the cheese at the table.

tip KEEP THE PASTA AND THE BOWL HOT

A great way to heat the pasta serving bowl is to set it in the sink and set the colander for draining the pasta inside the bowl. That way, the boiling pasta water heats up the bowl as the pasta drains. When ready to serve, simply pour the water from the bowl and the bowl will be hot.

FLUFFY YUKON GOLD POTATOES with GOAT CHEESE and GREEN ONIONS

PREP 20 min | COOK TIME 15 to 20 min | SERVES 4–6

The Yukon Gold potato has become our all-purpose potato. Once available only on a limited basis, it's now found in almost every supermarket. Because the flesh has more moisture and less starch than russet (baking) potatoes, it is dense, creamy, and very rich when mashed, rather than light and fluffy. The goat cheese adds extra creaminess and surprisingly pleasant tartness to this dish. Do not be tempted to mash potatoes in a food processor, or they'll be gluey.

Implements Medium Saucepan, Colander, Small Saucepan, Food Mill, Rubber Spatula, Wooden Spoon

Ingredients

3 pounds Yukon Gold potatoes, peeled and cut into 1-inch cubes

2 cloves garlic, peeled and left whole

Coarse salt

1 cup milk

2 tablespoons unsalted butter

4 ounces cold fresh goat cheese, crumbled, brought to room temperature

Freshly ground black pepper

4 tablespoons thinly sliced green onions, both white and parts

1. In a medium saucepan, combine the potatoes, garlic, 2 teaspoons salt, and water to cover by 1 inch. Bring to a boil over high heat, adjust the heat to a simmer, and cook, uncovered, for 15 to 20 minutes, until the potatoes are tender when pierced with a fork. Drain in a colander.

2. Meanwhile, in a small saucepan, combine the milk and butter over medium-low heat and heat just until the butter melts. Remove from the heat.

3. Fit a food mill with the medium disk, and set the mill on the rim of the saucepan used to cook the potatoes. Working in batches, put the potatoes in the mill and puree. Occasionally stop to clean the underside of the mill with a rubber spatula, so the puree falls freely.

4. With a wooden spoon, gradually stir the hot milk mixture into the potatoes until blended. Add the goat cheese and stir until partially blended. Season to taste with salt and a grinding of pepper. Stir 2 tablespoons of the green onions into the potatoes.

5. Mound the potatoes in a warmed serving bowl and sprinkle with the remaining 2 tablespoons of green onions. Serve hot.

Use an all-purpose four-sided box grater for grating cheese (coarse or fine) and slicing and shredding vegetables.

Martha Stewart, AUTHOR, *MARTHA STEWART'S HOMEKEEPING HANDBOOK*

Miniature Zucchini Pancakes with Asian Dipping Sauce

Grater

There are dozens of types of graters, each with a specific use. The metal box grater usually made of stainless steel is the classic. Its design is now more sophisticated, but it still has at least four, and sometimes more, different surfaces. It also has comfy handless and a removable plastic bottom for capturing the grated food. Flat graters with different surfaces are also available.

The rotary grater, another classic, usually comes with two removable cylinders, typically one for fine and one for coarse grating. The cylinders are held in place with a long-armed grating surface that presses down on a square of hard cheese or a chunk of bread as you turn the crank.

The rasp grater, sometimes called a zester, is the newest type of grater and is ideal for removing the zest from citrus. The original design was a long, thin strip of stainless steel with small, sharp perforations. But newer designs have introduced wider grating areas and perforations in a variety of sizes and shapes suitable for nearly any food that needs to be grated or shredded. These contemporary flat graters also have ergonomically designed handles and finger shields to protect against scraped knuckles.

Tips for Using

In the basic kitchen it's useful to have three kinds of graters: a box grater, a cheese grater (rotary or other), and a rasp grater.

The weight of what you grate varies depending on the type of grater you are using. For example, ½ cup of grated cheese prepared on a rasp grater will usually weigh less than ½ cup of grated prepared on a box grater.

Use the fine punctures of a box grater for citrus zest and fine shreds of carrot; use the basic grate for hard cheeses; use the slicing blade for semisoft cheeses, hard-cooked eggs, and for shredding lettuce; use the coarse punctures for semisoft to semifirm cheeses, raw potatoes, and cabbage.

A rotary grater is handy for grating chocolate to top your morning cappuccino, toasted nuts for salad, or a small chunk of hard cheese for pasta or other dishes.

Use a fine rasp grater, the same one you use for citrus, for grating garlic or nutmeg; medium (¼ inch) is good for cabbage, carrots, and other vegetables; extra-wide is good for semisoft cheeses.

If you're comfortable eyeballing the amount of citrus zest you add to a dish, hold the fruit in one hand and with the other hand pull the rasp grater across the skin to collect the gratings on the underside of the rasp. Then turn the zester over and gently tap it on the rim of the bowl.

Care in Using

Rinse well in warm water and use a stiff brush to clean thoroughly.

Most graters are dishwasher safe.

Always consult the manufacturer's instructions.

Alternatives

It's difficult to replace a grater, but the food processor with its numerous attachments can do just about any grating job. Follow the manufacturer's instructions carefully.

recipes

Shredded Cabbage Salad with Rice Vinegar, Ginger, and Sesame | Miniature Zucchini Pancakes with Asian Dipping Sauce

SHREDDED CABBAGE SALAD with RICE VINEGAR, GINGER, and SESAME

PREP 20 min | SERVES 4

Quickly shred the cabbage with the wide (¼ inch) shredding blade on a box or flat grater directly into a large bowl. A rasp grater is the perfect tool for grating ginger because it effortlessly cuts through ginger's fine tough strings. Top the salad with a sprinkling of crunchy, mildly nutty brown or black sesame seeds. Look for them in Asian groceries and well-stocked supermarkets. Serve this refreshing salad with grilled or pan-seared soy-glazed salmon or tuna.

Implements Box or Flat Grater, Two Large Bowls, Standard or Flat Whisk

Ingredients

1-pound wedge green cabbage, cored and halved or quartered (about 4 cups)

½ red onion

DRESSING

⅓ cup unseasoned rice vinegar

¼ cup canola or other flavorless vegetable oil

2 tablespoons freshly squeezed lemon or lime juice

1 tablespoon toasted sesame oil

1-inch piece fresh ginger, peeled and grated (about 2 teaspoons)

1 teaspoon coarse salt

½ teaspoon sugar

2 tablespoons finely chopped fresh mint

1 teaspoon brown or black sesame seeds

1. Using the wide shredding blade on a box or flat grater, shred the cabbage and onion directly into a large bowl.

2. **MAKE THE DRESSING:** In another large bowl, whisk together the vinegar, canola oil, lemon juice, sesame oil, ginger, salt, and sugar until blended.

3. Add the cabbage, onion, and mint to the dressing and stir with a large fork to blend. Sprinkle with the sesame seeds and serve chilled or at room temperature.

MINIATURE ZUCCHINI PANCAKES with ASIAN DIPPING SAUCE

PREP 25 min | COOK TIME 20 min | SERVES 4

Serve these tiny pancakes for a snack or hors d'oeuvre during the summer when zucchini are abundant at farmers' markets. They are delicious with a chilled glass of pinot gris or other crisp white wine. Use the wide (¼ inch) shredding blade on a box or flat grater for the zucchini—they are soft and shred quickly and easily—and carrot, and a rasp grater for the onion, garlic, and ginger.

Implements Small Bowl, Spiral or Flat Whisk, Grater with Wide Shredding Blade, Rasp Grater, Large Bowl, Rubber Spatula , Rimmed Sheet Pan, Wire Rack, 10-inch Cast-Iron or Other Heavy Skillet (Not Nonstick), Slotted Spoon or Spatula, Wire Rack

Ingredients

ASIAN DIPPING SAUCE

¼ cup light soy sauce

¼ cup freshly squeezed lime juice

¼ cup water

¼ cup Asian fish sauce

2 tablespoons sugar

1 tablespoon thinly sliced jalapeño or serrano chile

1 clove garlic, grated

PANCAKES

3 small zucchini

1 large carrot, peeled

2-inch piece fresh ginger, peeled

1-inch wedge yellow onion

¼ cup cracker meal or matzo meal

1 tablespoon minced fresh cilantro

2 large eggs, lightly beaten

½ teaspoon coarse salt

Canola or other flavorless vegetable oil, for frying

1. **MAKE THE DIPPING SAUCE:** In a small bowl, combine the soy sauce, lime juice, water, fish sauce, sugar, chile, and garlic. Whisk to blend. Cover with plastic wrap and set aside until ready to serve. The sauce can be refrigerated for up to 5 days before serving.

2. **MAKE THE PANCAKES:** Trim the stem and blossom ends from the zucchini. Working over a large bowl, rub the cut end of the zucchini over the wide shredding blade on a box or flat grater. You should have about 2 cups. Repeat with the carrot. You should have about ½ cup. Grate enough ginger on a rasp grater to yield about 2 tablespoons. Then grate the onion on a rasp grater to yield about 1 tablespoon. Add the ginger and onion to the zucchini, along with the cracker meal and cilantro.

3. Add the eggs and salt to the zucchini and stir with a rubber spatula until well blended. Let stand for 10 minutes.

4. Place a wire rack on a rimmed sheet pan. Add oil to a depth of ½ inch to a 10-inch cast-iron or other heavy skillet. Heat over medium heat until a small crust of bread dropped into the hot oil lightly browns on contact. Drop rounded tablespoons of the zucchini mixture into the hot oil, forming pancakes about 1½ inches in diameter and being careful not to crowd the pan. Fry, turning once with a slotted spoon or spatula and adjusting the heat between medium and medium-low as needed to keep the pancakes gently sizzling, for 2 to 3 minutes per side, until golden brown. Using the slotted spoon, transfer the pancakes to the rack. Repeat with the remaining zucchini mixture in 2 or 3 more batches. (The pancakes can be cooled completely, arranged in a single layer in a resealable plastic freezer bag, and frozen for up to six weeks. To serve, transfer while still frozen to a rimmed sheet pan and place in a preheated 300°F oven for about 20 minutes, or until sizzling.)

5. Serve the pancakes while they are warm, and accompany them with the dipping sauce.

Not as powerful as a stand blender, but so convenient.

Kabocha Squash Soup with
Toasted Cumin and Chiles

Immersion Blender

The immersion blender is a scaled-down version of the yard-long model used in professional kitchens. The latter's ability to emulsify multigallon tubs of salad dressing and puree enormous pots of soup in minutes caught the attention of manufacturers of kitchen equipment, who created the lightweight home version, also known as a wand hand blender. It does everything that a stand blender does, plus more. Its main advantage is that the food stays in the pot in which it is cooked or in the bowl in which it is mixed, eliminating the need to pour foods back and forth between a stand blender and the pot or bowl. Consequently, cleanup is easy. Its primary disadvantage is that it keeps one hand occupied with moving the wand back and forth through the food, so you can't turn to other tasks as you can with a stand blender.

Before buying an immersion blender, make sure that it feels comfortable in your hand and that the weight is okay. Some models are cordless, and some have various attachments, such as a small chopper for fresh herbs and garlic and a whisk for whipping cream. Yet another occasional feature is a tall, narrow measuring cup for blending salad dressings, smoothies, or other small batches of liquids.

Tips for Using

To avoid splattering, have the blade well below the surface of the food before engaging the motor, do not lift it from the food while the motor is running, and always wait for a few seconds after turning off the motor before removing it.

For the best results, place the food in a deep, rather than shallow, pot or bowl.

Use a gentle, barely perceptible up-and-down motion as you guide the blade through the liquid.

This blender is a must-have for making pureed soups right in the pot, for smoothing out gravies, and for blending smoothies, berry sauces, and emulsified salad dressings.

If your custard or other egg-based sauce has gotten too hot and threatens to curdle, the immersion blender can often save it.

When your hosting a party, keep the blender near the bar for making pureed or blended fruit drinks.

Care in Using

Some models have detachable blending shafts that are dishwasher safe.

The gearbox and motor housing should be wiped clean with a hot, soapy cloth, and not immersed in water

Always consult the manufacturer's instructions.

Alternatives

A blender, food processor, or food mill can do many of the same tasks as a immersion blender, but require additional pouring steps.

recipes

Lemon Chickpea Dip with Mint and Dill | Kabocha Squash Soup with Toasted Cumin and Chiles

LEMON CHICKPEA DIP with MINT and DILL

PREP 10 min | SERVES 6–8

Here is a bright-tasting puree of chickpeas (garbanzo beans) inspired by Middle Eastern hummus. This chunky version prepared with a hand wand blender omits the tahini (sesame paste) sometimes added to the classic and substitutes a generous measure of lemon juice in its place. The result is a much lighter dip. The dill and mint mimic typical herbs used in Middle Eastern dishes. Serve with crisp triangles of pita bread (see right) and red bell peppers, cut into wedges, for scoops.

Implements Deep Narrow Bowl, Immersion Blender, Rubber Spatula

Ingredients

2 (14-ounce) cans chickpeas, rinsed and well drained

⅓ cup freshly squeezed lemon juice

¼ cup extra-virgin olive oil, plus more for garnish

1 teaspoon coarse salt

1 clove garlic, minced or grated

Pinch of cayenne pepper

1 tablespoon packed chopped fresh mint, for garnish

1 tablespoon packed chopped fresh dill, for garnish

1. Put the chickpeas, lemon juice, olive oil, salt, garlic, and red pepper in a deep, narrow bowl. Place the bowl on a folded towel or a nonskid mat.

2. Use an immersion blender to blend the mixture to a light, coarse puree. Alternatively, coarsely puree the mixture in a food processor. Taste and adjust the seasoning with more lemon juice and salt.

3. Spread the mixture with a rubber spatula on a shallow serving plate. Finely chop the mint and dill together and sprinkle evenly on top. Drizzle with a thin stream of olive oil.

TOASTED PITA CHIPS

Preheat the oven to 400°F. Split white or whole-wheat pita bread rounds horizontally into two rounds. Lightly brush one side of each round with olive oil, and stack the rounds. Using a utility or chef's knife, cut through the stack to yield 6 or 8 wedge-shaped chips from each round. Spread the wedges on rimmed baking sheet(s). Bake for 10 minutes, or until lightly browned. Stir the chips to redistribute and turn them over. Bake for 5 minutes more, or until crisp. Let cool, then store in resealable plastic bags at room temperature. The chips will keep for up to 2 weeks.

KABOCHA SQUASH SOUP with TOASTED CUMIN and CHILES

PREP 20 min | COOK TIME 20 min | SERVES 4–6

The Japanese *kabocha* squash is squat and round, and has nubby, dark green skin and dense, sweet flesh. Use a large, heavy chef's knife to cut the squash into big chunks. Because the skin is too thick and brittle to peel, the squash is cooked and then the flesh is scooped from the skin. Pureed with coconut milk, it makes a rich, golden soup. Balance the richness with a generous addition of fresh lime juice, slivered chiles, and a shower of finely chopped cilantro.

Implements
Large Pot and Matching Steamer Insert, Oven Mitt, Flat-Edged Wooden Spoon, Immersion Blender

Ingredients

1 (4-pound) kabocha squash, cut into large chunks and seeds and membranes removed

1 tablespoon flavorless vegetable oil

½ cup chopped yellow onion

1 clove garlic, minced or grated

2½ teaspoons ground cumin

2 (14-ounce) cans light or regular coconut milk

2 teaspoons coarse salt

⅛ teaspoon freshly ground black pepper

¼ cup freshly squeezed lime juice

1 red or green jalapeño chile, halved lengthwise, seeded, and slivered crosswise

2 tablespoons finely chopped fresh cilantro

1. Place the squash in a steamer insert set over a large pot of gently boiling water. Cover and cook for 20 minutes, or until tender when pierced with a fork. Lift the steamer from over the water, using an oven mitt, and let the squash cool. Discard the water in the pot and wipe the pot dry.

2. Add the oil to the pot, place over medium heat, and heat the oil until hot enough to sizzle a piece of onion. Add the onion and cook over low heat, stirring with a wooden spoon, for 3 minutes, or until the onion is translucent. Stir in the garlic and cook for 30 seconds. Add the cumin and cook, stirring, for 1 minute. Remove from the heat.

3. Use a tablespoon to scoop the cooled squash from the brittle skins and add it to the pot with the onion. Stir in the coconut milk.

4. Use immersion blender to puree the soup right in the pot. Alternatively, puree soup in batches in a blender. Add the salt and pepper.

5. Reheat the soup over medium-low heat, stirring to prevent sticking, until steaming. Do not allow to boil. Stir in the lime juice, half of the chile, and 1 tablespoon of the cilantro. Taste and adjust the seasoning with salt. Ladle into warmed bowls. Garnish with the remaining chile and the remaining tablespoon of cilantro.

Unless you're very handy with a knife, and few of us are, it's much faster and easier to slice certain vegetables with a vegetable slicer. The mandoline, the fanciest of these slicers, is almost indispensable, not only for thin slices of potatoes, but for julienning, cutting different French fry sizes, and for slicing ruffled potato chips.

James Peterson, AUTHOR, *VEGETABLES*

Jicama and Carrot Slaw with
Fresh Pineapple and Cilantro

Mandoline

The mandoline is a hand-operated precision slicer for fruits and vegetables. The first culinary mandoline was made, like the musical instrument, from wood. It wasn't until the mid-twentieth century that the all-metal mandoline was manufactured.

Today, the all-stainless-steel version found in most professional kitchens is the gold standard for this family of slicers. It has hinged legs with nonskid feet to support it, freeing your hands to operate the slicer. There is a round, dimpled food pusher that simultaneously holds the food in place—gliding along tracks above the blade—and protects your fingers from the razor-sharp blades. This super-duper mandoline comes with a wide assortment of blades that produce crinkle cuts, julienne strips, paper-thin slices, and waffle cuts.

Just a notch below is a slicer made of steel and plastic composite. It has some of the attributes of the high-end slicer, such as a reversible blade and adjustable slice, at a much lower price. There are other less elaborate—and less expensive—slicers on the market, too, that are perfect for small jobs, such as slicing cucumbers or carrots. Some, like the V-slicer, perch at an angle on just one set of legs and some are legless and balance over a bowl as you slice. All have razor-sharp blades that will cut through any firm vegetable or fruit.

Tips for Using

You'll need some practice with your mandoline before you master the technique, but once you get it, they'll be no stopping you.

For the best results, only attempt to cut firm, crisp fruits and vegetables.

Use the mandoline when you need a large quantity of paper-thin slices of one or more firm fruits, such as apples, pears, or plums for galettes, pies, and tarts. It also makes quick work of slicing potatoes for scalloped potatoes and *pommes Anna,* onions for onion soup, and all kinds of vegetables for gratins.

Never use the mandoline without the combination food holder–finger guard.

Care in Using

Wash carefully with warm, soapy water.

Some models are dishwasher safe, but always consult the manufacturer's instructions.

Use caution when cleaning the blades.

Do not towel-dry the blades; allow them to air-dry.

Pack away carefully after each use.

Alternatives

There are many types of slicers on the market, but none will match the power or precision of a mandoline, except perhaps a well-sharpened chef's knife.

recipes

Jicama and Carrot Slaw with Fresh Pineapple and Cilantro | Zucchini and Crecenza Gratin with Mint

JICAMA and CARROT SLAW with FRESH PINEAPPLE and CILANTRO

PREP 30 min | SERVES 6

The task of cutting perfect julienne strips for this sprightly slaw is accomplished quickly and easily with a mandoline. Handheld julienne slicers can be used to cut the jicama and carrots, but jicama flesh is slightly stringy, so it will be slow going. If all else fails, use the shredding attachment that comes with your food processor. The slaw will have a different appearance, but the great flavor will still be there. Or, if you're in the mood, turn on some music, pour yourself a tall glass of something cool, and carefully and methodically cut thin matchsticks of jicama and carrot with a sharp chef's knife. Serve the salad with pan-seared jumbo shrimp, salmon, swordfish, or tuna.

Implements Chef's Knife, Serrated Peeler, Mandoline, Cutting Board, Large Bowl, Small Bowl, Spiral or Flat Whisk

Ingredients

1 (1-pound) jicama

3 or 4 carrots, peeled

½ ripe pineapple (cut lengthwise through the crown)

2 green onions, white and green parts, thinly sliced on the diagonal

¼ cup coarsely chopped fresh cilantro leaves and tender stems

⅓ cup unseasoned rice vinegar

⅓ cup canola or other flavorless vegetable oil

½ teaspoon coarse salt

1. Trim the ends from the jicama and remove the skin. A regular vegetable peeler doesn't work on the thick, leathery skin, but a serrated-edged swivel-blade peeler or a small paring knife will do the job. Cut the jicama in half through the stem end. With the flat side down, cut each half into julienne strips with the julienne blade of a mandoline. There should be about 2 cups.

2. Cut the carrots in half lengthwise. With the rounded side down, cut each half into julienne strips with the julienne blade of the mandoline. There should be about 2 cups.

3. Using a chef's knife, divide the pineapple half in half lengthwise. Place 1 wedge cut edge down and slice away the center core. Slice off the rough outside skin and remove any spines with the tip of a paring knife or vegetable peeler. Cut the wedge crosswise into ⅛-inch-thick slices. Stack a few slices at a time, cut the stack into ⅛-inch-wide julienne strips. There should be about 2 cups.

4. In a large bowl, combine the jicama, carrots, pineapple, green onions, and cilantro. In a small bowl, whisk together the vinegar, oil, and salt until blended. Pour the dressing over the vegetables and toss to coat evenly. Cover and refrigerate for 1 hour, or until chilled, before serving.

tip  A SPRIG? A STEM? A LEAF?

A sprig is a thin stem with just a few leaves attached. A stem is a long stem with several sprigs attached. And a leaf? Is a leaf!

ZUCCHINI and CRESCENZA GRATIN with MINT

PREP 45 min | **COOK TIME** 45 min | **SERVES** 4–6

Zucchini layered with crunchy fresh bread crumbs and *crescenza,* a soft, creamy fresh cow's milk cheese, makes a luscious gratin. Select tender, young zucchini if available. Smaller ones tend to have less water than their more mature cousins. To guard against a watery dish, drain the sautéed zucchini well before layering it in the gratin. If *crescenza,* made by Bellwether Farms in Sonoma County, California, is unavailable, use fresh mozzarella. Unfortunately, Italian *crescenza,* which originated in the Lombardy region, is not typically exported to the United States. Serve the gratin with grilled or broiled lamb chops or steaks or broiled leg of lamb.

Implements Mandoline, Large Sauté Pan or Skillet, Colander, Strainer, Medium Bowl, Large Spoon, Wide Spatula, 7-by-11-inch (1½-Quart) Baking Dish or Gratin

Ingredients

2 pounds small zucchini

4 tablespoons unsalted butter

2 tablespoons finely chopped fresh mint

1 clove garlic, grated or minced

1 teaspoon coarse salt

Freshly ground black pepper

2 cups fresh bread crumbs

⅓ cup finely chopped red onion

8 ounces *crescenza* or fresh mozzarella cheese, cut into thin strips

1 cup heavy cream

1. Trim the stem and blossom ends from the zucchini. With a mandoline, handheld slicer, or chef's knife, slice the zucchini into thin rounds. Set aside.

2. Heat 2 tablespoons of the butter in a large sauté pan or skillet over medium heat until the butter begins to foam. Add the zucchini, cover, and cook for 10 minutes, or until the liquid is released. Transfer the zucchini to a colander set over a medium bowl. Press on the zucchini with the back of a spatula or large spoon to release any excess moisture. Let stand for 10 minutes and then discard the liquid. Transfer the drained zucchini to the bowl and add the mint, garlic, salt, and a generous grinding of pepper. Toss to combine.

3. Rinse and dry the sauté pan. Heat the remaining 2 tablespoons of butter over medium-low heat until the butter begins to foam. Add the bread crumbs and cook, stirring, for 5 minutes, or until golden.

4. Preheat the oven to 350°F. Lightly butter a shallow 7-by-11-inch (1½-quart) baking dish or gratin. Sprinkle with half of the bread crumbs.

5. Spread half of the zucchini on top of the bread crumbs. Sprinkle with the onion. Arrange half of the cheese on top, and then the remaining bread crumbs. Spread the remaining zucchini on top of the bread crumbs, followed by the remaining cheese. Pour the cream evenly over the top.

6. Bake for 45 minutes, or until the top is browned and the cheese is melted. Serve immediately.

A meat pounder comes in handy for a bunch of cooking tasks, from crushing a few nuts to sprinkle on salad to flattening pork tenderloin medallions into thin cutlets for a quick sauté.

Bruce Aidells, AUTHOR, *BRUCE AIDELLS'S COMPLETE BOOK OF PORK*

Pork Medallion Sauté with Figs

Meat Pounder

A meat pounder, sometimes called a meat mallet, is a useful tool for flattening chicken breasts for Milanese, veal slices for piccata, and beef slices for carpaccio. It has a smooth surface that flattens but doesn't tenderize, and should not be confused with the waffle-surfaced meat tenderizer.

Three basic models are available. One type is a smooth disk with softly rounded edges (so it won't tear or cut into the meat) about 3½ inches in diameter and ½ inch thick. It has a 4- to 5-inch handle rising from the center of the disk, and it weighs about 1½ pounds. The handle is either all metal or is metal with a cushioned covering. The second type is designed like a mallet. It sometimes has two different surfaces, a smooth one for pounding and a waffled one for tenderizing. A third type, also a mallet design, has two opposing heads, one smooth and one waffled.

Always consider weight and balance when selecting a meat pounder. Like a hammer, it needs some heft to do the job, so the heavier, the better. And also like a hammer, it needs to feel balanced as you maneuver it.

Tips for Using

Place whatever is to be pounded between two sheets of plastic wrap and pound firmly but gently, beginning in the center and working your way to the edges.

Do not pound hard or the impact of the pounder will tear the food.

Remove the plastic wrap and rearrange the meat periodically while pounding. The food will spread out more readily if the plastic wrap, which will begin to stick to the food, is released.

Pound slices of meat or chicken until thin enough to make quick-cooking sautéed dishes such as Italian scaloppine, French escalopes, and German Wiener schnitzel. Or, stuff, roll, and tie the slices into bundles for Italian *braciole* or French *oiseaux sans têtes* or *roulades*.

Pound slices of beef round steak or filet mignon for beef carpaccio and serve drizzled with truffle oil and topped with curls of Parmigiano-Reggiano cheese.

The meat pounder can be used for crushing cookies or crackers into crumbs and whole or broken nuts into small pieces. (Remember to slip the ingredient into a heavy-duty plastic bag first.)

Care in Using

Stainless-steel meat pounders are dishwasher safe.

Always consult the manufacturer's instructions.

Alternatives

The smooth underside of a small, heavy saucepan, a rolling pin, or a wooden mallet from the hardware store can be used in a pinch.

recipes

Panko-Crusted Chicken Cutlets with Arugula Salad | Pork Medallion Sauté with Figs

PANKO-CRUSTED CHICKEN CUTLETS with ARUGULA SALAD

PREP 25 min | COOK TIME 10 min | SERVES 4

Panko, sold in Asian groceries and in many super-markets, develops a golden, crunchy crust when fried that stays crisp. Here, the *panko* are tossed with grated Parmigiano-Reggiano cheese to give them an Italian profile and extra flavor.

Implements
Paring or Utility Knife, Meat Pounder, Spiral or Small Whisk, Medium Shallow Bowl, Shallow Baking Dish, Large Rectangular Wire Rack, Rimmed Sheet Pan, 10- to 12-inch Skillet, Tongs, Medium Bowl

Ingredients

4 (4- to 5-ounce) boneless, skinless chicken breast halves
Coarse salt
Freshly ground black pepper
4 paper-thin slices prosciutto
1 large egg
¼ cup milk
1¼ cups *panko*
⅓ cup grated Parmigiano-Reggiano
Canola or other flavorless vegetable oil, for frying

ARUGULA SALAD

1 tablespoon red wine vinegar
½ clove garlic, grated or minced
½ teaspoon coarse salt
2 tablespoons extra-virgin olive oil
2 tomatoes, cut into thin wedges
2 cups packed arugula or baby spinach leaves, rinsed and dried

1. Trim any bits of tendon or fat from the chicken. Make sure the fillet, or tenderloin, attached to the underside of each breast has been removed. If it hasn't, gently pull it away from the breast and reserve for another recipe.

2. Cut 2 sheets of plastic wrap each about 10 inches long. Place a chicken breast on 1 sheet and cover with the second sheet. Gently pound the chicken until evenly flattened to between ¼ and ⅓ inch thick. Repeat with the remaining breasts. When all of the breasts have been pounded into cutlets, sprinkle them lightly on both sides with salt and pepper. Pat a slice of prosciutto on top of each cutlet and trim any excess.

3. Whisk the egg in a shallow bowl and then whisk in the milk. Combine the panko and grated cheese in a shallow baking dish and stir to mix. Dip the chicken in the egg and let the excess drip back into the bowl. Lay the chicken on the *panko* mixture, turn to coat, and press the crumbs into the chicken with your fingertips.

4. Place a rectangular wire rack on a rimmed sheet pan. Heat a heavy 10- to 12-inch skillet over medium-low heat. Pour in vegetable oil to a depth of about ½ inch and heat until hot. To test the heat of the oil, add a pinch of *panko*. It should sizzle and turn golden brown on contact. When the oil is ready, add the chicken 1 or 2 pieces at a time, depending on the size of the skillet. Cook, turning once, for 2 minutes per side, or until the *panko* turns a deep gold. Use tongs to lift the chicken from the oil and place on the wire rack.

5. MEANWHILE, MAKE THE SALAD: In a medium bowl, whisk together the vinegar, garlic, and salt. Slowly whisk in the olive oil in a slow, steady stream. Add the tomatoes and arugula and toss to coat evenly.

6. Place a chicken cutlet in the center of each dinner plate. Distribute the salad evenly on top of the cutlets. Serve at once.

PORK MEDALLION SAUTÉ with FIGS

PREP 25 min | COOK TIME 15 to 20 min | SERVES 4

Make this dish with fresh figs when they're in season. Green-skinned figs are the prettiest, as the purple ones tend to tint the sauce a rosy pink. If it isn't fig season, use either dried Black Mission or the lighter-skinned Calimyrna. For the pan sauce, use an inexpensive dry Marsala, a fortified Italian wine.

Implements
Kitchen Scissors, Small Saucepan (Optional), Cutting Board, Paring or Utility Knife, Chef's Knife, Meat Pounder, 10- to 12-inch Skillet, Tongs, Strainer (Optional), Wide Spatula

Ingredients

12 figs, fresh or dried (see headnote)

1 cup dry Marsala

1½ pork tenderloins (about 1¼ pounds total)

Coarse salt

Freshly ground black pepper

2 teaspoons finely chopped fresh thyme

About ½ cup all-purpose flour

2 tablespoons unsalted butter

2 tablespoons extra-virgin olive oil

½ cup finely chopped shallots

1 to 2 tablespoons fig balsamic or regular aged balsamic vinegar

Thyme sprigs, cut into 1-inch pieces, for garnish

1. Snip the stems from the figs with kitchen scissors. Cut the small figs into halves or the large ones into quarters. Set aside. If using dried figs, place them in a small saucepan with the Marsala and heat gently until warmed. Set aside to soak while preparing the pork cutlets.

2. Remove the silverskin from the pork tenderloin: Lay the whole tenderloin on a cutting board and trim any excess fat. Locate the silverskin, which is a long, narrow, shiny white membrane that runs along the surface of the meat. With the tip of a thin, sharp knife, make a small cut at the top of the silverskin long enough for you to hold onto the skin with the fingertips of one hand. With the other hand, pull the knife, its blade leaning toward the skin, along the skin and parallel to the meat to separate it from the meat. Discard the skin. Repeat with the half tenderloin. Slice the tenderloins into 12 slices each ¾ inch thick.

3. Cut 2 sheets of plastic wrap each about 10 inches long. Lay 2 or 3 tenderloin slices on 1 sheet and cover with the second sheet. Gently pound the slices until evenly flattened to between ⅛ and ¼ inch thick. Repeat with the remaining slices. When all of the slices have been pounded into cutlets, sprinkle them lightly on both sides with salt and pepper, then sprinkle them on one side only with 1 teaspoon of the chopped thyme. Place the flour on a sheet of plastic wrap, and dip each cutlet in the flour, lightly coating on both sides and shaking off the excess.

4. Heat a 10- to 12-inch skillet over medium heat. Add the butter and oil and heat until the butter foams. Add the pork a few slices at a time and sauté, turning once with tongs, for 1 to 2 minutes per side, or until lightly browned. Using the tongs, transfer to a plate and cover with aluminum foil to keep warm. Repeat with the remaining pork slices.

5. Add the shallots to the pan and sauté over medium-low heat, stirring, for 3 minutes, or until softened. If the dried figs are soaking, strain and reserve the Marsala separately. Add the figs, increase the heat to medium-high, and cook, turning them with a spatula as they brown, for about 3 minutes (turn fresh figs gently, as stirring might crush them). Add the Marsala and boil, gently turning the fruit, for about 3 minutes, or until the sauce thickens. Sprinkle 1 tablespoon of the vinegar and the remaining 1 teaspoon of chopped thyme on top. Taste and add more vinegar, if needed. Season the sauce with salt and pepper. Return the pork to the pan and quickly reheat, turning the pork in the sauce.

6. Arrange the pork slices on a warmed platter and spoon the figs and sauce on top. Garnish with the thyme sprigs and serve at once.

i admit it gives me enormous pleasure to imagine the powers of alchemy and sorcery that the mortar suggests—it's as if i have the ability to transform matter and mix magic potions.

Penelope Casas, AUTHOR, *DELICIOSO*

Green Bean, Tomato, and Potato Salad with Almond and Basil Pesto

Mortar and Pestle

There are many societies—unlike our own, which is hopelessly plugged in—where the mortar and pestle are still used on a daily basis. These tools are used to grind spices and legumes in India, to reduce chiles to a paste in Thailand, to mill grains in Africa, and to grind corn in Central America. Unplug your appliances and give the mortar and pestle a try. Basil leaves pounded into pesto have a more complex taste, spices ground to a powder are more fragrant, and garlic pulverized in a deep mortar is juicier.

The bowl-shaped mortar comes in many sizes and materials, including stone, marble, wood, and brass. The bat-shaped pestle, the pounding instrument, typically comes in marble, wood, or granite. For big jobs, such as making pesto, sauces, or shrimp paste, you'll need a large (2- to 3-cup capacity), heavy mortar and pestle. For pounding spices and herbs to a powder, a smaller (about 1-cup capacity) mortar will work. But to accomplish any task, big or small, quickly and efficiently, you'll need a sturdy mortar and a weighty pestle.

Tips for Using

Place the food to be crushed in the mortar and pound on it gently but firmly with an up-and-down motion. The power of the action is determined by the stubbornness of the food being reduced.

To make salad dressing, mash garlic with salt to a paste. Add mustard and vinegar and work them in with the pestle. Slowly add the olive oil, stirring and pounding with the pestle until the dressing emulsifies.

The next time a recipe calls for crushed garlic, reach for you mortar and pestle. They work as well as your garlic press.

Use your mortar and pestle to crush whole spices (cloves, allspice, cumin, coriander, peppercorns) to a coarse grind or fine powder.

For dry ingredients, a wooden mortar and pestle are best. For wet ingredients, use a nonabsorbent stone mortar and pestle.

Break walnuts or other nuts into coarse pieces by lightly pounding them in a mortar with a pestle.

The pounding and grinding slowly releases the natural oils and other flavor elements in foods, which heightens their flavor when combined with other ingredients.

You'll be amazed at how quickly a mound of fresh basil leaves will collapse into a soft paste when pounded in a mortar, making this tool ideal for pesto.

Care in Using

Wash with warm, soapy water and a brush. Rinse well and air dry.

Always consult the manufacturer's instructions.

Alternatives

If you enjoy cooking, the mortar and pestle will be a natural and pleasurable extension of your craft. But if you simply need to get the job done, plug in your food processor or blender.

recipes

Grilled Butterflied Leg of Lamb | Green Bean, Tomato, and Potato Salad with Almond and Basil Pesto

GRILLED BUTTERFLIED LEG of LAMB

PREP 25 min | MARINATING 2 hr or overnight |
COOK TIME 25 min | SERVES 8

For entertaining, almost nothing beats a butterflied leg of lamb. Its preparation is simpler than simple, and the cooking time is short. Plus, great meals can be planned around the leftovers, including a Greek-style sandwich of sliced lamb, crumbled feta, sliced cucumbers, and tomatoes, or a salad of bulgur, chopped romaine, lemon juice, olive oil, and garlic topped with sliced lamb. Serve the grilled lamb with bulgur pilaf (page 85) and Marinated Grilled Zucchini (page 71).

Implements Large Mortar and Pestle, Rimmed Sheet Pan or Large Baking Dish, Paring Knife, Instant-Read Thermometer, Cutting Board, Carving Knife, Small Saucepan

Ingredients

12 large cloves garlic

3 tablespoons chopped fresh rosemary, or 1 tablespoon dried

1 tablespoon coarse salt

½ teaspoon freshly ground black pepper

1 (4- to 6-pound) leg of lamb, boned
and butterflied (see Tip, right)

2 large lemons

3 or 4 sprigs rosemary, for garnish

1. In a large, heavy mortar, combine the garlic, rosemary, salt, and pepper. Pound the garlic to a paste, stirring it with the other ingredients until combined. Alternatively, grate or press the garlic onto a plate and use a fork to mash the other ingredients into the garlic until blended.

2. Place the lamb on a rimmed sheet pan or in a large baking dish. With your fingertips, rub half of the garlic paste on the surface of the lamb, spreading it evenly into all of the crevices. Turn the lamb over and repeat on the other side.

3. Thinly slice and seed 1 lemon and spread the slices on the lamb. Halve the remaining lemon and squeeze the juice over the surface of the lamb. Cover the pan with plastic wrap and refrigerate for at least 2 hours or as long as overnight. Remove the lamb from the refrigerator 1 hour before grilling or broiling.

4. Heat a charcoal or gas grill to medium. Scrape the lemon slices off the lamb and reserve. Grill the lamb for 10 to 12 minutes per side for the thickest piece and for 8 minutes per side for the thinner pieces, or until an instant-read thermometer registers 140°F for medium-rare. Toward the end of the grilling time, arrange the lemon slices on the grill and heat just until golden. Reserve the lemon slices for garnishing the lamb.

5. Alternatively, the lamb can be broiled: Position an oven rack in the top of the oven so that the top of the broiler pan will be about 5 inches from the heat source, and pre-heat the broiler. Place the lamb on a broiler pan and broil using the same time and internal temperature guidelines used for grilling. Toward the end of the broiling time, place the lemon slices on the surface of the lamb and broil just until golden. Reserve the lemon for garnishing the lamb.

6. Transfer the meat to a wooden board and let rest for 5 to 10 minutes. Carve the meat across the grain into thin slices. Arrange the slices on a warmed serving platter in neat overlapping rows. Pour the meat juices and the seasonings that have accumulated on the board into a small saucepan, reheat briefly, and pour over the meat slices. Garnish with rosemary sprigs and the grilled or broiled lemon slices and serve at once.

tip LEG OF LAMB, ANATOMICALLY SPEAKING

Because a butterflied leg of lamb is a rather free-form mass of muscle and flesh, and thus thicker in some spots than others, there is no way to grill or broil it in one piece successfully. The solution is to divide the lamb into pieces following the anatomy of the leg. To do this, position the lamb, smooth side down, on a cutting board and divide it following the natural separations. Then turn the pieces of lamb over and make sure the butcher has trimmed off all but a thin layer of fat. If not, use a thin, sharp knife or a boning knife to trim away any excess.

GREEN BEAN, TOMATO, and POTATO SALAD with ALMOND and BASIL PESTO

PREP 30 min | COOK TIME 18 min | SERVES 4–6

The Italian word *pesto* translates roughly as "pounded" and typically refers to any food mashed in a mortar. But the best-known pesto is a sauce made with fresh basil leaves, garlic, olive oil, pine nuts, and grated cheese. It is traditionally the sauce for a pasta dish that also includes green beans and potatoes, but here the pasta has been left out and the pesto is instead served over a salad of warm cubed potatoes and green beans. In another departure from tradition, dry-roasted almonds are used in place of the pine nuts. Make this recipe in the summer when the markets are well stocked with beautiful fresh basil.

Implements Large Mortar and Pestle, 6-Quart Dutch Oven, Colander, Rubber Spatula, Chef's Knife

Ingredients

1 clove garlic

1 teaspoon plus ½ teaspoon coarse salt

4 tablespoons coarsely chopped unsalted dry-roasted almonds

1 cup lightly packed fresh basil leaves, stemmed

¼ cup grated Parmigiano-Reggiano cheese

¼ cup grated pecorino romano cheese

¼ cup extra-virgin olive oil

1 pound Yukon Gold or other boiling potatoes, peeled and cut into ¾-inch cubes

12 ounces thin green beans, trimmed and cut into 1-inch lengths

1 large, ripe tomato, cut into thin wedges, for garnish

1. Place the garlic, ½ teaspoon of the salt, and 2 tablespoons of the almonds in a large mortar. Pound with the pestle to a smooth paste. Gradually add the basil leaves while pounding, adding more only after each batch has been reduced to a paste. This will take only 2 to 3 minutes.

2. When all of the basil leaves are pounded to a smooth paste, gradually add both cheeses, stirring with the pestle to blend them with the basil paste. Then drizzle in the olive oil with one hand while stirring and pounding with the pestle in the other hand until the mixture is smooth. Set aside.

3. Fill a 6-quart Dutch oven or other large, wide pan two-thirds full of water and bring to a boil. Add the remaining 1 tablespoon of salt and the potatoes. Boil, uncovered, for 10 minutes. Add the green beans and boil for 6 to 8 minutes, until both the beans and potatoes are tender. Drain in a colander.

4. Place the beans and potatoes in a large serving bowl, spoon the pesto on top, and fold together gently with a rubber spatula until blended. Sprinkle with the remaining 2 tablespoons of almonds. Garnish the bowl with the tomato wedges. Serve warm or at room temperature.

Apple-and-Ginger-Spiced
Sweet Potatoes

If you're making mashed potatoes for a holiday crowd, a potato ricer will help you make mounds without the elbow grease required by a potato masher. Another advantage: You can cream your potatoes directly into a saucepan, reheating them as you add the milk and butter.

Alton Brown, AUTHOR, *ALTON BROWN'S GEAR FOR YOUR KITCHEN*

Potato Ricer

Old-fashioned mashed potatoes, evocative of hearth and home, are a matter of great pride for many cooks. But the term *mashed* is misleading because velvety-smooth "mashed" potatoes are more likely pushed through either a ricer or a food mill. The potato ricer is a curious piece of cookware comprised of a canlike canister with perforations on the bottom. Attached to the canister are two long handles that operate a lever. When the handles are compressed, the lever presses on the potatoes, forcing them through the holes in the bottom. They emerge in thin, delicate strands that somewhat resemble rice, which is perhaps how this handy tool got its name.

The ricer is highly efficient, with no morsel of potato going unmashed. The best-designed models have comfortable, easy-grip handles and wings that allow you to rest the canister on the rim of a bowl or a saucepan. Ricers come two sizes, 1 cup and 2 cup, so you can choose the one that suits your needs.

Tips for Using

Not just for potatoes, a ricer can press cooked parsnips, turnips, carrots, and even apples, on their own or in combination with potatoes.

A ricer is a good choice for making small batches (two or three servings) of potatoes or pureed vegetables, while the food mill works better for larger batches (four or more servings).

A favorite French chestnut dessert known as Mont Blanc, after the tallest mountain in Western Europe, is a made by passing sweetened cooked chestnuts through a ricer, forming a mound, and then topping the "mountain" with a cloud of whipped cream.

Try using your potato ricer to press moisture from cooked spinach, salted zucchini, or cucumber slices. It will even squeeze juice from pomegranate seeds.

Care in Using

Warm, soapy water and a brush usually does the job.

Check the manufacturer's instructions to see if your ricer is dishwasher safe.

Alternatives

The food mill can easily take the place of a potato ricer, but it is better suited for larger portions.

recipes

Apple-and-Ginger-Spiced Sweet Potatoes | Roasted Garlic Mashed Russets with Olive Oil | Roasted Garlic

APPLE-and-GINGER-SPICED SWEET POTATOES

PREP 10 min **|** **COOK TIME** 35 min **|** **SERVES** 4

The potatoes for this simple mashed sweet potato dish can be boiled or baked. Cook them in their skins and then peel them and pass the soft flesh through a potato ricer. If you lack a ricer, you can use a food mill or even an old-fashioned potato masher. Any color sweet potato or any mix of colors can be used, such as orange-fleshed Red Garnets or Jewels and cream-colored Hannas. A splash of apple juice and a bit of finely grated ginger add a fresh spark to this old favorite.

Implements Large Saucepan, Colander, Paring Knife, Wooden Spoon, Potato Ricer, Pepper Mill

Ingredients

2 pounds sweet potatoes (see headnote)

1 cup unsweetened apple juice

2 tablespoons unsalted butter

1 teaspoon peeled, grated fresh ginger

Coarse salt

Freshly ground black pepper

1 tablespoon minced fresh chives or thinly sliced green onion tops, for garnish

1. Place the sweet potatoes in a large saucepan and add water to cover. Bring to a boil over high heat, cover partially, reduce heat to medium-low, and cook for 30 minutes, or until tender when pierced with a skewer. Drain in a colander and let cool. Use a paring knife to pull off the skins. Cut the potatoes into 1-inch chunks.

2. Rinse and dry the saucepan you used for cooking the potatoes. Add the apple juice, butter, and ginger, place over low heat, and warm, stirring with a wooden spoon, until the butter is melted. Remove from the heat.

3. Rest the potato ricer on the rim of the pan holding the apple juice mixture. Half fill the ricer with cooked potatoes and press them through. Repeat until all the potatoes have been pureed.

4. Season the potatoes with salt and a grinding of pepper. Reheat over low heat, stirring with a wooden spoon, until hot. Spoon into a warmed serving dish and garnish with the chives.

ROASTED GARLIC MASHED RUSSETS with OLIVE OIL

PREP 25 min | COOK TIME 15 to 20 min | SERVES 4

The russet potato, also known as the baking or Idaho potato, has low moisture and high starch, qualities that yield wonderfully light, fluffy mashed potatoes. Drizzle them sparingly with truffle oil or a garlic- or herb-infused extra-virgin olive oil.

Implements Large Pot, Colander, Potato Ricer, Medium Bowl, Wooden Spoon

Ingredients

2½ pounds russet potatoes, peeled and cut into 1-inch chunks

2 bay leaves

Coarse salt

1 or 2 heads Roasted Garlic (right), mashed

¼ cup extra-virgin olive oil, plus more for garnish

Freshly ground black pepper

1. In a large pot, combine the potatoes and bay leaf and add water to cover. Bring to a boil over high heat and add 1 tablespoon of salt. Lower the heat to medium, cover partially, and cook for 15 to 20 minutes, until the potatoes are tender when pierced with a fork. Drain in a colander and discard the bay leaf.

2. Set the potato ricer on the rim of a medium bowl. Half fill the ricer with cooked potatoes and press them through. Repeat until all the potatoes have been pureed.

3. Add half of the roasted garlic and all of the olive oil to the potatoes and beat with a wooden spoon until blended. Season to taste with salt and pepper. If you want a more pronounced garlic flavor, add the remaining mashed garlic.

4. Mound the potatoes in a warmed serving bowl. Pass the olive oil at the table for guests to add to taste.

ROASTED GARLIC

PREP 10 min | COOK TIME 1 hr | MAKES about ¼ cup

Roasted garlic is easy to make and is delicious whisked into a vinaigrette, rubbed under the skin of chicken breasts, spread on sandwiches or crostini, swirled into a steaming bowl of chicken-vegetable soup, or added to freshly mashed potatoes. To store it, cover it with a thin layer of olive oil, cap tightly, and refrigerate. It will keep for several weeks.

Implements Chef's Knife, Garlic Roaster or Small Baking Dish, Oven Mitt, Small Bowl, Fork

Ingredients

2 heads garlic

2 tablespoons extra-virgin olive oil

Coarse salt and freshly ground black pepper

1. Preheat the oven to 350°F.

2. Rub the outside of each garlic head to remove the papery outer skins. Place each garlic head on its side and cut ½ inch off the top. Place the heads, cut side up, in a garlic roaster or small baking dish (a small *cocotte* or gratin, no bigger than 4 inches, will also do). Drizzle each head with 1 tablespoon of the olive oil. Cover the garlic roaster, or cover the baking dish with aluminum foil. You can also dispense with the dish and wrap each garlic head in a piece of heavy-duty aluminum foil. Roast for 1 hour, or until the cloves are soft when squeezed with a mitted hand. Remove from the oven and let cool.

3. Separate the cloves of garlic. Have ready a small bowl. One at a time, pinch each clove at the stem end and then press on the clove to squeeze the softened garlic out into the bowl. Add a pinch of salt and a grinding of pepper and mash with a fork until blended.

Also known as a whip, this tool is essential if you want smooth sauces, emulsified vinaigrettes, and fluffy, fully elevated egg whites or whipped cream.

Alton Brown, AUTHOR, *ALTON BROWN'S GEAR FOR YOUR KITCHEN*

Soufflé Omelet with Spinach, Feta, and Tomatoes

Whisk

The gracefully curved wires of whisks are used to stir mixtures or to combine or aerate ingredients. Classic whisks are made from sturdy stainless steel. What defines a specific type of whisk it the number and thickness of the wires and its overall shape. The classic French sauce whisk has approximately ten slightly curved thick stainless-steel wires. It comes in a variety of lengths and can be used to mix salad dressings or stir soups and thick sauces. The balloon whisk has approximately twice as many thin stainless-steel wires curved to follow the shape of a ball. The bulbous shape and many thin wires are necessary to quickly whip air into egg whites and heavy cream. The standard whisk is similar to the French sauce whisk, but has thinner wires. It is a good all-around whisk that can do most jobs from stirring a sauce to whipping cream.

A flat or roux whisk has only a few thick wires arranged in a spatula-like design that easily cleans the bottom or sides of a bowl or saucepan. It is most often used to blend salad dressings, make sauces right in a roasting pan, or to mix a roux, the flour and butter paste used for thickening cooked sauces. The long-handled coiled or spiral whisk has a circular frame covered with medium-thin spiraled wire, a design that makes contact with the entire surface of a saucepan or bowl. It is good for stirring light batters, beating an egg or two, or blending salad dressing.

Tips for Using

Whisks are handy for many jobs, and every kitchen should have the three basic types: sauce, balloon, and flat.

Whisk handles are made from smooth stainless steel or wood, but newer molded plastic handles are especially comfortable to grasp when you're faced with extended whisking.

For use in nonstick pots, select a whisk with nylon- or silicone-coated wires that won't scratch the surface. Lightweight and flexible, these whisks work best for stirring thin mixtures.

Small, narrow sauce whisks, 6 to 8 inches long, are handy for beating small amounts of ingredients, such as one egg; reaching down into small jars or containers; or emulsifying small quantities of salad dressing.

To prevent muscle fatigue during long whisking, set the bowl or pan on a folded kitchen towel on a low table or in a dry sink.

Care in Using

Wash in warm, soapy water or in the dishwasher.

Always consult the manufacturer's instructions.

Alternatives

The inspired design of the whisk makes it difficult to replace, but a fork will work for beating eggs, salad dressings, or mayonnaise, and a stand or handheld mixer can replace a balloon whisk for beating egg whites or cream.

recipes

Soufflé Omelet with Spinach, Feta, and Tomatoes | Sautéed Fish Fillets with Herb Butter Sauce and Mango

SOUFFLÉ OMELET with SPINACH, FETA, and TOMATOES

PREP 25 min | COOK TIME 20 min | SERVES 2–4

For soufflé omelets—sometimes called puffed omelets—egg whites are whisked into soft, fluffy peaks and then gently folded into lightly whisked egg yolks. A small amount of water added to the whites turns to steam when the mixture is heated, encouraging the omelet to inflate. Started on the stove top and finished in the oven, soufflé omelets are versatile, adapting easily to almost any classic omelet filling.

Implements
Two Large Bowls, Sauce or Flat Whisk, Balloon Whisk, Large and Small Rubber Spatulas, 10-inch Ovenproof Skillet, Sauté Pan or Dutch Oven, Tongs, Small Bowl, Oven Mitts

Ingredients

5 large eggs, separated
Freshly ground black pepper
¼ cup water
½ teaspoon coarse salt
1 tablespoon extra-virgin olive oil

FILLING
1 tablespoon extra-virgin olive oil
1 small clove garlic, grated
1 (5-ounce) bag baby spinach, rinsed and dried
¾ cup diced ripe plum tomatoes
1 tablespoon chopped fresh dill
1 tablespoon minced fresh chives or green onion tops
½ cup crumbled feta cheese
Coarse salt and freshly ground black pepper

1. Preheat the oven to 350°F. In a large bowl, combine the egg yolks and pepper. With a sauce or flat whisk, stir the yolks and pepper until well blended; set aside. In a second large bowl, beat the eggs whites until foamy with a balloon whisk. Add the water and salt, and whisk until soft peaks form. With a large rubber spatula, gently fold the whites into the yolks until evenly distributed.

2. Heat the oil in a 10-inch ovenproof skillet with low, sloping sides (preferably nonstick) over low heat. Swirl the oil to coat the bottom and sides of the skillet. Gently pour the egg mixture into the skillet.

3. Increase the heat to medium-low and cook, without stirring, for 3 minutes, or until the edges begin to pull away from the sides of the pan. Transfer the skillet to the oven and bake for 10 to 12 minutes, until golden and puffy.

4. MEANWHILE, MAKE THE FILLING: In a sauté pan or Dutch oven, combine the oil and garlic and heat over low heat just until the garlic begins to sizzle. Add the spinach, cover, and cook for 2 minutes, or until the spinach is wilted. Remove from the heat, use tongs to toss, and let stand uncovered.

5. In a small bowl, combine the tomatoes, dill, chives, and cheese, and mix gently. Taste and add a pinch of salt, if needed, and a grinding of pepper.

6. Remove the omelet from the oven and spoon the spinach on half. Top with the tomato mixture. Loosen the edges of the omelet from the pan with a small rubber spatula. Use a wide rubber spatula to lift one side of the omelet and fold it in half over the filling.

7. Slide the omelet onto a serving platter. Cut into 4 wedges and serve warm.

SAUTÉED FISH FILLETS with HERB BUTTER SAUCE and MANGO

PREP 30 min | COOK TIME 20 min | SERVES 4

The basis for this sauce is the French *beurre blanc*, here jazzed up with lots of minced fresh herbs and finely diced mango. Use any skinless fish fillet, from wild salmon to farm-raised tilapia.

Implements
1½- to 2-Quart Heavy Saucepan, Small Strainer, Two Small Bowls, Large Heavy Skillet, Wide Slotted Spatula, Flat Whisk, Salad Spinner

Ingredients

⅓ cup dry white wine

⅓ cup plus 1 teaspoon freshly squeezed lemon juice

2 tablespoons minced shallot

1 ripe mango, peeled, pitted, and cut into ⅛-inch dice

2 tablespoons minced fresh mint

1 tablespoon minced fresh Italian parsley

Coarse salt

4 (4- to 6-ounce) skinless fish fillets

Freshly ground black pepper

½ cup all-purpose flour

1 tablespoon unsalted butter, plus ½ cup (1 stick) cold unsalted butter, cut into ⅛-inch-thick slices and refrigerated

1 tablespoon extra-virgin olive oil

1 tablespoon water

1 small red bell pepper, seeded and cut lengthwise into narrow strips, for garnish

1. Combine the wine, ⅓ cup of the lemon juice, and the shallots in a heavy 1½- to 2-quart saucepan and bring to a gentle boil over medium heat. Decrease the heat to medium-low and simmer for 3 to 4 minutes, or until reduced by half. Set a small strainer over a small bowl and pour the contents of the pan into the strainer. Press down on the shallots with a rubber spatula to extract its flavor, then discard the shallots and return the liquid to the saucepan. Set aside.

2. In a small bowl, combine the mango, mint, parsley, the remaining 1 teaspoon of lemon juice, and a pinch of salt, and mix gently. Set aside.

3. Sprinkle the fish generously on both sides with salt and pepper. Place flour on a plate or a sheet of waxed paper. Dip the fish in the flour to coat evenly and tap gently with fingertips to shake off the excess.

4. In a large, heavy skillet, combine the 1 tablespoon of butter and the olive oil over medium heat and heat until the butter melts and sizzles. Tip the skillet to coat. Add the fish and cook, adjusting the heat to maintain a steady sizzle, for 2 minutes, or until lightly colored. Turn the fish with a wide slotted spatula and cook for 2 to 3 minutes more, or until cooked through and opaque at the thickest part. Transfer to 4 warmed plates and cover with aluminum foil.

5. Return the wine mixture to medium heat and bring to a boil. Adjust the heat to low, and use a flat whisk to stir in the water.

6. Add the remaining ½ cup of cold butter one piece at a time to the wine mixture, whisking constantly until each piece is melted before adding the next one. Keep the heat low and periodically lift the pan from the heat to prevent overheating the sauce. (If overheated, the sauce will separate.) After about 10 minutes, the sauce will be slightly thickened. Once all of the butter is incorporated, remove the saucepan from the heat and gently fold in the mango mixture.

7. Spoon the sauce evenly over the fish. Garnish with the bell pepper and serve at once.

tip HOW TO CUT A MANGO

Place the mango on its side. With a sharp knife, cut it lengthwise, just grazing one side of the large central pit. Do the same on the other side of the pit, and then discard the pit. With the tip of a paring knife, score each mango "cheek" in a grid pattern, without cutting through the skin. (For the sauce above, make the grid ¼-inch dice.) Using your fingers, press against the skin, forcing the flesh up and outward. Cut along the base of the mango flesh, freeing the diced pieces from the skin.

GLOBE-TROTTING
KITCHEN ESSENTIALS

5 | The ASIAN KITCHEN

The Asian Pantry

Many of us love Asian food but don't necessarily feel comfortable cooking it at home. However, many Asian recipes rely on a minimum of tools and cookware, use techniques that are easy to master, and call for only a handful of ingredients. In this chapter, you'll take a closer look at a few classic pieces of cookware found in Chinese and Japanese kitchens, such as the wok, *suribachi*, and bamboo steamer. The fascinating ingredients typically found in an Asian pantry include pickled ginger, tamari, and *umeboshi*, and then accompanying recipes put them to use. You'll also find suggestions for substitute cookware if you don't have the authentic piece on hand. Soon the thought of cooking Asian food at home will no longer seem impossible.

Chile-Pepper Oil

Sold in small bottles in Asian grocers, chile oil is vegetable oil that has been steeped with hot red chiles. It's used as a seasoning in dipping sauces, stir-fries, soups, and other dishes. Buy it in a small bottle and store in the refrigerator to preserve its heat and keep it from turning rancid.

Chinese Rice Wine

Sometimes called yellow wine, rice wine is made from fermented rice. It has a slightly nutty taste and is used in many Chinese dishes. It is available both salted for cooking and unsalted for cooking and drinking. Look for *Shao hsing*, which can be purchased in Asian markets. If Chinese rice wine is unavailable, dry sherry, sake, or dry white vermouth can be substituted.

Chinese Salted Black Beans

These small, fermented, very salty black soybeans are used to flavor steamed and stir-fried seafood, chicken, or vegetables. They come in small plastic bags. They can be rinsed before using to remove some of the salt. Store at room temperature.

Fish Sauce

Pungent and salty, fish sauce, made by allowing salted fish, usually anchovies, to ferment in large earthenware crocks or barrels in the sun, is used as both a flavoring and a condiment in Southeast Asia. There is a wide variety of brands to choose from in Asian groceries and well-stocked supermarkets, most of them from Thailand. Once opened, store fish sauce in the refrigerator. Buy a small bottle as a little goes a long way.

Five-Spice Powder

The spices used in this aromatic blend vary among manufacturers, but can include any combination of cinnamon, fennel, star anise, clove, ginger, and Sichuan peppercorns. It is a popular ingredient in southern China and in Vietnam, where it is used in rubs, marinades, and as a seasoning.

Fresh Ginger

A knobby-looking rhizome with thin, tan skin and creamy white, somewhat fibrous flesh, fresh ginger is used in marinades, stir-fries, soups, and countless other ways. The skin is easily peeled with a paring knife or scraped off with the edge of a teaspoon. Once peeled, the flesh is grated, slivered, or chopped. Ginger, which has a pleasantly spicy, peppery yet sweet flavor, is stocked in the produce section of most supermarkets. Store unwrapped in the vegetable bin in the refrigerator. For longer storage, slip ginger into a resealable plastic freezer bag and freeze for up to four months, then peel and grate or chop while still frozen.

Hoisin Sauce

Hoisin sauce is a slightly sweet, spicy, thick soybean-based sauce typically flavored with sugar, garlic, chiles, and many other seasonings. It is used as a glaze or basting sauce for grilled, roasted, or slow-cooked meat and poultry; to flavor stir-fries; and as a dipping sauce, often thinned with soy sauce or Chinese rice wine (or dry sherry). Once open, store in the refrigerator; it will keep indefinitely.

Japanese Rice

When properly cooked, Japanese medium-grain rice, also called sushi or short-grain rice, yields moist and slightly sticky yet firm kernels. It must be rinsed well before cooking to remove some of the starch, and because it absorbs some of the rinse water, it requires less water for cooking. Excellent-quality Japanese rice is grown in the United States. Look for Kokuho Rose, CalRose, and Nishiki brands. Japanese-grown rice is not exported to this country.

Miso

A versatile fermented soybean paste found in every Japanese pantry, miso is available in jars or plastic containers in the refrigerated section of the market. There are many different types of miso, each with its own color and flavor. Light-colored, mild misos are used in delicate soups, sauces, and salad dressings, whereas darker, stronger-tasting types are used in more robust soups and for all-purpose cooking. Stored in the refrigerator, miso will keep for months.

Nori

These thin sheets of dried, dark green to black seaweed, with a flavor reminiscent of the sea, are primarily used for wrapping sushi and for snipping into small pieces for garnishing all kinds of dishes. Toasting nori improves its flavor and texture, emphasizing its nutty, salty taste. It can be purchased already toasted, or it can be briefly toasted over a gas burner or with a chef's torch. Nori is typically sold in cellophane-packaged sheets, either whole or perforated.

Pickled Ginger

Cut into paper-thin slices and preserved in sweet vinegar, pickled ginger, or *gari,* is available in plastic containers or jars in the refrigerated section of Japanese or Asian markets. Available in its natural color or dyed pale pink, it is always served alongside sushi.

Rice Vinegar

Japanese rice vinegar is colorless, generally quite mild, and versatile. Look for Marukan brand, which is light enough for dressing leafy greens and rice salads. It comes both seasoned and unseasoned, although unseasoned vinegar is preferred by many cooks because of its pure, clean taste. Chinese rice vinegars, available in black, red, and white, are usually stronger tasting than Japanese vinegars and are used mostly for braised dishes; for stir-fries, such as sweet-and-sour pork; and as a table condiment.

Sesame Seeds

White, tan, and black sesame seeds are used in Chinese and Japanese cooking. The white are unhulled and have a mild taste. The tan and black are hulled and have a more assertive, nutty flavor. They are used as a condiment and in salads, stir-fries, sushi, and other dishes. Because sesame seeds are high in fat, they should be refrigerated to avoid rancidity. They're available in jars or cellophane packages in Asian or other well-supplied grocery stores.

Sesame Soy Marinade

Available in specialty grocers, this Shanghai-style bottled soy-based mixture of sesame oil, spices, and sherry is used to marinate poultry and meat or as a seasoning for stir-fried rice or vegetable dishes. It's the familiar flavor in stir-fried beef and broccoli.

Shiitake Mushrooms

These mushrooms are sold whole or sliced, dried in cellophane packages or boxes as Chinese black mushrooms in Chinese stores and shiitake mushrooms in Japanese stores and must be rehydrated in boiling water (for a quicker result) or tepid water before using. The flavor and aroma are both smoky and pungent, and the texture is thick and meaty. In contrast, fresh shiitake—available in most supermarkets—are mild and soft. Before using whole fresh or dried, discard the tough, inedible stems.

Shiso Leaves

Related to the mint and basil family, shiso is a popular herb in Japanese cooking. The heart-shaped, jagged-edged, aromatic leaves are used in recipes for Japanese sashimi, sushi, and salads. Small plastic bags holding about six fresh leaves are sometimes found in produce sections of Japanese markets. Refrigerated, they'll keep about one week. It is sometimes called *perilla* or Japanese basil.

Soy Sauce

Used as a condiment or seasoning, this familiar Asian sauce is made from fermented soybeans combined with roasted wheat or occasionally barley and is available in a variety of strengths. Light or thin soy, used primarily with milder foods such as fish and poultry, is often saltier than dark soy, which is aged longer, giving it a deeper, more caramel-like color and flavor well suited to use with meats. Bottles labeled simply "soy sauce" hold a pleasantly strong and salty all-purpose sauce. Low-sodium soy sauce has the mildest taste and is recommended for people watching their sodium intake. Mushroom soy, a popular Chinese sauce, is soy sauce flavored with dried Chinese black mushrooms.

Tamari

Similar to soy sauce and traditionally made without wheat, tamari, which originated in Japan, is slightly thicker and has a mellower, richer flavor. Today, tamari made both with and without wheat is sold. If you are following a wheat-free diet, check the label before purchase.

Toasted Sesame Oil

This aromatic, amber-colored oil is pressed from toasted sesame seeds. It is a seasoning oil, not a cooking oil, and it adds a delicious depth of flavor to steamed vegetables, soups, stir-fries, marinades, and dipping sauces. Buy small bottles and store in the refrigerator because it quickly turns rancid.

Tofu

Tofu is made from soy milk. It is sold in square white cakes in the refrigerator section of almost all markets. Sometimes called soybean curd or bean curd, it has a custardlike texture and bland flavor, which helps it to blend well with spicy or highly flavored foods. In Chinese and Japanese cooking it is often stir fried, deep-fried, or added to broth. It can be diced, sliced, mashed, or pureed. Many types of tofu are available, including soft, firm, and extra firm. In Western-style cooking it is used in casseroles, soups, smoothies, salads, stir-fries, sandwiches, and puddings and other desserts. Tofu should be kept refrigerated. It stays fresh for about one week.

Umeboshi

These brined, unripe plums are a delicacy in Japan. They are deep red—which comes from including red *shiso* leaves along with the brine—and have a mouth-puckering tartness. Believed to aid digestion, *umeboshi* are used as a stuffing in *onigiri* (rice balls wrapped in *nori*) and as a condiment at most meals. These are available as whole plums or as a paste in jars, tubes, and cans in Asian or Japanese food shops.

Wasabi

Wasabi, a Japanese root commonly compared to Western horseradish (the two are unrelated), has a memorable eye-watering, sinus-clearing kick. Sold as a pale green paste or powder (the fresh root is rarely available in the United States), it is lightly applied—just a tiny dot is sufficient—to *maki-zushi* and other sushi and is mixed with soy sauce as a dip for raw fish. The paste is available in a convenient small tube, whereas the powder, which must be reconstituted with water (follow the directions on the label), comes in a can.

The shallow dome-shaped bamboo lid absorbs water, so one never needs to worry about condensation sprinkling down on the food. The woven steamer tiers are simultaneously cooking tools and sewing pieces.

Barbara Tropp, AUTHOR, *THE MODERN ART OF CHINESE COOKING*

**Shrimp and Pork Dumplings
with Spicy Dipping Sauce**

Bamboo Steamer

The bamboo steamer is a perfect example of beauty and practicality in a single package. Long ago, the Chinese learned to adapt to a limited supply of cooking fuel, relying on steaming and stir-frying over small, intensely hot fires. The bamboo steamers—and woks—born of that necessity have endured.

Each steamer is handcrafted by weaving bamboo strands into a mesh tray secured to a circular bamboo frame, with the tray's tight-fitting cover made essentially the same way. The steamers are designed for stacking, so that more than one dish can be cooked at the same time, and although a tower of steamers is possible, one or two trays is usually adequate for the home kitchen. The tray is set over boiling water—usually inside a wok—covered, and the steam rises up through the mesh, filling the interior of the steamer with gentle heat that cooks the food. Because bamboo is absorbent, any excess moisture doesn't drip onto the food. A delicate, pleasant scent of wet bamboo permeates the kitchen and adds a lovely fragrance to the food. The steamers come in a variety of sizes, from small (6 to 9 inches in diameter) to large (10 to 12 inches in diameter).

Tips for Using

Food can be steamed directly on the bamboo surface, but to keep the bamboo clean and to collect flavorful juices, place a heat-resistant plate, pie dish, or disposable foil pan in the steamer, leaving ample space (at least ½ inch) around the edges for the steam to enter.

For foods that won't release a lot of juice, such as dumplings, line the steamer with a circle of oiled parchment paper or aluminum foil (leave at least a 1½-inch border), or use blanched Napa cabbage or romaine lettuce leaves.

Set the bamboo steamer in a wok with enough water to reach the bottom rim of the steamer, but not touch the mesh. Keep water simmering in a teakettle, to replenish the water if the wok threatens to boil dry.

If you are using more than one tray, you don't need to switch their positions. The steam will be hot enough to cook the food in multiple trays evenly.

Care in Using

Wash with a soft brush and warm water and mild soap and rinse thoroughly. Air dry at room temperature before reassembling and storing. Do not store in a plastic bag.

Always consult the manufacturer's instructions.

Alternatives

To improvise a bamboo steamer, put a wok ring (or collar), a wide, latticed bamboo wok insert or two crossed chopsticks, a round cake rack, or one or two shallow empty cans with the top and bottom removed (tuna-fish cans are the perfect size) in a wok, a wide, deep pot, or a deep sauté pan. Place a tight-fitting lid on whatever vessel you're using. Add water, cover tightly, and bring to a boil. Set a heat-resistant plate or shallow bowl with the food on top of the insert, re-cover, and steam until cooked.

recipes
Shrimp and Pork Dumplings with Spicy Dipping Sauce | Steamed Sea Bass in a Ginger and Scallion "Net"

SHRIMP and PORK DUMPLINGS with SPICY DIPPING SAUCE

PREP 30 to 45 min | COOK TIME (per batch) 20 minutes | MAKES about 40 dumplings | SERVES 4–6

Asian dumplings are fun to make and to eat, and ready-made wrappers can be found in the refrigerated or frozen-food section of many supermarkets. Asian dumplings can be boiled, braised and browned in a skillet, or steamed. These are complemented by a spicy dipping sauce.

Implements
Small Saucepan, Small Strainer, Food Processor, Rimmed Sheet Pan, Parchment Paper, Large Skillet, Tongs, 1 or 2 Bamboo Steamers, Pot Holder

Ingredients

FILLING
½ cup dried (about ½ ounce) shiitake mushroom slices

4 ounces shrimp, shelled and deveined

4 ounces ground pork (not too lean)

2 tablespoons finely chopped shallot

2 teaspoons peeled, finely chopped fresh ginger

2 teaspoons soy sauce

2 teaspoons Chinese rice wine or dry sherry

½ teaspoon toasted sesame oil

½ teaspoon crushed or grated garlic

¼ teaspoon sugar

⅛ teaspoon freshly ground black pepper

All-purpose flour, for dusting

1 (10-ounce) package refrigerated or frozen round wonton wrappers or square *gyoza* skins (about 50)

6 to 8 whole Napa cabbage leaves

SPICY DIPPING SAUCE
⅓ cup soy sauce

2 tablespoons Chinese black vinegar or balsamic vinegar

2 tablespoons water

¼ teaspoon chile oil

1. MAKE THE FILLING: In a small saucepan, combine the mushrooms with water to cover (about 1 cup) and bring to a boil. Remove from the heat, cover, and let stand for 20 minutes, or until softened. Drain in a small strainer placed over a bowl, reserving the soaking liquid for soup. Spread the mushrooms on a clean kitchen towel and blot dry. Finely chop the mushrooms.

2. In a food processor, pulse the shrimp until finely chopped but not pureed. In a large bowl, combine the mushrooms, shrimp, pork, shallot, ginger, soy sauce, rice wine, sesame oil, garlic, sugar, and black pepper. Insert a chopstick or the round handle of a wooden spoon into the mixture and pull it straight across once or twice to mix the ingredients. Then use the chopstick or handle to stir the mixture gently in one direction until well mixed.

3. Have ready a small bowl of warm water. Line a rimmed baking sheet with parchment paper or waxed paper. Lightly flour a flat work surface, and lay a wrapper on the surface. Top the wrapper with a rounded teaspoon of the filling, placing it off center. Using your fingertip or a small brush, moisten half of the edge of the wrapper with the warm water. If using a round wrapper, fold it in half to make a half circle. If using a square wrapper, fold it in half to make a triangle. Pinch the center closed first. Using your fingertips, make 2 pleats on the front (side facing you) flap of the wrapper and press to close. (You can skip the pleats, see Tips, following). Alternatively, bring the corners of both sides of the bottom of the triangle together and seal. Stand the dumpling on the prepared sheet pan. Repeat to make more dumplings until you have used up all of the filling. As you put the dumplings on the sheet pan, make sure they are not touching, or they will stick together. If you have leftover wrappers, they can be frozen for another use. At this point, the dumplings can be frozen. Place them on a rimmed sheet pan lined with heavy-duty aluminum foil and freeze solid, then peel them off the foil and store them in a resealable plastic freezer bag in the freezer for up to 2 months. Thaw before steaming.

4. Half fill a large skillet or sauté pan with water and bring to a boil. Add the cabbage leaves a few at a time and blanch for 1 minute, or until wilted. Using tongs, transfer

the leaves to a plate and let cool. Lay the cooled leaves in a single layer, overlapping them slightly, in the bottom of 1 or 2 bamboo steamers. Arrange as many dumplings as will fit comfortably, without touching, on top of the leaves.

5. Place the bottom of a steamer in a large wok and add just enough water so that the rim, but not the mesh, of the steamer touches the water. If using a second tier, place it on top of the first and cover it; otherwise, just press the top in place. Place the wok on the stove and bring to a boil over high heat. Reduce the heat to medium-high and steam the dumplings for 18 minutes.

6. **MEANWHILE, MAKE THE DIPPING SAUCE.** In a small bowl, combine the soy, vinegar, water, and chile oil and stir to mix. Set aside in small serving bowls.

7. When the time is up, test the dumplings for doneness: Uncover the steamer, remove 1 dumpling, and cut it open. The filling should be cooked through and the dumpling light and tender.

8. To serve, slide the steamer (or each steamer) onto a round platter using a pot holder. Serve the dumplings directly from the baskets, and eat the cabbage leaves along with the dumplings. Either spoon the sauce over the dumplings once they're served or place individual bowls of sauce on the table for dipping.

tips THE MANY WAYS TO WRAP A DUMPLING

Dumpling wrappers are variously called dumpling skins, wonton wrappers, and *gyoza* wrappers. Examine them carefully before buying. The thicker wrappers are good for boiled dumplings, whereas the thinner ones are better for steamed or fried dumplings. Although round and square wrappers are traditionally used for different fillings, they can be used interchangeably.

Chinese steamed dumplings are typically pleated along their edges, so that the steam can puff them up without the delicate wrapper tearing. (If they do break open during steaming, you have probably used too much filling.) The pleating can be omitted in favor of simply pressing the edges together firmly; be sure you underfill the dumplings slightly, or they will break open while steaming. Or, look for a molded plastic dumpling maker, a hinged tool that pleats and presses a Chinese dumpling with one easy motion.

WHY STIR IN ONE DIRECTION? It may sound overly fussy, but stirring the dumpling filling in one direction is important. It blends the ingredients together thoroughly without compacting them, which is what happens if you stir them in more than one direction. Your filling will be lighter and more tender as a result. Apply this same technique to meat loaf, meatball, and pâté mixtures.

STEAMED SEA BASS in a GINGER and SCALLION "NET"

PREP 15 min | COOK TIME 5 to 10 min | SERVES 4

You can use other lean, mild fish in this recipe, such as halibut, tilapia, or striped bass, which, like the sea bass, will complement, rather than challenge, the seasonings. To ensure even cooking, select uniform pieces. If you have two bamboo steamers, put the fish on the bottom tier and put a vegetable, such as snow peas, on the top tier. Serve the fish atop a bowl of hot rice, and spoon the cooking juices from the fish over the top to moisten and flavor the rice.

Implements Bamboo Steamer, Wok, Plate, Paring Knife

Ingredients

4 (6-ounce) pieces sea bass fillet (with or without skin)

1 tablespoon soy sauce

2 teaspoons toasted sesame oil

1 teaspoon minced jalapeño chile, or pinch of crushed red pepper

1 tablespoon packed peeled, julienned fresh ginger

2 green onions, white and green parts, cut into 2-inch-long julienne

½ teaspoon black sesame seeds

Hot cooked white or brown rice, for serving

1. Place the fish in a single layer on a heatproof plate that will fit in your bamboo steamer (see Alternatives, page 149, for other options).

2. Slowly spoon the soy sauce about ½ teaspoon at a time over the fish, so that it soaks into the flesh. Then spoon ½ teaspoon of the sesame oil over each piece of fish. Sprinkle the chile and then the ginger evenly over the fish.

3. Place the bottom of the steamer in a large wok and add just enough water so that the rim, but not the mesh, of the steamer touches the water. Place on the stove and bring to a boil over medium-high heat. Reduce the heat to medium.

4. Place the plate in the steamer, making sure there is at least ½ inch between the edge of the plate and the steamer rim, so the steam will surround the food. Cover the steamer.

5. Steam the fish until it is opaque in the center when tested with a knife tip. Thin pieces will take about 5 minutes, while thicker pieces will take 8 to 10 minutes.

6. To serve, spoon the rice into deep bowls. Top each bowl with a piece of fish. Spoon the juices that collected in the plate over the top to moisten the rice. Arrange the green onions in a net pattern over the fish, then sprinkle with the black sesame seeds. Serve immediately.

Chopping, Dicing, and Slicing

Chop To chop is to cut food into ¼-inch irregular pieces about the size of peas. To finely chop is to cut food into ⅛-inch irregular pieces. To coarsely chop is to cut food into ⅓- to ½-inch irregular pieces.

Dice To dice is to cut food into small squares. Finely diced pieces are ⅛ inch or smaller; Regular dice is about ¼ inch. Large dice, which is about ½-inch pieces, is sometimes referred to as cubes.

Julienne To make julienne strips, sometimes called matchstick strips, cut the food into slices between ⅛ inch and ¼ inch thick and about 2 inches long. Stack the slices and cut the slices lengthwise into ⅛- to ¼-inch-wide strips.

Rice Cooker

This amazing piece of cookware guarantees a perfect pot of rice every time. It is compact, and has a removable insert or bowl usually with a nonstick finish. Under the bowl is a spring-loaded thermostat that senses when the water has been absorbed, which means the rice is done. The cooker then announces the rice is ready with a click, a bell, or a bell-like melody. The finished rice will remain warm in the rice cooker for a period of time that varies with the manufacturer and model.

A rice cooker is a liberating appliance. It allows you to put the rice on to cook without worrying about scorching or overcooking. You may have to experiment a bit with the correct ratio of rice to water (see "Tips for Using" below), depending on the type of rice and how you like it. The features vary by model, so before purchase, decide on the features you want and on the size that will work for the number of people in your household.

Tips for Using

Rinsing raw rice or soaking it in water before cooking to remove excess starch is optional. Either step will shorten the cooking time and produce rice with a softer texture.

Rice cookers come with lines printed vertically on the inside of the bowl that indicate water level. The smaller-than-standard rice measuring cup (it's typically 6 ounces) that comes with the cooker is calibrated to match these measurements.

The following measures will work in any rice cooker for rice that has not been rinsed or soaked: For rice with a soft texture, use 1¾ cups liquid (14 fluid ounces) to 8 ounces rice (1 cup dry measure). For rice with a slight bite (al dente), use 1½ cups liquid (12 fluid ounces) to 8 ounces rice (1 cup dry measure).

Once the rice cooker shuts off, the warming mode keeps the rice warm, and also functions as a resting time, which improves the texture of the rice. 10 to 15 minutes is adequate. A rice paddle is ideal for transferring rice to a serving bowl.

Some rice cookers have a special setting for brown rice. But for the best texture, it's always a good idea to soak brown rice in water for an hour or more before putting it in a rice cooker.

Water or chicken, beef, vegetable, or mushroom broth can be used to cook rice.

Some models can also be used for cooking cereal, steaming vegetables; consult your instruction manual.

Care in Using

Unplug the rice cooker before wiping down the outside.

The insert can be washed by hand with soap and water or in a dishwasher.

Use a soft brush or sponge on inserts with a nonstick surface.

Alternatives

A 6-quart Dutch oven, 5-quart sauté pan, 4-quart wide, shallow saucepan with a lid can be used in place of a rice cooker.

recipes

Jasmine Tea–Cooked Rice with Rice Vinegar and Scallions | Green Rice with Tomatoes and Coconut

JASMINE TEA-COOKED RICE with RICE VINEGAR and SCALLIONS

PREP (brew and cool tea) 30 min | COOK TIME 15 min |
SERVES 4

Cooking rice in jasmine tea is a whimsical idea that adds extra flavor to this dish. The rice vinegar and ginger add a mild tang and heat to the softly floral flavor of the jasmine rice.

Implements Small Saucepan, Rice Cooker

Ingredients

1¾ cups water

1 jasmine tea bag

1 cup jasmine rice

3 tablespoons rice vinegar

½ teaspoon sugar

¼ teaspoon peeled, grated fresh ginger

1 teaspoon salt

1 tablespoon thin, diagonally sliced green onion tops, for garnish

1. In a small saucepan, bring the water to a boil, remove from the heat, add the tea bag, cover, and steep for 5 minutes. Discard the tea bag and let the tea cool to room temperature.

2. While the tea is cooling, in a small bowl, stir together the rice vinegar, sugar, and ginger until the sugar has dissolved. Set aside.

3. Place the insert in the rice cooker and add the brewed tea, rice, and salt. Stir to distribute the rice evenly. Cover, plug in the rice cooker, and press the lever to begin cooking. The lever will disengage in about 15 minutes, or when the water is absorbed and the rice is tender. Remove from heat and let stand, uncovered, for 10 minutes.

4. Alternatively, cook the rice in a saucepan: Transfer the tea (it doesn't need to be cool) to a wide, shallow saucepan and bring to a gentle boil. Stir in the rice and salt, decrease the heat to low, cover, and cook for 12 minutes, or until the water is absorbed and the rice is tender.

5. Drizzle the vinegar mixture over the hot rice and fluff with a chopstick or a fork. Spoon into a serving dish, garnish with the green onion tops, and serve at once.

tips CRISPED RICE CRUST AS A DELICACY

If you keep rice warm for more than a few hours in a rice cooker, a thin layer of crisped golden rice will form on the bottom of the insert. In China, this sheet of crunchy rice is broken into pieces and served as an edible garnish on top of the rice. The Chinese think of this crispy layer as a delicacy, and Chinese youngsters consider it a special treat.

PERFECT PILAF

To make pilaf, heat 1 to 2 tablespoons olive oil in the rice cooker insert. Add onion and garlic and sauté until softened. Then add rice and seasonings, such as a cinnamon stick, whole cardamom pods, grated lemon zest, or saffron threads, stirring until blended. Add the liquid, stirring to blend, then cover and cook. Once the rice is cooked, if desired, add raisins, minced dried apricots or other dried fruits, or minced Preserved Lemons (page 328), toasted nuts (page 85), sautéed mushrooms, toasted coconut, grated Parmigiano-Reggiano cheese, or chopped herbs.

GREEN RICE with TOMATOES and COCONUT

PREP 20 min | COOK TIME 15 min | SERVES 4

Here, distinctively flavored cilantro turns fragrant jasmine rice a beautiful bright green. Serve this rice with stir-fried shrimp or grilled seafood, or spoon it onto individual plates, top with a grilled soy-glazed salmon fillet, and garnish with lime wedges.

Implements Rice Cooker, Medium Skillet, Wooden Spoon, Blender

Ingredients

1½ cups water

1 cup jasmine rice

1 teaspoon coarse salt

⅓ cup unsweetened shredded dried coconut

1 cup packed coarsely chopped fresh cilantro, plus 1 tablespoon chopped, for garnish

½ cup coconut milk

2 tablespoons freshly squeezed lime juice

1 tablespoon peeled, minced fresh ginger

1 clove garlic, chopped

1 large, ripe tomato, cut into ½-inch chunks

1. Place the insert in a rice cooker and add the water, rice, and salt. Stir to distribute the rice evenly. Cover, plug in the rice cooker, and press the lever to begin cooking. The lever will disengage after about 15 minutes, when the water is absorbed and the rice is tender.

2. Alternatively, cook the rice in a saucepan: Bring the water to a gentle boil in a wide, shallow saucepan or a sauté pan. Stir in the rice and salt, cover, decrease the heat to low, and cook for 15 minutes, or until the water is absorbed and the rice is tender. Remove from heat and let stand, covered, for 10 minutes.

3. Meanwhile, spread the coconut in a medium skillet, place over medium-low heat, and heat, stirring constantly with a wooden spoon, for about 5 minutes, or until golden. Remove from the heat and set aside.

4. Place 1 cup of the cilantro and the coconut milk, lime juice, ginger, and garlic in a blender and puree until smooth. Alternatively, combine the ingredients in a deep bowl and puree with an immersion blender.

5. When the rice is cooked, remove the insert from the rice cooker, or leave the rice in the saucepan. Pour the cilantro puree over the rice and use a chopstick or the round handle of a wooden spoon to mix. Transfer the rice to a shallow serving bowl and garnish with the tomatoes. Sprinkle with the toasted coconut and the remaining 1 tablespoon of cilantro and serve at once.

Avocado, Persimmon, and Butter Lettuce Salad with Ginger, Garlic, and Rice Vinegar Dressing

In the traditional Japanese kitchen, grinding, crushing, and mashing are performed in a suribachi (grooved mortar). Unlike contemporary tools like the food processor, blender, and spice mill, the old-fashioned suribachi performs as both a mixing bowl and a serving bowl at the table.

Elizabeth Andoh, AUTHOR, *WASHOKU*

Suribachi

The *suribachi* is a Japanese earthenware mortar used for grinding sesame seeds, tofu, miso, herbs, nuts, spices, and other foods and seasonings to a paste. The exterior of the mortar is glazed, traditionally a rich brown, while the unglazed interior has rough ridges, often in an artfully designed pattern. This textured surface helps to pulverize the food quickly and with minimal exertion as it is worked with a carved wooden pestle, or *surikogi*.

The earliest Japanese *suribachi* was crudely made from stone and used in the preparation of medicines, then flour, and finally food, originally miso (page 146). Today's *suribachi* is lightweight and carefully crafted and used for countless preparations, from dressings to fish pastes. The *suribachi* and the *surikogi* are usually sold as a set.

Tips for Using

The base of the mortar is unglazed, so set it on a folded towel or silicone mat to protect your countertop.

Before each use, soak the wooden pestle in cold water for 10 minutes to discourage sticking.

When grinding, hold the pestle near the top with one hand and near the bottom with your other hand. Then rotate the bottom of the pestle, guiding it against the sides of the mortar or bowl to crush the food.

The *suribachi* can be used for preparing ingredients for other cuisines, too, such as onions, garlic, herbs, and nuts for salsas and pureed sauces.

Care in Using

Clean the *suribachi* with a stiff brush in warm, soapy water. Wipe and then air dry the *surikogi* before storing. Most models are not dishwasher safe.

Alternatives

A conventional mortar and pestle can be substituted for a *suribachi* and *surikogi*. For grinding spices, use an electric spice grinder (page 247).

recipes

Asparagus with Miso-Sesame Sauce | Avocado, Persimmon, and Butter Lettuce Salad with Ginger, Garlic, and Rice Vinegar Dressing

ASPARAGUS with MISO-SESAME SAUCE

PREP 20 min | COOK TIME 3 to 5 min | SERVES 4

Here, asparagus spears are lightly coated with a tangy sauce of ground sesame seeds, miso, and rice vinegar. Mild *shiro* miso, or white miso, has a slightly sweet taste that nicely balances the acidity of the vinegar. Both flavors are a pleasant foil for the richness of the sesame seeds. Look for tan, unhulled sesame seeds in large jars in Asian markets and some supermarkets. Store them in the freezer, so they won't turn rancid before you can use them up, and sprinkle them on vegetables and salads for a rich, nutty crunch. The miso-sesame sauce can also be tossed with salad greens or spooned over sliced tomatoes or steamed green beans.

Implements Serrated Peeler, 6-Quart Saucepan, Tongs, Cooking String or Silicone Ties, Colander, Suribachi and Pestle

Ingredients

1 bunch (about 1 pound) asparagus, stems trimmed

1 tablespoon coarse salt

MISO-SESAME SAUCE

2 tablespoons tan, unhulled sesame seeds

2 tablespoons *shiro* miso (white miso)

3 tablespoons unseasoned rice vinegar

1 teaspoon toasted sesame seeds, for garnish

1. Trim the tough stem ends from the asparagus. Use a serrated peeler to remove the scales from the lower section of the stalks.

2. Fill a 6-quart saucepan or other large pan three-fourths full of water and bring to a boil over high heat. While the water heats, lay two 12-inch lengths of cooking string or silicone ties on a counter, spacing them 3 to 4 inches apart. Place the asparagus in a pile perpendicular to the strings. Tie the strings firmly—but not too tightly—around the asparagus to make a bundle. Lower the asparagus bundle into the boiling water, add the salt, and cook for 3 to 5 minutes, depending on the thickness of the spears, until crisp-tender.

3. Meanwhile, fill a large bowl with ice water. When the asparagus are cooked, lift the bundle from the water with tongs and immediately plunge them into the ice water, and leave them for 3 minutes, or until they are well chilled and bright green. Pour off the cold water, remove the string or silicone ties, and drain in a colander. Spread the asparagus on a clean dish towel to absorb excess water.

4. MAKE THE SAUCE: Place 2 tablespoons of the sesame seeds in a *suribachi*. Holding the pestle in one hand, rotate the base of the *suribachi* with the other hand to grind the seeds along the ridges, pulverizing them to a powder. Add the miso, ½ tablespoon at a time, blending well with the pestle after each addition. Gradually add the vinegar, ½ tablespoon at a time, blending well after each addition.

5. Arrange the asparagus on a large serving platter. Drizzle the sauce across the asparagus in a zigzag design. Sprinkle with the sesame seeds. Serve chilled or at room temperature.

AVOCADO, PERSIMMON, and BUTTER LETTUCE SALAD with GINGER, GARLIC, and RICE VINEGAR DRESSING

PREP 20 min | SERVES 6

The Fuyu persimmon, a wintertime treat, is small, orange, and tomato shaped. Unlike its well-known cousin, the heart-shaped Hachiya, the Fuyu is neither tart when underripe nor supersweet and soft when ripe. Instead, a ready-to-eat Fuyu has a mildly sweet taste and a pleasant crunch. Fuyus are a great addition to winter salads when decent tomatoes are scarce. Use a mandoline or other slicer to make paper-thin slices of the red onion, persimmon, and cucumbers.

Implements Suribachi and Pestle, Rasp Grater

Ingredients

4 paper-thin slices red onion

DRESSING

1-inch cube fresh ginger, peeled

1 small clove garlic

½ teaspoon coarse salt

½ teaspoon sugar

3 tablespoons unseasoned rice vinegar

4 tablespoons flavorless vegetable oil

1 head Bibb or Boston lettuce, cored, separated into leaves, rinsed, and dried

2 small or 1 large, ripe Fuyu persimmon, stem and blossom ends trimmed, sliced into paper-thin rounds

1 firm, ripe avocado, halved, pitted, peeled, and cut into ⅛-inch wedges

1 slender Japanese cucumber, unpeeled, sliced paper-thin, or 1 cup thinly sliced unpeeled English (seedless) cucumber

1 tablespoon sliced almonds, toasted (page 85), for garnish

1. Separate the red onion slices into rings and soak in a small bowl of ice water for 10 minutes.

2. WHILE THE ONIONS ARE SOAKING, MAKE THE DRESSING: Place the ginger, garlic, salt, and sugar in a *suribachi* and grind with a pestle until reduced to a paste. Add the salt and sugar and stir with the pestle until dissolved. Then gradually stir in the vinegar and oil until blended. Alternatively, use a rasp grater to grate the ginger and garlic into a small bowl, and then stir in the other ingredients.

3. Tear the largest lettuce leaves into 2-inch pieces. Combine the lettuce, persimmon, avocado, and cucumber in a large bowl. Drizzle with the dressing and toss to coat.

4. Set out 4 salad plates. Distribute the salad ingredients evenly among the plates, tucking in the slices of persimmon, avocado, and cucumber among the lettuce leaves. Drain the onions and pat dry. Top each salad with the crisped onion rings and the almonds, dividing them evenly. Serve at once.

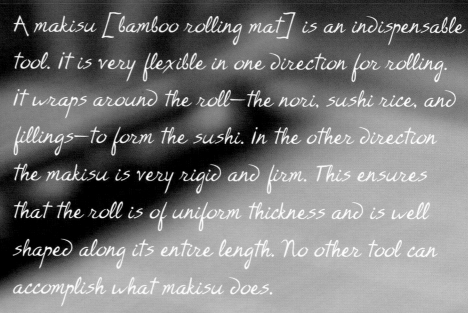

A makisu [bamboo rolling mat] is an indispensable tool. It is very flexible in one direction for rolling. It wraps around the roll—the nori, sushi rice, and fillings—to form the sushi. In the other direction the makisu is very rigid and firm. This ensures that the roll is of uniform thickness and is well shaped along its entire length. No other tool can accomplish what makisu does.

Hiroko Shimbo, AUTHOR, *THE SUSHI EXPERIENCE*

Sushi Rolls

Sushi Tools

Two tools are essential for making *maki-zushi,* or sushi rolls: the rice paddle and the bamboo mat. The rice paddle is used to flip the hot cooked sushi rice as it cools, and then to incorporate the rice vinegar seasoning. The paddle is traditionally made of bamboo, which is handsome and feels good in your hand, but many Japanese cooks recommend the more modern molded-plastic paddle because the rice doesn't stick to it as it does to the bamboo.

The bamboo mat, or *makisu,* is made by weaving thin, parallel bamboo rods together with cotton string into a flexible 9-inch square. It looks like a miniature bamboo window shade and is used to help guide the nori (seaweed) into a roll around the rice and filling ingredients.

Tips for Using

To help prevent the rice from sticking to the paddle, sprinkle it with a little water, or use the hand vinegar (page 163).

The flat rice paddle is perfectly shaped for scooping rice out of the cooking pot without crushing the delicate grains.

A wooden bowl is the best type to use for cooling the rice because it absorbs the excess moisture (see headnote, page 162). Moisten the bowl or platters used to cool and season the rice to keep the rice from sticking.

When making sushi rolls make sure the slats of the bamboo mat are facing horizontal.

Care in Using

Rinse a wooden or plastic rice paddle in a mild solution of soap and water. Rinse the mat in water and clean off any sticky rice with a stiff brush.

Air-dry both the wooden paddle and the mat before storing.

Alternatives

Any flat spoon or server can be substituted for a rice paddle. A dampened dish towel or linen napkin can be used in place of the *makisu.*

recipes

Vinegar Rice for Sushi | Sushi Rolls

VINEGAR RICE for SUSHI

PREP 10 min | **COOK TIME** 10 to 14 min |
STAND TIME 5 min | **COOLING TIME** 5 min |
MAKES 3 cups cooked rice

When the Japanese want a quick bite, they often buy sushi in a *bento,* the equivalent of the American lunch box. The simplest *bento* is made of plain wooden slats and sold by vendors on the street or in train stations. More elaborate boxes are made of exquisite lacquered wood and sold in chic food shops. The sushi in a *bento* may be *maki-zushi* (rolled in seaweed), *nigiri-zushi* (hand shaped), *oshi-zushi* (pressed in a mold), or other types. Not all types of sushi include nori, but nearly every kind includes vinegar rice, the preparation of which is a time-honored Japanese ritual. First, the rice is rinsed several times in cold water to remove the excess starch before cooking. Next, the rice is cooked and transferred to a *handai,* a shallow wooden bowl (the wood absorbs moisture from the hot rice). Finally, one hand is used to fold the seasoned vinegar into the rice with a rice paddle, while the other hand cools the rice as quickly as possible with a paper fan. The vinegar is slowly folded, never stirred, which would make the rice too sticky.

Implements Strainer, 6-Quart Dutch Oven or Rice Cooker, Shallow, Wooden Bowl or Platter, Rice Paddle

Ingredients

1½ cups Japanese-style medium-grain rice

1¾ cups water

VINEGAR RICE SEASONING

⅓ cup unseasoned rice vinegar

2 tablespoons sugar

2 teaspoons sea salt or other coarse salt

1. Put the rice in a large bowl and add cold water to cover. Gently stir the rice with your fingertips and then drain the rice in a strainer held over the sink. Return the rice to the bowl, add fresh water to cover, stir, and drain again. Repeat this step two or three more times. The Japanese traditionally rinse their rice until the water runs clear.

2. Transfer the rinsed rice to a 6-quart Dutch oven or other large pot and add the water. Set the pot over high heat and bring to a boil. Reduce the heat to low, cover, and cook for 10 to 14 minutes, until all of the water has been absorbed and the surface of the rice is dimpled. Remove the pot from the heat and let stand, covered, for 5 minutes.

3. Alternatively, use a rice cooker: Place the rice in the rice cooker, add the water, cover, and press the cook lever or button. The rice cooker will automatically shut off after about 10 minutes, when all the water is absorbed. Let the rice stand, covered, for 5 minutes.

4. **MAKE THE VINEGAR RICE SEASONING:** In a small bowl, stir together the vinegar, sugar, and salt until the sugar and salt are dissolved.

5. Rinse the rice paddle or other large, flat spoon with cold water and use it to transfer the cooked hot rice to a large, shallow bowl or platter, preferably wood. Rinse the spoon again to keep the rice from sticking to it, and then gently fold the rice repeatedly. As you fold, use your other hand to fan the rice with a paper fan or a square of stiff cardboard. After about 5 minutes of folding and fanning, the rice will be tepid. Then, while continuing to fold the rice gently, quickly splash the vinegar mixture into the rice, tipping about 1 tablespoon at a time into the bowl and distributing each addition evenly before adding more. Stop to rinse the rice paddle with water as needed to keep the rice from sticking to it. Finally, continue fanning the rice for about 5 minutes longer, or until it has a glossy sheen.

6. Cover the rice with a kitchen towel or other cloth, and let stand at room temperature 5 minutes, or until ready to make the sushi rolls. Do not use plastic wrap or foil because you don't want any condensation to form, and don't refrigerate the rice, or it will harden. Rice can stand at room temperature for 1 to 2 hours.

tip SUSHI RICE SALAD

If you're not making sushi rolls, use the vinegar rice in a bright-tasting rice salad. Add to the rice diced seedless cucumber, crisply cooked snow peas, impeccably fresh raw corn kernels, and a splash of toasted sesame oil, and then season it with finely chopped *shiso* leaf, brown or black sesame seeds, and/or peeled, grated fresh ginger and garlic. Garnish with about 1 tablespoon crumbled toasted nori.

SUSHI ROLLS

PREP time 45 min | MAKES about 36 pieces | SERVES 4–6

The primary tools you need to make these popular Japanese rolls are a bamboo mat, or *makisu,* and agile fingers. Typically, the fillings for sushi rolls are simple. First, fiery wasabi (see page 147) is added sparingly to the rice, and then the rice is topped with pieces of raw tuna, cucumber, green onion, cooked fish, mushroom, avocado, or many other options. Here, the rice is treated to a smear of *umeboshi,* or pickled plum paste (see page 147), and then you have a choice of fillings. You can prepare 6 rolls with a single filling, or you prepare one-half or one-third of each of the suggested fillings and serve rolls with an assortment of fillings. You can even get creative and come up with your own fillings. Serve the rolls as a snack, appetizer, or a full meal with pickled ginger or *shiso* (see page 147). Both are available in many Japanese markets.

Implements Bamboo Mat, Spatula, Chopstick

Ingredients

3 cups Vinegar Rice for Sushi (page 162)

HAND VINEGAR

1 cup water

¼ cup unseasoned rice vinegar

3 sheets untoasted or toasted nori, each about 7 by 8 inches

Umeboshi **paste, for spreading sparingly**

Walnut-sized mound wasabi paste

CUCUMBER FILLING

8 (8-by-¼-inch) peeled strips Japanese or other unwaxed seedless cucumber

TUNA FILLING

6 ounces sushi-grade tuna (*ahi***), cut into long, ¼- to ½-inch-wide strips**

2 tablespoons finely chopped green onions, white and green parts, or more to taste

AVOCADO FILLING

1 avocado, diced

1 tablespoon minced *shiso* or basil leaves, or more to taste

Japanese soy sauce

Pickled ginger

1. **HAVE THE RICE READY. MAKE THE HAND VINEGAR:** In a medium bowl, combine the water and rice vinegar and set aside.

2. Cut the nori sheets in half to make 6 pieces each about 8 by 3½ inches. If using untoasted nori, pass each sheet over a medium-high gas flame or electric stove burner for 1 to 2 seconds, or in front of a chef's torch. Set aside.

3. **PREPARE THE FILLINGS:** Select a single filling, or make rolls with assorted fillings (see headnote). If using the cucumber filling, set cucumber strips on a plate so they're ready to use. If using the tuna filling, combine the tuna and green onion in a small bowl and stir with a chopstick. If using the avocado filling, combine the avocado and *shiso* in a small bowl and stir gently with a chopstick to combine.

4. Place a bamboo mat, with the slots crosswise, on a work surface. Have the wasabi and *umeboshi* nearby. Place 1 sheet of the nori shiny side down lengthwise on top of the mat. Dampen your hands in the hand vinegar, scoop up a scant ¼ cup of the rice, and gently form it into a log. Place the log in the center of the seaweed, redampen your fingertips in the hand vinegar, and push the rice evenly to the edge of 3 sides of the nori, leaving a ½-inch border uncovered on the edge farthest from you. Use your fingertip to lightly spread a scant lengthwise stripe of wasabi paste down the center of the rice. (If filling with cucumber, you might want to substitute *umeboshi* for the wasabi.)

5. If using the cucumber, place a strip or two on top of the *umeboshi*. Keeping the cucumber in place, pick up the edge of the mat nearest you and slowly lift the rice-covered nori around the cucumber, pressing gently against the mat to make a nori roll filled with rice, with the cucumber in the center. Let the roll stand in the mat for a couple of minutes so the rice can set. Then fold down the mat and roll the extra margin of seaweed so that it overlaps the roll, to form a tube of rice-filled nori. Gently transfer the sushi roll to a tray and cover tightly with plastic wrap to keep it moist. Repeat with the remaining nori, rice, and filling ingredients. You won't need all of the wasabi (it is very hot). Reserve the remainder to serve with the sushi.

6. If using the tuna or the avocado filling, proceed as directed in step 5, dividing the filling ingredients evenly and placing them in a strip down the center of the rice. There will be plenty of rice to make a minimum of 6 rolls each about 8 inches long, and 1 or 2 extra, if needed.

7. To serve, cut each roll in half with a sharp knife, and then cut each half into 3 equal pieces. Arrange the slices, cut side up, on a platter, and serve with small bowls of pickled ginger, wasabi, and soy sauce. Provide diners with small saucers for mixing a dab of the wasabi in a little soy sauce for dipping the slices.

A World of Rice

Rice is a staple grain of over half the world's population, and thousands of varieties are cultivated. The following brief list includes the most popular types available in American markets.

Arborio This is the primary rice used to make risotto. The round, medium grains turn creamy as they are stirred with broth over heat, but the heart, or pearl, of each kernel remains firm to the bite even when fully cooked. Carnaroli and Vialone Nano are also good choices for risotto.

Basmati This fragrant long-grain rice is used in dishes throughout India and the Middle East. It elongates as it cooks, giving it a distinctive appearance. It is available as white or brown rice.

Black Black rice can be short grain with a sticky texture or medium grain and not sticky. The sticky rice is eaten in Thailand, often served with coconut milk and sliced mango. The Chinese grow a medium-grain black rice with a small but slender grain and a nutty flavor that can be used in savory and sweet dishes.

Brown Brown rice has not had its bran layers removed. It takes about three times longer to cook than white rice, but the bran contributes nutrients and a wonderful nutty taste and chewy texture.

Jasmine This fragrant medium- or long-grain white or brown rice cooks up moist and tender. White jasmine rice is used in Thai cooking served with full-flavored dishes. American- grown brown jasmine rice makes a delicious pilaf or side dish sprinkled with toasted almonds and sautéed onion and garlic.

Green Imported from China, green rice is typically medium-grain, and colored and flavored with the juice of bamboo. Green rice is steamed and served plain as a side dish.

Red The term *red rice* is used for any rice that is covered with red, instead of brown, bran. Red rice imported from Bhutan is short grain, whereas the red rice imported from the Himalayas has long, slender grains, and the red rice grown in the Carmargue, in southern France, has plump, medium-sized grains. All of these rices have a nutty taste and chewy consistency and are excellent in salads, soups, stews, pilaf, and other side dishes.

Spanish Rice Three varieties of Spanish rice exported to the United States are Bomba, Calasparra, and Valencia. Although sometimes labeled as short-grain rice, these rices are technically medium-grain. Bomba and Calasparra are prized for their ability to absorb large quantities of liquid without losing their shape and becoming sticky, so they are ideal for paella. Valencia rice has a slightly smaller grain, but also makes an excellent paella. (See page 295 for more details.)

Sushi Rice Japanese medium-grain white rice, also known as sushi, or short-grain rice, cooks up moist and slightly sticky yet firm. It should be rinsed repeatedly before cooking to remove some of the starch and requires relatively little water for cooking. (See page 162 for more details.)

Wild Rice Wild rice is botanically a grass, but when cooked the dark, chewy hull expands and the kernel pops, exposing the soft, white center. This contrast in textures is part of the appeal. It is good in salads, stuffings, and side dishes.

In old China, the versatile wok was used for every cooking technique: stir-frying, smoking, pan-frying, braising, boiling, poaching, steaming, and deep frying—creating eight distinct and treasured tastes.

Grace Young, COAUTHOR, *THE BREATH OF A WOK*

Three-Alarm Tofu with Oyster Mushrooms and Spinach

Wok

The Chinese wok was originally made of iron and only later of carbon steel, an excellent conductor of heat. Today, woks are available in carbon steel, stainless steel, enameled caste iron, aluminum, and other materials. The pan's classic shape—a deep bowl with sloping sides—is ideal for the rapid stirring and flipping over high heat that defines stir-frying. The most useful size is 12 to 14 inches in diameter. Woks are often sold with a set of wok tools (see page 30).

The round-bottomed wok is designed for use on a gas stove, but it can also be used on an electric burner with a wok ring, a metal band that surrounds the burner and stabilizes the wok. The flat-bottomed wok, also known as a stir-fry pan, can be used on both gas and electric stoves, but is better suited to the flat burner of an electric stove.

Traditional woks have two opposing metal loop handles to facilitate lifting and tilting. Newer woks often have two opposing wooden spool handles, or a single long handle made from molded metal, smooth-finished wood, or a heat-resistant covering and helper handle on the opposite side. Before purchasing any wok, test the handles for comfort.

Tips for Using

New carbon steel and iron woks must be seasoned before using in any way. If your wok did not include seasoning instructions, wash it well in plenty of hot water with a mild dish soap, and then scrub it both inside and outside with a scouring pad to completely remove the manufacturer's protective coating of sticky oil. Then, place the wok on the stove top over high heat and heat until very hot. Remove from the heat and rub the interior with a thick wad of paper towels coated with vegetable oil. Let the wok cool completely and repeat the process at least twice. Rub the wok dry with a paper towel before using.

An all stainless-steel wok requires more oil to keep food from sticking than a carbon-steel wok.

The wok is a versatile piece of cookware. In addition to stir-frying, steaming, and deep-frying, it can be used for sautéing, braising meats, boiling shrimp, and even smoking.

Frequent use will be help the wok develop its own natural nonstick finish, or patina.

Woks are available with a nonstick finish and should only be used with wooden or other nonmetallic heatproof tools to protect the surface from nicks and scratches.

Care in Using

Always clean a wok immediately after use, following the manufacturer's instructions. Not recommended for dishwashers.

Do not use a metal scouring pad or detergent on a seasoned carbon-steel wok. Loosen any cooked-on bits with very hot water and a plastic scrubber. Dry thoroughly with a paper towel or cloth and rub the surface with a little vegetable oil. Store in a dry place.

recipes

Three-Alarm Tofu with Oyster Mushrooms and Spinach | Pork, Pineapple, and Snow Peas with Sesame Soy Sauce Marinade

THREE-ALARM TOFU with OYSTER MUSHROOMS and SPINACH

PREP 15 min | **MARINATING** 30 min | **COOK TIME** 5 min | **SERVES** 4

Tofu absorbs the flavors of other ingredients with which it is cooked. In this dish, it takes on the earthiness of the mushrooms and the spice of the ginger, garlic, and chiles. To save time, chop the ginger and garlic and prepare the other ingredients while the tofu is marinating.

Implements
Cutting Board, Wok, Slotted Spoon, Wire Skimmer, Wok Spatula

Ingredients

12 ounces firm tofu, in a single block, well drained

MARINADE

2 tablespoons soy sauce

2 tablespoons unseasoned rice vinegar

1 tablespoon honey

1 tablespoon cornstarch

2 teaspoon toasted sesame oil

¼ teaspoon crushed red pepper

8 ounces oyster mushrooms

3 tablespoons peanut, canola, or other oil with a high smoking point

1 tablespoon peeled, finely chopped fresh ginger

1 tablespoon finely chopped garlic

6 ounces baby spinach

⅓ cup thinly, diagonally sliced green onions, green and white parts, for garnish

Hot cooked white or brown rice, for serving

1. Set the tofu block on one end and cut it into two ¾-inch-thick slices. Place the slices on half of a clean kitchen towel, top with the other half of the towel, and press the tofu gently with your palm to coax out excess moisture. Uncover the tofu, transfer to a cutting board, and cut into ½-inch squares. Set aside.

2. **MAKE THE MARINADE:** In a large bowl, combine the soy sauce, vinegar, honey, cornstarch, sesame oil, and red pepper, and mix well. Add the tofu and stir gently to coat. Marinate for 30 minutes, or longer, if preferred. Using a slotted spoon, transfer the tofu to a plate and set aside. Reserve the marinade.

3. Trim the base of each mushroom stem. Cut the mushroom caps and the remaining tender stems into ½-inch pieces. Set aside.

4. Heat the wok over high heat until hot enough for a drop of water to sizzle and evaporate on contact, then add 2 tablespoons of the oil. When the oil is hot, add the tofu a small batch at a time, shaking the wok and flipping the tofu over with a wok spatula for 2 minutes, or until evenly browned. Using a wire skimmer or slotted spoon, transfer the tofu back to its plate.

5. Add the remaining 1 tablespoon oil to the wok. Add the mushrooms, ginger, and garlic, and stir-fry over high heat for 1 minute, or until heated through. Return the tofu to the wok and add the reserved marinade and spinach. Stir-fry for 10 seconds, or until the spinach wilts.

6. Transfer the stir-fry to a serving platter and sprinkle with the green onions. Serve at once with the rice.

 **tip** WHERE THERE'S SMOKE

Because you'll be cooking in your wok over high heat, the kind of oil you use is important. Some vegetable oils with a low smoking point, such as extra-virgin olive oil, are not well-suited for high-temperature cooking. Peanut oil, grape seed oil, and canola oil are recommended for high-temperature frying.

PORK, PINEAPPLE, and SNOW PEAS with SESAME SOY SAUCE MARINADE

PREP 20 min | **COOK TIME** 5 min | **SERVES** 4

Excellent Shanghai-style sesame soy sauce marinades are available in some supermarkets and many specialty cookware shops (for more details, see page 146). Use them as a marinade for meat, poultry, or seafood; a glaze for broiled or grilled foods; or as a sauce to flavor stir-fries. Here, it is mixed with the pork before it goes into the wok, and then more is added to the dish just before it is ready.

Implements Wok, Wok Spatula

Ingredients

12 ounces pork tenderloin or boneless pork loin, cut into 1-by-¼-by-¼-inch strips

4 tablespoons sesame soy sauce marinade

2 tablespoons peanut, canola, or other oil with a high smoking point

1 tablespoon packed julienned, peeled, fresh ginger

6 ounces snow peas, trimmed and strings pulls off

1 cup slivered red bell pepper

1 cup ¼-inch-dice fresh pineapple

2 cloves garlic, minced or grated

Hot cooked white or brown rice, for serving

¼ cup thin, diagonally sliced green onions, including tender green tops, for garnish

2 tablespoons finely chopped fresh cilantro, for garnish

1. In a medium bowl, stir together the pork and 2 tablespoons of the sesame soy marinade, mixing well. Let stand for about 15 minutes while you prepare the remaining ingredients.

2. Heat the wok over high heat until hot enough for a drop of water to sizzle and evaporate on contact, then add the oil. When the oil is hot enough to sizzle a piece of pork, gradually add the pork in three or four additions, stirring briskly with a wok spatula for 10 seconds after each addition. Add any marinade left in the bottom of the bowl and stir-fry for 1 minute, or until the meat begins to brown. Using the wok spatula, transfer the pork to a plate.

3. Add the ginger, snow peas, and bell pepper to the wok and stir-fry over high heat for 2 minutes. Return the meat to the wok, add the pineapple, garlic, and the remaining 2 tablespoons of sesame soy marinade, and stir-fry for 30 seconds, or until heated through.

4. Mound the rice in a shallow serving bowl and spoon the stir-fry on top. Drizzle any juices left in the bottom of the wok over the top. Sprinkle with the green onions and cilantro and serve at once.

tip CRISP UP THE SNOW PEAS

Snow peas are delicate and lose moisture quickly once they are picked. But perking them up is easy. Place the snow peas in a bowl, add a handful of ice, and then add cold water to cover. A 15-minute soak will revive them to their original crispy selves.

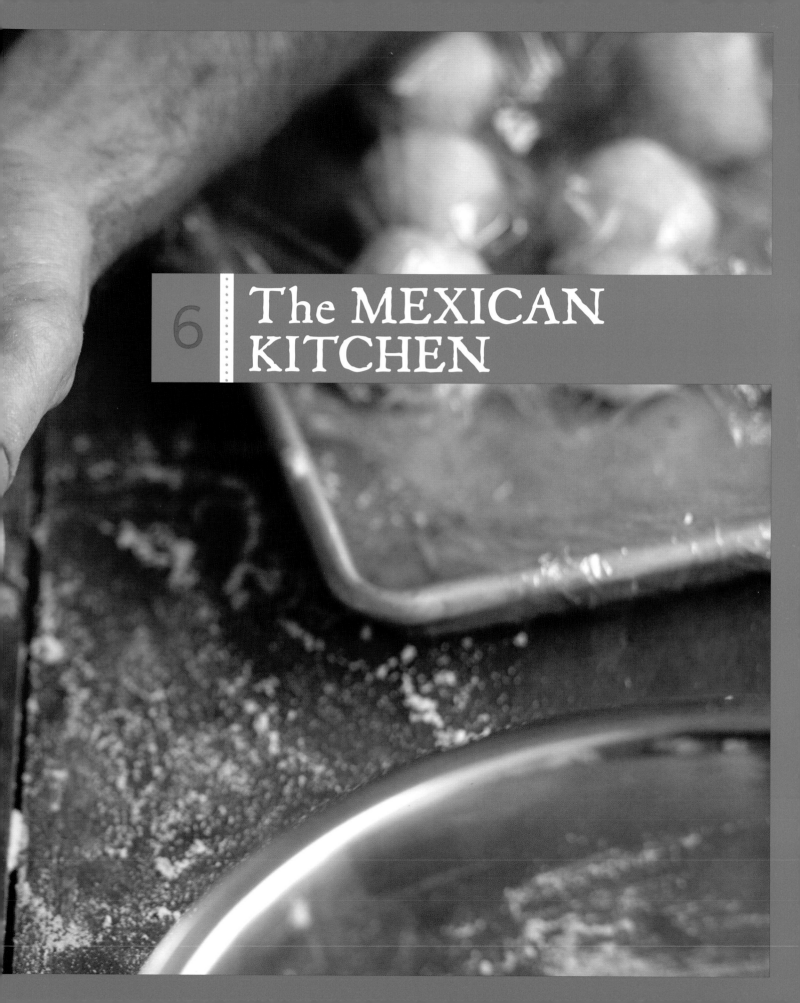

6 The MEXICAN KITCHEN

The Mexican Pantry

From warm soft tortillas to piquant chiles to scores of complex sauces, the Mexican kitchen boasts a broad palette of remarkable flavors drawn from many cultures. The indigenous foods of the New World—corn, chocolate, chiles, beans, squashes, avocados, tomatoes, potatoes, and more—are the heart of Mexican cuisine, while new foods such as wheat, onions, cilantro, cattle, and pigs have been introduced. Discover the *molcajete*, a rustic mortar carved from volcanic rock and used to grind seasonings, pound ingredients for sauces, and crush chiles. Learn to use the wonderfully practical tortilla press and beautifully handcrafted terra-cotta bakeware found in every Mexican kitchen. If you are open to experimenting with intriguing new ingredients, try recipes using achiote, pepitas, tomatillos, and chipotles. The following pages will put an exciting array of colorful dishes on your table.

Achiote and Anchiote Paste

Achiote is the name for both the deep red seeds of the annatto tree and the spice made from them. The seeds are rock hard, and must be soaked before they can be ground to a paste. Typically used in the cooking of the Yucatán, achiote seeds are available whole in small jars and already ground into a paste (with other spices) that is sold in cellophane-wrapped blocks. The spice adds an earthy taste and a pretty reddish yellow color to dishes. (It's also what makes Cheddar cheese yellow.)

Cheeses

QUESO AÑEJO

This hard, aged, salty cheese is primarily used as a garnish, crumbled over such dishes as enchiladas. Salted fresh farmer cheese can be substituted, or grated pecorino romano, Asiago, or crumbled feta can be used in a pinch.

QUESO ASADERO

Made from cow's milk, this semisoft, mild cheese is an excellent melting cheese. Monterey Jack can be substituted.

QUESO CHIHUAHUA

Pale yellow, rich, and tangy, this semisoft cheese is a good melting cheese. Mozzarella, Monterey Jack, or Muenster cheese can be substituted.

QUESO FRESCO

This salty, moist cheese has a coarse, crumbly texture. Salted farmer cheese or a mild French feta can be substituted.

Chile Powder

This popular, wildly available mixture of powdered seasonings is used for Mexican dishes. The mixture usually includes some ground dried chiles, cumin, and coriander.

Dried Chiles

ANCHO

The ancho chile is a dried poblano. Popular throughout Mexico, it is medium hot, dark red, short and rounded, and has a complex flavor reminiscent of dried fruit. Sometimes mislabeled a *pasilla* chile, it is most often used in sauces and moles.

CHIPOTLE

Chipotles are jalapeño chiles that have been smoked-dried over a wood fire. Dark brown, about 3 inches long, and with an unsurpassed smoky aroma, they carry a good wallop of heat that is balanced by a complex, almost chocolate-like taste. Chipotles are also available in cans in adobo sauce, a vinegar-based sauce that helps to offset the heat of the chiles (page 94).

PASILLA

This long, wrinkle-skinned black chile, the dried form of the *chilaca* chile, is occasionally called *pasilla negro,* and is sometimes confused with the ancho and the *mulato* (another dried chile) on the West Coast. About 5 inches long, the *pasilla* has a rich, complex taste that often flavors moles and other sauces.

Fresh Chiles

ANAHEIM

Also known as the California chile, the anaheim is typically bright green, about 7 inches long, and has a green-vegetable, mildly hot flavor. It is often used for stuffed chiles (*chiles rellenos*) and to make *rajas* (page 180).

HABANERO

This small, lantern-shaped chile, related to the Scotch bonnet chile, is considered one of the hottest chiles on the planet. It is available in a range of colors, and is most frequently used in hot sauces.

JALAPEÑO

Sold in almost every supermarket, the jalapeño is medium to dark green—and sometimes red—2 to 3 inches long, and has a rounded tip. Always buy more than one jalapeño, because a handful often includes a chile as sweet as a bell pepper.

POBLANO

This mildly hot, dark green chile is wide at the stem end, about 5 inches long, and tapers off to a point. Sometimes it's erroneously called a *pasilla*. Always eaten cooked, it is used for stuffing (*chiles rellenos*) and roasting (*rajas,* page 180).

SERRANO

The popular serrano is only about 2 inches long, and is available both dark green and red. It resembles a smaller, hotter jalapeño and can be used in place of the jalapeño if you want a bit more heat. It is frequently used in salsas and sauces and is excellent roasted.

Cilantro

This leafy green herb, also called fresh coriander or Chinese parsley, has a delicate, scalloped leaf and a big, fresh, distinctive taste. Used widely in Mexican, Chinese, and Indian cooking, it's truly a global herb.

Epazote

Pungent and aromatic, epazote is sold dried in cellophane bags and fresh by the bunch in Mexican markets and well-stocked supermarkets. It is added to stews, bean dishes, and to some meats, but it should be used sparingly, because it can be bitter.

Masa Harina

Masa harina is corn flour made from corn that has been processed with flaked lime, causing it to swell. When *masa harina* is moistened and worked into a dough, it is called simply *masa* and is used to make tortillas and tamales. It is not the same as cornmeal, and they cannot be used interchangeably.

Mexican Oregano

Slightly stronger than the more readily available Mediterranean oregano, Mexican oregano, of which there are more than a dozen different species, is thought to be more closely related to lemon verbena than to its Mediterranean namesake. Mexican oregano is aggressively flavored and should be used sparingly.

Pepitas

Pepitas are raw or toasted, salted or unsalted pumpkin seeds that are used ground in sauces. Store them in the freezer to keep them fresh.

Tomatillos

These small, green fruits covered with a papery husk look like tomatoes, but are related to the gooseberry. Available fresh and canned, they are used primarily as a base for sauces and salsas. Fresh tomatillos, which can be found wherever Mexican or other Latin American produce is sold, are very tart and must be simmered in boiling water for several minutes because using.

Molcajete

The *molcajete* and the *tejolote* are the Mexican mortar and pestle, respectively. Both terms are from Nahuatl, the language of the Aztecs, and for centuries these tools have been used to crush chiles, herbs, and spices for moles, salsas, and other dishes. The *molcajete* is hand carved from a solid chunk of rough-textured basalt, a type of volcanic rock. The shallow bowl averages 6 to 8 inches in diameter and sits on three stubby legs, and the *tejolote* is usually about 4 inches long and 2 inches wide at the base. Some *molcajete* bases are whimsically designed to resemble a pig or a bull.

In the United States, *molcajetes* are sold in Mexican markets and in large supermarkets that cater to the Latin American community. The production of *molcajetes* in Mexico is a cottage industry, so their quality can vary. Also, although they may be labeled "preseasoned," further seasoning may be needed.

Tips for Using

To season a *molcajete,* scrub the interior repeatedly with a stiff brush and rinse with water. Then place the *molcajete* on a folded towel, and put a tablespoon of raw rice in the bowl. Using the *tejolote,* pound the rice for about 5 minutes, or until pulverized. Repeat with additional batches of fresh rice until there are no longer gray flecks of grit in the rice. Depending on how well the *molcajete* was "preseasoned," it may take 5, 10 or even 20 separate rice treatments.

To check the progress of seasoning, add 1 cup water to the bowl and rub the surface of the *molcajete* with the *tejolote.* Pour the water into a clear glass or bowl, let stand for a minute or two, and then slowly pour off the water and search the bottom of the glass for heavy particles of gray grit. If there is still grit coming from the *molcajete,* take a break and begin again.

Some *molcajetes* are impossible to season properly, but are handsome enough to be used for serving salsa, guacamole, tortilla chips, or fresh fruit.

The heavy pestle and rough surface of the bowl make quick work of crushing garlic, onions, herbs, dried chiles, and spices.

Care in Using

Wash with warm water and a small amount of very mild soap. Rinse the *molcajete* thoroughly and air dry.

Alternatives

A large granite mortar and pestle can be substituted for the *molcajete* and *tejolote,* and won't require the laborious seasoning steps needed to make some *molcajetes* grit free. You can use a spice grinder for spices, a chef's knife for chopping tomatoes for salsa, the back of a fork to mash avocado for guacamole, and a blender or food processor for mole and smooth sauces.

recipes   Mango and Chipotle Chile Guacamole | Oven-Braised Duck Legs with Toasted Pumpkin Seed Sauce

MANGO and CHIPOTLE CHILE GUACAMOLE

PREP 15 min | **SERVES** 4–6

In modern Mexico, making guacamole in a *molcajete* is reserved for special occasions. But anyone who has eaten guacamole made the traditional way insists that its texture and taste are superior to its counterpart made with any other tool, especially the food processor. If you don't have a *molcajete,* mash the ingredients with the back of a fork or a potato masher, and finely chop the onion, garlic, and chipotle before adding them. Or, use any large mortar and pestle.

Implements *Molcajete,* Small Rubber Spatula

Ingredients

> 2 sprigs cilantro, coarsely chopped
> ¼ cup chopped white onion
> 1 chipotle chile in adobo sauce, plus
> 1 to 2 teaspoons adobo sauce
> 1 clove garlic
> ½ teaspoon coarse salt
> 2 large, ripe avocados, halved, pitted, and scooped from skins
> 1 to 2 tablespoons freshly squeezed lime juice
> 1 ripe mango, peeled, pitted, and cut into ¼-inch dice (see Tip, page 139)
> Tortillas chips, warm flour tortillas, or raw vegetables (such as cucumber, carrot, red bell pepper, or celery), for serving

1. Place the cilantro, onion, chipotle, garlic, and salt in a *molcajete* or other mortar and mash until blended and the mixture becomes a paste. Alternatively, finely chop together all the ingredients and place in a bowl.

2. Add the avocado, lime juice, and adobo sauce to taste and roughly mash with the *tejolote* until the avocado is coarse but creamy and the mixture is blended. Alternatively, use a potato masher, pastry blender, or the back of a fork to make a coarse, creamy mixture. Using a small rubber spatula, gently fold in the mango.

3. Taste and adjust the seasoning with salt. Serve directly from the *molcajete* or transfer to a deep, wide serving bowl. Serve with tortilla chips or raw vegetables.

OVEN-BRAISED DUCK LEGS with TOASTED PUMPKIN SEED SAUCE

PREP 45 min | **COOK TIME** 2 hr | **SERVES** 4

Sometimes called green mole, toasted pumpkin seed sauce is often served over braised or roasted chicken or duck. The primary ingredients of the sauce are *pepitas,* or pumpkin seeds, and tomato-like, tangy tomatillos. Chicken or duck can be used for this dish, but because duck parts are now conveniently sold in many markets, they make a nice change from the more usual chicken. Duck legs are not very meaty, so plan on 1½ legs or more per person, depending on the appetites of your guests. Serve the braised duck legs with rice.

Implements Braiser, Stovetop Pepper Roaster, Small Skillet, Medium Saucepan, *Molcajete,* Blender, Tongs, Spatula or Flat-Edged Wooden Spoon

Ingredients

> 6 to 8 whole duck legs, excess skin and fat trimmed
> Coarse salt and freshly ground black pepper
> 1 large white onion, halved thinly sliced
> 1 cup dry white wine
> **PUMPKIN SEED SAUCE**
> 2 poblano chiles
> ½ cup raw hulled *pepitas*
> ½ cup low-sodium chicken broth

½ pound tomatillos, husks removed, rinsed, and coarsely chopped

½ cup packed fresh cilantro leaves

¼ cup chopped white onion

1 clove garlic, chopped

1 teaspoon coarse salt

¼ teaspoon dried Mexican oregano

1 large tomato, cut into ½-inch cubes, for garnish

Cilantro sprigs, for garnish

1. Preheat the oven to 350°F. Pat the duck legs dry, place skin side down on a work surface, and rub the flesh with a sprinkling of salt and pepper. Heat a braiser or other shallow 11- to 12-inch stove top–to–oven pan with a tight-fitting lid over medium heat until hot enough for a drop of water to sizzle on contact. Working in batches if necessary, add the duck legs skin side down and cook for 8 to 10 minutes, until the skin is golden brown and the legs can be easily lifted and turned without sticking to the pan. Use tongs to turn the legs over and cook on the other side for 8 minutes more, or until browned on the second side. Transfer the legs to a plate. Discard half of the rendered duck fat in the pan.

2. Add the onion to the fat left in the pan and, over medium-low heat, cook, stirring, for 5 to 8 minutes, until golden. Add the wine and boil for 3 minutes, or until reduced by half, scraping up the brown bits in the pan with the flat edge of a spatula or wooden spoon. Return the duck legs, skin side up, to the pan and spoon the onion and wine over them. Cover and transfer to the oven. Bake for 1 hour, or until the duck is very tender when pierced with a skewer.

3. **WHILE THE DUCK IS COOKING, MAKE THE PUMPKIN SEED SAUCE:** Preheat a stove-top pepper roaster or a grill pan over medium-high heat or preheat a broiler. Char the skins of the chiles, turning the chiles as needed with tongs, for 10 to 15 minutes, until evenly blackened and blistered. Place the charred chiles in a bowl, cover with aluminum foil or plastic wrap, and let stand for about 20 minutes, or until cool enough to handle and the skins have loosened. Rub the charred skins off the cooled chiles with your fingertips, or use the tip of a small knife. Rinse with water, then slit each chile along its length and open it flat. Cut out and discard the stem and scrape away the seeds and white membrane with the tip of a spoon. Coarsely chop the chiles. Set aside.

4. Spread the pumpkin seeds in a small, dry skillet, place over medium-low heat, and heat, shaking the pan, for 3 to 4 minutes, or until lightly browned. Transfer to a bowl and let cool. Then pour the cooled seeds into a *molcajete* and pound into fine particles. Alternatively, use a spice grinder, blender, or mortar and pestle.

5. In a medium saucepan, combine the chicken broth, chiles, tomatillos, cilantro, onion, garlic, salt, and oregano over medium heat and bring to a gentle boil. Reduce the heat to low, cover, and simmer for 10 minutes, or until the vegetables have softened. Remove from the heat and let cool.

6. Remove the braiser from the oven. Transfer the duck to a plate. Add the remaining contents of the braiser and the tomatillos mixture into a blender or food processor, and reserve the braiser to reheat the sauce. Process until the sauce is smooth.

7. Pour the pureed sauce back into the braiser. Reheat over medium-low heat, stirring, for 5 minutes, or until the sauce boils. Gradually stir in the finely ground *pepitas* until blended. Return the duck and any juices that have accumulated on the plate to the sauce. Stir to coat the duck with the sauce. Cover and reheat for 5 minutes, or until heated through.

8. Taste the sauce and adjust the seasoning with salt. Transfer the duck and the sauce to a deep platter, garnish with the tomato and cilantro sprigs, and serve at once.

tip KEEPING THE STOVE TOP TIDY

A splatter screen is a round frame fitted with a windowlike screen and a long handle. It fits on top of skillets and saucepans and helps contain the splatter that's inevitable when simmering a sauce (like tomato sauce), frying chicken, or browning duck legs. A large splatter screen can be used on different-sized pans.

Fresh chiles, tomatoes, tomatillos, onions, and garlic are fire-roasted to begin the cooking process before they are added to a dish, and to give them a smoky and slightly sweeter flavor.

Daniel Hoyer, AUTHOR, *CULINARY MEXICO: AUTHENTIC RECIPES AND TRADITIONS*

Stove-Top Pepper Roaster

This is typically a heavy-gauge, stainless-steel-mesh round utensil with a sturdy rim and a black baked-on finish that ensures even cooking over high heat, and removable, stay-cool wooden handles. It does a great job on *rajas,* or roasted chiles, for Mexican dishes, but it is also convenient for charring the skins on other fresh chiles and on bell peppers, saving you the trouble of preheating the broiler or firing up the outdoor grill. It's great for blistering tomatoes, onions, garlic, and eggplants, too.

The versatile tool can also take the place of the *comal,* the flat, round metal or terra-cotta griddle traditionally used to cook or heat up tortillas so they won't dry out. Most models are about 10½ inches in diameter, which fits comfortably on the burner of a gas or electric stove.

Tips for Using

Season once before using: Remove wooden handles, rub vegetable oil on both sides of the mesh, and place in a 400°F oven for 2½ hours.

When ready to cook, preheat the roaster over medium-high heat until hot enough for a chile to sizzle when it is laid on the mesh.

The roaster is especially handy if you're roasting small batches (one or two bell peppers, chiles, or tomatoes), saving you time and conserving energy over using the oven or broiler.

Always turn on the exhaust fan when roasting chiles, as the "fumes" can sear your throat and make your eyes tear.

Use the pepper roaster as a stove-top grill for cooking aluminum foil–wrapped chicken or fish, to heat up tortillas or pita bread, or to prepare quesadillas.

Care in Using

Wash with warm, soapy water and air dry.

Always consult the manufacturer's instructions.

Alternatives

A stove-top grill pan or a chef's torch can be used for charring vegetables.

recipes

Rajas (Poblano Chile Strips) | **Fresh-Fruit Quesadillas**

RAJAS (Poblano Chile Strips)

PREP 25 min I **STAND TIME** (chiles) 20 min I **COOK TIME**
10 min I **SERVES** 2–4

In the Mexican kitchen, narrow strips of roasted
and peeled poblano chiles, sometimes sautéed with
onions, garlic, tomatoes, and seasonings, are called
rajas. They make a delicious side dish or a topping
for fried or roasted fish, roasted potatoes, grilled
steak, cooked rice, or scrambled eggs, and will keep
in the refrigerator for up to a week.

Implements Stove-top Pepper Roaster, Tongs, 10-inch Skillet

Ingredients

2 to 4 poblano chiles

2 tablespoons flavorless vegetable oil

1 white onion, cut into thinly sliced wedges

1 clove garlic, finely chopped

Pinch of dried Mexican oregano

Coarse salt

1. Preheat a stove-top pepper roaster over medium-high
   heat until hot enough for a chile to sizzle when it is laid
   on the hot mesh. Arrange the chiles on the roaster and
   roast, turning the peppers often with tongs, for 5 to 15
   minutes, until the skin is evenly blackened and blistered.
   Alternatively, preheat the broiler or a grill pan or fire up
   an outdoor grill and grill the peppers.

2. Place the charred chiles in a bowl, cover with aluminum
   foil or plastic wrap, and let stand for about 20 minutes,
   or until cool enough to handle and the skins have loosened. Rub the charred skins off the cooled chiles with
   your fingertips, or use the tip of a small knife. Rinse with
   water, then slit each chile along its length and open it
   flat. Cut out and discard the stem and scrape away the
   seeds and white membranes with the tip of a spoon. Cut
   the peppers into ½-inch-wide strips and set aside until
   ready to use. These are the *rajas.*

3. In a 10-inch skillet, heat the oil over medium-low heat.
   Add the onion and cook, stirring, for 5 minutes, or until
   softened. Add the poblano strips and garlic and cook,
   stirring, for 5 minutes, or until the onion begins to turn
   golden. Add the oregano and season to taste with salt
   and stir to blend.

4. Serve at once, or cool and refrigerate until ready to use.

tip HANDLING FRESH CHILES

When handling fresh chiles, be sure to wear disposable plastic
gloves to protect your hands. The membranes and seeds of
the chile contain capsaicin, an oily compound that carries the
pepper's heat, and if capsaicin is transferred to sensitive skin or
your eyes, it will cause painful burning. Also, thoroughly wash
your hands and any tools—knife, cutting board—used for chiles
as soon as you have finished working with them.

In general, the smaller the chile, the hotter it will be.
But when it comes to chiles and the heat factor, there are no
hard-and-fast rules. If you buy a handful of chiles, chances are
there will be one or two that are searingly hot and one or two
that are almost sweet. Even chiles that have been left on the
plant to ripen fully, turning red, do not follow any rules. Some
varieties will get hotter and others will not. The flavor of chiles,
both fresh and dried, intensifies when they are roasted before
using. (See page 179 for details on the Stove-Top Pepper
Roaster).

FRESH-FRUIT QUESADILLAS

PREP 15 min | **COOK TIME** 8 to 10 min | **SERVES** 4

Quesadillas are the classic bread and cheese snack. Here, instead of a skillet or *comal,* use the pepper roaster to toast the filled quesadillas and melt the cheese. The simplest quesadilla is made with just cheese, but it can be dressed up with a spoonful of salsa, chopped chiles, or slivered avocado. This recipe departs from the traditional, with thin peach slices added to the cheese, chiles, and cilantro.

Implements Cutting Board, Stove-top Pepper Roaster, Wide Spatula

Ingredients

4 (9-inch) corn or flour tortillas

1½ teaspoons flavorless vegetable oil

2 cups (4 ounces) shredded *queso asadero* or Monterey Jack cheese

2 large or 3 medium peaches (peeled) or nectarines (unpeeled), halved, pitted, and very thinly sliced (about 2 cups)

2 tablespoons finely chopped fresh cilantro

1 jalapeño chile, seeded and thinly sliced into rounds

1. Lay the tortillas on a cutting board. Lightly brush the tops with oil. Turn the tortillas oiled side down.

2. Divide the cheese evenly among the tortillas. Make a visual line down the center of each tortilla. Arrange a layer of the peach slices to the right of the visual line, so the fruit covers half of the opened tortilla. Sprinkle the peaches with the cilantro and chile, dividing them evenly. Fold the tortillas in half over the filling.

3. Preheat a stove-top pepper roaster, griddle, or skillet over medium-high heat until hot enough for a drop of water to sizzle on contact. Add as many folded tortillas as will fit without crowding. Adjust the heat to medium-low and grill for 2 to 3 minutes, until the underside is lightly browned. Use a wide spatula to turn the tortillas over and grill for 1 to 2 minutes more, until lightly browned on the second side and the cheese is melted. Using the spatula, return the quesadillas to the cutting board. Repeat with the remaining folded tortillas.

4. To serve, cut each half circle into 3 wedges and arrange on a platter or a tray. Serve hot.

The highly glazed dark brown terra-cotta and earthenware casseroles (cazuelas y ollas) are still used by traditional and country cooks who swear that the flavor of the food cooked in them is superior to that cooked in metal pots—and, of course, i tend to agree.

Diana Kennedy, AUTHOR, *THE ART OF MEXICAN COOKING*

Roasted Fish Fillet with Achiote, Potatoes, Chile Strips, and Orange Salsa

Terra-Cotta Bakeware

Rustic and homey, these baking dishes are made from red clay in a wide variety of shapes and sizes, from small enough to hold olives to large enough to accommodate a recipe that serves eight. They're perfect for both baking and serving the sunny flavors of Mexico and the Iberian Peninsula (page 291).

Called *cazuelas* in Mexico and Spain and *tacho de barro* in Portugal, these earthenware dishes typically have unglazed bottoms. Some are fired at a high temperature, which makes them dry and brittle until they have been seasoned, while others are ready to use. If you purchase a dish that needs seasoning, all you need to do is soak it in water for six to twelve hours before using the first time.

Terra-cotta dishes are ideal for oven use, especially for recipes that call for long, slow cooking, but they can also be used directly on a burner (gas or electric) with a heat diffuser. Some larger, round pieces dishes come with lids. Refer to manufacturer's instructions for stove-top cooking. Most terra-cotta dishes are imported from Portugal, Spain, or Mexico.

Tips for Using

Read the manufacturer's instructions to find out if your terra-cotta baking dish must be seasoned before you use it for the first time.

Don't restrict your large terra-cotta dishes to cooking only. Use them for serving salads, fruits, and desserts.

Not all terra-cotta baking dishes are of the same weight and quality. Read the manufacturer's instructions to find out if the piece is lead free, strong enough to resist direct heat on a stove top or under a broiler, and is recommended for oven baking.

Small terra-cotta dishes are great for serving salsa or guacamole, olives or nuts, and other small bites. In Spain, they are used to serve tapas.

Care in Using

If you live in a dry climate, you may need to soak your dishes to season them more than once to restore moisture to the terra-cotta.

Always consult the manufacturer's instructions.

Alternatives

Any gratin or oval baking dish can be used in place of a terra-cotta baking dish.

recipes

Roasted Fish Fillet with Achiote, Potatoes, Chile Strips, and Orange Salsa | Red Rice with Roasted Poblano Chiles and *Queso Chihuahua*

ROASTED FISH with ACHIOTE, POTATOES, CHILE STRIPS, and ORANGE SALSA

PREP 30 min | **COOK TIME** 50 min | **SERVES** 4

For this recipe, use achiote paste (*adobo de achiote*). This typical dish of the Yucatán combines the earthy-tasting achiote with fish, potatoes, and a pretty, refreshing citrus salsa. Serve with a green vegetable or a tossed salad.

Implements *Molcajete,* 9-by-13-inch Terra-Cotta Baking Dish

Ingredients

ACHIOTE SAUCE

1 clove garlic

1 tablespoon chopped white onion

½ teaspoon coarse salt

½ teaspoon chile powder

½ teaspoon grated orange zest

1 (½-by-¼-inch) piece achiote paste

2 tablespoons freshly squeezed orange juice

1 tablespoon flavorless vegetable oil

Rajas (Poblano Chile Strips), page 180

1 pound Yukon Gold or any potatoes, unpeeled, cut into ½-inch wedges

1 large white onion, cut into ⅛-inch wedges

ORANGE SALSA

1 large navel orange

1 plum tomato, seeded and chopped

1 tablespoon finely chopped red onion

1 tablespoon freshly squeezed lime juice

1 tablespoon finely chopped fresh cilantro

Pinch of coarse salt

1¼ pounds skinless firm fish fillet (such as halibut, ling cod, or red snapper), preferably in a single piece

1. **MAKE THE ACHIOTE SAUCE:** Place the garlic, onion, salt, chile powder, orange zest, and achiote in a *molcajete* or other mortar and mash with a pestle until blended and the mixture becomes a paste. Gradually work in the orange juice and oil with the pestle. Alternatively, combine the ingredients in a blender or small food processor and process until smooth. Set aside.

2. Make the *rajas* and set aside.

3. Preheat the oven to 400°F. In a medium bowl, combine the potatoes, onion slices, and half of the achiote sauce and stir to coat the potatoes. Spread the potato mixture in a 9-by-13-inch terra-cotta baking dish or another type of baking dish. Roast the potatoes, turning once at the midpoint, for 35 minutes, or until golden and almost tender. Remove the baking dish from the oven.

4. **WHILE THE POTATOES ARE ROASTING, MAKE THE ORANGE SALSA:** Use a sharp, thin knife to cut the peel and all the white pith from the orange. Working over a bowl, cut along both sides of each segment to release it from the membrane, allowing the segments and the juices to drop into the bowl.

    Coarsely chop the orange segments and return them to the bowl with the juices. Add the tomato, onion, lime juice, cilantro, and salt, and stir gently to combine. Taste and adjust the seasoning with salt. Let stand at room temperature until ready to serve.

5. Brush one side of the fish with half of the remaining achiote sauce mixture. Push the potatoes to the edges of the baking dish, and place the fish, sauce side down, in the center of the dish. Brush the top of the fish with the remaining sauce. Arrange the *rajas* on top of the fish, spacing them about ½ inch apart. Rearrange the potatoes, placing some of them on top of the fish.

6. Return the baking dish to the oven and roast for 15 minutes, or until the fish is opaque when cut into at the thickest part with a knife.

7. Spoon the salsa over the fish and serve from the baking dish or transfer the fish to a platter and serve.

RED RICE with ROASTED POBLANO CHILES and QUESO CHIHUAHUA

PREP 25 min | COOK TIME (peppers) 10 min | COOL TIME (peppers) 20 min | COOK TIME (casserole) 30 min | STAND TIME (rice) 10 min | SERVES 4

The secret to tender, shimmering individual rice grains is to coat them thoroughly with hot fat before adding the tomatoes and broth. If you're using a baking dish that can't be put directly on a burner, start the recipe in a skillet and then transfer the contents to a baking dish, or use a braiser. Use a serrated peeler to peel the tomatoes, or peel them as described in the sidebar on page 305. Serve the rice with roasted chicken or other meats or with fish.

Implements
Stove-top Pepper Roaster, Tongs, 9-inch or 1½ to 2-Quart Terra-cotta Baking Dish, Large Skillet, Heat Diffuser

Ingredients

2 poblano chiles

2 tomatoes, peeled

2 tablespoons vegetable oil or lard

½ cup chopped white onion

1 clove garlic

½ teaspoon ground cumin

1½ cups long-grain white rice (not parboiled)

2 cups boiling water or low-sodium chicken broth

1 teaspoon salt

1 cup slivered or shredded *queso Chihuahua* or other semisoft melting cheese (such as mozzarella, Monterey Jack, or Muenster)

1. Preheat a stove-top pepper roaster or a grill pan over medium-high heat or preheat a broiler. Char the skins of the chiles, turning the chiles as needed with tongs, for 10 to 15 minutes, until evenly blackened and blistered. Place the charred chiles in a bowl, cover with aluminum foil or plastic wrap, and let stand for about 20 minutes, or until cool enough to handle and the skins have loosened. Rub the charred skins off the cooled chiles with your fingertips, or use the tip of a small knife. Rinse with water, then slit each chile along its length and open it flat. Cut out and discard the stem and scrape away the seeds and white membranes with the tip of a spoon. Coarsely chop the chiles. Set aside.

2. Halve the tomatoes and gently squeeze over a bowl or the sink to remove the juice and seeds. Coarsely chop the flesh and add to the chiles. Set aside.

3. Preheat the oven to 400°F.

4. Heat the oil in a 9-inch terra-cotta baking dish on a heat diffuser or in a large, heavy skillet over medium heat. Add the onion, decrease the heat to low, and cook, stirring, for 5 minutes, or until softened. Add the garlic and cook for 1 minute, or until fragrant. Stir in the cumin and toast in the hot oil for 30 seconds. Add the rice and sauté, stirring, for 5 minutes, or until some of the grains appear to be a different color than the others.

5. Add the reserved chiles and tomatoes and stir to blend. If using a large skillet, transfer the mixture to a lightly oiled 1½- to 2-quart baking dish. Add the boiling water and the salt and smooth the rice with a rubber spatula or the back of a spoon. Cover tightly (use aluminum foil if you don't have a cover or lid) and bake for 15 minutes. Uncover and scatter the cheese evenly on top. Bake, uncovered, for 5 minutes more, or until the cheese is melted and all the liquid has been absorbed.

6. Remove from the oven and let stand for 10 minutes before serving.

Simply put, without years of hand-patting experience, the easiest way for most of us to get a consistently flat tortilla is to press it out between the plates of an inexpensive tortilla press.

Rick Bayless, AUTHOR, *RICK BAYLESS'S MEXICAN KITCHEN*

Corn Tortillas

Tortilla Press

When the Spanish arrived in Mexico in the sixteenth century, they found the Indians eating thin, round cakes of unleavened corn dough. Today, those same cakes, or tortillas, remain an indispensable element of the Mexican diet. Prepared *masa,* the dough for tortillas, is sold in many Mexican groceries, or you can make the dough yourself by mixing *masa harina* (corn treated with lime and ground to a flour) and water. Once the dough has rested briefly, the tortillas are shaped by either clapping a small ball of the dough between your palms—a technique only for the experienced—or by flattening it in a tortilla press.

Sadly, handmade tortillas are a dying art, but two types of tortilla press are still available for those who like to make—or want to learn how to make—tortillas from scratch. One type is handcrafted of wood and the other is made of metal. The metal press, made of heavyweight cast aluminum or iron, is the one most often recommended by experts. Heavy and compact, it has two round plates about 7 inches in diameter connected by a hinge. Directly across from the hinge is a long handle that acts as a lever: when you pull it down, the top plate presses the ball of *masa* against the bottom plate, flattening it into a thin tortilla.

Tips for Using

To prevent the dough from sticking to the metal plates, line them with squares or rounds of cut-up 1-quart heavy-duty plastic bags.

If the dough cracks while it's being shaped into a ball, or while the plastic is being peeled off, it is too dry. Add moisture by dampening your hands with water and kneading it into the dough.

Once the tortilla is formed, peel the plastic from the dough, not the other way around.

Cook each tortilla as soon as it is formed.

Making tortillas goes more quickly if you use two skillets. Keep them both over medium-low heat, adjusting the heat as necessary.

The tortilla press can also be used to shape Chinese green onion pancakes or some Indian breads, such as chapati.

Care in Using

Wipe the press clean with a damp cloth.

Do not immerse the press in water or subject it to abrasive cleaners.

Always consult the manufacturer's instructions.

Alternatives

Corn tortillas cannot be made with a rolling pin. You might want to try patting them between your palms, as Mexican cooks do.

recipes

Corn Tortillas | Corn Tortillas Casserole

CORN TORTILLAS

PREP 5 min | REST TIME (dough) 30 min | SHAPE AND
COOK TIME 45 min | MAKES 18 (6-inch) corn tortillas

If you live in a community where you can buy fresh
prepared *masa,* use it here. Otherwise, be sure to buy
masa harina (page 174). Don't try to substitute regular
cornmeal. In Mexico, tortillas are consumed countless ways: as scoops for stews, beans, and eggs; as
wrappers for meats and vegetables; and like pasta in
casseroles (called dry soup; see next recipe).

Implements Tortilla Press, Two Heavy Medium
Skillets, Wide Spatula, Rimmed Sheet Pan

Ingredients

2 cups *masa harina*
½ teaspoon coarse salt
1½ cups warm water

1. Place the *masa harina* and salt in a large bowl. Add the
   water and stir until combined. The mixture will be lumpy.
   Reach into the bowl with your hands and work the dough
   into a smooth ball. If the dough is crumbly, add more
   moisture by dampening your hands with water and working it into the dough. The dough should be moist and
   smooth but not sticky. Wrap the dough tightly in plastic
   wrap and let stand at room temperature for 30 minutes.

2. Place two 8- to 10-inch heavy skillets over medium-low
   heat. Dampen 2 dish towels and squeeze dry. Fold one
   in half on a rimmed sheet pan; reserve the other.

3. Divide the dough into 18 equal portions and shape each
   portion into a ball between your palms. Cover the balls
   with plastic wrap to prevent drying. Cut open a 1-quart
   plastic food storage bag, and divide it into 2 equal pieces. Lay 1 piece over the bottom plate of the tortilla press.
   Place 1 ball of dough on top of the plastic in the center
   of the plate and press lightly with the heel of your hand
   to flatten slightly. Lay the second piece of plastic on top

of the dough. Close the press, pulling the handle down
gently to flatten the ball. Open the press, rotate the plastic a quarter turn, and press again.

4. Open the press and peel the top layer of plastic off the
   tortilla. Flip the tortilla onto your hand, plastic side up,
   and very gently pull the remaining plastic off the tortilla.
   If the tortilla tears, the dough may need more water. Or,
   you may have to begin at another corner and pull more
   gently. Slide the tortilla into a skillet and cook for 1 minute.
   Using a wide spatula, turn the tortilla over. Increase the
   temperature to medium and cook for 1 minute more. Turn
   the tortilla back onto the first side and cook for 30 seconds
   more, or until lightly speckled with brown spots. Tap the
   surface of the tortilla with your fingertips and it should puff
   up. Using the spatula, transfer the tortilla to the sheet pan,
   slipping it into the fold of the towel. (The puffed tortilla will
   quickly deflate.) Repeat with the remaining dough balls.

5. When all the tortillas are cooked and have cooled, stack
   them, place in a plastic bag, and store in the refrigerator
   for up to 1 week. Use a stove-top pepper roaster and
   tortilla grill or a skillet to reheat the tortillas one at a time.
   Or, wrap the stacked tortillas in aluminum foil and heat
   in a preheated 350°F oven for 10 minutes.

CORN TORTILLAS
CASSEROLE

PREP time 30 min | COOK TIME (sauce and chiles) 20 min |
COOK TIME (casserole) 35 min | SERVES 6

Known as a *sopa seca,* or "dry soup," this casserole is
the definition of Mexican comfort food. Corn tortillas
cut into strips are layered with spicy tomato sauce,
roasted poblano chiles, and two types of cheese, one
soft and melting and the other dry and sharp. The top
is spiced with sour cream or Mexican *crema,* a rich,
thick cream available in Mexican grocers, and then the
whole thing is baked.

Implements
Large Sauté Pan, Stove-top Pepper Roaster, Tongs, Heavy 10-inch Skillet, Slotted Spoon, Round or Rectangular Terra-cotta Baking Dish

Ingredients

TOMATO SAUCE WITH CHIPOTLE CHILES

2 tablespoons flavorless vegetable oil

¼ cup chopped white onion

1 clove garlic, chopped

3 cups canned tomato puree

1 canned chipotle chile in adobo sauce, finely chopped, plus 1 teaspoon adobo sauce

½ teaspoon coarse salt

1 poblano chile

Canola oil, for frying

12 to 15 day-old corn tortillas, cut into 1-inch-wide strips

1 cup (2 ounces) shredded *queso Chihuahua* or other semisoft melting cheese (such as Monterey Jack or Muenster)

1 cup grated *queso añejo* or other sharp grating cheese (such as pecorino romano or Asiago)

½ cup sour cream, preferably Mexican sour cream, called *crema*

1. **MAKE THE SAUCE:** Heat a large sauté pan or skillet over medium heat. Add the oil and onion to the pan and cook, stirring, for about 3 minutes, or until softened. Add the garlic and cook for 1 minute, or until fragrant. Add the tomato puree, chile and adobo sauce, and salt, and bring to a gentle boil, stirring. Decrease the heat to low and cook, uncovered, for 10 minutes, or until thickened. Set aside.

2. Preheat a stove-top pepper roaster or a grill pan over medium-high heat or preheat a broiler. Char the skin of the poblano, turning with tongs, for 10 to 15 minutes, until evenly blackened and blistered. Place the charred poblano in a bowl, cover with aluminum foil or plastic wrap, and let stand for about 20 minutes, or until cool enough to handle and the skin has loosened. Rub the charred skin off the cooled chile with your fingertips, or use the tip of a small knife. Rinse with water, then slit the chile along its length and open it flat. Cut out and discard the stem and scrape away the seeds and white membranes with the tip of a spoon. Cut the poblano lengthwise into ¼-inch-wide strips and set aside.

3. Line a tray with paper towels. Pour oil to a depth of ½ inch into a heavy 10-inch skillet, place over medium heat, and heat until a tortilla strip dropped into the oil sizzles on contact. Working in small batches, fry the tortilla strips for 20 to 30 seconds, until they begin to crisp but not brown. Use a slotted spoon or skimmer to transfer the tortilla strips to the prepared tray. Repeat until all the tortillas strips are fried.

4. Preheat the oven to 350°F. Spread one-third of the sauce in a 10-by-2-inch round or an 8½-by-10½-by-2-inch terra-cotta, ceramic, or enameled cast-iron baking dish. Layer half of the tortilla strips on top. Sprinkle with one-third each *queso Chihuahua* and *queso añejo* cheese. Layer half of the poblano strips on top. Spread with half of the remaining tomato sauce and layer with all of the remaining tortillas strips, half of each cheese, and all of the remaining poblano strips. Add a final layer of tomato sauce and then a layer of both cheeses. Spread the sour cream over the top.

5. Bake for 35 to 40 minutes, until the casserole is hot and bubbly. Let stand 10 minutes and serve.

7 | The FRENCH KITCHEN

The French Pantry

Almost every American cook has had some exposure to French cooking, and that made the selection of cookware, tools, and recipes for this chapter an exciting challenge. The French have had an amazing impact on what Americans eat and how we talk about cooking. You can hardly look at a cooking magazine, read a restaurant menu, or step into a fast-food joint without seeing the words soufflé, fondue, crème brûlée, pâté, quiche, and, of course, French fry. Discover specialized cookware such as the *cocotte*, the *chinois*, the raclette grill, the mussel pot, and the *pommes Anna* pan, and rediscover familiar pieces like the crepe pan, the omelet pan, and the fondue pot. Then you can serve up these Gallic specialties using the wonderful variety of cheeses, oils, vinegars, and other specialties of France.

Cheese

BRIE

This rich cow's milk cheese has a creamy, soft interior and is covered by a chalky, mildly flavored edible rind. Brie imitations are sold everywhere but, for a special meal, seek out an imported Brie de Meaux. (This is almost impossible to find in the United States because it is made from raw milk and aged less than the FDA-required sixty days. An excellent substitute is an imported knockoff called Fromage de Meaux that is almost as good as the real thing.)

CHÈVRE

The word *chèvre* means "goat," and is also used to describe a pure goat's milk cheese in France. Goat cheeses are made throughout the world, but the French probably have the widest range of types, shapes, and sizes. Typically, the cheeses have a tangy, almost lemony taste. Soft fresh goat cheeses are often melted

into sauces or cut into disks, browned, and served as the centerpiece of a salad. The semiaged log-shaped Bucheron has a tangier, more complex flavor than a fresh *chèvre,* and a drier, chalkier texture that makes it ideal for crumbling on top of salads.

COMTÉ

A cow's milk cheese from the Jura in eastern France, near the Swiss border. It has a sweet, nutty taste and, although it is a firm cheese, it has a soft feel in your mouth. Sometimes compared to Gruyère, it is both a great melting cheese and eating cheese.

EMMENTAL

Both France and Switzerland make Emmental (also known as Emmenthaler), a pale yellow cheese distinguished by its large holes, nutty taste, and rich flavor. Commonly known as Swiss cheese in the United States, it is considered the classic cheese for fondue.(Fondue purists insist that at least one-third of the cheese be Emmental.)

GRUYÈRE

Although this is traditionally a Swiss cheese, it is very commonly used in French cooking. This distinguished cow's milk cheese has been made since the thirteenth century, and the real thing is easy to find, so don't settle for an imitation. It has a rich, mildly salty, nutty flavor and is a great melting cheese, turning up in fondue pots, on top of onion soup, in sandwiches, and atop casseroles.

RACLETTE

Although this is traditionally a Swiss cheese, it is commonly used in French cooking. Like Comté, Emmental, and Gruyère, raclette is a semihard cow's milk cheese with a firm, buttery texture and rich, nutty taste. It is traditionally used for the dish of the same name, which is made by halving a whole raclette cheese through the center, setting it by a fire to soften, and then scraping off the semimelted cheese to eat along with boiled potatoes and small pickles.

ROQUEFORT

This celebrated blue-veined sheep's milk cheese is aged in natural caves where conditions encourage the development of its distinguishing mold. At its best, Roquefort is assertive but balanced, with a rich, salty taste. The saltiness makes it perfect for pairing with fresh and dried fruits.

BLEU D'AUVERGNE

Firm and creamy, with a rich, sweet, nutty taste, this blue-veined cow's milk cheese from south-central France is preferred by those who appreciate a relatively mild blue. It's a good eating cheese and is delicious sprinkled over salad greens.

Cornichon

Miniature crisp, tart pickle made from tiny gherkin cucumbers. Cornichons are traditionally served with pâté, ham, and smoked fish.

Crème Fraîche

Velvety and rich, this thick cream has a slightly tangy, nutty taste. It is used much like sour cream in both savory and sweet dishes, as a garnish for canapés, swirled into soups and sauces, and spooned on top of fresh fruit. Crème fraîche is available in specialty markets and some supermarkets, or you can make your own: Stir together 1 cup of heavy cream and 2 tablespoons of cultured buttermilk in a glass jar and let stand at room temperature for 1 or 2 days, or until thickened to the consistency of sour cream. Cover and refrigerate for up to 2 weeks.

Flageolets

Flageolets are mild-flavored, pale white or pale green French kidney beans. Smaller than American kidney beans, they are considered a delicacy and are usually only available dried and sometimes frozen in specialty-food shops.

Fleur de Sel

Fleur de sel, literally "salt of the sea," is slightly coarse, mineral-rich salt harvested by hand from evaporated seawater along the Atlantic coastline of France. (See "Salt," page 67, for more information.)

Herbs de Provence

A blend of dried herbs popular in Provence.

Lentilles du Puy

These are tiny, round green lentils grown in the area around Le Puy, in central France. Prized for their almost peppery taste and their firm, but delicate texture, they are often used in many French dishes, including the classic lentil salad with fresh spinach and chopped hard-cooked eggs.

Mustard

There are many types of French mustard, but clean-tasting, pungent Dijon, made from mildly spicy brown mustard seeds and good-quality wine vinegar, is the most famous. French mustard is used in sandwiches, with pâté, in salad dressings, as a condiment for steak, in sauces, and as a glaze for fish or meats.

Olive Oil

Olive oil is produced in France only in Provence, and only in limited quantities. The oils range from light and elegant to rich and buttery. (See "Olive Oil," page 45, for more information.)

Vinegar

The most famous French vinegar is Banyuls, made from a fortified wine in a town in the Pyrenees, both also named Banyuls. The vinegar is light and soft, and should be used with a very light extra-virgin olive oil, perhaps one from France as well. Not surprisingly, given the many excellent French wines, France makes many other delicious vinegars in addition to Banyuls. (See "Vinegar," page 195, for more information.)

Vinegar

Vinegar is made when tiny airborne bacteria develop in a fermented liquid and form into a gelatinous mass—the "vinegar mother"—which then converts the liquid into acetic acid, or vinegar. The quality of the final product depends on the quality of the original liquid, so inexpensive vinegars are typically made from cheap, poor-quality wine or other liquids, whereas flavorful vinegars are made from relatively expensive, high-quality wine or other liquids.

A fine vinegar is aged until the flavor is properly developed. Vinegar is available in different levels of acidity, from 4 percent (mild) to 7 percent (stronger). If the acidity is not on the label, taste it before using. A supply of vinegars in different flavors, types, and acidity levels is ideal.

Balsamic Italian balsamic vinegar is made from the cooked and concentrated freshly pressed must (or *mosto*) of the Trebbiano grape. The best and most expensive is labeled *aceto balsamico tradizionale*. It develops its deep concentrated flavor, heady aroma, and thick consistency by aging in a series of casks each made from a different aromatic wood. This vinegar is more sweet than acidic and the best—and most expensive—is sometimes served as a liqueur or as a condiment for sprinkling on fresh fruits.

Lesser-quality balsamic vinegars are more acidic and often used in salad dressings, or pan sauces. White balsamic is made with white wine vinegar and white grapes. Its mild flavor and clear color are useful when you want a colorless balsamic flavor, but its quality is no match for true *balsamico*.

Cider The best cider vinegar is made by fermenting apple juice made from fresh apples. It has a pleasant, fruity taste and roundness that makes it an excellent addition to coleslaw, potato salad, macaroni salad, or other mayonnaise-dressed salads.

Fruit Fruit vinegars are made either from fermented fruit juice or wine vinegar sweetened with fruit syrups. The former have the purest fruit taste without being overly sweet. Typically low in acid, fruit vinegar is great for splashing onto cooked greens, salads, or cut-up fruit, or for whisking into vinaigrettes.

Herb Herb vinegars are made by infusing pure vinegar with fresh or dried herbs or spices. Use herb vinegars in salad dressings, on fruit salads or steamed carrots, or stir a spoonful into a creamy carrot soup.

Malt Malt vinegar, made from roasted barley, has a caramelized, mild flavor and low acidity. Its uses are similar to cider vinegar.

Rice Made from fermented rice, rice vinegar of many different types is used throughout Asia. Japanese rice vinegar is the most versatile. Practically colorless, its distinctive, almost salty taste and mild acidity make it a good choice for salad dressing. (See page 146.)

Sherry Sherry wine makes a smooth, nutty vinegar with a complex taste. The highest-quality sherry vinegar is from Spain's Jerez region. Aged in oak barrels, great sherry vinegar has a distinctive taste of caramel and roasted nuts, and has a boldness that makes it a great match for tomato salad, gazpacho, and white beans.

Red and White Wine The best wine vinegars are aged in wood and begin with a top-notch wine—white, red, or even Champagne. Good wine vinegars aren't cheap, but their depth of flavor makes them worth the expense; just a little makes an exquisite salad dressing.

When a recipe calls for straining a sauce through a fine sieve, the best is a conical sieve, called a chinois.

Mary Risley, AUTHOR, *THE TANTE MARIE'S COOKING SCHOOLS COOKBOOK*

Tomato and Saffron Broth
with Saffron Cream

Chinois

This conical sieve is made with either a continuous sheet of finely perforated molded metal or of very fine stainless-steel mesh. The perforated type—sometimes called a China cap—is used for pureeing soups, vegetables, or fruits. The mesh type—always called a *chinois*—is used for refining creamed soups, stocks, sauces, and fruit purees.

Ideally, a wooden pestle to match the contours of the *chinois* is used to shove the foods through the small openings, but a wooden spoon can be substituted. Some models come with a metal stand, freeing both hands for pouring and working the food through the holes. All have a long metal handle with an opposing hook that rests over the rim of a pot or bowl for stability. A shallow *chinois*—about 7 inches deep—is practical for home use because it will clear the bottom of most large pots and bowls.

Tips for Using

Because of its exceptional depth, a *chinois* is good for straining large quantities without spilling.

The perforated *chinois* is good for mashed potatoes, applesauce, cooked winter squash, or a silky smooth bean puree.

The fine-mesh *chinois* helps to filter out fat, small bits of herbs, and even coarsely ground pepper from stocks and sauces. Because the mesh won't get plugged with tiny seeds, it is used to strain cooked or raw mashed fruits for a coulis (pureed fruit sauce) or fruit for jelly.

When shopping for a *chinois,* make sure it won't hit the bottom of the bowl or pot you plan to use it in.

Care in Using

Immediately after use, soak in warm, soapy water and scrub with a stiff brush to prevent small particles of food from lodging and drying in the perforations or mesh.

A stainless-steel *chinois* is dishwasher safe.

Always consult the manufacturer's instructions.

Alternatives

A fine-mesh strainer or a regular strainer lined with a double layer of dampened cheesecloth can be used in place of a *chinois*. For a pureed soup, process the soup in a blender and then push the puree through a fine-mesh strainer.

recipes
with Saffron Cream

Beef and Shiitake Broth | Tomato and Saffron Broth

BEEF and SHIITAKE BROTH

PREP 20 min | COOK TIME (browning) 45 min | COOK TIME (broth) 3 to 4 hr | MAKES about 2 quarts | SERVES 8

Use this broth as a base for soups, or pass it through a fine-mesh *chinois* and serve as a crystal-clear soup. To keep the broth as clear as possible, don't stir it as it simmers.

Implements
Large Roasting Pan, Wide Spatula, Tongs, Teakettle, Slotted Spoon, Flat-Edged Spatula, Fine-Mesh *Chinois,* 8-Quart Stockpot, Fine-Mesh Skimmer, Large Ladle, 6-Quart Dutch Oven

Ingredients

2 stalks celery with leaves, cut into ½-inch-thick slices

1 large carrot, peeled and sliced

1 large yellow onion, cut into thin wedges

2 tablespoons flavorless vegetable oil

2 to 3 pounds meaty beef shin bones (sometimes called shank)

2 pounds marrowbones, cracked by the butcher

Coarse salt

2 cups boiling water

2 ounces fresh shiitake mushrooms, stemmed and stems reserved for the broth, caps reserved for later

1 cup (about 1 ounce) dried shiitake mushroom slices

3 sprigs Italian parsley

2 bay leaves

1 sprig fresh or dried thyme

1 teaspoon black peppercorns

3 whole allspice

2 tablespoons tomato paste

¼ cup minced fresh chives

1. Preheat the oven to 400°F. Spread the celery, carrot, and onion in a large roasting pan. Drizzle with the oil and stir to coat. Push the vegetables aside and add the shin bones and marrowbones. Sprinkle the meat and vegetables with about 1 teaspoon salt. Roast, turning the vegetables with a wide spatula and the bones with tongs every 15 minutes, for 45 minutes, or until well browned. Remove the roasting pan from the oven. Set a teakettle half filled with water on the stove and bring to a low boil.

2. With the tongs, transfer the marrowbones and shin bones to an 8-quart stockpot or other large pot. With a slotted spoon, transfer the vegetables to the stockpot. Then tip the roasting pan and, with a solid spoon, remove as much of the fat as possible.

3. Add the boiling water to the roasting pan and use a flat-edged spatula or wooden spoon to scrape up the browned bits on the bottom. Pour the contents of the roasting pan into the stockpot. Add just enough water to cover the bones by about ½ inch (about 2 quarts). Add the fresh shiitake stems, the dried shiitake, parsley, bay leaves, thyme, peppercorns, and allspice. Bring to a simmer over medium-high heat, without stirring, and immediately decrease the heat to low. Use a fine-mesh skimmer or a solid spoon to remove any foam that rises to the surface. Continue to simmer the broth, still without stirring, for 3 to 4 hours. Periodically skim any foam that rises to the surface, and add small amounts of boiling water if the level drops below the bones.

4. Turn off the heat and let the broth cool to lukewarm in the pot without disturbing it. Then move the pot to the sink. Place a large heatproof bowl in the sink and rest a fine-mesh *chinois* on the rim of the bowl. Alternatively, line a large strainer with a triple layer of cheesecloth that has been dampened and squeezed dry. Use a large ladle to transfer the broth to the *chinois* or strainer. When you reach the bones, use tongs to remove them from the pot. Then pour the remaining broth in the pot through the *chinois* or strainer. Discard the solids. Transfer the broth to refrigerator containers, cover, and chill for several hours or overnight, so the fat rises and solidifies on top. Then, spoon off and discard the solid fat.

5. Transfer the broth to a 6-quart Dutch oven or other large pot, place over medium heat, and bring to a gentle simmer. While the broth is heating, thinly slice the fresh shiitake caps. When the broth is at a simmer, stir in the tomato paste and the sliced shiitake. Cover and cook

over low heat for 20 minutes, or until the shiitake are very tender. Taste and adjust the seasoning with salt.

6. Ladle the broth into warmed bowls. Top each bowl with a few shitake and a sprinkling of chives. Serve at once.

TOMATO and SAFFRON BROTH with SAFFRON CREAM

PREP 20 min | COOK TIME 45 min | STAND TIME 45 min | SERVES 4

This silken tomato soup—the elegant texture the result of pushing the soup through a *chinois*—carries a haunting hint of saffron and a pleasant hit of black pepper. Ideally, this soup is made at the height of summer when fresh tomatoes are at their best, but canned tomatoes can be substituted.

Implements 6-Quart Dutch Oven, Small Skillet, Large Slotted Spoon, Blender, *Chinois*, Ladle, Flat Whisk, Small, Fine-Mesh Strainer

Ingredients

2 tablespoons extra-virgin olive oil

1 large leek, white and pale green parts only, chopped

½ cup peeled, chopped carrot

1 clove garlic, finely chopped

1 teaspoon saffron threads

2 cups low-sodium chicken or vegetable broth

½ teaspoon coarse salt

¼ teaspoon freshly ground black pepper

1 cup heavy cream, at room temperature

2 teaspoons lemon juice

1. In a 6-quart Dutch oven or saucepan, combine the olive oil, leek, carrot, and garlic, place over medium heat, and heat, stirring, for about 10 minutes, or until the vegeta-

bles begin to sizzle. Decrease the heat to low, cover, and cook for 15 minutes, or until the vegetables are softened but not browned.

2. Meanwhile, put the saffron threads in a small, dry skillet, place over very low heat, and warm for about 1 minute. Remove from the heat.

3. When the vegetables are ready, add ½ teaspoon of the heated saffron threads to the pan, and reserve the remaining saffron in the skillet for the garnish. Heat the saffron in the vegetables, stirring, for 1 minute. Add the tomatoes, broth, and salt, and bring to a boil. Adjust the heat to medium-low, cover, and cook for 30 minutes, stirring occasionally and breaking up the tomatoes with the side of the spoon. Add the pepper and then taste and adjust the seasoning with salt.

4. While the soup is cooking, make the saffron cream garnish: Add ½ cup of the cream to the saffron remaining in the skillet, place over low heat, and heat, stirring, until the cream is hot. Remove from the heat, cover, and let stand until ready to serve.

5. Remove the soup from the heat and let cool for about 20 minutes. Working in batches, ladle the soup into a blender and process until smooth. Alternatively, use an immersion blender to puree the soup in the pot.

6. Set a fine-mesh *chinois* or a fine-mesh strainer over a large, deep bowl (or a 2-quart measuring cup with a spout if using a strainer). Ladle the soup into the *chinois* or strainer. Let stand about 45 minutes. Press on the solids to extract as much flavor as possible. Scrape the puree from the outside of the strainer or *chinois* into the broth. When the solids inside the *chinois* are pressed dry, discard them. Rinse out the pot and return the soup to it. Gradually add the remaining ½ cup of cream to the soup, stirring gently with a flat whisk until blended. Reheat, whisking gently, over low heat. Stir in the lemon juice. Do not allow to boil. Taste and add more salt and pepper if needed. Ladle into warmed soup plates.

7. Strain the saffron through a fine-mesh strainer and drizzle a scant tablespoon of the saffron cream into each bowl of soup. Serve at once.

The cocotte is one of my favorites. It's perfectly designed to go from oven to table, which I love because not only is it a beautiful dish, but it also reduces the number of dishes to wash.

Laurent Tourondel, AUTHOR, *BISTRO LAURENT TOURONDEL: NEW AMERICAN BISTRO COOKING*

Chicken with Preserved Lemon
and Moroccan Spices

Cocotte

Cocotte is the French word for "casserole," but the word is also widely used to refer to a variety of deep oval or round cooking pots or casseroles with heavy, tight-fitting lids that are perfect for slow-cooking moist and delectable stews and roasts. They are made from enameled cast iron, flame-resistant ceramic, or sturdy white porcelain, among other materials. The heavy-duty cast-iron or ceramic *cocotte* is sometimes referred to as a Dutch oven. It can be used to brown or sauté foods over direct heat before being placed in the oven.

Cocottes are available in a broad palette of colors and finishes and a wide range of sizes and shapes. The smallest *cocotte* is the right size for baking a single egg, as in the classic *eggs en cocotte*. The largest is big enough for slowly cooking a whole chicken or large pot roast.

Some *cocottes* have tiny spikes protruding from the underside of the lid. The weight of the flat lid traps moisture inside the pot, and the spikes collect condensation to baste the food while it cooks. The *doufou,* another type of *cocotte*, has a recessed lid designed to hold ice cubes. While in the oven the ice causes condensation to collect inside the lid and bastes the food with moisture in the same way the spikes do. A *cocotte,* made from sturdy white porcelain, with a slightly domed tight-fitting lid and two looped handles, is perfect for oven-only cooking.

Tips for Using

The oval *cocotte* is the perfect shape for a roast or a whole chicken. The round tends to be a more versatile shape as it has more space for browning stew meats or cut-up poultry.

The *cocotte* will retain heat for a long time, making it a good choice for keeping food warm once it comes out of the oven.

The flame-resistant ceramic *cocotte* is lighter than the enameled cast-iron one. Use it for soup, stove-top or oven-braised stews, roasts, ribs, and other dishes.

When using a porcelain *cocotte,* recipes that require browning over direct heat are first browned in a skillet and then transferred to the *cocotte* to finish cooking in the oven (see page 205).

The oven-only porcelain *cocotte* is not only good for baking casseroles and oven-braising beans and meat dishes but also makes an attractive serving dish.

Care in Using

Soak in warm, soapy water to loosen stubborn residue, then scrub with a stiff brush.

An automatic dishwasher is not recommended for some *cocottes.* Consult the manufacturer's instructions.

Alternatives

Any enameled cast-iron Dutch oven can be used in place of a *cocotte.* If the lid is domed, cut a round piece of parchment paper just large enough to fit in the pot on top of the food being braised. This will ensure the moisture will stay close to the food, rather than cook off.

recipes

Chicken with Preserved Lemon and Moroccan Spices |
Beef Daube with Zinfandel and Dried-Porcini Sauce

CHICKEN with PRESERVED LEMON and MOROCCAN SPICES

PREP time 30 min | **COOK TIME** 1¾ hr | **SERVES** 6

Using a classic pan of the French kitchen to cook the dish of another cuisine is an excellent example of the versatility of the cookware that makes up the global kitchen. For this recipe, Moroccan spices are used to delicately perfume a chicken roasted in a *cocotte*. The spice mixture is an exotic blend called *ras el hanout*, and every spice stall in a Moroccan *souk* (market) has its own blend of this mysterious mixture, which includes dozens of toasted and finely ground spices, dried roots, and alleged aphrodisiacs. Fortunately, it is becoming more widely available in specialty markets in the United States. Lemons preserved in salt can be made at home or purchased in specialty shops.

Implements
Colander, Two Large Bowls, Cooking String or Silicone Ties, *Cocotte,* Instant-Read Thermometer, Two Wide Spatulas, Fat Separator, Skillet, Carving Knife, Cutting Board

Ingredients

1 (4-pound) whole chicken

Coarse salt

Handful of ice cubes

6 sprigs cilantro, included long stems

4 cloves garlic, chopped

1 large yellow onion, cut lengthwise into ⅛-inch-thick slivers

1 large carrot, peeled and cut on the diagonal into ⅛-inch-thick slices

2 tablespoons coarsely chopped preserved lemon (page 328)

1 tablespoon peeled, finely slivered fresh ginger

2 teaspoons Moroccan spice blend (see headnote)

Pinch of saffron threads (about 15 strands)

1 cinnamon stick

½ cup water

1. Place the chicken in a colander in the sink and rinse well, inside and out, with cold water. Half fill a large bowl (large enough to accommodate the chicken) with water and dissolve ½ cup of salt in the water. Add the ice cubes and the chicken, and then add more water if needed to cover the chicken. Refrigerate for 1 hour.

2. If necessary, rearrange the oven racks to accommodate the large size of the pan. Preheat the oven to 400°F.

3. In a large bowl, combine the cilantro, garlic, onion, carrot, preserved lemon, ginger, 1 teaspoon of the spice blend, the saffron, and 1 teaspoon of coarse salt. Stir to mix. Spoon out and reserve about 1 cup of the mixture.

4. Lift the chicken from the water, turning the bird to make sure all the water drains from its cavity. Dry the chicken inside and out with paper towels. Place the chicken, breast side up, on a work surface.

5. Stuff the cinnamon stick and all but about ½ cup of the nonreserved onion mixture into the body cavity. Skewer the opening closed with a metal poultry-trussing skewer. Cross the tips of the drumsticks and tie them together with cooking string or silicone ties. With the neck opening facing you, carefully work your fingers between the breast skin and flesh to make a pocket under the skin. Gently shove the reserved 1 cup onion mixture under the breast skin, spreading it as flat as possible. Be careful not to stretch the skin taunt, or it will split during braising.

6. Spoon the reserved ½ cup onion mixture into the neck cavity, pull over the skin flap, and secure with a metal poultry-trussing skewer. Rub the skin on the breasts and legs with the remaining 1 teaspoon of the spice blend.

7. Select a 7- or 8-quart *cocotte* or other large, heavy pan (such as a Dutch oven). An oval pan is ideal for a whole chicken, but not essential. Add the water and place the chicken, breast side up, in the pot. Cover with the lid and place in the lower half of preheated oven. Roast for 1½ hours, or until an instant-read thermometer inserted in the thigh (without touching the bone) registers 170°F. Remove from the oven and let stand, uncovered, for 10 minutes. Turn off the oven.

8. Using 2 wide spatulas, transfer the chicken to a heat-proof platter. Cover with aluminum foil and place in the turned-off oven. Pour the juices in the pot into a fat separator and let stand for about 10 minutes, or until the fat rises to the surface. Carefully pour off the juices into a medium skillet or sauté pan, and then discard the fat in the bottom of the fat separator. Or, let the juices stand in the bowl until the fat rises to the surface, skim off and discard the fat with a spoon, and pour the defatted juices into a skillet or sauté pan.

9. Remove the chicken from the oven. Pull out the trussing skewers and remove the string or silicone ties. Spoon out the onion mixture from both cavities (the onions won't be as tender as the onions under the skin) and add to the juices in the skillet. Add to the skillet any other stuffing than may have fallen from the cavities onto the platter, too. Heat the onions in the juices over medium heat, stirring, for 5 minutes, or until the onions are limp and the juices are reduced. Keep warm over very low heat.

10. Use a carving knife to cut off the full leg at the thigh joint. Find the joint between the thigh and drumstick with the tip of the knife and divide the leg into 2 pieces. Arrange the pieces on the warmed platter. Remove each half breast in one large piece from the chicken, and transfer them to a cutting board. Carve each half breast crosswise into ½–inch-thick slices and arrange on the platter. Spoon the wilted onions and hot juices on top of the chicken. Serve at once.

BEEF DAUBE with ZINFANDEL and DRIED-PORCINI SAUCE

PREP (marinade) 30 min | **MARINATING** Overnight |
PREP (daube) 30 min | **COOK TIME** 2½ hr | **SERVES** 6

A daube is a fancy stew. In this beef daube, similar to *boeuf à la bourguignonne,* the meat cubes are marinated in wine that has been simmered with sautéed aromatic vegetables, herbs, spices, and strips of orange zest, and then cooled. For the best flavor and texture, select well-marbled beef chuck and ask the butcher—or you can do it yourself—to cut the meat into large cubes (about 1½ inches). Although there is a long list of ingredients, preparation can be done up to three days before serving. Not only will the flavors improve, but the slow-cooked juices will chill and all the fat will collect on the surface, where it can be easily removed and discarded. This is a great dish to serve to company. If using a porcelain *cocotte* that cannot be used over direct heat, see the alternative tip on page 205.

Implements Rimmed Sheet Pan, Large Skillet, Colander, Small Saucepan, *Cocotte,* Tongs, Slotted Spoon, Strainer, Fat Separator (Optional)

Ingredients

3 to 4 pounds well-marbled boneless beef chuck, excess fat trimmed and cut into 1½-inch cubes

Coarse salt and freshly ground black pepper

MARINADE

2 tablespoons extra-virgin olive oil

1 cup chopped yellow onion

½ cup peeled, chopped carrot

½ cup chopped celery

1 tablespoon chopped garlic

1 (750-milliliter) bottle zinfandel

¼ cup chopped fresh Italian parsley

2 (3-by-½-inch) strips orange zest

2 bay leaves

1 leafy thyme sprig

1 cinnamon stick

1 cup (1 ounce) dried porcini mushrooms

2 cups water

2 thick slices (¼ inch) lean slab or thick-cut bacon, cubed

4 tablespoons extra-virgin olive oil

1 yellow onion, cut into thin wedges

1 clove garlic, bruised with knife

1 cup drained canned Italian plum tomatoes

12 large shallots, halved lengthwise

12 large cremini mushrooms, halved through the caps

GARNISH

1 leafy sprig Italian parsley

1 teaspoon fresh thyme leaves

1 (3-by-½-inch) strip orange zest

1. Place the meat in a single layer on a rimmed sheet pan and sprinkle each piece generously on all sides with salt and pepper. Cover and refrigerate.

2. **MAKE THE MARINADE:** Heat a large skillet or sauté pan over medium heat until hot enough for a drop of water to sizzle on contact. Add 2 tablespoons of the oil and swirl to coat. Add the onion, carrot, celery, and garlic, decrease the heat to medium-low, and sauté, stirring, for 6 minutes, or until tender but not browned. Add the zinfandel, parsley, orange zest strips, bay leaves, thyme sprig, and the cinnamon stick and bring to a boil. Decrease the heat to low and simmer, without boiling, for 10 minutes. Remove from the heat and let cool to room temperature.

3. Place the beef in a large bowl and carefully add the cooled marinade. Arrange the beef so that it is totally covered by the marinade. Cover and refrigerate overnight.

4. **MAKE THE DAUBE:** Set a colander over a bowl and drain the meat. Reserve the strained marinade. Save the orange zest strips, bay leaves, thyme sprig, and cinnamon stick, but discard the other chopped vegetables. Pat each piece of meat dry with paper towels and spread out on the rimmed sheet pan. Add another sprinkling of salt and pepper.

5. In a small saucepan, combine the porcini and water and bring to a boil. Remove from the heat, cover, and let stand for 20 minutes, or until softened.

6. While the mushrooms are soaking, heat a large flame-resistant *cocotte* or other large, heavy pan (such as an 8-quart Dutch oven) over medium heat. Add the bacon, decrease the heat to medium-low, and cook, stirring, for 5 minutes, or until evenly browned. Use a slotted spoon to transfer the bacon to a plate. Discard almost all of the fat in the *cocotte,* leaving only a thin film on the bottom.

7. Add 2 tablespoons of the olive oil to the pan and heat over medium-high heat until hot enough for a piece of meat to sizzle on contact. Decrease the heat to medium. Working in batches, add the meat to the hot pan and sear, turning with tongs as necessary, for 3 to 5 minutes, until well browned on all sides. As each batch is ready, transfer it to a plate. When all of the meat has been browned, spoon off the excess fat from the pan and discard.

8. Strain the porcini through a fine strainer set over a small bowl and press on the mushrooms to expel the excess water. Coarsely chop the porcini and set aside. Save the porcini water.

9. If necessary, rearrange the oven racks to accommodate the large size of the pan. Preheat the oven to 325°F.

10. Return the pan to medium heat and heat until hot. Add the onion and garlic to the hot fat and sauté, stirring, for 5 minutes, or until golden. Add the tomatoes and break them into chunks with the side of a spoon. Add the reserved strained marinade, the chopped porcini and porcini liquid, and the orange zest strips, bay leaves, thyme sprig, and cinnamon stick reserved from the marinade.

Bring to a boil over high heat. Remove from the heat and add the browned meat and any juices that accumulated on the plate. Sprinkle the bacon on top. Cover and place in the lower half of the oven.

11. Cook for 2½ hours, or until the meat is fork-tender. Halfway through the cooking time, remove the cocotte from the oven and carefully lift the lid to check on the liquid in the pot. It should be simmering. If it is boiling, lower the oven temperature to 300°F. When the meat is fork-tender, remove the pot from the oven and let stand, covered, for 5 minutes.

12. If preparing the daube ahead, use a slotted spoon to transfer the meat to a storage bowl. Cover the meat and refrigerate until ready to reheat. Refrigerate the juices separately; the fat will solidify on the surface. Just before serving, place the cold meat in a shallow baking dish and cover tightly with aluminum foil. Preheat the oven to 350°F. Place the meat in the oven for 30 minutes, or until hot. Lift off and discard the fat from the refrigerated juices. Pour the defatted juices into a saucepan and heat to boiling; decrease the heat to low, cover, and keep warm until ready to serve. To finish the dish, proceed to step 15.

13. If serving the daube soon after it is cooked, transfer the meat to a deep, heatproof serving dish, cover with foil, and keep warm in the turned-off oven. Set a strainer over a bowl and pour the contents of the pan into the strainer. Remove the orange zest strips, bay leaves, thyme sprig, and cinnamon stick, and discard. Spoon the other solids in the strainer over the meat.

14. Pour the strained juices into a fat separator and let stand for about 10 minutes, or until the fat rises to the surface. Carefully pour off the juices into a small saucepan, and then discard the fat in the bottom of the fat separator. Or, let the juices stand in the bowl until the fat rises to the surface, skim off and discard the fat with a spoon, and pour the defatted juices into a small saucepan. Keep the juices warm over low heat.

15. Just before serving, heat a large skillet over medium-low heat and add the remaining 2 tablespoons of olive oil. Add the shallots, cut sides down, and sauté, turning with tongs as they brown, for 10 minutes, or until evenly browned. Push the shallots to one side of the skillet to continue cooking. Add the cremini mushrooms to the skillet and sauté, turning as necessary, for 5 minutes, or until the mushrooms are evenly browned and tender and the shallots are tender and browned. Sprinkle with salt and pepper.

16. **MAKE THE GARNISH:** Finely chop the parsley, thyme, and orange zest together. Set aside.

17. Spoon the shallots and mushrooms on top of the meat. Spoon the hot juices over the meat and vegetables. Sprinkle with garnish and serve at once.

tip ALTERNATIVE FOR PORCELAIN *COCOTTE*

If using a non-flame-resistant *cocotte* that cannot be used over direct heat, first brown the beef, sauté the vegetables, and boil the wine marinade in a separate large sauté pan. Transfer the ingredients to a large porcelain *cocotte* and bake in oven, as directed.

Once baked, skim the fat from the cooking juices as directed in the recipe and then return the meat and juices to the porcelain *cocotte* for serving.

A good crepe originates in a good frying pan, and nothing beats the traditional shallow black steel pan, available in several sizes.

Anne Willan, AUTHOR, *COOK IT RIGHT*

Buckwheat Crepes with Sautéed
Apples and Gruyère Cheese

Crepe Pan

The French took the basic pancake and created the paper-thin and meltingly tender crepe that is surprisingly simple to make, especially if you have the right pan. The French crepe pan is basically a frying pan with low sides and an easy-to-grasp long, narrow handle. They are primarily made of blue steel, nonstick aluminum, or other metals. The pan must conduct, distribute, and retain heat efficiently to turn out perfect crepes.

The crepe batter must evenly and completely cover the surface of the pan to ensure a great crepe. To help spread the batter, you'll need to lift the pan from the burner and rotate it several times. If the pan is not evenly balanced or if it is too heavy, this step will be difficult, so it is a good idea to simulate this motion before you purchase any pan. The French crepe pan comes in a range of sizes. The smaller pans (6 to 8 inches in diameter) are typically used for dessert crepes, whereas the larger pans (9 to 11 inches) pans are generally used for dinner crepes.

Tips for Using

Preheat the pan on low heat. Cook the crepes on medium-low heat. The batter should begin to set the moment it hits the pan.

Adjust the amount of batter to the pan size. Small (6- to 8-inch) pans require 2 to 3 tablespoons of batter, whereas larger pans will need up to ⅓ cup of batter.

Most pans require only one very light application of butter. Apply softened or melted butter by rubbing it into the warm pan with a paper towel, or a silicone brush.

Getting the batter to coat the bottom of the hot pan quickly and evenly takes practice. You need to rotate your wrist smoothly so that the batter swirls and flows outward simultaneously.

The first crepe is never perfect but, even if it tears or needs to be patched, it will still taste good.

Some pans come with a *rabot,* a T-shaped tool made from two wooden dowels, for spreading the batter. It works best in a large crepe pan.

Some crepe pan sets include a flat wooden slat with a pointed tip. Use the tip to release the set edges of the crepe, so you can easily lift and turn the crepe.

Care in Using

The traditional steel crepe pan must be seasoned before use. Follow the manufacturer's instructions carefully.

Crepe pans generally need little or no washing. Use a mild soap if necessary, but never use any abrasive detergents.

The best pans are cleaned by wiping them with a damp paper towel and then buffing them dry.

Never place any crepe pan in a dishwasher.

Always consult the manufacturer's instructions.

Alternatives

Although not ideal, a small, well-seasoned skillet or omelet pan can be used to make small crepes. For larger crepes, a large skillet would be too awkward and heavy for swirling the batter.

recipes
Buckwheat Crepes with Sautéed Apples and Gruyère Cheese | Spinach-and-Egg-Stuffed Semolina Crepes with Tomato Béchamel

BUCKWHEAT CREPES with SAUTÉED APPLES and GRUYÈRE CHEESE

PREP (batter) 10 min | RESTING TIME (batter) 1 hr |
PREP (filling) 30 min | COOK TIME 2 min per crepe |
SERVES 4–6

Throughout France, you will find small restaurants, often tucked away on side streets, specializing in crepes. In Brittany, the crepes are made with buckwheat flour and the typical filling is a smear of salted butter, cheese, ham or bacon, thinly sliced fruit, and/or eggs. In most of France, crepes are rolled up or folded into half or quarter circles, but in Brittany, where they are sometimes called galettes, they are folded differently. The filling is spread in the center of the pancake, the four rounded sides are folded in over the filling, forming a square, and then the crepe is inverted onto a serving plate.

Implements Standard Whisk, Large Skillet, 9- to 11-inch Crepe Pan, Small Ladle, Small, Narrow Rubber Spatula, Wide Spatula (Optional)

Ingredients

CREPE BATTER

1 cup buckwheat flour

½ cup all-purpose flour

1 teaspoon coarse salt

2 large eggs

1½ cups water

2 tablespoons salted or unsalted butter, melted

FILLING

4 tablespoons salted or unsalted butter

3 yellow onions, cut into ⅛-inch wedges

6 slightly green Golden Delicious apples, quartered, cored, and cut into ⅛-inch wedges

2 ounces smoked ham, thinly slivered (optional)

3 tablespoons freshly squeezed lemon juice

⅛ teaspoon freshly grated nutmeg

Pinch of coarse salt

1 tablespoon salted or unsalted butter, melted, plus 2 tablespoons, softened

3 cups (12 ounces) coarsely grated Gruyère or Comté cheese

1. **MAKE THE CREPE BATTER:** In a large bowl, stir together the buckwheat flour, all-purpose flour, and salt. In a small bowl, whisk the eggs until well blended; stir in the water and butter. Gradually whisk the egg mixture into the flour mixture until the batter is smooth. Cover and refrigerate for 1 hour. The batter should be the consistency of heavy cream. If it is too thick, whisk in additional water, 1 tablespoon at a time.

2. **WHILE THE BATTER IS RESTING, PREPARE THE FILLING:** In a large skillet, melt the butter over medium-low heat. Add the onions, increase the heat to medium, and cook, stirring, for 5 minutes. Add the apples and cook, stirring, for 10 to 15 minutes, until the apples begin to brown and have softened. Add the ham and sprinkle with the lemon juice, nutmeg, and salt. Cover and set aside until ready to fill the crepes.

3. Heat a 9- to 11-inch crepe pan over medium-low heat until hot enough for a drop of water to sizzle on contact. Brush the surface of the crepe pan with a thin film of the melted butter. Blot any excess with the tip of a paper towel. Stir the crepe batter well with the whisk. Ladle about ⅓ cup of the batter into the heated pan, and simultaneously tilt and roll the pan from side to side to coat the surface with a thin layer of batter. Cook for 1 minute, or until the edges begin to set. Run the tip of a small, narrow rubber spatula under the edges of the crepe to loosen it from the pan. Use your fingertips to lift the crepe and quickly flip it over. Cook the other side for 30 seconds, or until the batter is set into a thin pancake. Do not brown the crepe or cook it until crisp. Transfer the crepe to a large, round plate. Repeat with the remaining batter, brushing the pan with more butter if necessary. Stack the crepes as they are made. You should have 12

crepes. If making ahead, wrap the crepes in plastic wrap or aluminum foil to prevent drying out. The crepes can be refrigerated for up to 2 days.

4. If the crepes have been made ahead, fill them one at a time by first warming each crepe in the pan over low heat. While they are still in the pan, sprinkle about ¼ cup of the cheese in the center of the crepe. Top the cheese with a large spoonful of the warm apple filling, spreading it into a single layer. Fold in two opposite sides of the circle to cover the filling. Then fold in the remain-

ing two rounded sides, overlapping slightly, to form a square envelope. With a wide spatula, lift the crepe from the pan and invert it, so it is seam side down, onto a serving plate. Cover with aluminum foil to keep warm if not serving at once. Fill the remaining crepes in the same way. Reserve the remaining filling.

5. Just before serving, brush the smooth top of each crepe with a thin film of the softened butter. Reheat the remaining apple filling and spoon a portion on top of each crepe. Serve at once.

SPINACH-and-EGG-STUFFED SEMOLINA CREPES with TOMATO BÉCHAMEL

PREP 1½ hr | **RESTING TIME** (batter): 1 to 24 hr |
COOK TIME 45 min | **SERVES** 10 as a first course or 5 as a
main course

This recipe illustrates the versatility of the crepe pan.
Here, it is used to make *crespelle,* Italian-style crepes
that are traditionally used in place of pasta sheets
in manicotti and lasagna. These delicate crepes
are made with semolina flour, the same flour that
is used for some pastas, gnocchi, and couscous. A
hint of ground cloves in the crepe filling is an exotic
surprise. Make the béchamel, crepes, and tomato
sauce a day or two before assembling the dish. The
assembled dish can be baked immediately, or it can
be refrigerated up to overnight before baking.

Implements
**Standard Whisk, 9- to 11-inch Crepe
Pan, Small Ladle, Small, Narrow Rubber Spatula, 10-inch
Skillet, Food Mill, 1½- to 2-Quart Saucepan, Flat Whisk,
10-inch Sauté Pan, Strainer, 9-by-13-inch Baking Dish,
Small Saucepan**

Ingredients

CREPES
4 large eggs
1½ cups water
1 cup finely ground semolina flour
2 teaspoons coarse salt
1 tablespoon unsalted butter, melted

TOMATO SAUCE
2 tablespoons extra-virgin olive oil
¼ cup finely chopped yellow onion
1 clove garlic, grated or finely chopped

1 (28-ounce) can Italian plum tomatoes with juices
1 tablespoon torn fresh basil leaves
½ teaspoon coarse salt
Freshly ground black pepper

BÉCHAMEL SAUCE
2 tablespoons unsalted butter
2 tablespoons all-purpose flour
2 cups whole milk or half-and-half
1 teaspoon coarse salt

FILLING
4 large eggs
2 (5-ounce) bags baby spinach leaves, rinsed
1 (15-ounce) container whole-milk ricotta cheese
½ cup grated Parmigiano-Reggiano cheese
¼ teaspoon ground cloves
Freshly ground black pepper
½ cup grated Parmigiano-Reggiano cheese, for topping

1. **MAKE THE CREPES:** In a large bowl, whisk the eggs until
   blended. Whisk in 1 cup of the water. Gradually add the
   semolina, whisking well after each addition. Stir in the
   salt. Cover and refrigerate for 1 hour or up to overnight.
   When ready to cook the crepes, the batter should be the
   consistency of heavy cream. Whisk in the remaining ½
   cup of water, or as needed, to achieve the correct consistency.

2. Heat a 9- to 11-inch crepe pan over medium-low heat
   until hot enough for a drop of water to sizzle on contact.
   Brush the surface of the pan with a thin film of the butter. Blot any excess with the tip of a paper towel. Stir
   the crepe batter well with the whisk. Ladle about ⅓ cup
   of the batter into the heated pan, and then simultaneously tilt and roll the pan from side to side to coat the
   surface up to the rim with a thin layer of batter. Cook for
   1 minute, or until the edges begin to set. Run the tip of
   a small, narrow rubber spatula under the edges of the
   crepe to loosen it from the pan. Use your fingertips to lift
   the crepe and quickly flip it over. Cook the other side for
   30 seconds, or until the batter is set into a thin pancake.
   Do not brown the crepe or cook until crisp. Transfer the
   crepe to a plate. Repeat with remaining batter, brushing

the pan with more butter if necessary. Stack the crepes as they are made. You should have about 10 crepes. If making ahead, wrap the crepes in plastic wrap or aluminum foil to prevent drying out. The crepes can be refrigerated for up to 2 days.

3. **MAKE THE TOMATO SAUCE:** In a 10-inch skillet, heat the olive oil over medium-low heat. Add the onion and sauté, stirring, for 8 minutes, or until softened. Stir in the garlic and sauté for 1 minute, or until softened. Meanwhile, set a food mill, fitted with the medium disk, on the rim of a medium bowl, add the tomatoes with their juices, and puree. Or, puree the tomatoes in a food processor and then press though a fine-mesh strainer to remove the seeds. Add the puree to the skillet, increase the heat to medium, and cook, stirring, for 5 minutes, or until the mixture begins to boil. Decrease the heat to medium-low and simmer the sauce for 15 minutes, or until slightly thickened. Add the basil, salt, and a grinding of pepper and stir well. Set aside to cool.

4. **MAKE THE BÉCHAMEL SAUCE:** In a 1½- to 2-quart saucepan, melt the butter over low heat. Add the flour, stir with a flat whisk until the mixture is smooth, and then continue to cook, stirring, for 2 minutes. Gradually add the milk while whisking constantly until smooth. Continue cooking, whisking gently, for 5 minutes, or until the sauce boils and thickens. Stir in the salt and set aside to cool.

5. **MAKE THE FILLING:** Place 3 of the eggs in a small saucepan and add cold water to cover. Place over medium-high heat and bring to a boil. Remove the pan from the heat, cover, and let the eggs stand in the hot water for 15 minutes. Drain the eggs, rinse with cold water, and then crack and peel away the shells. Coarsely chop the hard-cooked eggs and set aside.

6. Place the spinach in a 10-inch sauté pan or other wide, shallow pan with a lid, place over medium heat, cover, and cook for 3 minutes, or until wilted. Transfer the spinach to a strainer and press firmly with the back of a spoon to extract the excess moisture. Set the spinach aside.

7. In a large bowl, whisk together the ricotta, the remaining uncooked egg, the Parmigiano-Reggiano, the cloves, and a generous grinding of pepper until blended. Fold in the spinach and the chopped eggs. Set aside.

8. Preheat the oven to 350°F. Gradually whisk the cooled tomato sauce into the cooled béchamel sauce until blended. Ladle half of the sauce mixture into the bottom of a shallow 9-by-13-inch baking dish.

9. Spoon about ⅓ cup of the filling across the center of each crepe and gently roll into a cylinder. Arrange the rolled crepes, seam side down, in a row in the baking dish. Spoon the remaining sauce mixture on top of the crepes. Sprinkle the Parmigiano-Reggiano evenly over the top.

10. Bake the crepes for 45 minutes, or until the sauce is bubbling and the cheese is melted. If the crepes have been assembled ahead of time and refrigerated, cover the baking dish with aluminum foil for the first 15 minutes of the baking time, and then add 15 minutes to the total baking time, or bake until the sauce is bubbling and the crepes are heated through. Let stand 10 minutes before serving.

Fontina Fondue with Grappa and
Chopped Broccoli

*Fondue is fun to eat and an easy way to
entertain. Folks love fondue because it satisfies
the primal act of sharing food with friends.
When i'm in the mood for a satisfying, informal
meal, i fire up my trusty fondue pot.*

Rick Rodgers, AUTHOR, FONDUE

Fondue Pot

The word *fondue* comes from the French *fondre,* or "to melt." The earliest fondues were Alpine shepherds' suppers of cheese melted with wine over a campfire and sopped up with hunks of bread. But that humble beginning has evolved into an international social ritual, its popularity fueled by the casual, pleasurable experience of people sharing a communal dish.

Today, three different types of fondue are regularly enjoyed: cheese fondue, fondue Bourguignonne, and chocolate fondue. Cheese fondue has its own wide, shallow heatproof ceramic pot called a *caquelon. Fondue bourguignonne* (tender beef chunks cooked in hot oil) calls for a tall, narrow iron, copper, or other metal pot that tapers inward as it nears the rim to prevent the hot oil from spattering. Chocolate fondue, first popular in the 1960s, is experiencing a revival. Special chocolate fondue pots are available, but any type of fondue pot can be used.

Fondue pots are sold with matching tabletop heaters, and some pots come with forks or skewers and sauce dishes.

Tips for Using

Gruyère and Emmental are the cheeses traditionally used for fondue, but almost any cheese with good melting properties (except mozzarella) can be used.

The bread chunks for dipping into cheese fondue are typically speared onto the tips of long-handled forks.

Some cheese fondue pots require a heat diffuser when used on the stove top.

When making *fondue bourguignonne,* heat the oil in the fondue pot on the stovetop and then transfer the pot to a tabletop heater to keep it hot for cooking the beef. Use skewers or forks with heatproof handles for spearing the beef.

Fondue bourguignonne is traditionally beef, but other foods can be used, such as shrimp, chunks of chicken breast or salmon fillet, or vegetables.

A ceramic or metal pot can be used for chocolate fondue. Be sure to adjust the heater to the lowest flame to prevent scorching.

Popular dippers for chocolate fondue are whole strawberries, banana chunks, orange segments, and other fruits; marshmallows; hunks of brownie; and cubes of pound cake.

Care in Using

Wash with warm, soapy water and a stiff brush.

Some pots are dishwasher safe.

Always consult the manufacturer's instructions.

Alternatives

Any heavy pot or chafing dish can be used for cheese or chocolate fondue. Use a deep, narrow 1½- to 2-quart saucepan for *fondue bourguignonne.*

recipes

Goat Cheese and Mascarpone Fondue with Crumbled Bacon | Fontina Fondue with Grappa and Chopped Broccoli

GOAT CHEESE and MASCARPONE FONDUE with CRUMBLED BACON

PREP 20 min | COOK TIME 10 min | SERVES 4

A new twist on the classic French fondue, this recipe uses three cheeses: a log of fresh goat cheese; a tub of mascarpone, an Italian cream cheese; and a small amount of aged blue-veined cheese, such as English Stilton. For dipping, use strawberries, seedless green grapes, crisp, thin apple slices, and/or crunchy Bosc pear wedges. The tanginess of the goat cheese pairs well with the natural sweetness of the fruits.

Implements 10-inch Skillet, Slotted Spoon, Kitchen Scissors, Fondue Pot, Flat Whisk

Ingredients

2 slices bacon

1 large clove garlic, halved lengthwise

1 (8-ounce) log fresh goat cheese

1 (8-ounce) container mascarpone cheese

¼ cup milk

½ cup (1 ounce) crumbled Stilton or other hard blue-veined cheese

½ teaspoon coarse salt

⅛ teaspoon freshly ground black pepper

Fruit, for dipping (see headnote)

1. In a 10-inch skillet, cook the bacon over medium heat for 8 to 10 minutes, or until crisp. Using a slotted spoon, transfer to a paper towel to drain. Snip with kitchen scissors or crumble into small bits.

2. Rub the inside of a flameproof ceramic fondue pot with the cut sides of the garlic. Discard the garlic, or reserve for another use. Add the goat cheese, mascarpone, and milk to the fondue pot and set over medium heat. (Check the manufacturer's instructions to see if a heat diffuser is necessary.) Heat, stirring constantly with a slotted spoon, for 5 minutes, or until melted and hot. Add the blue cheese and stir with a flat whisk until the mixture is light and creamy. Remove from the heat and sprinkle with the crumbled bacon.

3. Arrange the fruit on a platter and place it on the table. Place the tabletop heater in the center of the table and the fondue pot on top. Provide each diner with a fondue fork for spearing the fruit and dipping into the communal pot.

tip SHREDDING SEMI-SOFT CHEESE

To shred semi-soft cheese easily, wrap it in plastic wrap and place it in the freezer for 30 minutes, or until firm. Cold cheese shreds quickly with a handheld grater or in a food processor fit with a shredding blade.

FONTINA FONDUE with GRAPPA and CHOPPED BROCCOLI

PREP 30 min | COOK TIME (bread) 20 min | COOK TIME (fondue) 10 min | SERVES 4–6

The classic fondue is made with Gruyère and Emmental cheese melted with white wine and a splash of kirsch, a clear brandy distilled from cherry juice and pits. This riff on that tradition is made with imported Italian *fontina Val d'Aosta,* a rich, nutty cheese used to make *fonduta,* the famed fondue of northern Italy that combines cheese, egg yolks, and cream. The broccoli is a pretty touch but is optional, as is the crushed red pepper.

Implements Tongs, Rimmed Sheet Pan, 2- or 3-Quart Saucepan, Strainer, Fondue Pot, Slotted Spoon

Ingredients

1 loaf whole wheat Italian or French bread, cut into 1-inch cubes

¼ cup extra-virgin olive oil, plus more as needed

1 cup coarsely chopped (¼-inch pieces) broccoli florets, (optional)

½ teaspoon coarse salt

1 large clove garlic, halved lengthwise

1 cup pinot grigio or other dry white wine

1 tablespoon grappa or brandy

1 pound *fontina Val d'Aosta* cheese, rind removed and coarsely shredded (about 8 cups)

3 tablespoons all-purpose flour

Pinch of crushed red pepper (optional)

1. Preheat the oven to 350°F. Place the bread cubes in a large bowl and drizzle with the oil. Use tongs or your hands to toss the bread, coating it with the oil and adding a little more oil if the cubes aren't evenly coated. Spread the bread on a large rimmed sheet pan and bake for 20 minutes, or until very lightly toasted. Remove from the oven and let cool.

2. Heat to a boil a 2- or 3-quart saucepan half filled with water. Add the broccoli and salt and boil for 3 minutes, or until tender. Drain in a strainer and rinse with cold water. Set aside.

3. Rub the inside of a flameproof ceramic fondue pot with the cut sides of the garlic. Discard the garlic, or reserve for another use. Add the wine to the fondue pot and bring to a simmer over medium heat. (Check the manufacturer's instructions to see if a heat diffuser is necessary.) Add the grappa.

4. In a large bowl, combine the cheese and flour and toss to combine. Gradually add the cheese, a handful at a time, to the simmering wine, stirring vigorously with a slotted metal or wooden spoon after each addition until melted before adding more cheese. Fold the broccoli and red pepper into the melted cheese until blended.

5. Put the bread cubes on a platter or in a basket and place on the table. Place the tabletop heater in the center of the table and place the fondue pot on top. Provide each diner with a fondue fork for spearing the bread cubes and dipping into the communal pot.

Gratin

The word *gratin* is used for both the cookware and the food cooked in it, and to *gratinée* means to give a dish a crisp, golden brown top. Recipes that are *au gratin* have been baked (or broiled) in a shallow ovenproof dish or metal pan. The ingredients of a gratin are always topped with a generous shower of buttered bread crumbs, shredded or grated cheese, and/ or bits of butter. The shallow depth and broad surface of the dish ensures a generous ratio of crisped brown top to the rest of the ingredients.

The dishes are either round or oval and come in graduated sizes. White porcelain is classic, as is the handsome copper oval or round gratin with a stainless-steel interior surface and sturdy brass handles. But a gratin can be made of any heatproof material, including highly durable enameled cast iron, as long as the material can withstand the heat of both the oven and the broiler. The handiest sizes are the 12-inch oval with a capacity of 1½ quarts or the slightly larger oval with a capacity of 2½ quarts. The small (6- to 8-inch) oval or round gratin is perfect for individual gratinéed dishes, like creamed vegetables or creamed seafood.

Tips for Using

Porcelain gratins are handsome enough to double as serving dishes.

In classic gratin recipes, the ingredients are first cooked in another pan and then spread in the gratin dish and topped with a creamy sauce, buttered crumbs, and /or cheese.

To prevent messy spills, set a full gratin on a rimmed sheet pan before placing it in the oven to bake.

There are many variations on the gratin theme. Fish baked with a crumb topping, also and broiled peach halves topped with cookie crumbs and almonds, are both considered gratins.

To make a reduced-calorie gratin, omit the rich cream sauce, toss the ingredients with melted butter, and top with buttered crumbs and grated cheese. As long as the top is browned, it's a gratin.

Use gratins for cooking other dishes, such as baked apples, roasted fish fillets, baked stuffed tomatoes, or roasted potatoes.

Care in Using

Soak in warm water with dish detergent to loosen baked-on particles. A stiff dish brush will clean most gratins.

Porcelain gratins are dishwasher safe.

Always consult the manufacturer's instructions.

Alternatives

Baking dishes, preferably shallow, can be used in place of gratins. Be sure to check the manufacturer's instructions on whether they can withstand the heat of the broiler.

recipes

Yukon Gold and Sweet Potato Gratin with **Three Cheeses** | **Cauliflower, Shrimp, and Prosciutto Gratin**

YUKON GOLD and SWEET POTATO GRATIN with THREE CHEESES

PREP 30 min | COOK TIME 50 min | SERVES 6–8

Potato gratins are classic, but the combination of yellow Yukon Gold potatoes and orange sweet potatoes is novel. Quickly prepare the potatoes with two indispensable tools: the serrated peeler and a mandoline or other vegetable slicer. Rosemary gives the creamy sauce a distinctive profile that goes well with big flavors like grilled salmon, steaks, or lamb chops.

Implements 6-Quart Dutch Oven, 2-Quart Gratin Dish, Slotted Spoon, Ladle, Paring Knife, Square Spatula

Ingredients

2½ cups whole milk

1½ cups heavy cream

2 teaspoons coarse salt

2 teaspoons minced fresh rosemary

1 clove garlic, grated or finely chopped

⅛ teaspoon freshly ground black pepper

2 pounds Yukon Gold potatoes, peeled and sliced ¼ inch thick

2 pounds sweet potatoes, peeled and sliced ¼ inch thick

1½ teaspoons unsalted butter, softened

½ cup shredded Gruyère cheese

½ cup shredded white Cheddar cheese

½ cup grated Parmigiano-Reggiano cheese

1. In a 6-quart Dutch oven or other large, heavy pan, combine the milk, cream, salt, rosemary, garlic, and pepper. Place over medium heat and heat, stirring, for 3 minutes, or until small bubbles appear around the edges of the pan. Add the Yukon Gold and sweet potatoes, stir to coat with the milk mixture, and simmer gently, uncovered, for 10 to 12 minutes, until the potatoes are partially cooked. Remove from the heat.

2. Preheat the oven to 400°F. Rub the butter over the bottom and sides of a 2-quart gratin dish.

3. Use a slotted spoon to transfer half of the potatoes to the gratin dish. Sprinkle with half each of the Gruyère, Cheddar, and Parmigiano-Reggiano cheeses. Add the remaining potatoes. Use 2 forks to arrange the top layer of potatoes in a slightly overlapping design, evenly distributing the different-colored potatoes. Ladle the hot cream mixture over the potatoes and sprinkle with all of the remaining cheeses.

4. Bake for 35 minutes, or until the potatoes are tender when pierced with a skewer or the tip of a knife and the gratin is bubbling and golden.

5. Let the gratin rest for 10 minutes before serving. To serve, cut into squares and transfer to individual plates with a square spatula or server.

CAULIFLOWER, SHRIMP, and PROSCUITTO GRATIN

PREP 20 min | COOK TIME 40 min | SERVES 4

In this pretty gratin, cauliflower florets are blanketed with a thick béchamel and flavored with shrimp and slivers of prosciutto. The buttered bread crumbs and grated Parmigiano-Reggiano give the top both a golden glow and a crunchy texture, and the contrast of the soft cooked interior and the crisp topping is irresistible. Serve as a side dish with roasted fish, or as a light main dish, baking it in individual gratins and accompanying it with a green salad.

Implements 12-inch Oval Gratin Dish, 6-Quart Dutch Oven, Colander, 1½- to 2-Quart Saucepan, Flat Whisk, 10-inch Skillet, Large Spoon

Ingredients

1½ teaspoons unsalted butter, softened, plus 1 tablespoon

1 (1½- to 2-pound) head cauliflower, cut into 1- to 2-inch florets (6 to 8 cups)

2 teaspoons salt

BÉCHAMEL SAUCE

3 tablespoons unsalted butter

3 tablespoons all-purpose flour

1½ cups whole milk

½ cup heavy cream

2 tablespoons minced fresh chives

2 teaspoons grated lemon zest

1 teaspoon salt

⅛ teaspoon freshly ground black pepper

8 ounces uncooked frozen peeled small or medium shrimp, thawed

½ cup frozen peas, thawed

2 slices prosciutto or other ham, fat trimmed and slivered

½ cup fresh bread crumbs (see page 219)

3 tablespoons grated Parmigiano-Reggiano cheese

1. Preheat the oven to 400°F. Rub the 1½ teaspoons butter over the bottom and sides of a 12-inch oval gratin or 1½-quart shallow baking dish.

2. Half fill a 6-quart Dutch oven with water and bring to a boil. Add the cauliflower and salt and boil, uncovered, for 3 minutes, or until barely tender. Drain in a colander and set aside.

3. MAKE THE BÉCHAMEL SAUCE: In a 1½- to 2-quart saucepan, melt the butter over low heat. Add the flour, stir with a flat whisk until mixture is smooth, and then continue to cook, stirring, for 2 minutes. Gradually add the milk and cream while whisking constantly until smooth. Continue cooking, whisking gently, for 5 minutes, or until the sauce boils and thickens. Add the chives, lemon zest, salt, and pepper.

4. Spread the cauliflower in the prepared gratin. Sprinkle with the shrimp, peas, and prosciutto. Pour the béchamel sauce evenly over the top.

5. Melt the remaining 1 tablespoon of butter in a 10-inch skillet and remove from the heat. Add the bread crumbs and cheese to the butter and toss to coat. Sprinkle the crumbs evenly on the top of the gratin.

6. Bake for 35 minutes, or until the sauce is bubbling and the top is golden.

7. Let the gratin rest for 10 minutes before serving. Serve with a large spoon.

Making Fresh and Dried Toasted Bread Crumbs

To make fresh bread crumbs from soft (sandwich) bread, cut or tear the bread, including the crusts, into 1-inch pieces. To make fresh crumbs from Italian, French, or other crusty bread, cut off the bottom or other tough crust with a serrated knife. Cut or tear either type of bread into 1-inch pieces. Place the torn bread in a food processor and pulse until the crumbs are the desired consistency. It is difficult to determine the exact yield but, in general, 2 slices of sandwich bread or a 4-inch chunk of crusty bread will yield about 1 cup of coarse crumbs. To freeze leftover fresh bread crumbs, place them in a heavy-duty resealable plastic bag. They will keep for about 6 months.

To make dried toasted bread crumbs, spread coarse fresh bread crumbs on a rimmed sheet pan and toast in a preheated 350°F for 10 to 15 minutes, until golden. Let cool and grind in a food processor to the desired consistency. Store in an airtight container for up to 3 months.

Mussels in Fennel and
Orange Broth

*The weight of the mussel pot and the
heavy lid keeps all the heat and steam
inside the pot, helping the mussels to
steam evenly without having to stir.*

Laurent Tourondel CHEF AND AUTHOR, GO FISH

Mussel Pot

Rumor has it that Francis Staub designed his Staub Mussel Pot out of frustration at not being able to easily access the flavorful mussel juices at the bottom of a conventional pot. Made in France of enameled cast iron, the unique design—it's shaped like a giant mussel shell—has a removable stainless-steel strainer at the narrow end of the pot, making it easy to dip bread into the deep pool of juices. The smaller pot (2 quarts) has a matte black interior and gradated shades of Mediterranean blue on the exterior. The larger pot (6 quarts) is black matte inside and out. When the lid is inverted, it becomes a convenient receptacle for empty shells. Both pots are handsome enough to go from stove to table and are perfect for sharing.

Tips for Using

The small pot holds 2 pounds of mussels (or small clams), enough for one voracious appetite or two normal appetites. The larger, or family-sized, mussel pot holds up to 5 pounds of mussels, enough for 4 servings.

Because the space inside the mussel pot is restricted by the strainer, mussels cooked in the mussel pot will take longer to open than will mussels cooked in a Dutch oven, braiser, or other broad pan. But the slow, steady heat renders the mussels plump and juicy every time.

Don't be tempted to lift the lid and peek at their progress, as it will lengthen the cooking time.

To flavor the broth, sauté aromatics such as spices, herbs, and wine right in the pot over medium heat; bring the liquid to a boil to reduce slightly, and then add the mussels.

Slide the strainer out of the pot for sautéing. Slide it back into place before adding the mussels. It goes in easily, even when the pot is hot.

Use the mussel pot to steam clams, too. Because clams have thicker shells, 2½ pounds will take up about the same amount of space inside the pot as would 2 pounds of mussels.

The pot is also good for steaming clams and mussels for pasta, as the flavorful juices can be quickly poured off without danger of spilling the contents.

Care in Using

Wash in warm, soapy water. Putting it in the dishwasher is not recommended.

Alternatives

A 7- or 8-quart Dutch oven, a large braiser, or 5-quart sauté pan with lid can be substituted. Mussels will take less time to open because they will have more space to spread out in the pan.

recipes

Mussels in Fennel and Orange Broth | Manila Clams in Coconut Milk with Southeast Asian Flavors

MUSSELS in FENNEL and ORANGE BROTH

PREP 20 min | **COOK TIME** 20 min | **SERVES** 2 as a main course or 4 as an appetizer

In this recipe, fennel three ways—the fresh bulb, the fernlike fronds, and the dried seeds—are used to infuse both the mussels and their broth. The sweetness of the fennel is perfectly balanced with the addition of white wine and orange zest. You can easily increase the recipe and make it in the family-sized mussel pot, a 7- to 8-quart Dutch oven, or a 5-quart sauté pan with a lid. Don't forget the warm baguette for soaking up the broth.

Implements Mussel Pot, Mortar and Pestle, Oven Mitts, Tongs or Slotted Spoon, Large Bowl

Ingredients

2 pounds mussels (see Tip)

2 tablespoons unsalted butter

½ cup chopped yellow onion

½ cup chopped fennel

1 tablespoon coarsely chopped fresh Italian parsley

1 tablespoon chopped fennel fronds (optional)

2 teaspoons fennel seeds

1 tablespoon julienned orange zest

1 teaspoon chopped garlic

1 cup dry white wine

1 teaspoon coarse salt

1. Rinse and debeard the mussels and refrigerate until needed.

2. Remove the strainer from a 2-quart mussel pot and set aside. Heat the butter in the mussel pot over medium heat until sizzling. Add the onion, chopped fennel, parsley, and fennel fronds, and sauté, stirring occasionally, about 5 minutes until the vegetables are wilted.

3. While the vegetables are cooking, coarsely crush the fennel seeds with a mortar and pestle or bruise them by cutting into them with the sharp edge of a heavy knife. Add to the sautéed vegetables along with the orange zest and garlic and sauté for 1 minute. Add the wine, bring to a boil, and boil for 2 minutes. Add the salt.

4. With a mitted hand, slide the strainer back into the pot. Add the mussels. Cover and cook over medium heat for 8 to 10 minutes, until the mussels have opened. If not all of the mussels have opened, use tongs or a slotted spoon to transfer the opened mussels to a bowl and cover with aluminum foil. Then, re-cover and continue to cook the unopened mussels for 2 minutes, or until all are opened. Discard any mussels that do not open. Remove the pot from the heat, and return the mussels in the bowl to the mussel pot.

5. Bring the mussel pot to the table. Remove the lid and invert it on the table to hold the empty mussel shells. It's fun to share the mussels directly from the pot. Dip hunks of crusty warm baguette into the pot to sop up the flavorful juices that will pool through the strainer. Or spoon the mussels with a little bit of the juices into shallow individual bowls and serve with bread.

tip MUSSEL AND CLAM PRIMER

The number of mussels or clams in a pound can vary, but generally about 1 pound per person is an ample serving. Clams and mussels are sometimes gaping slightly when you buy them. This is natural, but the shell should close tightly when tapped lightly with a finger. If not, the mollusk is dead and must be discarded. Do not store live shellfish in a plastic bag. Instead, the moment you get them home, place them in a colander and rinse well with cold water. If they feel gritty, scrub them with a stiff brush and rinse them a few more times. Drain well and transfer to a bowl. Cover with a wet towel and refrigerate for up to 48 hours before cooking.

To remove the filaments, called the beard, that sometimes protrude from mussels, use a small pair of pliers, or protect your fingertips with the tip of a dish cloth, and pull firmly.

MANILA CLAMS in COCONUT MILK with SOUTHEAST ASIAN FLAVORS

PREP 20 min | **COOK TIME** 30 min | **SERVES** 2 as a main course or 4 as an appetizer

True, this isn't a French recipe. But it is a terrific way to put your French mussel pot to use. Select small, relatively thin-shelled Manila or other clams for this exotically spiced clam dish. Shop for the lemongrass and galangal in markets where fresh Asian produce is sold. Fresh galangal looks a little like fresh ginger, which can be substituted here, but the flavor of galangal is a bit more peppery. You can serve this dish with chunks of crusty bread to sop up the juices, but bowls of hot jasmine rice will complement the flavors better. If you have a larger pot, the recipe doubles easily.

Implements Mussel Pot, Oven Mitts, Tongs or Slotted Spoon, Ladle

Ingredients

2½ pounds Manila clams (see Tip, page 222)

2 stalks lemongrass

1 (14-ounce) can coconut milk

1 tablespoon thinly sliced fresh galangal or peeled fresh ginger

1 green onion, white and green parts, trimmed and cut on the diagonal into ¼-inch-thick slices

1 teaspoon coarse salt

2 cloves garlic, bruised with knife

1 serrano or other small green chile, halved lengthwise

1 cup chopped plum tomato

¼ cup chopped fresh cilantro

3 tablespoons freshly squeezed lime juice

4 cups hot cooked jasmine rice

1. Rinse and scrub the clams and refrigerate until needed.

2. Trim off and discard the woody ends from the lemongrass stalks. Peel away 2 or 3 layers of dry outer leaves from the bulblike portions, mash with the back of a heavy knife to loosen and tenderize the fibers, and then chop finely. You should have about 2 tablespoons of lemongrass. Set aside.

3. Remove the strainer from the mussel pot and set aside. Combine the coconut milk, lemongrass, galangal, green onion, salt, garlic, and chile in the mussel pot. Place over medium-low heat, cover, and cook for 20 minutes to blend the flavors.

4. In a small serving bowl, combine the tomato, cilantro, and 1 tablespoon of the lime juice and toss gently to mix. Reserve.

5. When the coconut milk mixture is ready, lift the lid and, with a mitted hand, slide the strainer back into the pot. Add the clams, cover, and cook over medium heat for 10 to 12 minutes, until the clams have opened. If not all of the clams have opened, use tongs or a slotted spoon to transfer the opened clams to a bowl and cover with aluminum foil. Then, re-cover and continue to cook the unopened clams for 2 minutes, or until all are opened. Discard any clams that do not open. Remove the pot from the heat. Add the remaining 2 tablespoons of lime juice to the coconut and clam broth, and return the clams in the bowl to the mussel pot. Top the clams with the tomato mixture.

6. Divide the rice among 4 shallow bowls. Bring the mussel pot to the table. Invert the mussel pot lid on the table to hold the empty clam shells. Tip the pot and ladle some of the coconut and clam juice onto the rice. Transfer a few clams at a time to the bowl of rice or eat the clams right out of the pot. While eating the clams, dip them into the broth left in the mussel pot.

Omelet Pan

An omelet pan is similar to a skillet but, for ease in handling, the sides should slope continuously (without a ridge) so the cooked omelet can roll out of the pan easily. It also has a super-comfortable handle that comes straight out of the side of the pan, rather than tilting upward. They are typically made from various stainless-steel constructions, cast iron, and cast aluminum. A 7- to 8-inch pan is perfect for a two- or three-egg omelet, just enough for one serving. A 9- or 10-inch pan is good for an omelet for two.

Some cooks prefer a nonstick finish for cooking omelets, while others favor the classic French iron pan. If you decide on an iron or steel pan, you will need to season and maintain it carefully. Other choices include anodized aluminum, stainless-clad aluminum, and stainless-clad copper.

Tips for Using

If you prefer a French iron omelet pan, follow the manufacturer's instructions carefully for seasoning it. In general, seasoning is simple: scour the pan with steel wool, rinse it in warm, soapy water, dry it well, heat it until hot, rub it with an oil-soaked paper towel, and let stand overnight before using.

An omelet is made in a matter of minutes, so everything must be ready to go. Have the warm filling in a side pan or at room temperature in a small bowl, and have the eggs beaten.

Using the correct temperature is important. When the butter foams and then the foam begins to subside, the pan is hot enough to add the eggs.

Care in Using

An improperly cleaned omelet pan will become sticky. To clean a sticky pan, rub it hard with a teaspoon of table salt and a handful of paper towels.

Once a French iron pan has been seasoned, it can be wiped clean with a paper towel. If it needs to be washed with soap and water, you must reseason it before using.

Always consult the manufacturer's instructions.

Alternatives

Any well-seasoned 8-inch cast-iron or other heavy skillet with a nonstick finish will work for omelets.

recipes

Bacon, Spinach, and Brie Omelet | Potato, Caramelized Onion, and Salmon Omelet

BACON, SPINACH, and BRIE OMELET

PREP 15 min | COOK TIME 10 min | SERVES 1

A tablespoon of water is added to the beaten eggs because once they hit the heat, the water will be converted to steam, giving the eggs an extra lift for a fluffier omelet. Read the entire recipe before beginning, make sure all of the ingredients are ready, and have a plate nearby to catch the omelet as it rolls out of the pan. To serve two, double the recipe and use a 9- to 10-inch pan.

Implements 10-inch Skillet, Slotted Spoon, Tongs, Flat Whisk, Medium Bowl, 7- or 8-inch Omelet Pan, Flat-Edged Rubber or Silicone Spatula

Ingredients

2 slices bacon

¾ cup lightly packed torn spinach leaves

Coarse salt and freshly ground black pepper

1-inch square Brie cheese, including the rind, cut into ⅛-inch-thick slices

2 or 3 large eggs

1 tablespoon water

1 tablespoon unsalted butter

1. In a 10-inch skillet, cook the bacon over medium heat for 8 to 10 minutes, or until crisp. Using a slotted spoon, transfer to paper towels to drain. When cool, chop coarsely and set aside.

2. Pour out the fat, leaving just a thin film in the bottom of the hot skillet. Add the spinach and cook, stirring, for about 45 seconds, or until wilted. Using tongs, transfer the spinach to a small bowl. Add a pinch of salt and a grinding of pepper to the spinach. Place the Brie in a separate small bowl.

3. Break the eggs into a medium bowl and add the water. Stir with a flat whisk, spiral whisk, or a fork just until blended. Add a pinch of salt and a grinding of pepper.

4. Heat a 7- or 8-inch omelet pan or skillet over medium heat for about 1 minute, or until hot. Add the butter and heat for 10 seconds, or until the butter foams and then begins to subside. Immediately pour the eggs into the center of the pan. They should sizzle on contact. Cook for about 10 seconds, or until the bottom is just set. Using a flat-edged rubber or silicone spatula, pull the set edges from the sides of the pan toward the center and tilt the pan to allow the unset egg to run toward the sides of the pan. Cook for 1 to 2 minutes, until the eggs are soft set.

5. Sprinkle the bacon on top of the eggs. Place the Brie slices down the center of the eggs. Use tongs or a fork to put the spinach on top of the cheese.

6. Remove the pan from the heat. Using a flat-edged rubber or silicone spatula, turn the one-third of the omelet nearest the handle over the filling in the center. Holding the pan by the handle, tilt the pan. With the edge of the spatula guide the omelet as it rolls out onto a plate, forming a seam-side-down envelope. Serve at once.

POTATO, CARAMELIZED ONION, and SALMON OMELET

PREP 15 min | COOK TIME about 35 min | SERVES 1

The potatoes and onions in this hearty omelet can be the starting point for many omelet fillings. Substitute bits of smoked ham, prosciutto, smoked trout, even bacon for the salmon. You can also omit the potatoes and instead add a couple of sliced cooked asparagus.

Implements 8- or 9-inch Skillet, Flat-Edged Spatula, Flat Whisk, Medium Bowl, 7- or 8-inch Omelet Pan, Flat-Edged Rubber or Silicone Spatula

Ingredients

1 tablespoon unsalted butter

1½ teaspoons olive oil

1 small Yukon Gold or other potato, cooked, peeled, and sliced ¼ inch thick

1 cup thinly, vertically sliced yellow onion

Pinch of coarse salt

Freshly ground black pepper

2 or 3 large eggs

1 tablespoon water

1 (2 x 6-inch) slice smoked salmon, cut into ¼-inch-wide strips

1½ teaspoons tablespoon minced fresh chives

1. In an 8- or 9-inch skillet, heat ½ tablespoon of the butter with the oil over medium heat until the butter has melted. Add the potatoes and cook, without turning, for 7 to 8 minutes, or until browned. Turn the potatoes over with a flat spatula and push to one side. Add the onion, decrease the heat to medium–low, and cook, stirring, for 10 to 12 minutes, until the onion is golden. Sprinkle with salt and pepper. Remove the pan from the heat and set aside.

2. Place the eggs in a medium bowl and add the water. Stir with a flat whisk, spiral whisk, or a fork just until blended. Add a pinch of salt and a grinding of pepper.

3. Heat a 7- or 8-inch omelet pan over medium heat for about 1 minute, or until hot. Add the remaining ½ table-spoon of butter and heat for 10 seconds, or until the butter foams and then begins to subside. Immediately pour the eggs into the center of the pan. They should sizzle on contact. Cook for about 10 seconds, or until the bottom is just set. Using a flat-edged silicone spatula, pull the set edges from the sides of the pan toward the center and tilt the pan to allow the unset egg to run toward the sides of the pan. Cook for 1 to 2 minutes, or until the eggs are soft set.

4. With a spoon, spread the potatoes and onions in the center of the omelet. Top with the pieces of salmon.

5. Remove the pan from the heat. Using a flat-edged rubber or silicone spatula, turn the third of the omelet nearest the handle over the filling in the center. Holding the pan by the handle, tilt the pan. With the edge of the spatula, guide the omelet as it rolls out onto a plate, forming a seam-side-down envelope. Serve at once.

Mushrooms

Prized for their rich, almost meaty flavor, mushrooms are fungi, not plants. Both wild and cultivated mushrooms are prized for their distinctive shapes, colors, and tastes. Here is a small selection of favorites.

Chanterelle The most common chanterelles are golden yellow, have an earthy, fruity taste and peppery bite; a long, edible shank; and a top that opens with a gentle curve, like a flower. These wild mushrooms are available dried year-round and fresh from midsummer through fall.

Cremini This cultivated mushroom, also known as "baby bella," related to the white button, is widely available in produce markets. It has a large, light brown, firm cap and a robust flavor. Use in soups or stews, or sauté as a side dish.

King Oyster Also known as the royal trumpet or king trumpet, the king oyster mushroom grows in clusters in tall, thick-stemmed trumpet shapes. The completely edible stems are white and the flat cap is dark gray; both have a meaty flavor and texture. Slice these lengthwise into 1/4-inch-thick "steaks," flour or bread the slices lightly, and fry or grill them.

Morel Famous for its nutty, earthy flavor, the highly prized wild morel has a long, conical, crevice-laced cap and tender, hollow stem. It ranges in color from light tan to dark brown or black. Both the cap and stem are edible, although the larger the morel, the tougher the stem. Always available dried, the morel is one of the first mushrooms to appear in the spring. Sauté them in butter and then simmer them in heavy cream and serve as a sauce on pan-browned veal chops.

Oyster Also known as the pleurotus, the cultivated oyster mushroom, available fresh and dried, has a delicate flavor and softly ruffled cap that resembles an oyster shell. The entire mushroom is edible, raw or cooked. Cook these with white wine to make a simple pan sauce for serving over sautéed chicken breasts.

Portobello A cultivated mushroom with a large (4 to 6 inches), flat cap, the portobello, which is a mature cremini, has an intense, woodsy, almost meaty taste. It can be grilled and served on a bun like a hamburger. The stems are edible, but are best finely chopped and sautéed or added to soups and stews.

Shiitake The shiitake has a broad cap, spongy texture, and woodsy taste. These widely cultivated mushrooms, available fresh and dried, have tough stems that must be discarded (or reserved to flavor stock). Their meaty taste is appreciated in mushroom or reduced wine sauces, or thinly sliced, sautéed in olive oil with garlic, and tossed with pasta.

When you bake sliced potatoes with butter in a very heavy pan in a very hot oven, you can turn them out onto a platter and they form a cake that is crisp and brown on the outside, tender and buttery inside. The only trick is that the potatoes must crust on the outside and not stick to the pan.

Julia Child, AUTHOR, T*HE FRENCH CHEF COOKBOOK*

Classic Pommes Anna

Pommes Anna Pan

Buttery *pommes Anna* and this handsome tin-lined copper pan of the same name are classic French inventions. Famed French chef Adolphe Duglére invented the dish for the celebrated beauty Anna Deslions during the reign of Napoleon III. It's a simple recipe of thinly sliced potatoes layered with clarified butter and baked until the exterior is crisp and golden and the interior is ethereally soft and creamy.

The pan is actually comprised of two round pans, one about ½ inch larger than the other. The smaller, deeper half is piled high with layers of sliced potatoes coated with butter. The larger half is inverted on top and used as both a cover while the potatoes are baking and as a serving dish for the finished potato cake. Both pans have beautiful solid brass handles, and are available in small (individual servings), medium (four to six servings), and large (six to eight servings) sizes.

Tips for Using

You can use the pan both on the stove top and in the oven.

Use a mandoline, a handheld slicer, or food processor to thinly slice the potatoes.

Use russet or other baking potatoes. If you rinse or soak the slices in water, drain well and dry with kitchen towels. If the potatoes are wet, they won't stick together properly.

Use the large inverted lid for serving the potatoes. Protect your fingers with oven mitts and invert the smaller pan into the larger one. Or, if you prefer, invert the potatoes onto a serving platter.

If using the lid for serving, do not cut the *pommes Anna*. The tin lining is soft and scratches easily.

Many recipes, including the classic, use clarified butter, but it's not a necessity.

Care in Using

Wash in warm, soapy water and scrub clean with a soft plastic brush.

Washing in a dishwasher is not recommended.

Shine the copper like French chefs do: rub it with a halved lemon dipped in coarse salt.

Always consult the manufacturer's instructions.

Alternatives

Use an iron or other heavy ovenproof skillet. Cover the potatoes with buttered aluminum foil and weight them with a heavy ovenproof lid while cooking on top of the stove.

recipes

Classic Pommes Anna | Pommes Anna with Herbs and Mushrooms

CLASSIC POMMES ANNA

PREP 30 min | COOK TIME 1 hr 15 min | SERVES 6–8

Nothing more than thinly sliced potatoes slowly cooked in butter, *pommes Anna* is both simple and sophisticated.

Implements Small Saucepan, Mandoline, Colander, Silicone Brush, 9½-inch *Pommes Anna* Pan, Large Spatula, Thin Nonmetal Spoon

Ingredients

4 pounds russet potatoes, peeled

1 cup (2 sticks) unsalted butter, melted or clarified (page 323)

Coarse salt

Freshly ground pepper

1. Place one oven rack in the lowest position in the oven. Preheat the oven to 425°F.

2. Using a mandoline, a handheld slicer, or a food processor, slice the potatoes into rounds ⅛ inch thick. (There will be approximately 8 cups of sliced potatoes.) Place the slices in a bowl, add cold water to cover, and then drain well in a colander. Spread the slices on two kitchen towels and pat them dry with another towel.

3. Brush the bottom and sides of the smaller and deeper half (bottom) of a 9½-inch *pommes Anna* pan with a generous film of the butter. Butter only the bottom of the larger half (top), which is the lid. If using an ovenproof skillet instead, butter both the sides and bottom of the pan, as well as one side of a sheet of aluminum foil cut large enough to cover the top of the skillet.

4. Heat the bottom of the *pommes Anna* pan or the skillet over low heat. When the pan is hot enough for a potato slice to sizzle on contact, quickly arrange a layer of potato slices in concentric circles to cover the bottom of the pan or skillet. The slices should overlap slightly. Drizzle with about 2 tablespoons of the butter and brush to distribute it evenly on the surface of the potatoes. Sprinkle generously with salt and pepper. With the pan or skillet still on the heat, repeat with additional layers, adding about 2 tablespoons of the butter and a sprinkling of salt and pepper to each layer, slightly mounding the slices in the center until you have used all of the potatoes, ending with a layer of potatoes and butter on top.

5. Increase the heat to medium and cook 10 minutes, occasionally press down on the potatoes with a large spatula. Cover the pan with the buttered lid or, if using the skillet, the foil, buttered side down, and press a flat ovenproof lid on top of the foil to weight the potatoes. Transfer the pan or skillet to the lowest rack in the oven and bake for 25 minutes. Uncover the pan and bake for 25 to 30 minutes more, or until the top is golden.

6. Remove from the oven and let stand undisturbed for 10 minutes. Run a thin, nonmetal spatula around the edges to loosen the potatoes. If using the *pommes Anna* pan, place the top back on the pan, invert the pans, and lift off the smaller pan. If using a skillet, place an inverted platter over the skillet, invert the skillet and platter, and lift off the skillet. If some of the potatoes have stuck to the pan or skillet, simply use a spatula to scoop them out and push them back into place.

7. Cut into wedges with a knife and serve with a spatula. Alternatively, the potatoes can be served directly from the pan, using a nonmetal spoon. Serve at once.

tip AVOID STICKING POTATOES

To guarantee that no potatoes stick to the bottom of the pan, cut a circle of parchment paper the size of the bottom of the pan and place it in the well-buttered pan. Butter the paper and arrange the potatoes directly on the buttered parchment.

POMMES ANNA with HERBS and MUSHROOMS

PREP 30 min I COOK TIME 1 hr 15 min I SERVES 6–8

Some extravagant mushrooms make this classic dish even more special.

Implements
Small Saucepan, Mandoline, Colander, Silicone Brush, 9½-inch *Pommes Anna* Pan, Large Spatula, Thin Nonmetal Spoon

Ingredients

4 pounds russet potatoes, peeled

1 cup (2 sticks) unsalted butter, melted or clarified (page 323)

1½ cups (4 ounces) fresh chanterelle, morel, or other wild or cultivated mushrooms, finely chopped

¼ cup finely chopped shallots

1 tablespoon finely chopped fresh Italian parsley

1 teaspoon minced fresh thyme

1 teaspoon minced fresh rosemary

Coarse salt and freshly ground pepper

1. Place one oven rack in the lowest position in the oven. Preheat the oven to 425°F.

2. Using a mandoline, a handheld slicer, or a food processor, slice the potatoes into rounds ⅛ inch thick. (There will be approximately 8 cups of sliced potatoes.) Place the slices in a bowl, add cold water to cover, and then drain well in a colander. Spread the slices on two kitchen towels and pat them dry with another towel.

3. Heat 1 tablespoon of the butter in a large heavy skillet over medium heat until hot enough to sizzle a pinch of the mushrooms. Add the remaining mushrooms, the shallots, parsley, thyme, and rosemary, and cook, stirring, over medium-low heat for 10 minutes, or until the mushrooms are tender. Remove from the heat and set aside.

4. Brush the bottom and sides of the smaller and deeper half (bottom) of a 9½-inch *pommes Anna* pan with a generous film of the butter. Butter only the bottom of the larger half (top), which is the lid. If using an oven-proof skillet instead, butter both the sides and bottom of the pan, as well as one side of a sheet of aluminum foil cut large enough to cover the top of the skillet.

5. Heat the bottom half of the *pommes Anna* pan or skillet over low heat. When the pan is hot enough for a potato slice to sizzle on contact, quickly arrange a layer of potato slices in concentric circles to cover the bottom of the pan. The slices should overlap slightly. Drizzle with about 2 tablespoons of the butter and brush to distribute it evenly on the surface of the potatoes. Sprinkle generously with salt and pepper. Sprinkle with about one-third of the mushroom mixture. With the pan or skillet still on the heat, repeat with additional layers, adding about 2 tablespoons of the butter, a sprinkling of salt and pepper, and one-third of the remaining mushrooms to each layer, slightly mounding the slices in the center until you have used all the potatoes, mushrooms, and butter, ending with a layer of potatoes on top.

6. Increase the heat to medium and cook for 10 minutes; occasionally press down on the potatoes with a large spatula. Cover the pan with the buttered lid or, If using the skillet, the foil, buttered side down, and press a flat ovenproof lid on top of the foil to weight the potatoes. Transfer the pan or skillet to the lowest rack in the oven and bake for 25 minutes. Uncover and bake for 25 to 30 minutes more, or until the top is golden.

7. Remove from the oven and let stand undisturbed for 10 minutes. Run a thin, nonmetal spatula around the edges to loosen the potatoes. If using the *pommes Anna* pan, place the top back on the pan, invert the pans, and lift off the smaller pan. If using a skillet, place an inverted platter over the skillet, invert the skillet and platter, and lift off the skillet. If some of the potatoes have stuck to the pan or skillet, simply use a spatula to scoop them out and push them back into place, so you have a perfectly round cake with a layer of browned crispy potatoes on top.

8. Cut into wedges with a knife and serve with a spatula. Alternatively, the potatoes can be served directly from the pan, using a nonmetal spoon. Serve at once.

Raclette Grill

Raclette is the name of a cheese, the name of a dish of melted cheese with boiled potatoes, and the name of an electric grill for preparing the dish. The dish dates back hundreds of years to when Alpine shepherds spent days in the mountains with their herds. There, they would eat simple meals of cheese melted on hot rocks and potatoes cooked in a campfire. They would warm the entire round of cheese and, as it melted, they would scrape it—*raclette* is from the French *racler,* "to scrape"—onto the hot potatoes.

A modern electric raclette grill makes it possible to reproduce this dish in today's kitchen. Instead of using a whole round of cheese, cheese slices are melted in eight small individual trays under the heating element. Meanwhile, foods such as shrimp, thin fish fillets, thin slices of filet mignon or other tender cuts, or strips of pounded chicken breasts slowly cook on the grill above the element. The potatoes, classic for raclette, are boiled until tender, halved, and kept warm on the grill.

This versatile, efficient appliance also comes with eight heat-resistant spatulas for scraping the cheese from the trays and onto potatoes or other foods.

Tips for Using

The traditional raclette meal is melted cheese, boiled potatoes, and cornichons and/or pickled onions.

Slices of *speck* (Italian brine or smoke-cured pork), *bresaola* (Italian dried, salted beef), prosciutto, or *serrano* ham are delicious served with the raclette and potatoes.

Have ready ⅛-inch-thick cheese slices arranged on a platter, for melting in the individual trays.

Cheeses other than raclette can be melted on the trays, including Cheddar, mozzarella, Gruyère, Comté, Emmental, Manchego, *scamorza,* or Fontina.

Because it must be plugged into an electrical outlet, the raclette grill is perfect for a buffet party.

Ready all the foods in small bowls or on platters and let people select what appeals to them.

Care in Using

When the grill unit is cool, wipe it clean with a damp cloth.

Wash the grill plate, individual trays, and scrapers in warm, soapy water.

Always consult the manufacturer's instructions.

Alternatives

The cheese can be thinly sliced, layered in a baking dish, and heated in a 375°F oven for 6 to 8 minutes, until melted. Use a small, wide spatula to transfer portions of the cheese to individual plates. Pass a bowl of hot potatoes and assorted pickles to eat with the melted cheese. Or, use a toaster oven to melt the cheese and prepare the variations (pages 234–35).

recipes

Classic Cheese and Potato Raclette | Shrimp with Tomatoes, Basil, and Brie | Miniature Bell Peppers with Thyme and Comté Cheese | Fresh Fruit with Walnuts and Roquefort

CLASSIC CHEESE and POTATO RACLETTE

PREP time 30 min | COOK TIME 30 min | SERVES 8

This popular après-ski treat is the perfect winter meal for a casual get-together. Do as much preparation ahead of time as possible. Boil the potatoes and keep them warm in an oven set to the lowest temperature. Slice all the cheese and have it arranged on a platter, and ready all the other accompaniments. A big green salad will round out the menu. Pour a full-bodied red wine.

Implements Large Saucepan, Colander, Cheese Knife (Optional), Strainer, Raclette Grill

Ingredients

16 small Yukon Gold or other boiling potatoes, unpeeled

1 to 1½ pounds raclette cheese

2 (5-ounce) jars small pickled onions

1 (15-ounce) jar French cornichons, or
2 cups chopped sour pickles

1 pound assorted thinly sliced cured meat such as prosciutto, *bresaola* (Italian air-dried beef), *speck* (Italian brine or smoke-cured ham), and/or *serrano* ham

Freshly ground black pepper

1. In a large saucepan, combine the potatoes with water to cover. Bring to a boil over medium heat, cover, then cook over low heat for 20 minutes, or until a skewer slides easily into the center of a potato. Drain in a colander, transfer to a baking dish, and keep warm in an oven turned to the lowest setting.

2. With a large knife, trim off the rind from the cheese and discard. Use the same knife or a cheese knife to cut the cheese into ⅛- to ¼-inch-thick slices. Cut the slices into 3-inch squares and arrange on a platter. Place the platter on the table.

3. Drain the onions in a strainer and transfer to a small serving bowl. Drain the cornichons in the strainer, and transfer to a second small serving bowl. Arrange the meats on 1 or 2 platters. Place the pickles and the meats on the table.

4. Place the raclette grill on a buffet table or dining table and plug it in. It will take 20 minutes to heat fully. Pile the boiled potatoes on top of the grill portion of the raclette to keep warm, or leave them in the baking dish and place on the table.

5. Outfit each diner with a plate. Then invite each diner to place a slice or two of cheese in an individual tray and place it under the heating element for 2 to 3 minutes, until fully melted.

6. To eat, slice a potato on the plate and, using a scraper, spread the melted cheese over the potatoes. Add a generous grinding of pepper, if desired. Accompany with the onions, cornichons, and meats.

SHRIMP with TOMATOES, BASIL, and BRIE

PREP 20 min | COOK TIME 6 to 8 min | SERVES 8 as part of a raclette buffet

Implements Large Saucepan, Colander, Raclette Grill

Ingredients

16 small Yukon Gold or other boiling
potatoes, unpeeled (optional)

24 large shrimp, peeled and deveined, tails left on

2 tablespoons extra-virgin olive oil

1 clove garlic, grated or finely chopped

2 tablespoons torn fresh basil leaves

6 to 8 ripe plum tomatoes, cut into ½-inch chunks

Coarse salt

8 ounces Brie cheese

1. Combine the potatoes with water to cover. Bring to a boil over medium heat, cover, then cook over low heat for 20 minutes, or until a skewer slides easily into the center of a potato. Drain in a colander, transfer to a baking dish, and keep warm in an oven turned to the lowest setting.

2. In a large bowl, combine the shrimp, olive oil, garlic, and 1 tablespoon of the basil and stir to coat. Refrigerate until ready to cook. Place the tomatoes in a small bowl, add the remaining 1 tablespoon of basil and a pinch of salt, and stir gently to mix.

3. Cut the Brie, including the rind, into 8 slices each ¼ inch thick. Cut each slice into 3-inch lengths and set aside.

4. Place the raclette grill on a buffet table or dining table and plug it in. It will take 20 minutes to heat fully. Pile the boiled potatoes on top of the grill portion of the raclette to keep warm, or leave them in the baking dish for a few minutes longer before putting them on the table.

5. When ready to cook, divide the shrimp evenly among the raclette trays. Top with a spoonful of the tomatoes. Place two 3-inch lengths of cheese on top of each portion of shrimp and tomatoes.

6. Place the trays under the heating element and cook for 6 to 8 minutes, until the shrimp are fully cooked and the cheese is melted. Let guests help themselves to the potatoes and use a scraper to scrape the contents of the trays onto their plates.

MINIATURE BELL PEPPERS with THYME and COMTÉ CHEESE

PREP 20 min | COOK TIME 10 to 12 min | SERVES 8 as part of a raclette buffet

Implements Raclette Grill

Ingredients

16 small Yukon Gold or other boiling
potatoes, unpeeled (optional)

1 (1-pound) box multicolored miniature bell
peppers, halved lengthwise and stems removed,
or 2 large red and/or yellow bell peppers, seeded
and cut lengthwise into ¼-inch-wide strips

1 tablespoon extra-virgin olive oil

1 teaspoon fresh thyme leaves

Coarse salt and freshly ground black pepper

4 ounces Comté or Gruyère cheese, shaved into curls

1. Combine the potatoes with water to cover. Bring to a boil over medium heat, cover, then cook over low heat for 20 minutes, or until a skewer slides easily into the center of a potato. Drain in a colander, transfer to a baking dish, and keep warm in an oven turned to the lowest setting.

2. Combine the peppers, olive oil, thyme leaves, a sprinkling of salt and a grinding of pepper in a bowl and toss to mix.

3. Place the raclette grill on a buffet table or dining table and plug it in. It will take 20 minutes to heat fully. Pile the boiled potatoes on top of the grill portion of the raclette to keep warm, or leave them in the baking dish for a few minutes longer before putting them on the table.

4. When ready to cook, divide the peppers evenly among the raclette trays, spreading them in a single layer. Place the trays under the heating element and cook for 6 to 8 minutes, until the peppers begin to blister. Remove each tray and place 2 curls of cheese on each portion of peppers. Place the trays back under the heating element and cook for 3 to 4 minutes, until the cheese begins to melt.

5. Let guests help themselves to the potatoes and use a scraper to scrape the contents of the trays onto their plates.

FRESH FRUIT with WALNUTS and ROQUEFORT

PREP 15 min | **COOK TIME** 6 to 8 min | **SERVES** 8 as part of a raclette buffet

This warm fruit raclette can be served as dessert at the end of an all raclette feast.

Implements Raclette Grill

Ingredients

3 or 4 ripe Bartlett pears, or 4 ripe peaches or figs
2 teaspoons balsamic vinegar
½ cup broken walnuts
4 ounces Roquefort cheese, crumbled
1 French baguette, thinly sliced

1. Place the raclette grill on a buffet table or dining table and plug it in. It will take 20 minutes to heat fully.

2. If serving pears, peel, halve, and core and cut into ¼-inch wedges. If serving peaches, peel, halve, and pit and cut into ¼-inch wedges. If serving figs, halve lengthwise. Divide the prepared fruit evenly among the raclette trays. Drizzle each portion with ¼ teaspoon of the vinegar. Sprinkle each portion with 1 tablespoon of the walnuts. Top each portion with an equal amount of the cheese.

3. Place the trays under the heating element and cook for 6 to 8 minutes, until the cheese has melted and the fruit is warmed.

4. Let guests use a scraper to scrape the contents of the trays onto their plates. Serve with the bread.

8 | The INDIAN KITCHEN

The Indian Pantry

India is a country of contrasts, with cool mountains in the north, tropical plains in the south, and a heady mix of religions and customs in every corner. Not surprisingly, this cauldron of differences has produced a varied, complex cuisine that inevitably attracts the adventurous cook. The diversity of Indian cooking is melded into a single culinary tradition by the importance of spices in every dish. To stitch the culinary quilt together the following pages focus on the *tawa* and *karahi*, two pieces of cookware found in every Indian kitchen, along with the electric spice grinder. The Indian kitchen's most commonly used spices and ingredients include cumin, garam masala, and ghee, and as each pinch of spice hits the hot *tawa*, you draw closer to the heart and soul of Indian cooking.

Ghee

This staple of the Indian pantry is what Western cooks call clarified butter. Ghee can be bought in tins, but the flavor is better if you make it yourself. The process is simple: melt butter, let the milk solids separate from the fat and sink to the bottom of the pan, and then pour off the clear liquid, or ghee. The solids have a lower smoking point than the fat, so they burn at high temperatures, plus they promote rancidity, especially if refrigeration is not available. (See page 323 for the technique.)

Spices
BLACK PEPPER

Native to India, this pungent dried berry is thought to be the most widely consumed spice in the world. It has been used in India since ancient times, usually cracked or ground and added to foods to give them a touch of heat.

CARDAMOM

A member of the ginger family, cardamom is a small pod with a thin, crackly covering and a number of tiny, round dark seeds inside. The pods can be green or bleached white. The seeds can be removed and the pod discarded, or the entire pod can be ground. Ground cardamon is also available, but some recipes may call for using the seeds whole. Cardamom, which is pungent and spicy with sweet tones, is used in both sweet and savory dishes.

CHILE

With the introduction of chiles to India in the sixteenth century, the "heat" in Indian cooking began to change, moving away from black pepper. Indians love their food spiced with chiles, and grow many different varieties. The Mexican chiles available in most supermarkets can be substituted. Typically, the smaller the chile, the hotter it will be.

CINNAMON

The cinnamon used in India is from the bark of the cassia tree, which is milder than the bark of true cinnamon. In northern India, rice is often seasoned with a cinnamon stick. Cinnamon is also used in garam masala, a custom blend of spices specific to every cook in India.

CLOVE

The dried flower bud of a tropical tree, clove has a powerful flavor and scent. It's one of the spices in garam masala; is used in sauces, especially with tomatoes; and is added to rice dishes.

CORIANDER

Coriander is used extensively in Indian cooking, both as a fresh leaf (cilantro) and a dried seed. The seeds are small, hard spheres that give off an intoxicating floral scent when ground. The mild flavor of coriander goes well with vegetable dishes, especially those made with tomatoes, eggplant, and carrots.

CUMIN

Cumin is considered the most important spice in Indian cooking. It is a small, curved, highly aromatic light brown seed that looks a bit like caraway. It is sold whole or ground. Toasting cumin seeds before grinding brings out their flavor. Cumin has strong citrus notes and is often added to neutral-tasting vegetables, such as beans, potatoes, and rice.

CURRY POWDER

Indian cooks typically mix up their own curry powders, choosing spices and proportions to their taste and according to the dish being seasoned. Curry powder is considered the original masala, or blend, of the southern Indian kitchen, whereas garam masala is the blend favored in the north. According to Indian food expert Julie Sahni, another blend, *panch phoron,* is popular in the kitchens of eastern India. Curry powder is used to flavor sauces and goes well with meat, seafood, and vegetable dishes, especially tomatoes.

FENNEL

Fennel seeds look a little like cumin, without the curve, but the sweet licorice aroma and flavor couldn't be more different. It is used to season vegetables and for sweets.

GARAM MASALA

In Hindi, *garam* means "warm" or "hot" and *masala* means "a blend of spices." The spices included in this blend vary by region, by cook, and by the dish to which it is being added. Every Indian cook creates his or her own blend, which can have as few as ten or as many as thirty different spices. In the United States, you can buy already-ground garam masala in jars or packets or mixtures of whole spices. Whole-spice mixtures typically include bay leaf, cinnamon stick, brown mustard seeds, green cardamom pods, whole cloves, and cumin seeds. The spices are always dry roasted on a griddle (*tawa*) or small skillet before they are ground in an electric spice grinder or, for smaller amounts, in a mortar and pestle (see page 129).

GINGER

Fresh ginger, with its familiar pungency and heat, is used widely in Indian cooking. It is typically peeled and then grated, chopped, or thinly sliced before adding to dishes. It is a popular seasoning in lentil dishes, various curries, and chutneys.

MUSTARD SEEDS

Mustard seeds come in several colors, but small brown seeds are most often used in Indian cooking, especially in the vegetarian cooking of the south and in traditional Indian pickles.

NIGELLA SEEDS

These small, black, pungent seeds are sometimes called black onion seeds, though the onion is not a relative. They are used in stir-fried vegetables, pickles, and in dals, dishes made with dried split lentils, peas, and/or beans.

TURMERIC

Turmeric, a rhizome like ginger, is commonly dried and ground into a brilliant golden yellow powder with a strong earthy taste. It is the spice that gives curry powder its distinctive color. It is also a common addition to vegetable, rice, seafood, and meat dishes and to pickles.

All About Nuts

Nuts add crunch, flavor, variety, and a big wallop of nutrients to many dishes. Because of their high (mostly good) fat content, they spoil quickly unless refrigerated or frozen. Use them directly from the freezer, or toasted (page 85) for a more intense taste. To enhance their flavor, pair nuts with a matching oil.

Almond Almonds are available with shells and without, raw, roasted, salted, with skins and without (blanched), slivered, ground, chopped, sliced, and made into paste. Almonds are a popular snack and a common ingredient in savory and sweet dishes. Sprinkle sliced, slivered, or chopped almonds on green salads, steamed green beans, roasted asparagus, rice pilaf, or fish. Whole almonds are ground into dips and sauces, including the classic Spanish *romesco*, a mixture of tomatoes, chile, garlic, olive oil and almonds (or hazelnuts), and into a paste for desserts.

Hazelnut Hazelnuts, also known as filberts, are popular in both desserts and savory dishes. Hazelnuts can be purchased in the shell or shelled, peeled or unpeeled, peeled and toasted, and peeled and chopped. Their flavor is distinctly sweet, with a pleasant earthiness. Hazelnuts are classically paired with chocolate in Europe, but they are also enjoyed in many savory recipes. The Egyptians eat them in a spicy paste called *dukkah*. You can coat chicken, meat cutlets, or fish fillets with finely chopped hazelnuts; toss chopped nuts into pilaf or into mushroom and wild rice salad; or mix ground nuts with garlic and olive oil and toss with boiled potatoes or pasta. Toasting and peeling hazelnuts is time consuming, but worth the effort (page 288).

Pine Nut This tiny nut with a resinlike flavor is called *pinoli* (or *pignoli*) in Italian and *piñon* in Spanish. Harvested from the cones of specific varieties of pine, the ivory nuts have a high oil content that gives them a particularly rich flavor. Toasting them to a shade just slightly darker than golden intensifies the richness. Pine nuts are used in confections, pastries, salads, stuffings, meatballs, and, of course, with basil in Liguria's famed pesto. They brown quickly because of their high fat content, so watch carefully when toasting.

Pistachio Pistachios are prized for their pretty green color. Sold shelled and unshelled, raw or roasted, and salted or unsalted, pistachios add a pale apple green hue to ice creams, sauces, and puddings. The color contrast is particularly stunning on sliced beets, in tomato salad, in pâté or sausage, or on top of a chocolate-frosted cake. Toast them over low heat, as high heat will alter the bright green color.

Walnut These popular nuts are sold as halves, broken (called meats), chopped, or in the shell. They are high in healthy fats and are often pressed for their oil (page 259). Walnuts are used in baked goods, confections, and savory dishes in many cuisines. Try walnuts in *muhummara*, a red pepper–walnut spread, or *tarator*, a pureed sauce of bread, olive oil, vinegar, and walnuts or other nuts, both popular in the Middle East, or in baklava, the familiar Greek and Turkish sweet made of layered phyllo and ground walnuts.

if i had to choose one cooking pot over all others, it would be the karahi. This versatile concave vessel can be used to make everything from deep-fried pakoras to a quick stir-fry of vegetables to a long simmered curry. **Ruta Kahate,** AUTHOR, *5 SPICES, 50 DISHES*

Cauliflower and Sweet Potatoes In
Spicy Tomato Sauce with Cashews

Karahi

The *karahi* looks a bit like a small wok, but with higher sides and two opposing high-looped handles. It is an indispensable piece of cookware in the Indian kitchen, used for everything from stir-frying to deep-frying to braising. Originally made with a narrow, rounded bottom that fit down into Indian cooktops, the modern version has a flat bottom, making it stable for use on a range of cooking surfaces.

The depth and bowl-like shape of the *karahi* make it perfect for deep-frying Indian snacks in a minimum of oil and for slowly simmering stews and curries. These are available in a variety of sizes, from 10 to 13 inches, but the 10-inch is most commonly used. Cast iron is the most typical material, but copper, stainless steel, and anodized metal, some with with a nonstick finish, are also available.

Tips for Using

Before using, season a cast-iron *karahi* as you would a cast-iron skillet (page 87).

Always wear oven mitts when grasping the looped handles, as they can get very hot.

The *karahi* can also be used in the oven at temperatures up to 450°F.

An attractive enameled cast-iron *karahi,* or one designed with beautifully sculpted handles, can double as an attractive serving dish.

If using a round-bottomed *karahi,* be sure to stabilize it on the stovetop with a wok ring (page 30) to prevent tipping.

You can use the *karahi* for deep-frying dishes from other cuisines, too, such as zucchini blossoms, corn fritters, and even breaded, stuffed olives.

Its smaller size makes the *karahi* more versatile than a wok—just the right size for sautéing a modest batch of spinach, broccoli, or other vegetables.

When using the *karahi* for braises or stews—the 10-inch *karahi* is good for slow cooking—use a lid from another pan of the same size.

Care in Using

If used for deep frying, simply rub clean with dry paper towels.

For braising and stir-frying, use warm, soapy water and a stiff brush, but avoid harsh cleansers.

Some models must be seasoned before use and reseasoned after washing.

Always consult the manufacturer's instructions.

Some materials are dishwasher safe. Consult the manufacturer's instructions.

Alternatives

A stir-fry pan (a wok with a flat bottom and high sides), a skillet, or a Dutch oven is a good substitute.

recipes

Cauliflower and Sweet Potatoes in Spicy Tomato Sauce with Cashews | Coconut and Curry Lamb Stew with Green Beans and Potatoes | Vegetable Fritters

CAULIFLOWER and SWEET POTATOES in SPICY TOMATO SAUCE with CASHEWS

PREP 25 min | COOK TIME 30 min | SERVES 4–6

The flavor in this vegetable stew comes from frying the whole spices in hot oil before adding the tomatoes. Serve this hearty dish as a vegetarian main course with rice and a green vegetable, or as a side dish with grilled chicken or meat.

Implements *Karahi*, Slotted Spoon

Ingredients

2 tablespoons canola oil

½ cup unsalted raw cashews

1½ teaspoons cumin seeds

1 teaspoon brown mustard seeds

1 cup chopped yellow onion

4 teaspoons peeled, finely chopped fresh ginger

1 (14½-ounce) can diced tomatoes with juices

1 serrano or other small green chile, halved or quartered lengthwise and seeded

1 (1½-pound) head cauliflower, cut into 1-inch florets

1 pound sweet potatoes, peeled and cut into 1-inch chunks

¼ cup water

1 teaspoon coarse salt

1 cup frozen peas, thawed

1 tablespoon finely chopped fresh cilantro

1. Add the canola oil to the *karahi*, a large skillet, a wok, or a Dutch oven and heat over medium heat. When the oil is hot, add the cashews and fry for 30 seconds, or until lightly browned. Use a slotted spoon or skimmer to transfer the nuts to a plate. Add the cumin and mustard seeds to the oil and fry for 30 seconds, or until lightly browned. Add the onion and ginger and cook, stirring, for 3 to 5 minutes, or until the onion is golden.

2. Add the tomatoes and chile, increase the heat to medium-high, and bring to a boil. Cook, stirring, for 5 minutes, or until slightly reduced and the oil begins to separate from the tomatoes. Add the cauliflower, sweet potatoes, water, and salt, and stir with a large spoon until thoroughly blended. Decrease the heat to medium-low, cover, and cook, stirring once halfway through the cooking time, for 15 minutes, or until the vegetables are almost tender. Add the peas, re-cover, and cook for 3 minutes, or until all the vegetables are tender.

3. Transfer to a warmed platter or bowl and sprinkle with the reserved cashews and the cilantro. Serve warm.

COCONUT and CURRY LAMB STEW with GREEN BEANS and POTATOES

PREP 20 min | **MARINATING** 30 min | **COOK TIME** 45 min |
SERVES 4

The primary seasoning in this fragrant lamb stew is curry powder. Most Indian cooks blend their own spices for seasoning, but you can use a favorite commercial blend. The lamb sirloin is tender and quick cooking. In just over a half hour, this succulent, savory stew is ready to eat. Prepare a pot of fragrant basmati rice to serve with it.

Implements Mortar and Pestle, Large Bowl, *Karahi,* Tongs, *Tawa,* Spatula

Ingredients

2 teaspoons peeled, finely chopped fresh ginger

2 cloves garlic

1 teaspoon coarse salt

1¼ pounds boneless lamb sirloin, excess fat trimmed and cut into 1-inch cubes

3 tablespoons canola oil or other flavorless oil

1 cup chopped yellow onion

1 tablespoon curry powder

½ cup water

2 tablespoons tomato paste

1 cup coconut milk

1 pound sweet potatoes, peeled and cut into 1-inch chunks

8 ounces green beans, trimmed and cut into 1-inch lengths

Freshly ground black pepper

3 tablespoons unsweetened grated dried coconut

1. Combine the ginger, garlic, and salt in a mortar and crush to a paste with a pestle. Or, grate the garlic and ginger with a rasp grater, transfer to a saucer, and use the back of a fork to mash with the salt until blended.

2. In a large bowl, combine the lamb and the ginger paste and toss to coat evenly, rubbing the paste into the meat. Cover, and refrigerate for 30 minutes.

3. Add 2 tablespoons of the canola oil to a *karahi,* a large skillet, or a wok and heat over medium heat. When the oil is hot, add half of the meat, spreading it out in a single layer, and fry, turning once with tongs, for about 2 minutes per side, or until lightly browned. Adjust the heat to keep the ginger and garlic from burning and sticking to the bottom of the pan. Using the tongs, transfer the lamb to a plate. Repeat with the remaining lamb.

4. Add the remaining 1 tablespoon of oil to the pan over medium heat. Add the onion and cook, stirring, for 5 minutes, or until golden. Decrease the heat to low, stir in the curry powder, and cook, stirring, for 2 minutes. Add the water and tomato paste, increase the heat to high, and heat, stirring, until the mixture reaches a boil. Add the coconut milk and the lamb and any juices that have accumulated on the plate. Stir to blend.

5. Decrease the heat to low, cover, and cook at a gentle simmer for 20 minutes. Add the sweet potatoes and green beans, and taste and adjust the seasoning with salt and a grinding of pepper. Cover and cook for 15 minutes, or until all the vegetables are tender.

6. Meanwhile, spread the coconut in a *tawa* or small skillet, place over medium-low heat, heat and, stirring frequently, heat for about 3 minutes, or until golden. Remove from the heat and pour onto a plate to cool.

7. Spoon the stew into a warmed serving bowl and sprinkle the coconut over the top. Serve hot.

VEGETABLE FRITTERS

PREP 35 min | STAND TIME (batter) 15 min | COOK
TIME (per batch) 3 to 5 min | MAKES about 20 fritters |
SERVES 4–6

In India, these crisp, full-flavored fritters are known
as *pakora.* They get their distinctive taste and texture
from chickpea flour (*besan*), which can be purchased
in health-food stores or wherever Indian products
are sold. A small amount of baking soda gives the
batter a little lift, and the generous addition of
spices will make it either flavorful or hot and spicy,
depending on which ones you select. There are two
types of *pakora*: large pieces of vegetable are dipped
into batter and dropped into hot oil, or finely cut
vegetables are stirred into batter and then dropped
from a spoon into hot oil. This recipe makes the latter
type. If you decide to add chiles to the batter, serve
the spicy fritters with a cooling *raita* of Ginger Mint
Yogurt Sauce.

Implements Wooden Spoon, *Karahi*, Deep-frying
Thermometer, Rimmed Sheet Pan, Slotted Spoon

Ingredients

Ginger and Mint Yogurt Sauce (page 248)
2 cups chickpea flour
½ teaspoon baking soda
1 teaspoon *garam masala* (page 248)
1½ teaspoons coarse salt
1 small fresh green chile, halved, seeded,
and finely chopped, or more to taste
½ cup finely chopped yellow onion
½ cup frozen peas, thawed
¼ cup peeled, coarsely shredded carrot
2 tablespoons finely chopped fresh cilantro
Canola oil, for frying

1. Prepare the Ginger and Mint Yogurt Sauce (page 248).
   Cover and refrigerate until ready to serve.

2. In a large bowl, stir together the flour, baking soda, garam masala, and salt until blended.

3. With a wooden spoon, beat in water ¼ cup at a time until
   the batter is thick enough to drop off the tip of the spoon
   in clumps. You will need about ¾ cup of water total. Let
   the batter stand for 15 minutes.

4. Add the chile, onion, peas, carrot, and cilantro to the
   batter and fold gently to distribute all of the ingredients
   evenly.

5. Pour the canola oil to a depth of 2 to 3 inches into a
   karahi, wok, or 6-quart Dutch oven, and heat over
   medium-high heat to 350°F on a deep-frying thermometer. Line a rimmed sheet pan or a tray with a thick layer
   of paper towels.

6. With a tablespoon, scoop up a 1½-inch clump of the
   batter. Holding the spoon near the surface of the hot oil,
   use the tip of a second spoon to push the batter into the
   oil. Alternatively, use a 1½-inch spring-loaded ice-cream
   scoop to scoop up and release the batter into the oil. Repeat until there are 3 or 4 fritters in the oil, and then fry,
   turning the fritters occasionally with the tip of a spoon so
   they cook evenly, for 3 to 5 minutes, until golden brown.
   Using a slotted spoon, transfer the fritters to the towel-
   lined pan to drain. Repeat until all the batter has been
   used.

7. Serve the fritters immediately while they are still piping
   hot, or drain and keep warm on a rimmed sheet pan in
   a 300°F oven until ready to serve.

Spice Grinder

Spices that you roast whole and grind finely just before using are far more fragrant and flavorful than spices you purchase already ground. You can do as Indian cooks do and roast whole spices on a *tawa* (page 251), or you can use a small skillet. The quickest and easiest way to grind your roasted spices is with a superefficient, inexpensive electric spice grinder, most commonly sold as a coffee grinder.

These readily available grinders measure about 6½ inches tall and 3½ inches wide and weigh in at just under 1½ pounds, making them easy to store in a drawer or to tuck into a corner on the kitchen counter. To grind whole spices, you simply put them in the grinding chamber, which is centered by a small, sharp blade; secure the oval plastic lid in place, and press the power button on the side of the lid. In seconds, the spices are reduced to a powder.

Tips for Using

Reserve one grinder for spices, and a second grinder for coffee. Spices and coffee both have big profiles, and you don't want to mingle their flavors.

Never fill the grinding chamber more than half full.

Plug in the grinder after you add the spices and secure the lid. Unplug the grinder before you remove the lid.

You can control the texture of the ground spice by how long you grind. A shorter time produces a coarse grind, and a longer time produces a fine grind.

It's easier and safer to measure the spices from the lid than from the grinder. To retrieve the ground spices, hold the lid closed, invert the grinder—the spices will fall into the lid—and lift away the grinder.

Be careful not to touch the sharp blade.

Care in Using

Wash the lid in warm, soapy water.

Do not immerse the rest of the grinder in water.

Clean around the blade with a soft brush or very carefully with a damp cloth.

Always consult the manufacturer's instructions.

Alternatives

A mortar and pestle are the time-honored tools for grinding spices.

recipes Garam Masala | Ground Lamb Kebabs with Ginger and Mint Yogurt Sauce

GARAM MASALA

PREP 10 min | **COOK TIME** 3 min | **MAKES** about ⅓ cup

This aromatic spice blend is used in northern India. It is commercially available, but homemade garam masala has a much livelier flavor.

Implements *Tawa,* Spice Grinder or Mortar and Pestle

Ingredients

- 2 tablespoons cumin seeds
- 2 tablespoons coriander seeds
- 1 tablespoon cardamom seeds
- 1 tablespoon black peppercorns
- 1 teaspoon fennel seeds
- 2 whole cloves
- ½ cinnamon stick, broken into small pieces in a mortar

1. Place a *tawa* or small, heavy skillet over medium heat and add the cumin, coriander, cardamom, peppercorns, fennel, cloves, and cinnamon. Heat, stirring constantly, for 2 to 3 minutes, until the spices turn a shade darker and become fragrant. Pour into a small bowl and let cool.

2. Transfer the cooled spices to a spice grinder or mortar and pestle and grind or pound to a powder. Store in a glass jar or a spice tin with a tight-fitting lid. The blend will keep for up to 2 months before its flavor begins to dissipate.

 **tip** STRONG SPICES

To rid the grinder of the aroma of a particularly strong-smelling spice, grind 2 tablespoons raw white rice, discard, and repeat until the grinder is odor free.

GROUND LAMB KEBABS with GINGER and MINT YOGURT SAUCE

PREP 30 min | **STAND TIME** 15 min | **COOK TIME** 20 min | **MAKES** 16 kebabs | **SERVES** 4

A kebab can be solid pieces of meat threaded onto a skewer, ground meat formed around a skewer like a big sausage, or ground meat shaped into thin fingers or patties and cooked in a shallow pool of oil. In this recipe, the meat is seasoned with a spice mixture called *garam masala* and shaped into patties. Make your own spice blend from the recipe at left, or buy a prepackaged mixture of whole spices, toast in a tawa (or small skillet), and grind in an electric spice grinder as needed.

Implements Mortar and Pestle, *Tawa,* Electric Spice Grinder, Blender or Food Processor, Spatula

Ingredients

GINGER AND MINT YOGURT SAUCE

- ½ cup lightly packed fresh mint leaves
- 2 tablespoons peeled, coarsely chopped fresh ginger
- 1 clove garlic
- 1 teaspoon coarse salt
- 1 cup plain whole-milk yogurt

LAMB KEBABS

1 tablespoon whole-spice garam masala blend (see headnote), or 1 teaspoon ground garam masala (page 248)

1 tablespoon peeled, chopped fresh ginger

2 cloves garlic

1 teaspoon coarse salt

3 tablespoons canola oil

½ cup coarsely chopped yellow onion

¼ cup water

1 pound ground lamb

2 tablespoons finely chopped fresh mint

1 egg yolk

Mango chutney, for serving

1. **MAKE THE YOGURT SAUCE:** Combine the mint, ginger, garlic, and salt in a large mortar and crush to a paste with a pestle. Alternatively, process the mint, ginger, garlic, and salt to a paste in a food processor. Transfer to a serving bowl and fold in the yogurt. Cover and refrigerate until ready to serve.

2. **MAKE THE KEBABS:** If using a store-bought whole garam masala blend, spread it in a *tawa* or small, heavy skillet. Examine the mixture carefully. If there is more than 1 clove, remove the other cloves. Place the *tawa* over medium heat and heat, stirring constantly, for 2 to 3 minutes, until the spices turn a shade darker and become fragrant. Pour into a small bowl and let cool. Transfer to an electric spice grinder, grind to a fine powder, and set aside. If using homemade garam masala, set it aside.

3. Combine the ginger, garlic, and salt in the mortar and crush to a paste with the pestle. Or, grate the garlic and ginger with a rasp grater, transfer to a saucer, and use the back of a fork to mash with the salt until blended.

4. In the *tawa* or a medium skillet, heat 1 tablespoon of the canola oil over medium-low heat. Add the ginger paste and cook, stirring, for 1 minute. Add the garam masala and cook, stirring, for 30 seconds. Transfer the spice mixture to a small bowl. Wash and dry the *tawa*.

5. In a blender or food processor, combine the onion and water and process to a smooth puree. Transfer the puree to a large bowl and add the lamb, mint, spice mixture, and egg yolk. Stir with your hand or a wooden spoon until the mixture is thoroughly blended. At first, the mixture may seem too wet, but stir it for another 30 seconds and it will tighten. Cover and refrigerate for 15 minutes.

6. Line a platter with a double thickness of paper towels. Heat the *tawa* or skillet over medium heat. Coat the surface with the remaining 2 tablespoons of oil and heat the oil. Using a measuring tablespoon as a guide, scoop up a generous 1-inch ball of meat, flatten it slightly to make a patty, and carefully place it in the hot oil. Repeat to make more patties, being carefully not to crowd the pan and rinsing your hands with cold water as needed to prevent the meat mixture from sticking to them. Fry the patties, turning once with a spatula, for 2 minutes per side, or until nicely browned and cooked through. Transfer the patties to the towel-lined platter to drain. Repeat with the remaining meat mixture in one or two batches.

7. Serve the patties hot with the yogurt sauce and the chutney.

Spice blends, called masalas, toasted in the traditional way, in a tawa, are what give Indian food its characteristic flavor, texture, and aroma.

Julie Sahni, AUTHOR, *CLASSIC INDIAN COOKING*

Chapatis

Tawa

The *tawa*, an iron griddle with slightly raised sides, is used to roast spices, cook flatbreads, and grill small batches of kebabs or cutlets called *tikki*. Sometimes spelled *tava*, the two most basic models are one with two opposing handles and one with a single long handle. Tavas with no handles are also available.

The *tawa* comes in a wide range of sizes, shapes, and materials, from heavy cast iron to brightly colored enameled cast iron to plain steel. A specially designed large, flat *tawa* is used for making *dosa*, the paper-thin, crisp southern Indian pancake.

Tips for Using

These pans are traditionally used on top of the stove, but newer enameled cast-iron models can withstand oven temperatures up to 450°F.

Always use protective oven mitts when touching the piping-hot handles.

The smaller, or oval, *tawa* with opposing handles can be used to oven roast or quickly sauté asparagus, bell pepper strips, cauliflower slices, and other vegetables.

The round, long-handled *tawa* can be used for cooking spice-rubbed or marinated chicken, meat cutlets or strips, kebabs, or fish fillets.

The brightly colored enameled cast-iron models are attractive enough for serving.

Care in Using

If used for frying breads, rub clean with dry paper towels.

If you need to clean stubborn stains, use warm, soapy water and a stiff brush, but avoid harsh cleansers.

Some models must be seasoned before use and reseasoned after washing, whereas other materials are dishwasher safe. Consult the manufacturer's instructions for details.

Alternatives

Any flat (smooth) griddle or large, wide skillet with low sides can be used in place of a *tawa*.

recipes

Yogurt-Marinated Chicken Cutlets | Chapatis

YOGURT-MARINATED CHICKEN CUTLETS

PREP 15 min | **COOK TIME** 25 to 30 min | **SERVES** 4–6

The *tawa* does double duty here: it is used to roast the spices for the marinade and then it is used to cook the marinated chicken. If you prefer to cook the chicken on an outdoor grill or in the broiler, cut the marinated thighs into 2-inch pieces and thread them onto metal skewers. This dish is called *tikki,* the Hindi word for both seared chunks of meat cooked on skewers and for meat cutlets seared without skewers. Serve the chicken with lime wedges on a bed of Basmati rice (page 165) garnished with cherry tomatoes and chopped cilantro.

Implements *Tawa,* Spice Grinder or Mortar and Pestle, Kitchen Scissors, Wide Spatula

Ingredients

1 teaspoon fennel seeds

1 teaspoon coriander seeds

1 teaspoon cardamom seeds

8 boneless, skinless chicken thighs (about 2 pounds)

⅓ cup plain yogurt

1 teaspoons peeled, grated fresh ginger

¼ teaspoon ground turmeric

¼ teaspoon coarse salt

⅛ teaspoon cayenne

2 tablespoons canola oil

½ cup tiny grape tomatoes, for garnish

1 tablespoon chopped fresh cilantro leaves, for garnish

1 lime, cut into wedges, for garnish

1. Place a tawa or small, heavy skillet over medium heat and add the fennel, coriander, and cardamom. Heat, stirring constantly, for 5 to 7 minutes, until the spices turn a shade darker and become fragrant. Pour into a small bowl and let cool, then grind finely in a spice grinder or mortar and pestle and set aside.

2. Use kitchen scissors to trim any fat and excess skin from the chicken thighs. Cut each thigh lengthwise into 3 rectangular pieces.

3. In a large bowl, stir together the ground toasted spices, yogurt, ginger, turmeric, salt, and cayenne until blended. Add the chicken and stir to coat. Cover with plastic wrap and refrigerate for 1 to 2 hours.

4. Remove the chicken from the refrigerator and scrape off and discard the marinade. Heat the *tawa* or a medium skillet over medium-high heat until hot enough for a drop of water to sizzle on contact. Add the oil to the pan. When the oil is hot, add about one-third of the chicken pieces and cook, adjusting the temperature to maintain a steady sizzle, for about 3 to 5 minutes, or until golden brown on first side. Use a wide spatula to turn the chicken and cook for about 3 minutes on the second side, or until browned. Transfer to a serving plate and repeat with the remaining chicken.

5. Garnish the chicken with the tomatoes, cilantro, and lime wedges and serve.

CHAPATIS

PREP 15 min | **REST TIME** 20 min | **COOK TIME** (each) 5 min | **MAKES** 12 flat breads

Chapatis are small, round disks of unleavened whole wheat bread cooked on a *tawa* or similar griddle. Chapati flour, a blend of wheat and barley flours, is available in Indian grocery stores and some Middle Eastern markets. If you can't find it, you can use equal parts all-purpose flour and whole wheat flour. Serve the chapatis warm brushed with melted ghee or plain butter.

Implements Wooden Spoon, Rolling Pin, *Tawa* or 8- to 10-inch Heavy Skillet, Tongs

Ingredients

2 cups chapati flour, or 1 cup each whole wheat flour and unbleached all-purpose flour, plus more for dusting

1 teaspoon coarse salt

¾ cup warm water

4 tablespoons ghee, clarified butter (page 323), or unsalted butter, melted

1. Place the chapati flour and salt in a large bowl. If using 2 different flours, stir with a wooden spoon until blended. Add the water and 1 tablespoon of the ghee and stir with the wooden spoon until the dough comes together in a sticky ball. Lightly dust a work surface with flour, and transfer the dough to it. Knead for about 4 minutes, or until smooth. Invert the bowl over the dough and let rest for 20 minutes. Meanwhile, clean the work surface.

2. Divide the dough into 12 equal pieces. With floured hands, form each piece into a ball. Lightly dust the work surface with flour. Place 1 ball on the work surface and press it with your palm into a disk about ½ inch thick. Using a rolling pin, roll out the disk into a round about 5 inches in diameter. Set the round aside and repeat with the remaining balls. As the rounds are rolled out, set them aside, without touching, and cover with a kitchen towel so they won't dry out.

3. Heat a *tawa* or an 8- to 10-inch heavy skillet over medium to medium-high heat until hot enough for a drop of water to sizzle on contact. Add a dough round and cook for 2 to 3 minutes, until brown spots appear on the underside. Turn with tongs and cook for 2 minutes longer, or until cooked through. Use the tongs to transfer the bread to a rimmed sheet pan and then cover with a towel to keep warm. Repeat with the remaining dough rounds.

4. Brush the warm breads with the remaining 3 tablespoons of ghee and serve at once.

9 | The ITALIAN KITCHEN

The Italian Pantry

Americans are passionate about the robust flavors, beautiful olive oils, great cheeses, and superb wines of Italy. The sheer joy Italians express through every meal, whether simple or lavish, is what makes their food so comfortable and so universally appealing. Simplicity defines Italian cookware. The *mezzaluna*, an inspired curved knife that quickly reduces a pile of herb sprigs to a minced mound and the venerable *chitarra*, a rustic wire-strung frame from the Abruzzo for cutting pasta strands are classics of the Italian kitchen. From the pantry to the recipes to the cookware, the Italian kitchen is all about *abbondanza*—"abundance."

Anchovies

Anchovies, small, silvery-skinned fishes, are typically sold filleted and preserved either in salt or olive oil, or whole, preserved in salt. Soak preserved anchovies in cold water for 10 minutes before using. Enjoy them warmed in butter or oil and tossed with pasta; or made into *bagna cauda,* a dip for raw vegetables.

Capers

Capers, the unopened flower buds of a plant native to the Mediterranean region, are sold preserved in mild vinegar brine and in salt. Drain brine-packed capers well, taste one, and, if too tart, place in a small strainer and rinse briefly with cold water. Soak salt-packed capers in a few changes of cold water until their flavor is to your taste.

Cheeses

ASIAGO

This cow's milk cheese has a sharp, tangy cooked-milk taste. Whereas a soft, young Asiago is a good melting cheese, aged Asiago is grated over pasta, shredded and sprinkled on pizza, or shaved on salads.

FONTINA

A semisoft cow's milk cheese with a nutty, earthy taste, Fontina has excellent melting properties. It is made in other countries, but the most flavorful is the true *fontina Val d'Aosta* of the Italian Alps. Fontina is used for *fonduta,* a type of Italian fondue, and is delicious melted on top of baked dishes and on bread for sandwiches.

GORGONZOLA

This premium blue-veined cow's milk cheese comes in two basic types, the mild *dolce,* or "sweet," and the aged, drier, assertively flavored *piccante.* Both can be tossed with hot pasta, crumbled on top of pizza or crostini, or served with nuts and fruit for a snack or dessert.

MOZZARELLA

There are two basic types of mozzarella cheese. One is mild and creamy, made from cow's milk; the other is fattier and stronger tasting, made from water buffalo milk in the regions of southern Italy. Both are used in *insalata caprese,* or salad in the style of Capri, which marries the cheese with tomatoes, basil, and olive oil. Both are also favorites on pizza, especially *pizza Margherita,* topped with tomato, mozzarella, and basil.

PARMIGIANO-REGGIANO

An aged (12 to 36 months) and firm cow's milk cheese, Parmigiano-Reggiano is a pale straw yellow and has a rich taste, with hints of nut and caramel. Production of the large wheels is limited to designated areas in the Emilia-Romagna region. Parmigiano-Reggiano is the grating cheese of northern Italy, and it is also a popular table or snacking cheese. *Grana padano,* a similar grating cheese usually aged for only 15 months and produced in Lombardy, is sometimes used in place of Parmigiano-Reggiano.

PECORINO ROMANO

This aged sheep's milk cheese comes from the Lazio region, near Rome. A similar cheese, *pecorino sardo,* is made in Sardinia. Both cheeses have a nutty, sharp flavor and complement the tomato sauces of the south.

PROVOLONE

Rich and spicy, this popular cow's milk cheese, produced primarily in the north, comes in two types, the mild *dolce,* or "sweet," and the drier, sharp-flavored *piccante.* Both cheeses are delicious shaved over salad greens, pizza, or for snacking.

RICOTTA

This soft, creamy fresh cheese is made by heating the whey—*ricotta* means "recooked"—left over from making other cheeses, such as mozzarella. The freshest is sweet enough to be enjoyed with a drizzle of rosemary or chestnut honey and a crunchy Bosc pear. In cooking, ricotta is typically used as a filling in ravioli and lasagna.

RICOTTA SALATA

Firm but crumbly, *ricotta salata* is made by salting and pressing fresh ricotta. Its taste and texture is similar to Greek feta, and it is delicious in tomato or green bean salad, tossed with pasta, or served with fruit.

Olives

Table olives are enjoyed all over Italy, with each region boasting its own variety and style. Sicily is famous for its fennel-seasoned green olives; Rome, for its black Gaeta olive; Liguria for small, black brine-cured olives; and Puglia for large, green Cerignola olives. (To read more about olives, see page 269.)

Olivada

This paste of ground olives and olive oil can be spread on sandwiches or crostini. It is sold in small jars, or it can be made at home by pureeing pitted black or green olives with olive oil in a food processor. Sometimes a bit of anchovy, orange zest, or other seasoning is added.

Olive Oils

Olive oil is produced in many parts of Italy, but each region has a distinctive flavor. Tuscan oils tend to be spicy and peppery and are particularly good with ripe, juicy tomatoes or other big flavors. Umbrian oils are fruity and buttery and are perfect for dressing sweet, fresh salad greens. Oils from Veneto are soft, fragrant, and nutty, and complement salads and cooked vegetables. Ligurian oils are typically mild, but with a full mouthfeel. Oils from the south—Puglia, Calabria, Campania, Sicily—have big flavors with notes of sweet and spice, and go well with the foods of these regions.

Pasta

DRIED PASTA

Fettuccine and Linguine These two flat, long ribbon pastas have a broad surface for holding a sauce, which means they work well with cream or other dairy-based sauces, pesto or other oil-based sauces, and smooth, rich marinara or other smooth tomato sauces.

Spaghetti, Bucatini, and Capelli d'Angelo Spaghetti is popular with light tomato, olive oil, and light cream sauces. Added vegetables or meat should be finely chopped or julienned. *Bucatini* is an especially sturdy pasta and pairs well with a robust sauce made from olive oil, bits of fried pancetta, ground black pepper or chile flakes, garlic, and a strongly flavored cheese, such as Pecorino Romano or Asiago. It also goes well with the rich egg, cheese, and bacon sauce called carbonara. Angel hair is more delicate and pairs nicely with butter or light cream sauces flavored with seafood, minced herbs, or finely chopped toasted nuts.

Lasagna, Manicotti, and Jumbo Shells These are known as oven shapes. They are classically combined with cheese and sauce; layered or stuffed with vegetables, cheese, and/ or meat; and baked, or prepared *al forno.*

Ancini di Pepe, Stelline, and Orzo These tiny pastas are known as soup shapes, although they also make a delicious side dish tossed with grated cheese and butter.

Gemelli, Campanelle, Orecchiette, Farfalle, and Conchiglie These are all boxy shapes that go well with sturdy tomato-based meat sauces or olive oil sauces with cooked vegetables. Cut up the vegetables to match the size and shape of the pasta. For example, broccoli and cauliflower florets match the size and shape of *orecchiette, campanelle,* and *conchiglie.* Green beans or asparagus spears pair well with the short twisted strands of Gemelli.

Rigatoni, Penne, Ziti, Mostaccioli These tube shapes are sturdy enough to stand up to thick tomato, olive oil, and dairy sauces. The ridged pastas, including *penne rigate* and rigatoni, hold sauces both in the ridges and inside the tubes. Pair these with cream-based sauces enriched with cheeses, such as *quattro formaggi,* or with spicy sauces, such as *arrabbiata* made with tomatoes, pancetta, and chiles. Cut vegetables to match the shapes.

FRESH PASTA

Cannelloni These are wide (3- to 4-inch) rectangles of pasta that are briefly boiled and then wrapped around fillings of cheese, vegetables, and/or meats and baked with a sauce.

Fettuccine This flat ribbon noodle ranges from ⅛ to ¼ inch wide. Just slightly thicker than tagliatelle, it can be paired with a light tomato or cream sauce, or olive oil and sautéed vegetables.

Lasagna Long and about 2 inches wide, these noodles are partially cooked in boiling water and then layered with cheese, vegetables, and/or meat, and sauce in a baking dish and baked to make the popular dish known as lasagna.

Pappardelle Flat, thin, and ¾ to 1 inch wide, *pappardelle* work well with heavier sauces because of their width, including rabbit or wild boar sauce in Tuscany.

Tagliatelle Flat, very thin, and delicate, tagliatelle measure about ¼ inch wide. Although similar to fettuccine, tagliatelle are thinner and slightly wider. Tagliatelle are partnered with light cream or tomato sauces, often with seafood.

Trenette These narrow (about ⅛ inch) noodles are typically rolled a little thicker than both tagliatelle and fettuccine. These are usually paired with light tomato sauces or other moderately light sauces.

Polenta

Polenta is the name for both the cornmeal and the dish made from it. The grain can be coarsely or finely ground and yellow or white, but the classic dish, popular in northern Italy, is made from coarse yellow cornmeal (see recipe on page 57).

Rice

Rice is cultivated in the Po River Valley located in northern Italy. The round, medium-grain kernels are distinguished by their naturally high amount of sticky starch, which is what gives risotto, the classic Italian rice dish, its distinctive creamy character. The three varieties of rice most popularly used for risotto are Arborio, Carnaroli, and Vialone Nano. (Read more about rice on page 165.)

Pancetta

Pancetta, a cut from the belly, or *pancia,* of the pig, is an unsmoked Italian bacon cured with salt, pepper, and spices. It is often diced and sautéed in oil to lend a sweet, earthy flavor to stews, risottos, or pasta sauces.

Prosciutto

Prosciutto, salt-cured, air-dried ham, is made throughout Italy, but *prosciutto* from Parma, in the Emilia-Romagna region, aged a minimum of 10 months with a sweet, complex flavor, is considered to be the best. The fat surrounding the pink meat is considered a delicacy and is almost never trimmed.

Semolina Flour

Ground from durum, a hard wheat, semolina flour has more gluten than does flour milled from soft wheat. This higher gluten, or protein, content is what gives some dried pastas, their chewy texture. If using semolina flour for making fresh pasta, be sure it is finely ground.

Tomatoes

The canned Italian tomato of choice has always been the San Marzano. But because of rising tariffs, the price of imported Italian tomatoes has skyrocketed. Fortunately, good-quality domestic canned Italian-style plum tomatoes packed in juice are available. Pick up a few different brands and compare the taste, texture, plumpness, and number of seeds.

Semolina and Egg Pasta Dough

*if one mentions the food of Abruzzo, the
first thing that comes to mind is la chitarra.
Not the musical instrument—although
you can play a tune on it—but the ancient
instrument illustrated in thirteenth-
century manuscripts that is used for cutting
macaroni to make maccheroni alla chitarra.*

Anna Teresa Callen, AUTHOR, *FOOD AND MEMORIES OF ABRUZZO*

Chitarra

Although the word *chitarra* translates as "guitar," the *chitarra* is not a musical instrument, but a wire-strung frame used to make a rustic fresh pasta called *maccheroni alla chitarra*. Found in kitchens and cookware shops throughout the region of Abruzzo, in central Italy, it consists of a roughly 16-by-8-inch birch-wood frame strung with fine wires fitted ⅛ or ¼ inch apart. Some models are double sided, with the narrow width on one side and the wider on the other side.

The *chitarra* is easy to use. You lay a sheet of pasta dough on top of the wires and press it with a special roller. The wires cut through the pasta sheet, forming strands squared on the sides. A tray beneath the wires catches the strands as they are cut. If the strings loosen with use, you can snug them up with screws at either end of the frame.

Tips for Using

The dough for the *maccheroni alla chitarra,* a mixture of fine semolina flour and all-purpose flour, is dense and can be difficult to knead and roll. To cut the kneading and rolling time by one-third, make the dough in a food processor and roll it out on a pasta machine (page 277).

Roll the dough on a pasta machine to the thickness indicated in the recipe, and then cut the sheets to fit just inside the wooden frame.

To cut the strands, lay the pasta on the wires, place the roller perpendicular to the wires, and roll the length of the frame. To encourage all of the strands to fall into the tray, strum the wires (like a guitar) with your finger, which will cause them to vibrate and release the strands.

Place a dampened towel or silicone mat under the *chitarra* to keep it from sliding on the counter while cutting the pasta.

In Abruzzo, this hearty, rustic pasta is typically paired with an equally hearty sauce, usually tomatoes with mushrooms, lamb, poultry giblets, beef, pork, rabbit, or other meats.

Care in Using

Do not get the *chitarra* wet.

Dust flour and any bits of dried pasta off the *chitarra* with a stiff brush or a dry towel.

Alternatives

Feed the sheets of pasta dough through the narrow cutters of a hand-cranked pasta machine.

recipes

Semolina and Egg Pasta Dough | Red Wine, Mushroom, and Tomato Ragù for Guitar Macaroni | Pork Sausage and Hot-Pepper Ragù for Guitar Macaroni

SEMOLINA and EGG PASTA DOUGH

PREP 45 min | **REST TIME** 30 min | **COOK TIME** 3–5 min | **MAKES** about 1 pound | **SERVES** 4–6

Look for fine semolina (durum-wheat) flour in large supermarkets, specialty-food stores, or health-food stores. If you can't find it, use bread flour, which has a higher percentage of gluten than does all-purpose flour, in its place. For flouring the work surface, your hands and the pasta machine, use a light dusting of all-purpose flour.

Implements
Food Processor, Pasta Machine, 2 Rimmed Sheet Pans, *Chitarra,* 8-Quart Stockpot, Colander

Ingredients

3 large eggs

½ teaspoon plus 3 tablespoons coarse salt

1 cup fine semolina flour, plus more for dusting sheet pans

1 cup unbleached all-purpose flour, plus more for dusting

1. Place the eggs and ½ teaspoon of the salt in a food processor and pulse until well blended. Gradually add the semolina and all-purpose flours, alternating between them and processing for a few seconds after each addition until a stiff dough forms. Remove the blade and, with floured hands, remove the dough from the food processor bowl.

2. Lightly dust a work surface with flour, and place the dough on it. Knead the dough, adding more flour to the surface as needed to prevent sticking, for at least 5 minutes, or until the dough springs back lightly when pressed with a fingertip. If the dough is too stiff, sprinkle it with a teaspoon of water and work the water into the dough to loosen it. Wrap the dough in plastic wrap and let rest for 30 minutes.

3. When ready to roll out the dough, follow the manufacturer's instructions to secure the pasta machine to one edge of a countertop or large table. Using a large knife or a bench scraper, divide the dough into 4 equal pieces, and cover 3 pieces with the bowl to prevent them from drying out. Use the heel of your hand to press the dough into an oval. Dust your hands with flour if the dough feels sticky.

4. Dust 2 rimmed sheet pans with semolina flour, and ready some clean kitchen towels. Position the pasta machine rollers at number 1, or at the widest opening. Dust the rollers lightly with flour. With one hand, guide the oval of dough between the rollers while turning the crank with the other hand. Fold the dough into thirds to make a rectangle and roll it through again. Repeat one more time. Then move the rollers one notch smaller and, without folding into thirds, roll the dough through this setting. As the dough comes through the rollers, hold it so it stays as smooth as possible. Continue rolling, narrowing the rollers by one notch each time, until you reach setting number 5, which is just about the right thickness for this dough. As you roll the dough, sprinkle it lightly with flour if it becomes sticky. When the pasta is ready, set it aside on a prepared sheet pan.

5. Repeat with the remaining dough pieces, stacking the pasta sheets on the pan and covering each layer with a clean kitchen towel to keep the dough from drying out or the sheets from sticking to one another.

6. When the pasta sheets are ready, carefully measure the wired surface of the *chitarra.* Cut the pasta sheets to fit down inside the wooden frame, and then lay a piece over the wires. Place the roller on the pasta perpendicular to the wires and roll and press to cut the sheet into long strands. Lift the roller and "strum" the wires to release any strands left on the wires. Transfer the pasta strands to the prepared sheet pans and cover with a kitchen towel. Repeat with the remaining dough sheets. The strands can be cooked right away or they can sit, covered with a towel, for several hours.

7. Place the pasta insert in an 8-quart stockpot or pasta-cooking pot and fill the pot three-fourths full with water. If not using the pasta insert, fill an 8-quart pot three-fourths full with water. Bring the water to a boil. Add the remaining 3 tablespoons of salt and the pasta. Cook, stirring gently once or twice to keep the strands from sticking to one another, for 3 to 5 minutes, until al dente (firm to the bite).

8. Place the pasta-serving bowl in the sink. If using the pasta-cooking insert, carefully lift it from the boiling water, allow the hot water to drain back into the pot, and then place it in the pasta-serving dish to finish draining. If not using the pasta-cooking insert, place a colander in the serving bowl in the sink and drain the pasta. Immediately tip any hot water out of the serving bowl so the pasta can continue to drain. When fully drained combine with a sauce and serve.

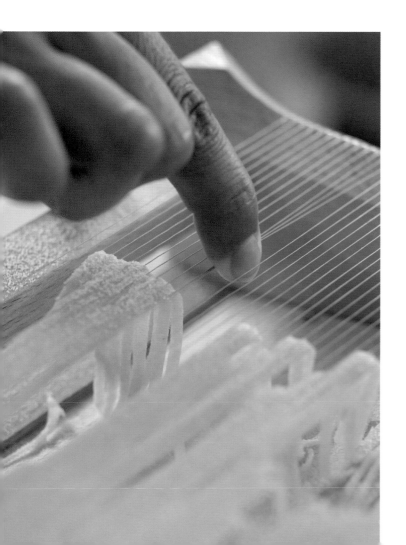

RED WINE, MUSHROOM, and TOMATO RAGÙ for GUITAR MACARONI

PREP 45 min | SOAK TIME (porcini) 20 min | COOK TIME 2 hr | SERVES 4–6

The mushroom flavor of this sauce is reinforced with the use of earthy, full-bodied dried porcini. Select the fresh mushrooms carefully for maximum flavor. Cremini and shiitake are among the best choices for cultivated mushrooms. Make the sauce a day or two ahead. Its flavor intensifies on standing.

Implements Strainer, 8-Quart Dutch Oven, Food Mill, Rubber Spatula, Large Ladle

Ingredients

1 cup (1 ounce) dried porcini

1 cup boiling water

4 tablespoons extra-virgin olive oil

1 cup chopped yellow onion

1½ pounds assorted fresh mushrooms (such as cremini, shiitake, chanterelle, king oyster, or others), tough stems discarded and coarsely chopped (about 8 cups)

Coarse salt and freshly ground black pepper

2 cloves garlic, finely chopped

1 cup full-bodied red wine (Zinfandel)

¼ cup lightly packed chopped fresh Italian parsley

1 tablespoon minced fresh oregano

2 (28-ounce) cans Italian plum tomatoes with juices

About 1 pound guitar macaroni (page 262) or long, round sturdy dried pasta (such as *bucatini* or linguine), for serving

Grated Parmigiano-Reggiano or *grana padano* cheese, for serving

1. Place the dried porcini in a small heatproof bowl and add the boiling water. Let stand for 20 minutes. Place a small strainer over a bowl and drain the mushrooms, reserving the soaking water. Finely chop the soaked porcini and add to the water.

2. In an 8-quart Dutch oven, heat 2 tablespoons of the olive oil over medium heat. Add the onion and cook, stirring, for 8 minutes, or until softened. Add the fresh mushrooms and season with 1 teaspoon salt and a generous grinding of pepper. Sauté the mushrooms over medium heat for 10 to 15 minutes, until they release their liquid and then reabsorb it and begin to brown. Add the garlic and cook for 2 minutes. Add reserved porcini and porcini water, wine, parsley, and oregano, and bring to a boil. Boil gently for 10 minutes, or until the wine is reduced by half.

3. Meanwhile, fit a food mill with the medium disk, and set the mill on the rim of a large bowl. Put the tomatoes with their juices in the food mill and puree. Reverse the crank to extract every bit of flavor from the tomato pulp, and occasionally stop to clean the underside of the mill with a rubber spatula, so the puree falls freely. Discard the pulp left in the strainer. Add the tomatoes to the mushroom mixture.

4. Bring the sauce to a boil over medium heat. Decrease the heat to low and cook the sauce, uncovered, for 2 hours, or until the sauce has reduced and thickened. Taste and adjust the seasoning with salt and pepper.

5. To serve, cook the pasta as directed in the guitar macaroni recipe, or according to package directions if using dried pasta, and drain (see page 264). Place 1 or 2 large ladlefuls of hot sauce in the bottom of a warmed pasta bowl or deep platter and add the drained pasta. Toss to coat the pasta with the sauce. Place another ladleful of sauce in the center of the pasta. Pass the remaining sauce and the cheese at the table.

PORK SAUSAGE and HOT-PEPPER RAGÙ for GUITAR MACARONI

PREP 30 min | **COOK TIME** 1½ hr | **SERVES** 6

The cooking of southern Italy is distinguished by the use of dried small whole red chiles (called *peperoncini*) in their cooking. The pod is usually added unbroken, so that it gently infuses the dish with a subtle, yet distinctive heat. Look for dried small chiles in cellophane bags in most supermarkets, or substitute crushed red pepper.

Implements Food Mill, Rubber Spatula, 8-Quart Dutch Oven, Wooden Spoon, Slotted Spoon, Large Ladle

Ingredients

2 (28-ounce) cans Italian plum tomatoes with juices

4 tablespoons extra-virgin olive oil

2 pounds sweet Italian sausage, preferably with fennel, casings removed

1 cup chopped yellow onion

3 cloves garlic, finely chopped

¼ cup lightly packed chopped fresh Italian parsley

1 teaspoon minced fresh rosemary or oregano

1 bay leaf

1 or 2 small dried whole red chiles, or ¼ teaspoon crushed red pepper, or to taste

½ cup full-bodied red wine (Zinfandel)

Coarse salt and freshly ground black pepper

About 1 pound guitar macaroni (page 262) or long, round sturdy dried pasta (such as *bucatini* or linguine), for serving

Grated Pecorino Romano cheese, for serving

1. Fit a food mill with the medium disk, and set the mill on the rim of a large bowl. Put the tomatoes with their juices in the food mill and puree. Reverse the crank to extract every bit of flavor from the tomato pulp, and occasionally stop to clean the underside of the mill with a rubber spatula, so the puree falls freely. Discard the pulp left in the strainer. Set the pureed tomatoes aside.

2. In an 8-quart Dutch oven, heat the olive oil over medium heat. Add half of the sausage and cook, stirring and breaking up the sausage with the side of a wooden spoon, for about 5 minutes or until no longer pink. Add the remaining sausage and cook, stirring and breaking up any chunks with the edge of the spoon, for 10 minutes, or until sausage is lightly browned. Add the onion, and cook, stirring, for 10 minutes, or until the sausage is browned and the onion is softened. Add the garlic and cook for 1 minute. Add the parsley, rosemary, bay leaf, and chile, and stir to blend.

3. Add the tomatoes and wine and bring to a boil. Decrease the heat to low and cook uncovered, stirring occasionally, for 1 to 1½ hours, until the sauce is reduced and thickened. Season to taste with salt and pepper. Retrieve the bay leaf with a slotted spoon and discard.

4. To serve, cook the pasta as directed in the guitar macaroni recipe, or according to package directions if using dried pasta, and drain. Place 1 or 2 large ladlefuls of hot sauce in the bottom of a warmed pasta bowl or deep platter and add the drained pasta. Toss to coat the pasta with the sauce. Place another ladleful of sauce in the center of the pasta. Pass the remaining sauce and the cheese at the table.

tip FRESH VERSUS DRIED HERBS

Add fresh herbs toward the end of cooking so they won't lose their potency, and add dried herbs at the beginning so they have time to rehydrate in the moisture of the dish. (This is especially true of bay leaves.)

Oregano, thyme, rosemary, tarragon, sage, and fennel are the best candidates for drying, as they retain their flavor better than other herbs.

Leave it to the Italians to come up with an ingenious way to cook chicken perfectly. But under a brick? The chicken ends up flat as a pancake. The meat is as moist as can be and the skin is incredibly crisp.

Joanne Weir, AUTHOR, *WEIR COOKING*

Cornish Hens with Basil and Mint

Mattone

Pollo al mattone, or "chicken under a brick," is served in trattorias throughout Tuscany. The traditional mattone is a round, glazed terra-cotta dish with a heavy disklike lid that weights down the chicken evenly as it cooks. The result is beautifully crisp skin and moist, succulent meat.

The more modern mattone is often called a *panini* pan and can be used for cooking chicken in much the same way. The *panini* pan for home use is a square, enameled cast-iron skillet with a black matte interior and a heavy lid that fits down inside the pan and holds the sandwich against the grilling ridge that line the bottom of the pan. It's the same concept as the *mattone,* making the pan useful for either *pollo al mattone,* grilled sandwiches, or other grilled foods.

Tips for Using

The *mattone* works on the stovetop or in the oven up to 350°F. A heat diffuser (page 27) is recommended when used on an electric or gas range. Check the manufacturer's instructions.

Soak the *mattone* in cold water for 2 hours before using it for the first time. Dry it thoroughly in a 350°F oven for 45 minutes, or at room temperature for 12 hours, and then rub with a rough cloth to remove any clay dust from the surface.

Hairline cracks in the surface of terra-cotta cookware are considered normal.

Use the *panini* pan for your favorite version of grilled cheese sandwiches.

Use just the bottom of the *panini* pan for hamburgers, pork chops, pan-seared vegetables, fish steaks, and other foods.

Care in Using

Soak the *mattone* or *panini* pan in warm, soapy water and scrub with a stiff brush. Never put the *mattone* in a dishwasher.

Do not store the *mattone,* or any terra-cotta equipment, in plastic.

Always consult the manufacturer's instructions.

Alternatives

Use any large, heavy skillet for the bottom part of the *mattone* or *panini* pan. For the heavy lid, wrap two bricks in a double layer of aluminum foil and place directly on the chicken, or use a smaller, heavy cast-iron skillet wrapped in foil that fits down into the larger skillet.

recipes

Grilled Provolone and Roasted Red Pepper Sandwiches with Olivada | **Cornish Hens with Basil and Mint** | **Goat Cheese–Stuffed Swiss Chard Bundles with Olives and Sun-Dried Tomatoes**

GRILLED PROVOLONE and ROASTED RED PEPPER SANDWICHES with OLIVADA

PREP 15 min | ROASTED PEPPERS PREP (optional) 1 hr | COOK TIME 10–12 min | SERVES 2

Perhaps because Americans love gooey melted cheese sandwiches, they have enthusiastically embraced the Italian concept of grilled *panini.* The secret of a good *panino* is to keep the ingredients to a minimum. If you like, use focaccia buns or soft rolls in place of the bread slices.

Implements Stove-top Pepper Roaster, Tongs, *Panini* Grill, Wide Spatula, Cutting Board, Silicone Brush

Ingredients

2 large red bell peppers or jarred roasted red peppers

4 (½–inch-thick) slices Italian bread, cut on the diagonal from a long loaf or straight across from a round loaf

4 slices (4 ounces) provolone cheese

4 to 6 large fresh basil leaves

2 tablespoons jarred black-olive *olivada*

2 tablespoons extra-virgin olive oil

1. Roast the peppers as directed in Tip at right. If using jarred peppers, drain, rinse and pat dry. Cut the peppers into ½-inch strips.

2. Place 2 of the bread slices on a work surface. Divide the cheese evenly between the slices. Top the cheese with 2 or 3 basil leaves. Divide the peppers evenly between the sandwiches. Spoon 1 tablespoon of the *olivada* on top of the peppers and spread in a thin layer. Place the remaining bread slices on top and press down firmly. Brush the top of sandwich bread lightly with oil.

3. Preheat a *panini* pan, a stove-top grill pan, or a griddle over medium heat. Arrange the sandwiches oiled side down in the hot pan. Brush the unoiled side of each sandwich lightly with olive oil. Place the cover on top, or use a heavy lid to weight the sandwiches down while grilling. Cook for 4 minutes, or until the sandwiches are toasted on the underside. Remove the lid and, using a wide spatula, turn the sandwiches over. Decrease the heat to medium-low and cook for 4 to 5 minutes more, or until the sandwiches are toasted on the other side and the cheese is melted.

4. Transfer the sandwiches to a cutting board and cut each sandwich in half and serve.

tip ROASTING PEPPERS

Position the broiler rack about 5 inches from the heat source and preheat the broiler. Place a large sheet of aluminum foil on a rimmed sheet pan, and arrange bell peppers shoulder to shoulder on the pan. Slide the pan under the broiler; the peppers should be 1 to 2 inches from the heat source. Broil, turning the peppers with tongs as they blister and darken, for about 20 minutes total, or until they are evenly blistered and blackened on all sides.

Remove the pan from the broiler, fold the foil up over the peppers, and seal tightly to lock in the steam. Let stand for 30 minutes, or until the peppers have cooled and the skins have loosened. Use your fingertips or a small paring knife to peel off the charred skin, working on the foil so all the precious juices will be captured. Separate each pepper into pieces, following its natural contours. Remove the stem and pull out the clump of seeds and the thick white membranes, or ribs. Do not rinse the peppers, or you will wash away flavor.

Place the peppers in a bowl. Place a strainer on the bowl, and pour the contents of the foil into the strainer. Press down to extract the flavorful juices. Discard the solids in the strainer. Use the reserved juices to season a soup, sauce, or the dressing that will be drizzled over the roasted peppers. One large pepper (8 to 10 ounces) will yield about ½ cup roasted pepper strips.

Olives

Olive trees are native to the Mediterranean, but today they are grown from California to South Africa to Australia. All olives are unpalatable until they are cured, usually in lye and then brine. In general, green olives—picked immature—have a crunchy texture, while black olives—the same fruit harvested when ripe—have a softer consistency and richer taste.

Green

ARBEQUINA (Spain) A small, khaki green olive with a sweet nutty taste. Serve with sherry (fino) and salted (preferably Spanish Marcona) almonds.

CERIGNOLA (Italy) A large, meaty, bright green olive with a sweet flavor. Serve with mozzarella di bufala.

GORDAL (Spain) Large, meaty olive sometimes called the queen olive. Serve with Manchego cheese.

MANZANILLA (Spain) Small, cracked or smooth olives with a mild, fruity taste; often stuffed with strips of pimiento.

NAPHLION (Greece) A slim, cracked olive with a meaty taste reminiscent of bacon. Serve with dried figs.

PICHOLINE (France) Small, lightly salted oval olives; used in cooking and wonderful marinated in a delicate French olive oil with crushed fennel seeds.

Black

ALPHONSO (South America) Fruity-tasting, plump purple olive grown in Chile. Serve warm heated in olive oil with orange zest and minced rosemary.

AMFISSA (Greece) Plump, purple-black, mildy sweet, rich olive. Serve with feta cheese.

GAETA (Italy) Small, round pleasantly bitter olive available oil cured (wrinkled) or brine cured (smooth). Marinate with crushed red pepper and crushed garlic, add to a tomato or greens pasta sauce, or use as a pizza topping.

KALAMATA (Greece) Popular almond-shaped purple-black olive cured in red wine vinegar. Good in salads, especially with tomatoes and fresh herbs.

LIGURIAN (Italy) Small, sometimes with stem attached, brine cured and intensely flavored. Similar to Niçoise (France) and difficult to pit.

MOROCCAN (Morocco) There are many types of Moroccan olives that fall into two categories: one is round, firm, meaty, and juicy, and the other is deep black, wrinkled, and oil cured.. Moroccan olives are sometimes available marinated in herbs and spices.

NIÇOISE (France) A tiny brine-cured, mild-tasting olive from Provence that ranges in color from dark brown to deep purple to black. The term à la niçoise suggests that a dish—such as salade niçoise—includes this popluar, nutty-tasting, oval-shaped olive.

CORNISH HENS with BASIL and MINT

PREP 20 min I **STAND TIME** 10 min I **MARINATING** 1 hr I
REST TIME 30 min I **COOK TIME** 30 min I **SERVES** 2–4

Cornish hens prepared *al mattone* cook more evenly and more quickly than a big chicken. In this recipe, the hens are treated to a marinade of white wine, lemon zest, garlic, mint, and basil to enhance their natural flavor. They make a delicious spring meal when accompanied with roasted asparagus and plain boiled potatoes for sopping up the juices.

Implements Kitchen Scissors, Skimmer, *Mattone,*
Tongs or Flat Metal Spatula, Chef's Knife

Ingredients

2 (1¼ pounds each) Cornish hens

4 cups water

Coarse salt and freshly ground black pepper

½ cup dry white wine

⅔ cup extra-virgin olive oil

Grated zest and juice of 1 lemon

2 tablespoons torn fresh basil leaves

2 tablespoons torn fresh mint leaves

2 cloves garlic, grated or finely chopped

1. Working with 1 hen at a time, and using kitchen scissors or poultry shears, cut along either side of backbone and remove. Turn the hen skin side up on a work surface and press down hard with the heel of your hand to flatten the breast and loosen the keel bone. (This is the slightly curved bone that separates the breasts.) Locate the keel bone and pull it free with your fingers. Twist and pull each leg until it pops out of its socket. With the scissors, remove the first and second sections of the wings; cut off the neck, if it's still attached; and trim away any extra skin and clumps of fat. Repeat with the second hen.

2. In a bowl large enough to hold the birds, combine the water and 2 tablespoons of the salt and stir to dissolve the salt. Add the hens, turn to rinse with the salted water, and let stand for 10 minutes. Drain well and pat dry.

3. Rub the hens generously with salt and pepper. Place the hens in a large, clean bowl and add the wine, ⅓ cup of the olive oil, the lemon zest and juice, and the basil, mint, and garlic. Turn to coat the hens. Cover and marinate the hens in the refrigerator for 1 to 2 hours. Remove from the refrigerator 30 minutes before cooking to bring to room temperature.

4. Add the remaining ⅓ cup of the olive oil to the bottom section of a *mattone* or *panini* pan and heat over medium heat for about 5 minutes, or until the oil is very hot but not smoking. Meanwhile, lift the hens from the marinade, reserving the marinade, and place on a platter. With fingertips, gently lift the breast and leg skin away from the flesh of the hens to form pockets. With a skimmer or perforated spoon, lift some of the chopped herb and lemon mixture from the marinade and spread the herb mixture under the skin.

5. When the oil is hot, add the hens, skin side down, to the pan. Cover with the lid and cook, adjusting the heat between medium and medium-low as needed to maintain a steady sizzle, for 15 minutes. Lift the lid and, with tongs or a flat metal spatula, turn the hens over. Cook for 10 minutes longer. Lift the lid again, turn the hens skin side down, and cook for 5 minutes more, or until the juices run clear when the hens are pierced in the leg with the tines of a fork.

6. Transfer the hens to a platter and let stand for 5 minutes before serving. Using a chef's knife, divide the hens into leg and breast portions and serve.

GOAT CHEESE-STUFFED SWISS CHARD BUNDLES with OLIVES and SUN-DRIED TOMATO

PREP 45 to 60 min | COOK TIME 6 min | MAKES 12

Each of these little cheese-stuffed chard bundles is lightly grilled on a *panini* pan, or on an outdoor grill if you like. They make a delicious appetizer, snack, or side dish. For a variation, substitute *ricotta salata,* feta, or a creamy cow's milk blue-veined cheese for the goat cheese.

Implements Rimmed Sheet Pan, 6-Quart Dutch Oven, Slotted Spoon, Cutting Board, *Panini* Pan, Tongs, Silicone Brush

Ingredients

12 large Swiss chard leaves, long stems trimmed

Coarse salt

6 to 8 ounces cold fresh goat cheese, cut into 12 (¼-inch) rounds or (1½-by-½-inch) rectangles

Freshly ground black pepper

½ cup finely chopped olive oil–packed sun-dried tomatoes

½ cup olivada or finely chopped brine-cured black or green olives

Extra-virgin olive oil

1. Line a rimmed sheet pan or large tray with a kitchen towel. Half fill a 6-quart Dutch oven with water and bring to a boil. If the Swiss chard leaves are very large, add them one at a time; otherwise, add two at a time. Cook for 1 minute, or just until limp, and then carefully lift from the water with a slotted spoon or wire skimmer and place on the towel-lined tray. Repeat with the remaining leaves.

2. When the leaves are cool enough to handle, place them, rib side up, on a cutting board. Cut along either side of the rib on each leaf and discard the rib (or save for soup or a pasta dish). Overlap the 2 sections of each leaf to make a solid surface. The leaf area needs to be about 3 to 4 inches wide and 10 to 12 inches long to accommodate the stuffing. Trim leaves that are larger than that.

3. Place a piece of the cheese about one-third of the way down from the top of each leaf. Top with a grinding of pepper. Place about ½ tablespoon of each the tomatoes and olivada on top of the cheese. Fold the top of the leaf over the cheese, fold in the sides, and then roll up the leaf to make a tight bundle about 2 inches square. Brush both sides of each bundle generously with olive oil. The bundles can be prepared up to this point 1 day ahead and cooked just before serving.

4. Place a *panini* pan or stove-top grill pan over medium heat until hot enough for a drop of water to sizzle on contact. Arrange the bundles, seam side down, on the pan and cook for 3 to 4 minutes, until grill marks appear on the underside. Turn with tongs and grill the other side for 3 to 4 minutes, until grill marks appear. Serve warm.

This is a crescent-shaped blade with a wooden knob at each end. It is rocked back and forth on a board to chop herbs and vegetables quickly and efficiently without bruising them. Once you have acquired the knack, you will find it much easier and more satisfactory to use than an ordinary knife.

Lorenza de'Medici, AUTHOR, *LORENZA'S PASTA*

Mezzaluna

This handy, curved-bladed knife, which is used for all kinds of chopping, comes with two basic handle designs. The one-handed model has a handle set in the center of the blade. The two-handed model has a handle at either end of the blade. A third type of *mezzaluna,* with no handle, is a single piece of stainless-steel curved into a double blade that works doubly fast. All of the designs are ideal for rocking the knife back and forth over the food without lifting the blade from the cutting surface.

The *mezzaluna* is good for both mincing and coarsely chopping, and works on a standard cutting board or on a specially designed board with a shallow indentation shaped to match the curve of the blade.

Tips for Using

To use a two-handled *mezzaluna,* place a hand on each handle and rock the blade back and forth without lifting it from the cutting surface.

To use a double-bladed *mezzaluna,* place one hand in the center and rock the blades by flexing your wrist, rather than rocking your hands.

The double-bladed *mezzaluna* with the matching *mezzaluna* cutting board is great for quickly mincing herbs.

The *mezzaluna* blade is razor sharp and should be covered with a blade guard when not in use.

Tips for Caring

Hand washing is recommended.

Always consult the manufacturer's instructions.

Alternatives

A well-sharpened chef's knife is an excellent substitute.

recipes

Tuna and Garden Vegetable Salad | Asparagus and Chopped Egg with Meyer Lemon Olive Oil

TUNA and GARDEN VEGETABLE SALAD

PREP 30 min | CHILL TIME 1 hr | STAND TIME 30 min |
SERVES 6–8

This mélange of coarsely chopped vegetables
and tuna, called *condiglione,* is eaten along the
Ligurian coast. Typically it's a mixture of tomatoes,
cucumbers, celery, green onions, red bell pepper, and
other seasonal vegetables marinated with olive oil,
mashed anchovies, and fresh herbs. Chopping all the
ingredients with the *mezzaluna* saves time and gives
the salad a more authentic quality.

Implements *Mezzaluna*, Cutting Board, Standard
Whisk, Rubber Spatula

Ingredients

4 (1¼ pounds) firm ripe tomatoes, cored and quartered

4 small, pale celery heart stalks with some leafy tops

½ English (seedless) hot house cucumber,
trimmed and quartered lengthwise

1 cup lightly packed fresh Italian parsley
leaves with tender stems

1 red bell pepper, quartered and seeded

1 bunch green onions, green and white parts, ends trimmed

2 (6-ounce) cans olive oil–packed tuna, well
drained and broken into pieces with a fork

3 oil-packed anchovy fillets, rinsed and dried

3 cloves garlic, grated or finely chopped

⅓ cup extra-virgin olive oil

3 tablespoons red wine vinegar

Freshly ground black pepper

Coarse salt

6 leaves romaine or other lettuce, rinsed and dried

¼ cup small black olives, preferably Ligurian, for garnish

1. Using a *mezzaluna* or a chef's knife, chop the tomatoes,
celery, cucumber, parsley, bell pepper, and green onions
into ½-inch pieces on a cutting board. As the vegetables
are cut, transfer them to a large bowl. Add the tuna to
the vegetables in the bowl.

2. Mince the anchovies with the *mezzaluna* on a *mezzaluna* cutting board or standard cutting board, or mince
with the chef's knife. Place in a small bowl. Add the garlic, olive oil, vinegar, 1 teaspoon of salt, and a generous
grinding of pepper. Whisk together until well blended.
Add to the vegetable and tuna in the large bowl. Using
a large rubber spatula, fold gently to blend. Cover tightly
with plastic wrap and refrigerate for up to 1 hour.

3. Take the salad from the refrigerator 30 minutes before
serving, so it has time to come to room temperature.
Taste and add salt, if needed.

4. Line a platter with the romaine leaves, and mound the
salad on top. Garnish with the olives and serve. Serve as
a main dish or side dish.

ASPARAGUS and CHOPPED EGG with MEYER LEMON OLIVE OIL

PREP 15 min | COOK TIME (eggs) 10 to 20 min | STAND TIME (eggs) 15 min | COOK TIME (asparagus) 3 min | SERVES 4 to 8

This recipe, while not traditionally Italian, illustrates the versatility of the *mezzaluna*. It is used to chop every element: the hard-cooked eggs, the asparagus, and the tarragon. The salad, which can be served as a main course, first course, or side dish, is dressed with Meyer lemon–infused olive oil. If you don't live where Meyer lemons grow, a bottle of Meyer lemon-infused olive oil is the next best thing. The lemons, which are especially fragrant, juicy, and sweet, are thought to be a cross between a regular lemon and a mandarin orange.

Implements
2-Quart Saucepan, Serrated Peeler, 5-Quart Sauté Pan, Tongs, *Mezzaluna,* Cutting Board, Rubber Spatula

Ingredients

4 large eggs

½ pound asparagus

1 cup ice cubes

Coarse salt

½ red onion

1 tablespoon packed fresh tarragon leaves, plus 4 small sprigs, for garnish

3 tablespoons Meyer lemon olive oil

2 tablespoons freshly squeezed Meyer lemon or regular lemon juice

Freshly ground black pepper

12 Bibb or other small lettuce leaves, rinsed and dried

10 small plum tomatoes, quartered, for garnish

1. Put the eggs in a 2-quart saucepan and add cold water to cover. Place over medium-high heat and bring to a gentle boil. Remove from the heat, cover, and let stand for 15 minutes. Pour off the hot water, and rinse the eggs with cold water until they are cool. Crack the shells against the sides of the pan, and let the eggs stand in the water for 10 minutes. Drain the eggs, peel, and set aside.

2. While the eggs are standing, trim the tough stem ends from the asparagus, and use a serrated peeler to remove the scales from the lower section of the stalks. Fill a wide bowl with water and add the ice cubes. Pour water to a depth of 1 inch into a 3- quart sauté pan or a deep skillet and bring to a boil. Add the asparagus and 1 teaspoon salt and cook for 3 minutes, or until crisp-tender. Lift the asparagus from the water with tongs and plunge into the iced water. Let stand for 2 minutes and drain.

3. Two at a time, coarsely chop the eggs with the *mezzaluna* on a *mezzaluna* cutting board or a standard cutting board and transfer to a large bowl. Coarsely chop the onion and add to the bowl with the eggs. Alternatively, chop the eggs and the onion with a chef's knife.

4. Pat the asparagus dry with paper towels. Place the spears a few at a time on the cutting board and cut into randomly sized ¼ to 1-inch slices with the *mezzaluna*. Add to the eggs. Put the tarragon leaves on the board, chop finely, and add to the eggs. Or, cut the asparagus and the tarragon with the chef's knife.

5. Drizzle the eggs and asparagus with the olive oil and lemon juice and sprinkle with ½ teaspoon salt and a grinding of pepper. Using a rubber spatula, fold gently to blend.

6. Arrange the lettuce leaves on individual plates or a platter and spoon the salad on top. Garnish with the tomatoes and tarragon sprigs.

With this pasta machine, you can quickly and easily roll out beautiful thin pasta sheets. Then snap on the cutting attachment and make perfect fettuccine. **Giuliano Hazan,** AUTHOR, *HOW TO COOK ITALIAN*

Spinach Pasta Dough

Pasta Machine

Made of chrome-plated steel, the pasta machine, with its easy-to-maneuver hand-cranked rollers, is a compact, sturdy tool for rolling out pasta dough quickly and efficiently. This smart, classic Italian import comes with a clamp to secure it to a countertop or table, so it won't slide while you turn the crank. The fluid rollers turn out 6½-inch-wide pasta sheets in a variety of thicknesses. Attachments for cutting ¼-inch-wide fettuccine and tagliatelle and ⅛-inch-wide trenette or other narrow pasta are included. A dial on the side of the machine adjusts to nine different thicknesses. Easy to store, the pasta machine comes in a 9-by-8-by-6½-inch box. An electric attachment for motorizing the machine is also available, as well as other attachments for making other shapes and sizes of pasta.

Tips for Using

Dust the dough and the rollers with all-purpose flour to help prevent sticking.

Roll a thick disk of dough through the widest setting once, then fold into thirds and roll once or twice more to finish the kneading process before you begin rolling out the sheets.

Do not pull the dough through the rollers. Instead, allow the rollers to flatten and push the dough out.

As you roll, periodically reach under the rollers and wipe off any dough from the pasta scrapers beneath them.

Work quickly and keep any dough you are not immediately rolling covered with either an inverted bowl or a damp kitchen towel. If the dough dries out, it will crack and tear.

Care in Using

Do not immerse the pasta machine in water.

To clean the rollers before use, pass a small disk of pasta dough through them and then discard the dough.

Brush flour and bits of dough from the machine with a stiff brush or a kitchen towel.

Never insert a knife between the rollers.

Always consult the manufacturer's instructions.

Alternatives

A rolling pin can be used to roll the pasta. A long, fat dowel (similar to a broom handle) is typical. To cut ribbons of pasta, roll up the sheet and cut across the roll with a floured knife.

recipes

Spinach Pasta Dough | Roasted Butternut Squash and Spinach Lasagna with Four Cheeses | Rosemary and Cheese Whole Wheat Breadsticks

SPINACH PASTA DOUGH

PREP 45 min | STAND TIME 30 min | MAKES about 1 lb.

Cooked spinach turns pasta dough a pretty jade green and adds a pleasant, albeit subtle, vegetable flavor. The spinach makes the dough softer, so it easier to knead and roll than plain egg pasta. This recipe makes enough pasta for Roasted Butternut Squash and Spinach Lasagna with Four Cheeses on page 279 or for four servings of spinach fettuccine or tagliatelle, which you can cut on the pasta machine with the appropriate attachment.

Implements
Colander, 6-Quart Dutch Oven, Food Processor, 1 or 2 Rimmed Sheet Pans, Paring Knife

Ingredients

8 ounces spinach, stemmed (see Tip, page 279)
2 large eggs
½ teaspoon coarse salt
1½ to 2 cups unbleached all-purpose flour, plus more as needed
Semolina flour or cornmeal, for dusting sheet pan

1. Rinse the spinach in a bowl of cold water and drain in a colander. Transfer to a 6-quart Dutch oven, place over medium-high heat, cover, and cook, stirring once, for 2 to 3 minutes, until the spinach is wilted and tender. Transfer to a colander and press with the back of a spoon to extract the water, or place the spinach in a potato ricer to press out the excess water. Transfer the spinach to a clean dish towel, fold the towel over the spinach, and press to blot out more moisture. Coarsely chop the spinach and set aside. You should have about ⅓ cup.

2. Place the spinach, eggs, and salt in a food processor and pulse until blended. Add 1½ cups of the flour, one heaping tablespoon at a time, pulsing after each addition, or until the dough clears the sides of the bowl and forms a ball, about 1 minute. If the dough seems sticky, add ¼ cup more flour as needed. Remove the blade and, with floured hands, remove the dough from the food processor bowl.

3. Lightly dust a work surface with any remaining flour, and place the dough on it. Knead the dough, using additional flour for your hands as needed to keep the dough smooth and moist but not sticky, for 5 minutes. Invert a bowl over the dough and let the dough rest for 30 minutes, or more.

4. When ready to roll out the dough, follow the manufacturer's instructions to secure the pasta machine to one edge of a countertop or large table. Using a large knife or a bench scraper, divide the dough into 6 equal pieces, and cover 5 pieces with the bowl to prevent them from drying out. Use the heel of your hand to press the dough into an oval. Dust your hands with flour if the dough feels sticky.

5. Dust a rimmed sheet pan with semolina flour, and have ready some clean kitchen towels. Position the pasta machine rollers at number 1, or at the widest opening. Dust the rollers lightly with flour. With one hand, guide the oval of dough between the rollers while turning the crank with the other hand. Fold the dough into thirds to make a rectangle and roll it through again. Repeat the folding and rolling one more time. Then move the rollers one notch smaller and roll the dough through this setting twice. (You don't need to fold the dough into thirds any longer.) As the dough comes through the rollers, hold it so it stays as smooth as possible. Continue rolling, feeding the dough through each setting twice before moving the dial to the next smaller opening, until the dough is ⅛ to 1/16 inch thick, or notch number 6. As you roll the dough, sprinkle it lightly with flour if it becomes sticky.

6. As the rolled sheet of dough emerges from the final setting, cut it into strips the length of the baking dish you will use for the lasagna (14 inches). Each strip should be 2½ to 3 inches wide. If it is wider, trim it with a paring knife or a fluted pasta cutter. Lay the pasta strips in a single layer on the prepared sheet pan and cover with a towel.

7. Repeat with the remaining dough, stacking the pasta strips (always arranged in a single layer) on the prepared pan and covering each layer with a clean kitchen towel to keep the dough from drying out or the pasta strips from sticking to one another. You should have 12 lasagna noodles.

8. When all the pasta dough has been rolled and cut into noodles, let them rest, covered with a towel, for at least 30 minutes or up to 2 hours before cooking.

tip COOK SPINACH ONCE FOR TWO RECIPES

If you are making the pasta to use in Roasted Butternut Squash and Spinach Lasagna with Four Cheeses (below), cook the spinach for both the dough and the filling at the same time and reserve ⅓ cup chopped spinach for the dough.

ROASTED BUTTERNUT SQUASH and SPINACH LASAGNA with FOUR CHEESES

PREP 1½ hr | COOK TIME (butternut squash) 30 min | COOK TIME (spinach) 3 min | COOK TIME (béchamel sauce) 20 min | COOK TIME (lasagna) 55 min | SERVES 8

This all-vegetable spinach-noodle lasagna, with its layers of butternut squash, ricotta cheese, cooked spinach, Gorgonzola, and cheese-rich béchamel, is an ideal main course for a fall or winter dinner party. If you are pressed for time, you can substitute store-bought spinach noodles.

Implements Large Baking Dish, Paring Knife, Colander, 6-Quart Dutch Oven, Large Spoon, 3-Quart Saucier, Flat Whisk, Sauce Whisk, Mesh Skimmer or Slotted Spoon, 9½-by-14-inch Baking Dish

Ingredients

1 (2½-pound) butternut squash, quartered, seeds and membranes removed

¼ cup water

2 pounds spinach, stemmed

PARMESAN BÉCHAMEL SAUCE

4 tablespoons unsalted butter

¼ cup all-purpose flour

1½ cups whole milk

1½ cups half-and-half

1 cup grated Parmigiano-Reggiano cheese

1 teaspoon coarse salt

¼ teaspoon freshly grated nutmeg

2 cups whole-milk ricotta cheese

½ cup grated Parmigiano-Reggiano cheese

2 large eggs

Freshly ground black pepper

1 pound Spinach Pasta Dough (page 278), cut into lasagna noodles, or 1 (10-ounce) box dried spinach noodles

Coarse salt

Freshly grated nutmeg, for dusting

2 cups (8 ounces) coarsely shredded Fontina cheese, preferably *fontina Val d'Aosta*

1 cup (5 ounces) cut-up or crumbled Gorgonzola cheese

1. Preheat the oven to 400°F. Place the squash quarters, cut side down, in a large baking dish and add the water to the dish. Roast the squash for 30 minutes, or until firm but tender when pierced with a fork. Let cool, peel away the skin with a paring knife, and cut each quarter crosswise into ¼-inch-thick slices. Set aside.

2. Rinse the spinach in a bowl of cold water and drain in a colander. Transfer to a 6-quart Dutch oven, place over medium-high heat, cover, and cook, stirring once, for 3 to 5 minutes, until the spinach is wilted and tender. Transfer to a colander and press with the back of a spoon to extract the water, or place the spinach in a potato ricer to press out the excess water. Transfer the spinach to a clean dish towel, fold the towel over the spinach, and press to blot out more moisture. Coarsely chop the spinach and set aside. You should have 1½ to 2 cups.

3. **MAKE THE BÉCHAMEL SAUCE:** In a 3-quart saucepan or saucier, melt the butter over medium-low heat. Add the flour, stir with a flat whisk until the mixture is smooth, and then continue to cook, stirring, for 5 minutes. Gradually add the milk and half-and-half while whisking constantly until smooth. Continue cooking over medium heat, whisking gently, for 5 minutes, or until the sauce boils and thickens. Remove the pan from the heat. Stir in the Parmigiano-Reggiano cheese, salt, and nutmeg.

4. In a medium bowl, combine the cooked spinach and ½ cup of the béchamel sauce and set aside.

5. In a large bowl, combine the ricotta cheese, Parmigiano-Reggiano cheese, eggs, and a generous grinding of pepper. Stir with a sauce whisk until well blended. Set aside.

6. Place the pasta insert in an 8-quart stockpot or pasta cooking pot and fill the pot three-fourths full with water. If not using the pasta insert, fill an 8-quart pot three-fourths full with water. Bring the water to a boil. Place a large, deep bowl (it must be large enough to accommodate the pasta insert, if using) next to the stove and half fill it with cold water. When the water boils, add 3 tablespoons coarse salt and gradually add the lasagna noodles. Cook the noodles until tender but slightly underdone. Fresh noodles will take about 3 minutes, and dried noodles will take about 8 minutes. If using the pasta cooking insert, carefully lift it from the boiling water, allowing the hot water to drain back into the pot, and then place it in the bowl of cold water. If not using the pasta insert, scoop the noodles with the mesh skimmer or slotted spoon from the boiling water and place them in the cold water. When the noodles are cool, lift them from the water and spread in a single layer on kitchen towels to blot dry.

7. Preheat the oven to 350°F. Generously butter a 9½-by-14-inch baking dish. Add a ladleful of the béchamel to the prepared dish, spreading it evenly over the bottom. Arrange 3 noodles side by side, or slightly overlapping if they are wide, on the bottom of the dish. Spoon about half of the ricotta mixture on top and spread evenly. Top with half of the squash slices, arranging them in a single layer. Sprinkle the squash with salt and pepper, dust with nutmeg, and scatter ½ cup of the Fontina evenly over the top. Arrange 3 more noodles on top. Add the spinach mixture by well-spaced spoonfuls and then spread in an even layer. Sprinkle the Gorgonzola evenly over the spinach layer. Arrange 3 more noodles on top. Spoon the remaining ricotta mixture on top and spread in an even layer. Top with the remaining squash slices in a single layer. Sprinkle the squash with salt and pepper, dust with nutmeg, and scatter ½ cup of Fontina over the top. Arrange the remaining 3 noodles on top. Pour the remaining béchamel sauce evenly over the noodles. Sprinkle the top evenly with the remaining 1 cup of Fontina cheese.

8. Bake for 55 minutes, or until the top is browned and bubbly. Remove from the oven and let stand for 15 minutes before serving. Cut into squares to serve.

ROSEMARY and CHEESE WHOLE WHEAT BREADSTICKS

PREP 30 min | **RISING TIME** 1 to 1½ hr | **REST TIME** 15 min | **COOK TIME** 18–20 min | **MAKES** about 6 dozen

A pasta machine fitted with the fettuccine cutter makes terrific breadsticks.

Implements Stand Mixer, Pasta Machine, Rimmed Sheet Pans and/or Baking Sheets

Ingredients

1 cup warm water (105° to 115°F)

1 package active dry yeast (about 2½ teaspoons)

½ teaspoon sugar

1½ cups unbleached all-purpose flour, plus more as needed

1 cup whole wheat flour

2 tablespoons extra-virgin olive oil, plus more for oiling bowl

2 teaspoons salt

1½ teaspoon finely chopped dried rosemary

1¾ cup (about 2 ounces) aged Asiago cheese

¼ cup yellow cornmeal, plus more as needed

1. In the large bowl of a stand mixer, or in a large bowl if mixing by hand, combine the warm water, yeast, and sugar, and stir to blend. Cover with plastic wrap and let stand for 5 minutes, or until foamy.

2. Fit the mixer with the paddle attachment. Add 1 cup of the all-purpose flour, the whole wheat flour, and the olive oil, salt, and rosemary to the yeast mixture. Beat on medium speed, or by hand with a wooden spoon, until well blended and a sticky dough begins to form. Gradually beat in the cheese. Beat in as much of the remaining ½ cup of flour as needed for the dough to pull away from the sides of the bowl and lose some of its stickiness.

3. Exchange the paddle attachment for the dough hook and knead the dough on low to medium speed, adding flour as needed if the dough is stickly, for about 10 minutes, or until smooth and elastic. Remove from the bowl onto a lightly floured work surface and knead for 1 minute, and set aside. Or, if kneading by hand, turn the dough out of the bowl onto a lightly floured work surface and knead, sprinkling the dough or the surface with extra flour as needed to prevent sticking, for 10 minutes, or until the dough is smooth and elastic.

4. Wash out the bowl and oil the inside with a light film of olive oil. Add the dough and turn to coat it with the oil. Cover the bowl with plastic wrap and let the dough rise in a warm place for 1 to 1½ hours, until doubled in bulk.

5. Punch down the dough and turn it out onto a lightly floured surface. Knead it once or twice. Using a large knife or a bench scraper, cut the dough into 8 equal pieces. Roll each piece into a smooth ball. Dust with additional flour, cover with a kitchen towel, and let stand while setting up the pasta machine.

6. Preheat the oven to 350°F. Divide the cornmeal between 2 rimmed sheet pans; shake to distribute it evenly.

7. When ready to shape the breadsticks, follow the manufacturer's instructions to secure the pasta machine to one edge of a countertop or large table and fit it with the fettuccine cutter.

8. On a floured surface, flatten 1 ball of the dough with the heel of your hand into an oval about 5 or 6 inches long and ¼ inch thick. Dust it generously with flour and insert a narrow end into the fettuccine cutter. Turn the crank with one hand and hold your other hand under the fettuccine cutter so that the cut dough will drape over your hand as it comes out. Lay the strips without touching on a prepared sheet pan.

9. Repeat with the remaining 7 balls of dough. If you run out of pans, lay the dough strips on dish towels dusted with cornmeal and transfer to cooled sheet pans as they become available.

10. Bake 2 sheet pans of breadsticks at a time on 2 racks, switching the racks and turning the pans 180 degrees after 8 minutes, for 18 to 20 minutes, or until lightly browned. Cool on the pans. The breadsticks will keep in an airtight container at room temperature for 3 to 4 weeks.

Baking stones, which provide thermal mass to absorb heat, can make a big difference in the effectiveness of a home oven.

Peter Reinhart, AUTHOR, *AMERICAN PIE*

Pizza with Radicchio, Pears, Gorgonzola, and Walnuts

Pizza Stone and Peel

If you enjoy making pizza, these two relatively inexpensive tools are indispensable. A pizza stone is a large, round or rectangular terra-cotta or stone slab for baking pizza or bread. You place it on the lowest rack of the oven, turn the oven on, and the stone preheats along with the oven, to approximate the radiant heat of the brick-lined ovens found in pizzerias and bread bakeries. When the pizza is slid onto the hot stone to bake, the stone distributes heat evenly throughout the pie and absorbs the moisture from the dough, to create a crispier crust. Look for a thick, heavy stone that will resist cracking.

A pizza peel is a long-handled, oversized spatula that simplifies sliding pizzas or breads into a hot oven and retrieving them when they are done. Also known as baker's peels, these handy tools are typically made of rock maple, basswood, alder, or another hardwood or aluminum and vary in size from about 12 by 14 inches to 16 by 18 inches, with a handle 8 to 10 inches long.

Tips for Using a Pizza Stone

Before its first use, wash the stone with cold water. Never use detergent.

Place the stone in a cold oven and then preheat the oven. Typically, pizza is baked at the maximum oven temperature, between 500° and 550°F.

Store the stone on the lowest rack of the oven, so it's always handy for baking pizza or bread.

Do not use the stone to bake breads with a high-fat content, because fat will stain the porous stone.

Tips for Using a Pizza Peel

To prevent sticking, sprinkle the peel with flour or cornmeal before sliding it under the uncooked pizza crust or loaf of bread.

Place the pizza-shaped dough on the peel and then add the toppings.

Reach the peel into the oven and angle it downward. Shake it gently until the pizza slowly slides off the peel and onto the stone.

To retrieve the finished pizza, slide the peel under the crust and guide it onto the peel.

Care in Using a Pizza Stone

Avoid spilling anything on the porous stone, as it readily stains.

To remove bits of burned-on food from a cooled stone, rub it with a detergent-free dry scouring pad.

Care in Using a Pizza Peel

Wipe a metal peel with a damp cloth. Wooden peels should be kept dry, or they will eventually warp, so wipe clean with a damp kitchen towel and dry thoroughly.

Alternatives

For a pizza stone, line the oven with unglazed clay tiles that have been rinsed in cold water, dried, and tempered in a hot oven for 15 minutes before the first use.

For a pizza peel, use a rimless sheet pan (cookie sheet) lightly dusted with flour.

recipes

Pizza with Radicchio, Pears, Gorgonzola, and Walnuts | Pizza with Mozzarella, Prosciutto, and Baby Arugula

PIZZA with RADICCHIO, PEARS, GORGONZOLA, and WALNUTS

PREP 30 min | **RISING TIME** 1½ hr and 1 hr | **COOK TIME** (per pizza) 8 to 10 min | **SERVES** 4

Pizza toppings can be classic, such as tomato, mozzarella, and fresh basil (*pizza Margherita*), or ultramodern, like smoked trout, goat cheese, and sun-dried tomatoes. This topping of torn radicchio leaves, thin pear slices, and a scattering of Gorgonzola falls somewhere in between. Here, four individual pizzas are made, but you can make one large or two medium-sized pizzas instead.

Implements Pizza Stone, Pizza Peel, Cutting Board, Cheese Grater, Kitchen Scissors

Ingredients

PIZZA DOUGH

1 cup warm water (105° to 115°F)

1 teaspoon active dry yeast

2½ cups unbleached all-purpose flour, plus more for dusting

½ cup cake flour (not self-rising)

1 teaspoon coarse salt

TOPPING

1 head radicchio, cored, leaves separated, and torn into 2- to 3-inch pieces

2 or 3 large, ripe Bosc or Bartlett pears, unpeeled, quartered, cored, and each quarter cut into 4 wedges

1 cup broken walnuts

10 ounces Gorgonzola cheese, coarsely crumbled (about 2 cups)

Freshly ground black pepper

4 tablespoons extra-virgin olive oil

Wedge of Parmigiano-Reggiano cheese, for grating

1. **MAKE THE DOUGH:** Place the warm water in a small bowl and sprinkle with the yeast. Cover with plastic wrap and let stand for 5 minutes, or until foamy. Stir to dissolve, if necessary.

2. In a large bowl, combine the all-purpose flour, cake flour, and salt, and stir to mix. Pour the yeast mixture over the flour mixture and stir with a wooden spoon until a soft dough forms.

3. Lightly dust a work surface with flour, and turn the dough out onto it. Knead the dough, sprinkling the dough or the work surface with extra flour as needed to prevent sticking, for 10 minutes, or until smooth and elastic. The dough can also be kneaded in a heavy-duty food processor, or in a stand mixer with a dough hook.

4. Shape the dough into a smooth ball, place it on a floured surface, and cover with an inverted bowl. Let rise, at room temperature, for about 1½ hours, or until doubled in bulk.

5. About 45 minutes before baking the pizza, place a pizza stone, unglazed quarry tiles, or a baking sheet on the lowest rack in the oven, and preheat the oven to 500°F.

6. When the dough is ready, use a large knife or a bench scraper to divide it into 4 equal pieces. With lightly floured hands, press out any bubbles that might have formed in the dough, and form each piece into a small smooth ball. Place about 4 inches apart on a lightly floured surface. Cover with a clean kitchen towel and let rise for 1 hour, or until doubled in bulk.

7. Generously dust a pizza peel or a rimless sheet pan (cookie sheet) with flour. On a lightly floured work surface, and with floured hands, pat out 1 ball of the dough, stretching gently and turning, into a round about 10 inches in diameter and ¼ inch thick, leaving the edges of the round slightly thicker. Gently slide the peel under the round of dough.

8. **TOP THE PIZZA:** Arrange about 6 pieces of torn radicchio leaves on the dough round. Top with 8 pear slices, evenly spaced in a sunburst pattern. Sprinkle with about ¼ cup of the walnuts, and top with about ½ cup of the Gorgonzola, distributing them evenly over the surface.

Add a grinding of pepper and drizzle with 1 tablespoon of the olive oil.

9. Open the oven door. Guide the peel onto the pizza stone, tilting the peel and gently shaking it so the pizza slowly slides off the peel and onto the center of the preheated stone. Close the oven door and bake the pizza for 8 to 10 minutes, until the crust is browned and crisp.

10. When the pizza is ready, open the oven door, carefully slide the peel under the pizza, retrieve the pizza from the oven, and slide it onto a cutting board. Using a cheese grater, grate about 1 tablespoon of Parmigiano-Reggiano over the top. Cut the pizza into wedges, using a pizza wheel or kitchen scissors, and serve.

11. Repeat steps 7, 8, 9, and 10 with the remaining dough and topping ingredients. Pizzas can be served as they are ready or all at once. If you have a second oven, you can keep the pizzas warm on baking sheets at 250°F until you are ready to serve them all at once.

PIZZA with MOZZARELLA, PROSCIUTTO, and BABY ARUGULA

PREP 30 min | **RISING TIME** 1½ hr and 1 hr | **COOK TIME** (per pizza) 6 to 8 min | **SERVES** 4

Pizza topped with milky sweet mozzarella, paper-thin slices of prosciutto, and tender, pepper arugula leaves is a favorite in the pizzerias of Naples. This one instead includes a scattering of red onion slices and a shower of Parmigiano-Reggiano cheese, too.

Implements Pizza Stone, Pizza Peel, Cutting Board, Cheese Grater, Kitchen Scissors

Ingredients

Pizza dough (page 284)
Unbleached all-purpose unbleached flour, for dusting

1 pound fresh mozzarella cheese, thinly sliced and patted dry with paper towels
1⅓ cups thin half slices red onion
Freshly ground black pepper
2 tablespoons extra-virgin olive oil
4 cups lightly packed baby arugula leaves, rinsed and dried
Wedge of Parmigiano-Reggiano cheese, for grating
6 to 8 thin slices prosciutto

1. Make the dough as directed in steps 1 through 6 (page 284).

2. Generously dust a pizza peel or a rimless sheet pan (cookie sheet) with flour. On a lightly floured work surface, and with floured hands, pat out 1 ball of the dough, stretching gently and turning, into a round about 10 inches in diameter and ¼ inch thick, leaving the edges of the round slightly thicker. Gently slide the peel under the round of dough.

3. Arrange about one-fourth of the mozzarella slices on the dough round. Evenly spread about ⅓ cup of the onion slices over the cheese. Add a grinding of black pepper and drizzle with 1½ teaspoons of the olive oil.

4. Open the oven door. Guide the peel onto the pizza stone, tilting the peel and gently shaking it so the pizza slowly slides off the peel and onto the center of the preheated stone. Close the oven door and bake the pizza for 6 to 8 minutes, until the crust is browned and crisp.

5. When the pizza is ready, open the oven door, carefully slide the peel under the pizza, retrieve the pizza from the oven, and slide it onto a cutting board. Top the pizza with 1 cup of the arugula leaves and grate about 1 tablespoon of Parmigiano-Reggiano cheese over the top. Arrange 1 or 1½ slices of prosciutto, torn into strips, on top of the arugula. Cut the pizza into wedges using a pizza wheel or kitchen scissors to serve.

6. Repeat steps 2, 3, 4, and 5 with the remaining dough and topping ingredients. Pizzas can be served as they are ready or all at once. If you have a second oven, you can keep the pizzas warm on baking sheets at 250°F until you are ready to serve them all at once.

Apple Risotto with
Prosciutto and Hazelnuts

Perfect risotto is easy to make at home as long as you have the right pan. A good risotto pan should be heavy to allow the rice to simmer without sticking and wide so the liquid evaporates easily. The sides of the pan should be low enough to enable you to thoroughly stir, yet high enough so that the liquid does not splash out.

Michele Scicolone, AUTHOR, *1,000 ITALIAN RECIPES*

Risotto Pan

The classic risotto pan is made of tin-lined copper, prized for its quick, even heat conduction. Some pans come with a detachable arced handle, and others sport a single long handle. Sizes range from a 4-quart capacity and about 10 inches in diameter to a 6-quart capacity and about 12 inches in diameter.

The pan's profile—low sides and broad surface—provides ample room for the purposeful and thorough stirring and rapid evaporation required to produce an exquisitely creamy risotto. A special risotto spoon has a pointed tip for reaching into the corners of the pot, and a unique hole in the bowl for the rice to flow through.

Tips for Using

Because copper is an excellent conductor of heat, keep the heat at medium to medium-low.

The pan's broad surface means the liquid will simmer and evaporate quickly, yielding shorter cooking times than in narrower pans.

Taste the rice periodically during cooking to check for doneness. Some varieties of Italian rice, including Carnaroli and Vialone Nano, take slightly longer to cook than others, such as Arborio.

Care in Using

Wash the pan with mild soap, warm water, and a soft brush.

Clean the copper with a halved lemon dipped in coarse salt.

Never put the pan in a dishwasher.

Always consult the manufacturer's instructions.

Alternatives

Any 6- to 8-quart broad Dutch oven or 5-quart sauté pan and a flat-edged wooden spoon can be used for making risotto.

recipes

Apple Risotto with Prosciutto and Hazelnuts |
Shrimp, Peas, and Saffron Risotto

APPLE RISOTTO with PROSCIUTTO and HAZELNUTS

PREP 15 min | COOK TIME 30 min | SERVES 4

Italian cooks are famous for being innovative with seasonal ingredients, so fruit in risotto is not unusual. Here, use tart green apples like Granny Smith. To ensure a creamy consistency, stir constantly while the risotto bubbles in the pan. As you stir, be sure to reach into the corners and evenly along the bottom to prevent sticking and scorching.

Implements 3-Quart Saucepan, Risotto Pan, Slotted Spoon, Large Ladle, Wooden Risotto Spoon

Ingredients

¼ cup hazelnuts

6 to 8 cups low-sodium chicken broth

2 tablespoons extra-virgin olive oil

4 thin slices prosciutto, cut crosswise into ¼-inch-wide strips

½ cup chopped yellow onion

½ cup dry white wine

1½ cups Carnaroli, Vialone Nano, or Arborio rice

3 Granny Smith or other tart green apples, peeled, cored, and diced (about 3 cups)

¼ teaspoon freshly grated nutmeg

½ cup grated Parmigiano-Reggiano cheese, plus more for serving

Coarse salt

tip TOASTING AND PEELING HAZELNUTS

Spread hazelnuts on a rimmed sheet pan and roast in 350°F oven for 15 to 20 minutes or until the skins crack. Wrap in a coarse kitchen towel to cool. Rub cooled nuts vigorously with towel to loosen skins. Don't worry if small bits of skin remain on the nuts.

1. Toast and peel the hazelnuts as directed. (See Tip below.) Coarsely chop and set aside.

2. In a 3-quart saucepan, heat the chicken broth over medium-low heat to a simmer. Decrease the heat to the lowest setting and cover to keep hot.

3. In a risotto pan, 8-quart Dutch oven, or 5-quart sauté pan, heat the olive oil over medium heat until hot enough to sizzle a piece of prosciutto. Add the prosciutto and cook, stirring, for about 3 minutes, or until lightly browned. With a slotted spoon or skimmer, transfer the prosciutto to a small bowl.

4. Add the onion to the oil left in the pan and sauté over medium-low heat, stirring, for 5 minutes, or until softened. Add the rice, decrease the heat to low, and cook, stirring, for 3 minutes, or until it is evenly coated with the oil and heated through. Add the wine, raise the heat to medium, bring to a boil, and stir until absorbed.

5. Using a large ladle, add about 1 cup of the hot broth and half of the diced apple to the rice. Cook over medium heat, stirring constantly with a risotto or flat-edged wooden spoon, until the broth is almost fully absorbed. Add the remaining broth ½ cup at a time, stirring constantly and adding more broth only after the previous addition has been absorbed, until the rice begins to pull away from the sides of the pan. Adjust the heat so the rice simmers rapidly throughout the cooking. Add the remaining apple during the last 10 minutes of cooking, and use as much of the hot broth as the rice will absorb. The total cooking time will be 20 to 30 minutes. The risotto is done when it is creamy and the grains are plump and tender with a slight resistance to the bite, not when the timer says it is. Stir in the nutmeg and cheese until fully blended and season to taste with salt.

6. Remove the risotto from the heat and let stand for 3 minutes before serving. Spoon into warmed shallow bowls and scatter the crisped prosciutto and the hazelnuts evenly over the top. Pass additional cheese at the table.

SHRIMP, PEAS, and SAFFRON RISOTTO

PREP 30 min | COOK TIME 30 min | SERVES 4

Rice tinted yellow and flavored by aromatic saffron looks pretty and has a haunting flavor. The color and taste of the pink shrimp and green peas add both a visual and textural contrast. Simmering the shrimp shells in the broth infuses it with the taste of the sea.

Implements 10-inch Skillet, Flat-Edged Wooden Spatula, Strainer, 3-Quart Saucepan, Risotto Pan, Large Ladle, Wooden Risotto Spoon

Ingredients

1 pound medium shrimp in the shell

2 tablespoons extra-virgin olive oil

1 clove garlic, grated or finely chopped

1 cup dry white wine

1 leafy sprig basil, plus 4 leaves

6 cups low-sodium chicken broth, plus boiling water if needed

1 teaspoon lightly packed saffron threads

3 tablespoons unsalted butter

½ cup chopped yellow onion

1½ cups Carnaroli, Vialone Nano, or Arborio rice

½ cup frozen peas, thawed

Coarse salt

1 to 2 tablespoons freshly squeezed lemon juice

1. Peel the shrimp and reserve the shells. Devein the shrimp, if necessary, then chop coarsely and refrigerate until needed.

2. Heat a 10-inch skillet over medium heat until hot enough for a drop of water to sizzle on contact. Add 1 tablespoon of the olive oil and the shrimp shells, increase the heat to medium-high, and cook, stirring, for 5 minutes, or until the shells turn dark red. Add the garlic and cook, stirring over low heat, for 1 minute. Add the wine and basil sprig, increase the heat to high, and bring to a boil. Boil,

stirring with a flat-edged wooden spatula, for 5 minutes, or until the wine is reduced by half.

3. Place a strainer over a bowl and add the shrimp mixture. Press down hard with the back of a large spoon to extract flavor from the shells. Discard the shells and add the shrimp broth to a 3-quart saucepan.

4. Add the chicken broth to the shrimp broth and bring to a boil over high heat. Decrease the heat to the lowest setting, stir in the saffron, cover, and keep hot.

5. In a risotto pan, 8-quart Dutch oven, or 5-quart sauté pan, heat the remaining 1 tablespoon olive oil and 1 tablespoon of the butter over medium-low heat until the butter has melted. Add the onion and sauté, stirring, for 5 minutes, or until softened. Add the rice, decrease the heat to low, and cook, stirring, for 3 minutes, or until it is evenly coated with the oil and butter and heated through.

6. Using a large ladle, add about 1 cup of hot broth to the rice and cook, stirring constantly, over medium heat until the broth is almost fully absorbed. Add the remaining broth ½ cup at a time, stirring constantly and adding more broth only after the previous addition has been absorbed, until the rice begins to pull away from the sides of the pan. Adjust the heat so the rice simmers rapidly throughout the cooking. Add the reserved shrimp and the peas during the last 10 minutes of cooking, and use as much of the hot broth as the rice will absorb. Or, use boiling water if you have used up all of the broth. The total cooking time will be 20 to 30 minutes. The risotto is done when it is creamy and the grains are plump and tender with a slight resistance to the bite, not when the timer says it is. Season to taste with salt. Remove from the heat, add the remaining 1 tablespoon butter and 1 tablespoon of the lemon juice, and stir constantly until fully blended. Taste and add the remaining lemon juice, if needed.

7. Remove the risotto from the heat and let stand for 3 minutes before serving. Meanwhile, stack the basil leaves, roll up lengthwise into a tight tube, and thinly slice crosswise to make a chiffonade. Spoon the risotto into warmed shallow bowls. Sprinkle an equal amount of the basil on top of each bowl and serve.

10 The IBERIAN KITCHEN

The Iberian Pantry

Spain and Portugal make up the Iberian peninsula at the western gate of the Mediterranean Sea. Both kitchens rely heavily on tomatoes, garlic, olive oil, and peppers, and they share a long history. The Moors, who occupied parts of the peninsula from the eighth to the fifteenth century, introduced lemon and orange trees, saffron, rice, eggplants, hazelnuts, and eastern spices. In Portugal, you find the strangely beautiful *cataplana*, a clam-shaped cooking pan that is perfect for slow cooking meats and shellfish to a succulent finish. Spain has its legendary paella that refers to both the large, round, shallow pan and the country's best-known dish invented by rural workers as a hearty midday lunch prepared outdoors from ingredients at hand. The culinary treasures in this chapter are guaranteed to entice you to explore dining adventures from Spain and Portugal.

Chorizo (Spanish) and Chouriço (Portuguese)

This dry, spicy pork sausage is typically flavored with paprika, garlic, and spices, with the spices varying from region to region. It is widely used in both countries as a seasoning in slow-cooked bean and meat stews and is also sautéed and grilled. In Spain, chorizo is often used to flavor paella.

Marcona Almonds

Spain grows many almonds, but the Marcona is considered the best. Flat and heart shaped, it has a milky, nutty flavor and texture that is crunchy but slightly softer than other almonds. Marcona almonds are peeled and roasted in sunflower oil, or roasted in olive oil and coated with fine salt. They are typically eaten as an accompaniment to wine or sherry with Manchego or another mild, flavorful Spanish cheese. Look for them in shops carrying Spanish foods and in specialty-food stores.

Paprika

In Spain, paprika is *pimentón,* or finely ground dried red pepper. It is available in different intensities, depending on the type of pepper used. Smoke-dried *pimentón (pimentón de la Vera)* has a complex smoked-wood aroma and flavor. Few traditional Portuguese recipes call for sweet paprika. Portuguese cooks instead prefer *massa de pimentão,* a paste of sweet red peppers, garlic, and olive oil, but because it is not readily available, adapted recipes often substitute sweet paprika.

Piquillo Peppers

A favorite of Spanish cooks, this 3-inch-long, triangular, intensely flavored, dark red pepper, known as *pimiento de piquillo,* takes its name from the word *pico,* or "beak," which describes its pointed tip. The peppers are sold, packed in jars or cans, in specialty-food shops. A popular dish calls for stuffing them with a puree of salt cod.

Quince Paste

Membrillo is the Spanish word for "quince," a yellow-skinned fruit that looks like a cross between an apple and a pear, with rough skin and tart, astringent flesh. The same word is used for the Spanish quince paste made by cooking down quince with sugar to a solid jelly. The paste is most commonly sold in plastic-wrapped blocks or rectangular tubs. It is often sliced and served with cheese, usually Manchego.

Saffron

This costly spice, the stigma of a specific variety of crocus, is painstakingly gathered by hand. Spanish saffron is world renowned for its high quality and pure taste. Always purchase saffron threads rather than ground saffron, as the threads retain their flavor better. Before adding the threads to a dish, some cooks crush them in a mortar and pestle and dissolve in boiling water or broth. Saffron contributes a distinctive flavor, alluring aroma, and pretty golden color to rice dishes or pale-colored sauces.

Salt Cod

Called *bacalao* in Spain and *bacalhau* in Portugal, salt cod is a favorite ingredient of both cuisines, with enough recipes for each to fill an entire book. Before cooking, the dried salt cod must be soaked in several changes of cold water for at least a day. Some popular uses for salt cod are baked with eggs and potatoes, flaked in salads, added to fritters, pureed with cream or olive oil, or stuffed into pastry.

Serrano Ham

This prized Spanish ham, known as *jamón serrano,* is salted and dry cured. The aging time, from as few as 12 months to as long as 30 months, is closely controlled. *Serrano* ham is typically thinly sliced and served much like Italians serve prosciutto.

Sherry Vinegar

The most impressive sherry vinegars in the world come from around the city of Jerez de la Frontera, in Andalusia in southwest Spain. Made from the best sherry wine and aged in wooden barrels, these vinegars have a great depth of flavor. Use them on tomato salads, mixed greens, or to finish a simple pan sauce. A favorite combination is sherry vinegar splashed on cooked beets and garnished with torn basil leaves.

Spanish Cheeses

CABRALES

This cave-aged blue-veined cheese, usually made from cow's milk, has a strong smell and big flavor. Sometimes the wheels are wrapped in maple leaves. It is served as a table cheese with sliced fruit and nuts or with thin slices of quince paste.

QUESO DE MURCIA AL VINO

Known in English as drunken goat cheese, this semisoft, mild, sweet cheese is washed with red wine. The interior remains white, but the outside turns pale purple. It is served as a table cheese with sliced fruit and/or nuts.

IDIAZÁBAL

A specialty of the Basque region, Idiazábal is a dense, ivory-colored sheep's milk cheese with a tan rind, a nutty flavor, and a buttery or firm texture depending on how long it has been aged. It is available smoked and unsmoked. Idiazábal is most often eaten as a snack or a table cheese and is perfect with a glass of hearty Spanish red wine.

MANCHEGO

This popular sheep's milk cheese has a mild to sharp taste and a rich, nutty flavor. The hard rind is impressed with a quickly recognizable zigzag pattern from the molds in which the cheese is aged. It is enjoyed as a table cheese and is also used in cooking because of its good melting properties.

Spanish Olives

Spain is a major producer of cured olives, both green and black. Among the most popular varieties are the Arbequina, a small, round, nutty-tasting greenish brown olive; the big, green Gordal (also known as the *gorda,* or "fat"), commonly called the queen olive; and the Manzanilla (sometimes spelled Manzanillo), a small, round greenish brown olive with a meaty taste.

Spanish Olive Oil

Spain is the world's largest producer of olive oil, with Andalusia, in the southern tier of the country, the primary area of production. Oil is also pressed to the east in Murcia and to the north in Catalonia. Differences in the varietals, the climate, and soil contribute to variations in the style and taste of the oils of these various areas.

In Catalonia, the oils tend to be elegant, with the gentle, sweet flavor of the olive, while Andalusian oils are full bodied and assertive, with a pronounced taste of the fruit. In the Andalusian province of Córdoba, which relies on a different olive that most of the region, the oils are smoother and more delicate. Murcian oils are robust and hearty, with a distinctive olive taste.

Olive oil is used for both cooking and as a condiment or flavoring oil. Spanish cooks, like cooks in most countries where olive oil is used, primarily rely on pure olive oil for cooking and extra-virgin olive oil for drizzling over a dish—seafood, meats, vegetables—just before serving.

Spanish Rice

The best rice for paella is Spanish medium-grain rice, although Italian Arborio or Carnaroli can be used in a pinch. Spanish rice, like Italian risotto rice, has a white center that keeps its bite as the softer outside soaks up the flavorful juices of a dish. The grains hold their shape well, whether cooked in paella or other rice dishes or in soups. The varieties to look for are Bomba, Calasparra, and Valencia. All of them are prized for their ability to absorb a large amount of liquid without becoming soft or sticky. Valencia has slightly smaller grains than the other two, and though all of them are good for making paella, Bomba and Calasparra are generally considered the best choice.

Nut Oils

Nut oils are pressed from toasted nuts. Because of their low smoke point, they should not be used for frying. Substitute nut oils for part or all of the oil in mayonnaise, drizzle over salad greens, or use in light vinaigrettes. Nut oils spoil easily, so buy them in small quantities and store them in the refrigerator for no more than 6 months. Bring to room temperature before using.

Almond Oil Almond oil has a delicate flavor. It is excellent on spinach salad with bacon and toasted almonds and drizzled over boiled potatoes or rice pilaf garnished with toasted almonds.

Hazelnut Oil Hazelnut oil has a deep amber color and complex flavor. Use in place of butter in pureed vegetables or mashed potatoes, add it to wild rice pilaf made with dried apricots and chopped toasted hazelnuts, or whisk it into an orange vinaigrette to dress a salad of greens, apples, and chopped toasted hazelnuts.

Macadamia Nut Oil Macadamia nut oil has a very mild nut taste. Unlike other nut oils, it has a high smoke point, which is why cooks like to use it for pan-frying potatoes, stir-frying vegetables, and other high-heat cooking.

Pistachio Oil Show off the luxurious green color and clean flavor of pistachio oil by drizzling it on a disk of fresh goat cheese or a salad of sliced beets and avocado wedges. Sprinkle the salads with chopped pistachios to reinforce the nut flavors in the oil. Use it as the oil in a pistachio-nut pesto or drizzle it on roasted fish or grilled or broiled lamb chops.

Walnut Oil Use this richly flavored oil to season fresh greens along with a squirt of lemon juice and a sprinkle of coarse sea salt. Add some roasted walnut halves and curls of nutty-tasting Gruyère or Comté cheese. Walnut oil is also good drizzled on freshly cooked asparagus spears or a walnut, pear, and goat cheese salad.

There's a reason the Portuguese embraced the cataplana: the name is used to describe two things, a clam, chorizo, and tomato stew or the copper cooking vessel that resembles two hinged clamshells. The process is simple, the results miraculous.

Joanne Weir, AUTHOR, *FROM TAPAS TO MEZE*

Clam, Pork, Sausage, and
Bacon Stew

Cataplana

Two side handles clamp this hinged domed classic Portuguese pan shut, creating a tight seal, so that foods cook in their own juices. The result is a memorably succulent dish. Originally the *cataplana* was used only for fish and shellfish—it looks like an outsized clam shell—but today's Portuguese cooks use it for everything from whole chickens to pork roasts to meat and seafood stews.

The most handsome *cataplana* is made of hammered copper lined with tin and ranges in size from 6½ to 11½ inches. Since tin-lined copper is soft, make sure to use cooking tools that won't scar the metal.

Tips for Using

Prepare the sauce in a separate pan, pour it over the shellfish, chicken, or meats in the *cataplana,* secure the lid, and cook the dish.

The steam heat that builds up in the *cataplana* creates the ideal moist environment for cooking clams and mussels.

Always use the *cataplana* on top of the stove. The rounded bottom makes the pan a little unsteady, but Portuguese food authority Jean Anderson suggests using a wok ring (page 30) to stabilize it.

Because of its attractive shape—and especially if it is hammered copper—the *cataplana* can be taken to the table for serving.

Wear oven mitts when opening the hot *cataplana.* Both the domes and the brass handles will be fiery to the touch.

Care in Using

Wash with warm, soapy water and a soft brush. Never wash in a dishwasher. Shine your copper *cataplana* by gently rubbing it with a special copper cleaner or with a halved lemon dipped in salt.

Alternatives

A Dutch oven or braiser with a tight-fitting lid is a successful stand-in for the *cataplana.*

recipes
Clam, Pork, Sausage, and Bacon Stew | Baby Back Ribs with Cannellini Beans

CLAM, PORK, SAUSAGE, and BACON STEW

PREP 30 min | COOK TIME 50 min | SERVES 4

A number of traditional Portuguese dishes are based on the unlikely, but flavorful, combination of pork and shellfish. This variation on *amêijoas na cataplana,* the classic clam and pork stew, calls for three types of pork: fresh pork cubes, spicy sausage, and bacon. The addition of Italian green beans, also known as romano beans, with the clams makes this recipe a one-pot meal. Serve with plenty of bread to sop up the flavorful sauce.

Implements Food Mill, Rubber Spatula, Large, Heavy Skillet, *Cataplana,* Oven Mitts

Ingredients

1 can (28-ounce) Italian plum tomatoes with juices

2 tablespoons extra-virgin olive oil

2 (¼-inch-thick) slices bacon, cut into ¼-inch dice

1 cup chopped yellow onion

1 cup chopped, seeded red bell pepper

½ cup chopped, seeded green bell pepper

3 cloves garlic, coarsely chopped

4 ounces *chouriço* or chorizo, casings removed and cut into ¼-inch dice

4 ounces pork tenderloin, loin, or shoulder, cut into ¼-inch dice (optional)

2 teaspoons sweet paprika

½ cup dry white wine

2 tablespoons finely chopped fresh Italian parsley

2 pounds littleneck or Manila clams, cleaned (see Tip, page 222)

8 ounces romano or other green beans, trimmed and cut into 1-inch lengths

1. Fit a food mill with the medium disk, and set the mill on the rim of a medium bowl. Put the tomatoes with their juices in the food mill and puree. Reverse the crank to extract every bit of flavor from the tomato pulp, and occasionally stop to clean the underside of the mill with a rubber spatula, so the puree falls freely. Discard the pulp left in the strainer. Set the puree aside.

2. In a large, heavy skillet, heat the olive oil over medium heat until hot enough to sizzle a piece of bacon. Add the bacon and cook, stirring, for 5 minutes, or until lightly browned. Add the onion and red and green peppers and sauté, stirring, for 8 minutes, or until the vegetables are wilted and beginning to turn golden. Add the garlic and sauté for 1 minute. Stir in the *chouriço* and pork and cook, stirring, for 3 minutes, or until lightly browned. Sprinkle with the paprika and cook, stirring, for 1 minute.

3. Add the wine, tomatoes, and parsley and bring to a boil. Decrease the heat to low and cook, uncovered, for 20 minutes, or until liquid is slightly reduced.

4. Spoon half of the sauce into the *cataplana;* spoon the clams on top and scatter the green beans over the clams. Spoon the remaining sauce on top. Secure the cover in place.

5. Place the *cataplana* over medium heat and cook for 10 minutes, or until the clams have opened. Bring the *cataplana* to the table and, using oven mitts, carefully lift the cover. Discard any clams that failed to open. Spoon the clams and rich sauce into warmed shallow bowls and serve at once.

tip PREPARATION IN ALTERNATIVE COOKWARE

Cook the sauce in a Dutch oven or braiser instead of the skillet. Add the clams, cover, and cook as directed for the *cataplana*.

BABY BACK RIBS with CANNELLINI BEANS

BRINING 30 min | PREP 30 min | COOK TIME 1 hr 25 min | SERVES 4

Small, meaty pork ribs, slowly cooked in a tomato-based sauce, are ideal candidates for the *cataplana.* Although paprika is not typical of *cataplana* recipes, it adds a pleasant depth of flavor to this rich sauce. Try smoked paprika for even more flavor. Once the ribs are tender, mix in the cooked cannellini beans and allow them to simmer long enough to absorb the flavors of the sauce.

Implements Large Skillet, Tongs, *Cataplana,* Oven Mitts

Ingredients

1 (2½-pound) rack baby back pork ribs

Coarse salt and freshly ground black pepper

2 tablespoons extra-virgin olive oil

1 cup chopped yellow onion

½ cup chopped green bell pepper

1 clove garlic, chopped

1½ teaspoons sweet or smoked paprika

2 cups crushed tomatoes

1 cup low-sodium chicken broth or water

1 cinnamon stick

¼ teaspoon crushed red pepper

1 (2-by-½-inch) strip orange zest

2 (15-ounce) cans cannellini beans, rinsed and drained, or 2½ cups cooked dried cannellini beans (page 61)

2 tablespoons finely chopped fresh Italian parsley

1. With a sharp knife, cut through the meaty portion between the ribs to separate them. There should be about 12 ribs. Place the ribs in a large bowl, add 3 tablespoons salt and cold water to cover, and stir to combine. Let stand for 30 minutes. Drain off the brining liquid, rinse with cold water, drain again, and pat dry. Sprinkle lightly with additional salt and pepper.

2. Heat a large skillet over medium-high heat until hot enough for a drop of water to sizzle on contact. Add 1 tablespoon of the olive oil and half of the ribs. Cook the ribs, turning as needed and adjusting the heat as necessary to maintain a steady sizzle, for about 10 minutes, or until evenly browned. Using tongs, transfer the ribs to a plate. Repeat with the remaining ribs.

3. Discard all but about 1 tablespoon of the fat from the skillet. Add the onion and green pepper and cook over medium-low heat, stirring, for about 10 minutes, or until golden. Add the garlic and cook for 1 minute. Stir in the paprika until blended. Add the tomatoes and broth and bring to a boil. Add the cinnamon, red pepper flakes, and orange zest, and stir to mix. Decrease the heat to low and cook, uncovered, for 5 minutes.

4. Transfer the ribs and any juices that have accumulated on the plate to the *cataplana.* Pour the sauce over the ribs. Secure the cover in place.

5. Place the *cataplana* over medium-low to low heat and cook for 1 hour, or until the meat is pulling away from the bones. Taste the sauce and adjust the seasoning with salt and pepper.

6. Add the beans to the ribs and use a large spoon to combine the sauce, ribs, and beans. Secure the cover in place and cook over low heat for 25 minutes, or until the beans have taken on the flavors of the sauce.

7. Bring the *cataplana* to the table and, using oven mitts, carefully lift the cover. Sprinkle with the parsley. Spoon the ribs, beans, and sauce into warmed shallow bowls and serve at once.

tip PREPARATION IN ALTERNATIVE COOKWARE

Brown the ribs and cook the sauce in a Dutch oven or braiser instead of the skillet. Return the browned ribs to the sauce and cook as directed for the *cataplana.*

Spanish chefs prefer cooking with earthenware,
the most ancient kind of cooking utensil known to
man, but they have a hard time explaining why.
"The food just tastes better," they are likely to say.

Penelope Casas, AUTHOR, *DELICIOSO! THE REGIONAL COOKING OF SPAIN*

Cazuela

The rustic earthenware *cazuela*—in Portugal, the same vessel is known as a *tacho de barro*—is found in the kitchen of every Spanish cook, though Catalonian cooks are especially renowned for their large repertoire of slow-cooked *cazuela* dishes. Glazed on the inside and unglazed on the outside, the versatile vessel is kiln-fired at a high temperature so that it can tolerate both the direct heat of a stove top and the radiant heat of an oven.

Cazuelas are usually only about 3 inches deep but come in a wide range of shapes—round, square, rectangular, oval—and sizes, including casseroles just large enough for a single serving. All of them are attractive and hold heat—and cold—well, which means they can travel from the stove to the table.

Tips for Using

Before using a *cazuela* for the first time, soak both the glazed and unglazed parts in cold water for several hours, or consult the manufacturer's instructions for details.

Always heat a *cazuela* slowly. Start in a cold oven, or warm over low heat before turning the heat higher.

To sauté or brown in a *cazuela,* add a shallow layer of olive oil to the cold casserole and then slowly heat over low heat before increasing the heat to medium. When the oil is hot, add the food to be sautéed or browned.

To prevent cracking, never heat an empty *cazuela* or set a hot cazuela on a cold surface.

A *cazuela* can be used as a serving dish for both hot and cold dishes. In Spain, it's not unusual for a host to ladle gazpacho from a large *cazuela* into single-serve *cazuelas*.

Some *cazuelas* are microwave safe. Consult the manufacturer's instructions.

Care in Using

Do not use harsh detergents or scouring pads.

Never wash a *cazuela* in a dishwasher.

Always consult the manufacturer's instructions.

Alternatives

A large skillet, a Dutch oven, a braiser, or an enameled cast-iron baking dish can be used in place of a *cazuela.*

recipes

Summer Vegetable Casserole with Manchego | Sea Bass Fillets with Tomatoes and Roasted Red Pepper and Almond Sauce

SUMMER VEGETABLE CASSEROLE with MANCHEGO

PREP 45 min | **COOK TIME** 1 hr 20 min | **SERVES** 6–8

Here, eggplants, red peppers, potatoes, tomatoes, onions and zucchini are cooked separately and then layered in a *cazuela* and baked until they melt together. This is a good dish for late summer when these vegetables are at their prime. You can cook the vegetables a day ahead, and then layer and bake them just before serving. The topping of Manchego cheese makes this dish hearty enough to be enjoyed as a main course. You can bake it in 1 large or 6 or more small *cazuelas*.

Implements
Two Large Rimmed Sheet Pans, Wide Spatula, Tongs, Medium Saucepan, 10- to 12-inch Skillet, Slotted Spoon, Colander, 10-inch *Cazuela* or 2-Quart Shallow Baking Dish

Ingredients

8 large (about 2 pounds) plum tomatoes, halved

2 red bell peppers, halved lengthwise and seeded

8 tablespoons extra-virgin olive oil

Coarse salt and freshly ground black pepper

1 (1-pound) eggplant, peeled and cut crosswise into 10 to 12 ½-inch-thick slices

1 pound all-purpose potatoes, peeled and halved

1 pound small zucchini, trimmed and cut lengthwise into ¼-inch-thick slices

2 cups yellow onion, cut vertically into ⅛-inch-thick slices

2 cloves garlic, minced

1 teaspoon sweet paprika, preferably smoked

2 tablespoons finely chopped fresh Italian parsley

1 cup (about 4 ounces) shredded Manchego cheese

1. Preheat the oven to 400°F.

2. Arrange the tomato halves and bell pepper halves, cut side down, on a on a large nonreactive rimmed sheet pan. Drizzle evenly with 2 tablespoons of the olive oil. Sprinkle with salt and pepper. Roast for 25 minutes.

3. Meanwhile, arrange the eggplant slices on a second rimmed sheet pan. Drizzle with 2 tablespoons of the olive oil and sprinkle with salt and pepper. Place in the oven with the tomatoes and peppers and roast for about 10 minutes, or until lightly browned on the bottoms. Remove the eggplant from the oven, and use a wide spatula to turn the slices over. Roast for about 10 minutes more, or until the eggplant is golden brown. Remove from the oven.

4. At this point, 25 minutes will have elapsed and the peppers will be ready to turn. Remove the sheet pan from the oven and use tongs to turn with them over. Return the pan to the oven and roast for 20 minutes more, or until the peppers are blistered and blackened and the tomatoes have collapsed. Remove the pan from the oven, cover with a sheet of aluminum foil, and let stand for about 20 minutes, or until slightly cooled. Turn the oven off.

5. While the peppers, tomatoes, and eggplant are roasting, place the potatoes in a medium saucepan and add water to cover. Bring to a boil and cook for 15 minutes, or until tender. Drain, let cool, and cut the potatoes into ½-inch-thick rounds.

6. Add the remaining 3 tablespoons of olive oil to the *cazuela* or a 10- to 12-inch skillet and heat over low heat. When the oil is hot, increase the heat to medium and add the zucchini in batches. Sauté for about 5 minutes per side, or until browned. Use a slotted spoon or spatula to transfer the zucchini to a colander to drain off the excess juices.

7. Add the onion slices to the *cazuela* or skillet and sauté, stirring over medium heat for 15 minutes, or until golden. Add the garlic and sauté for 1 minute. Add the paprika and parsley and remove from the heat. Season with ½ teaspoon of salt and a generous grinding of pepper. Transfer the onion mixture to a side dish.

8. Lift the foil from the rimmed sheet pan with the tomatoes and peppers. If the skins have loosened, peel them back with your fingertips and discard. If the skins are not loose, leave them on.

9. In the *cazuela* or 2-quart shallow baking dish, make single layers of the vegetables in the following order: the eggplant, onion slices, peppers, potatoes, zucchini, and tomatoes. Top evenly with the cheese.

10. Place the *cazuela* or baking dish in the hot oven (it's fine to put the *cazuela* in a hot oven because it has been preheated on the stove top) and bake for 30 to 35 minutes, or until the cheese has melted.

11. Remove from the oven and let stand for 5 minutes before serving. Serve directly from the *cazuela*.

SEA BASS FILLETS with TOMATOES and ROASTED RED PEPPER and ALMOND SAUCE

PREP 45 min | **COOK TIME** 55 min | **SERVES** 4

This recipe starts with the *cazuela* on the stove top for sautéing, and then, once the fish fillets are added, you slip the *cazuela* into the oven. The fish is served with a red pepper and almond sauce, a loose adaptation of the Spanish *romesco*. Any firm white fish fillets can be substituted for the sea bass.

Implements 12-inch *Cazuela* or 12-inch Skillet and 2-Quart Shallow Baking Dish, Strainer, Small Skillet, Blender

Ingredients

3 tablespoons extra-virgin olive oil

1 large sweet onion, cut into ⅛-inch wedges

1 clove garlic, sliced paper-thin

½ teaspoon sweet paprika

1 (28-ounce) can Italian plum tomatoes

Coarse salt and freshly ground black pepper

4 (6-ounce) skinless sea bass fillets

2 tablespoons finely chopped fresh Italian parsley or mint, or 1 tablespoon of each

PEPPER AND ALMOND SAUCE

½ cup whole natural (skin-on) almonds, coarsely chopped

1 clove garlic, coarsely chopped

8 jarred *piquillo* peppers, or 2 large roasted and peeled red bell pepper (page 268)

1 teaspoon coarse salt

½ teaspoon sweet paprika

4 to 6 tablespoons extra-virgin olive oil, or more as needed

1 tablespoon aged sherry vinegar

1. Add the olive oil to a 12-inch *cazuela* or skillet and heat slowly over medium-low heat. When the oil is hot enough to sizzle a piece of onion, increase the heat to medium, add the onion, and sauté, stirring, for 15 minutes, or until golden. Add the garlic and sauté for 5 minutes, or until softened. Stir in the paprika.

2. Set a strainer over a bowl and empty the can of tomatoes into the strainer. Use your hands to break the tomatoes into chunks, squeezing out and discarding the seeds. (Freeze the tomato juices for soup or another use.)

3. Add the broken, seeded tomatoes to the onion mixture and simmer over medium heat for 10 minutes, or until the mixture has cooked down. Add ½ teaspoon of salt and a grinding of pepper and remove from the heat.

4. While the tomato mixture is simmering, preheat the oven to 400°F.

5. If using a *cazuela*, arrange the fish fillets in a single layer on top of the tomato mixture. Season the fish with salt and pepper and sprinkle with the parsley. Place a spoonful of the tomato mixture on top of each fillet. If using a skillet, transfer the tomato mixture to a 2-quart shallow baking dish and arrange the fish fillets in a single layer on top. Season with salt and pepper and sprinkle with the parsley. Place a spoonful of the tomato mixture on top of each fillet.

6. Place the *cazuela* or baking dish in the hot oven (it's fine to put it in a hot oven because it has been preheated on the stove top) and bake the fish for 15 minutes, or until the thickest part of a fillet is opaque, rather than translucent, when tested with the tip of a small knife.

7. **WHILE THE FISH IS BAKING, MAKE THE SAUCE:** Put the almonds in a small, dry skillet, place over medium-low heat, and heat, shaking the pan, for 5 minutes, or until lightly toasted. Let the almonds cool slightly and then transfer to a blender. Add the garlic, peppers, salt, and paprika, and process until pureed, stopping to scrape down the sides of the blender as needed. With the motor running, add 4 tablespoons of the olive oil in a thin, steady stream. Taste and add more olive oil as needed to correct the balance. Add the vinegar and process to combine. Alternatively, make the sauce in a mortar: First crush the garlic and salt with a pestle. Then add the almonds and pound until the mixture forms a paste. Add the peppers and pound until blended. Slowly add the olive oil, pounding until the mixture is light and smooth. Add the vinegar and stir to blend. You should have about 1 cup of sauce. Taste and add more salt as needed. Transfer to a small serving bowl.

8. To serve, place the *cazuela* in the center of the table. Pass the sauce.

How to Peel Tomatoes and Peaches

A serrated peeler (page 14)—a relatively new tool—makes quick work of peeling tomatoes and peaches. Zip, zip, zip and the skins are gone. But if you're faced with peeling a big pile of tomatoes or peaches, immersing them in boiling water and then in an ice-water bath is more efficient.

Half fill a large, wide pot with water and bring to a boil. Prepare a large bowl of ice water. Use the tip of a paring knife to make a shallow X on the blossom end (bottom) of each tomato or peach. One at a time, gently lower the fruits into the boiling water, adding as many as will fit comfortably in the pot. Let simmer for about 20 seconds, or until the skins begin to curl away from the Xs. Use a slotted spoon to transfer the fruits to the bowl of ice water and then let them stand for about 30 seconds. Lift them from the water and set them on a large rimmed sheet pan or platter. The skins will slip right off.

The first key to paella is a paella pan, a round vessel with short, shallow sides, maybe an inch or so high and sloping outward at about a thirty-degree angle to its flat bottom. The shape is essential for good paella—the pan's shallowness and sloped sides allow the rice to cook without steaming and turning mushy.

Ari Weinzweig, AUTHOR, *ZINGERMAN'S GUIDE TO GOOD EATING*

Paella Pan

Paella, Spain's iconic dish of rice prepared with seafood, meats, poultry, and/or vegetables, originated in Valencia, where the Moors first planted rice. It was the midday meal for farm laborers who cooked it over an open fire and used ingredients on hand: rice grown nearby, frogs, snails, wild rabbit, and birds. These days it is cooked on top of the stove or on a grill in a broad, shallow pan with slightly flared sides about 2 inches deep and two opposing looped handles attached to the rim. The wide, low-slung design allows the rice to cook quickly over high heat.

Paella pans come in a range of sizes, from the smallest, about 13 inches, good for six to eight servings, to extra large, about 22 inches, big enough to feed a crowd. Materials vary from the classic Spanish dimple-bottomed steel pan with red handles to handsome stainless steel–lined copper and stainless-clad aluminum pans. Although paella pans traditionally have no lid, the stainless-clad aluminum model comes with one.

Tips for Using

On top of most stoves, even the smallest pan will span two burners.

The rice is always simmered uncovered in the broth. Keep additional broth simmering in a saucepan and add more, as needed, to keep the rice moist.

If you need to add more broth to the rice, do not stir it in. Instead, simply ladle it over the top.

The only reason to cover paella is to keep it warm before serving or to cook shellfish that needs trapped moisture to cook properly. If you don't have a lid, use a sheet of extra-wide aluminum foil.

When adding clams or mussels, push the hinged tips into the bubbling rice to encourage the mollusks to open toward the surface.

A grill is a great way to cook paella, and most grills are large enough to accommodate a good-sized paella pan.

For the best results, use Spanish rice, which will absorb more of the delicious juices.

Allow the rice on the bottom of the pan to cook to a rich golden crust, a delicacy known as the *socorrat*.

For feeding a crowd, invest in a specially designed paella burner and adjustable tripod for holding a 22-inch paella pan.

Care in Using

Soak in warm, soapy water and scrub with a stiff brush or scouring pad.

Always consult the manufacturer's instructions.

Alternatives

Use a braiser or other round, shallow pan with opposing handles.

recipes

Chicken, Shrimp, and Chorizo Paella | Mussel and Lima Bean Paella with Smoked Paprika

CHICKEN, SHRIMP, and CHORIZO PAELLA

PREP (chicken) 20 min | **MARINATING** 2 hr or overnight | **PREP** (paella) 45 min | **COOK TIME** 1 hour | **SERVES** 6–8

Every paella begins with a *sofrito,* a mixture of slowly cooked aromatic ingredients. Look for Spanish chorizo, which is cured, not fresh, and liberally seasoned with garlic and paprika.

Implements
Two 2½- to 3-Quart Saucepans, Strainer, 10-inch Skillet, Mortar and Pestle, 12- to 14-inch Paella Pan, Tongs, Wooden Spoon

Ingredients

8 bone-in chicken thighs, or 1 large chicken, cut into 8 serving pieces

Coarse salt and freshly ground black pepper

18 large shrimp, peeled, with shells reserved, and deveined

6 tablespoons extra-virgin olive oil

2 cloves garlic, bruised with knife, plus 2 teaspoons minced

2 teaspoons chopped fresh rosemary, plus sprigs, for garnish

5 to 6 cups low-sodium chicken broth

½ cup dry white wine

1 teaspoon saffron threads

½ cup chopped red bell pepper

½ cup chopped yellow onion

2 (3-ounce) chorizos, casings removed and cut into ¼-inch dice

1 teaspoon sweet paprika

1 (14½-ounce) can diced tomatoes with the juices

1½ cups Spanish rice

1 cup frozen peas, thawed

1 large lemon, cut into 6 to 8 wedges, for garnish

1. Generously sprinkle the chicken with salt and grind on some pepper. Place the chicken in a large bowl or large resealable plastic bag. Add the shrimp, 2 tablespoons of the olive oil, the bruised garlic, and the chopped rosemary. Cover the bowl, or seal the bag, and refrigerate for 2 hours or up to overnight.

2. In a 2½- to 3-quart saucepan, bring the chicken broth to a boil. Decrease the heat to low and cover to keep hot.

3. In a 10-inch skillet, heat 2 tablespoons of the olive oil over medium heat. When the oil is hot, add the shrimp shells and cook, stirring, for 3 minutes, or until they turn dark red. Add 1 teaspoon of the minced garlic and cook for 1 minute. Add the wine, bring to a boil, and boil for 1 minute. Add the shrimp mixture to the chicken broth, bring to a simmer, re-cover, and cook for 15 minutes. Set a strainer over a clean saucepan and strain the broth. Discard the shells. Keep the broth warm over low heat.

4. Crush the saffron in a mortar with a pestle, or place in a small cup and crush with the back of a spoon. Transfer to a small bowl and add a ladleful of the simmering broth. Cover and let stand until ready to use.

5. When ready to cook the paella, remove the chicken pieces from the marinade and place them on a plate. Heat the remaining 2 tablespoons of olive oil in 12- to 14-inch paella pan (set over two burners, if necessary) or an extra-large skillet over medium heat until hot enough to sizzle the chicken. Add the chicken, skin side down, and cook for 10 minutes, or until golden. Use tongs to turn the chicken and cook the other side for 5 to 8 minutes, or until browned. Return the chicken to the plate.

6. Add the bell pepper, onion, chorizos, and the remaining 1 teaspoon of minced garlic to the pan and cook over medium heat, stirring with a wooden spoon or spatula, for 5 minutes, or until the vegetables are browned. Add the paprika and cook, stirring, for 1 minute. Add the tomatoes and cook, stirring, for 3 minutes, or until the juices boil off and the tomato is dry. Add the rice and cook, stirring, for 2 minutes. Sprinkle with 1 teaspoon of salt. Bring the chicken broth to a boil and pour 4 cups of it over the rice. Add the reserved broth and stir into the other ingredients. Arrange the chicken around the outer edges of the pan.

7. Cook uncovered over medium heat, without stirring, for 15 minutes, or until most of the broth has been absorbed by the rice. Taste the rice and add more salt if needed.

8. Tuck the shrimp down into the partially cooked rice, concentrating them in the center area of the pan. Ladle 1 cup of the simmering broth over the rice and cook for 5 minutes more. As the rice cooks, it will continue to absorb the broth. Add more broth as needed, tasting the rice each time. It should be tender but firm. If you run out of broth before the rice is ready, use boiling water.

9. Sprinkle the peas on top and lay a piece of extra-wide aluminum foil over the paella for the last 5 minutes of cooking. Remove from the heat and let the paella stand covered for 5 to 10 minutes before serving.

10. Garnish with the lemon wedges and rosemary sprigs.

MUSSEL and LIMA BEAN PAELLA with SMOKED PAPRIKA

PREP 20 min | **COOK TIME** 30 min | **SERVES** 6–8

In this version large, plump Fordhooks, a favorite of lima bean aficionados are paired with Spain's celebrated air-cured *serrano* ham.

Implements 2½- to 3-Quart Saucepan, 12- to 14-inch Paella Pan, Ladle

Ingredients

1½ pounds small mussels (see Tip, page 222)

3 cups low-sodium chicken broth

2 cups water

¼ cup extra-virgin olive oil

1 (10-ounce box) frozen Fordhook lima beans, thawed

½ cup thinly sliced green onion, green and white parts

½ cup chopped red bell pepper

2 slices *serrano* ham or prosciutto, cut into 1-by-½-inch strips

1 clove garlic, minced

1 (2-by-½-inch) strip orange zest, cut into ⅛-inch-wide strips

2 teaspoons smoked Spanish paprika

1 (14½-ounce) can diced tomatoes, with juices

1½ cups Spanish rice

1 teaspoon coarse salt

2 tablespoons lightly packed torn fresh mint leaves

6 thin orange wedges, for garnish

1. Rinse, debeard, and refrigerate the mussels.

2. Heat the chicken broth and water in a 2½- to 3-quart saucepan. Cover and keep warm over low heat.

3. Heat the olive oil in a 12- to 14-inch paella pan (set over two burners, if necessary) or an extra-large skillet over medium heat until hot enough to sizzle a lima bean. Add the lima beans, green onion, and bell pepper, and cook, stirring, for 5 minutes, or until the pepper begins to brown. Add the ham, garlic, orange zest, and paprika, and cook, stirring, for 2 minutes.

4. Add the tomatoes and cook, stirring, for 3 minutes, or until the juice boils off and the tomato is dry. Add the rice and cook, stirring, for 2 minutes. Sprinkle the rice with the salt. Bring the broth to a boil and pour 3 cups of it over the rice. Stir the broth into the other ingredients. Cook uncovered over medium-high heat, without stirring, for 10 minutes, or until most of the broth has been absorbed by the rice. Taste the rice and add more salt, if needed.

5. Tuck the mussels, hinged side down, deep into the simmering rice, distributing them evenly. Ladle 1 cup of the simmering broth over the rice and cook for 5 more minutes. As the rice cooks, it will continue to absorb the broth. Add more broth as needed, tasting the rice each time. It should be tender but firm. If you run out of broth before the rice is ready, use boiling water.

6. Lay a piece of extra-wide aluminum foil over the paella for the last 5 minutes of cooking. All the mussels should be open. Discard any that aren't. Remove from the heat and let stand covered for 5 to 10 minutes before serving.

7. Sprinkle with the mint and garnish with the orange wedges.

11 | The MOROCCAN KITCHEN

The Moroccan Pantry

Morocco boasts a varied landscape: orchards of olives, almonds, and lemons; fishing boats crowding the seashore; and sheep and goats grazing on the mountainsides. Its colorful markets keep Moroccan pantries well stocked with exotic spices in every color and aroma. The intriguing cookware includes the *couscoussière*, a two-tiered metal pot for cooking couscous, and the *tagine*, a shallow earthenware pot with a tall, conical lid for cooking its famous stews. Here you will read about some of the staples of the Moroccan pantry and learn how to make *bisteeya*, a lavish savory pie with a buttery, paper-thin pastry, topped with a dusting of confectioners' sugar—an appropriately sweet finish to your journey through the global kitchen.

Cumin

Cumin is one of the most popular spices of the Moroccan kitchen. For the best flavor, always toast the whole seeds in a small, dry skillet to release their aroma before grinding them in either a mortar or an electric spice grinder.

Couscous

When uncooked, couscous, small beads of rolled semolina, look like tiny pellets. When steamed, they swell and become soft and fluffy. Boxes of precooked couscous—often labeled "instant" or "quick cooking"—hold the same couscous you see sold in bulk in specialty-food shops, health-food stores, and many supermarkets. The box directions produce a satisfying but heavy starch, but when steamed in the traditional way (page 316), the results are lighter, fluffier, and more tender.

Flower Waters

Orange-flower water and rose water are used to flavor desserts, sweets, and beverages. Both waters are distilled from blossoms or buds and are sold in small bottles in specialty-food shops and in some large liquor stores.

Harissa

Made from chiles, garlic, and caraway, coriander, and/or cumin, *harissa* is a fiery sauce found on tables throughout North Africa. It can be purchased in jars or tubes, or made at home in a blender or with a mortar and pestle. *Harissa* is used as a condiment to flavor soups, stews, couscous, and other dishes.

Preserved Lemons

Preserved lemons—slit whole lemons packed into jars with salt and lemon juice and left to mature—are indispensable in the Moroccan kitchen. The rinds are cut into small pieces to flavor *tagines* and other dishes, while the pulp is used to season sauces. They can be made at home (page 328) or purchased in specialty-food shops.

Ras el Hanout

This blend of exotic spices is primarily used to flavor meat dishes, but it is also used in rice dishes and couscous. It can be made with as few as ten spices or more than three times that amount. Home cooks typically roast whole spices and then grind them to a fine powder in a mortar or spice grinder. Look for *ras el hanout* in specialty-food shops.

Saffron

The orange-yellow stigma of a purple crocus, saffron is used in the cooking of many countries around the Mediterranean and in the Middle East, including Morocco, where local cooks regularly add it to *tagines*. Stored in an airtight container in a cool, dark place, it will keep for up to 6 months before it begins to lose its pungency. (For more on saffron, see page 293.)

Phyllo

These paper-thin Greek pastry leaves are widely available frozen, typically rolled in plastic and packed into a long, narrow box. Phyllo is an excellent substitute for traditional Moroccan pastry when making bisteeya.

The couscous concept is simple and it is brilliant. . . . When served together—the grain and the stew—the result is extraordinary; with the possible exception of bisteeya, couscous is the crowning achievement of Moroccan cuisine.

Paula Wolfert, AUTHOR, *COUSCOUS AND OTHER GOOD FOOD FROM MOROCCO*

Couscous with Raisins, Golden Onions, and Butternut Squash

Couscoussière

This curvaceous two-tiered pot is the traditional utensil for steaming couscous. The concept is similar to a double boiler, except that the pot is larger and the base of the top pan has perforations. Typically, broth or stew is simmered in the bottom pot and the steam, forced up through the perforations, is absorbed by the couscous, which causes the grains to swell.

Many recipes instruct you to line the bottom of the top section with cheesecloth, but it isn't necessary, as the steam will keep the pellets of couscous from dropping through the perforations. The *couscoussière* is tall and narrow, which gives the stew in the bottom section plenty of space in which to cook without touching the top pan. The *couscoussière* is typically made of stainless steel with a clad aluminum stainless-steel base. Tin-lined copper and unglazed earthenware models are also available. They come in a variety of sizes, typically 8-quart.

Tips for Using

For fluffy couscous, rinse it with water before steaming it.

Although the *couscoussière* comes with a lid, it's not necessary because coucous is cooked uncovered.

You can steam couscous over a stew, broth, or plain water.

Although you don't need to line the bottom of the upper pan (called the *kskas*) with dampened cheesecloth, you do need to use a strip of dampened cheesecloth to help seal the rim where the bottom pot (called the *gdra*) and top pot meet, to keep steam from escaping.

The couscous is steamed for several minutes, transferred to a platter, raked with fingertips to separate the granules, sprinkled with salted water, and steamed again—and again, if desired. (Some cooks steam it a half dozen times or more.) The more steamings, the lighter the couscous.

When the couscous is steamed to your satisfaction, add a lump of soft butter, a drizzle of olive oil, or whatever flavorings you like.

Care in Using

Wash with warm water and a mild detergent, and use a stiff brush to clean the perforations, if necessary.

Alternatives

You can rest a colander with small perforations over a deep pot. If the perforations are large, line the colander with dampened cheesecloth.

recipes

Couscous with Raisins, Golden Onions, and Butternut Squash | Classic Couscous with Butter and Fried Almonds | Couscous with Fish and Vegetable Kebabs and *Charmoula* Sauce

COUSCOUS with RAISINS, GOLDEN ONIONS, and BUTTERNUT SQUASH

PREP 30 min | COOK TIME (couscous) 1 hr 10 min |
COOK TIME (stew) 50 min | SERVES 6–8

Here, a simple vegetable stew of butternut squash and onions is spooned atop couscous flavored with cinnamon and dotted with raisins.

Implements Wide 3-Quart Saucepan, 8-Quart
Couscoussière, Dutch Oven

Ingredients

4 cups low-sodium vegetable or chicken broth

1 cinnamon stick

¼ cup raisins

1½ cups couscous

½ cup water

Coarse salt

3 tablespoons extra-virgin olive oil

**2 large yellow onions, halved lengthwise
and cut into vertical slices**

**1 (2½ to 3-pound) butternut squash, halved
lengthwise, seeds and membranes removed, and
cut into ½ to ¾-inch cubes (about 8 cups)**

2 teaspoons *ras el hanout*

⅛ teaspoon cayenne

1 (14½-ounce) can diced tomatoes with juices

About 1 tablespoon all-purpose flour

2 tablespoons chopped fresh cilantro

**2 tablespoons diced ⅛-inch preserved lemon peel (page
328) or 1 large lemon, cut into 8 thin wedges, for garnish**

***Harissa*, for serving**

1. In a wide 3-quart saucepan or sauté pan, combine 2 cups of the broth, cinnamon stick, and raisins, and bring to a boil. Decrease the heat to low, cover, and simmer for 5 minutes. Add the couscous and stir to blend. Remove from the heat and let stand for 10 minutes. Uncover and cool for 10 minutes. Combine ½ cup of water and 1 teaspoon of salt in a small bowl and stir to dissolve. Sprinkle the salted water on the couscous while simultaneously raking it with your fingers to break up the lumps. Let stand, uncovered, until ready to finish cooking.

2. Add the oil to the bottom section of the *couscoussière*, a Dutch oven, or 5-quart sauté pan. Heat the olive oil over medium low heat until hot enough to sizzle a piece of onion. Add the onions and cook, stirring, over low heat, for 15 to 20 minutes, or until the onions are golden brown. Add the squash and cook, stirring, until coated with the oil. Sprinkle with the *ras el hanout*, 1 teaspoon of salt, and the cayenne, and stir to blend. Add the remaining 2 cups of the chicken broth and the tomatoes and heat over low heat while preparing the top section of the *couscousière*.

3. If using a *couscoussière,* lightly butter the inside of the top section and set it on top of the bottom section holding the squash mixture. Cut a length of cheesecloth long enough to go around the rim of the bottom section with a slight overlap. Dampen the cheesecloth with water, squeeze dry, and sprinkle lightly with flour. Fold the cheesecloth into a 2-inch-wide band, and wrap the band around the rim between the top and bottom sections to seal the seam so no steam escapes.

4. Bring the stew in the bottom half of the *couscoussière* to a boil over medium heat. When the steam begins to rise through the perforations, add about one-half of the couscous in a layer. Then spoon the remaining couscous on top, piling it into a pyramid. Steam, uncovered, over medium-low heat, for 15 minutes.

5. Keeping the top and bottom sections sealed together with the cheesecloth, use a long handled spoon to transfer the couscous to a large platter, spreading it out with the spoon. Cool for 10 minutes, then rake it with your fingers to separate any clumps. (The couscous and stew can be prepared 1 to 2 hours ahead up to this step. Cover the couscous with a dampened towel to keep it from drying and remove the stew from the heat and proceed to steps 6 through 8 about 15 minutes before ready to serve.)

6. While the couscous is cooling, continue to cook the stew over medium-low heat for 10 minutes.

7. Return half of the couscous to the top of the *couscoussière* and spread in a layer. Then spoon the remaining couscous on top, piling into a pyramid. Steam the couscous while simultaneously continuing to cook the stew over low heat in the bottom portion for 10 to 15 minutes. Lift off the top portion and taste the stew and add salt, if needed.

8. Spoon the couscous onto a deep platter or shallow serving bowl. Make a well in the center and spoon the squash and its juices into the center. Sprinkle with the cilantro and add the preserved lemons or lemon wedges. Serve and pass the *harissa* at the table to be added to taste.

tip STEAM COUSCOUS AHEAD

You can steam the couscous the first time several hours before serving. Let it stand, covered with a damp towel, and then spoon it back into the *couscoussière* to warm just before serving.

CLASSIC COUSCOUS with BUTTER and FRIED ALMONDS

PREP AND REST TIME 30 min | **COOK TIME** 45 min | **SERVES** 4–6

Plain couscous is the ultimate comfort food. This version is seasoned with salt, melted butter, and fried almonds. Eat it for supper with a piece of grilled fish or sautéed chicken cutlets. Add a green vegetable and you have a meal.

Implements Strainer, 8-Quart *Couscoussière*, Cheesecloth, Wooden Spoon, Small Skillet, Slotted Spoon

Ingredients

1½ cups couscous

About 1 tablespoon all-purpose flour

½ cup water

½ teaspoon coarse salt

3 tablespoons unsalted butter

⅓ cup whole blanched almonds

1. Place the couscous in a strainer and hold it under cold running water for one minute. Shake out the excess water and spread the couscous on a platter. Let stand for 10 minutes.

2. Pull your fingertips through the couscous to separate the granules and break up any lumps that have formed. This is called "raking."

3. Half fill the bottom section of a *couscoussière* with water. Lightly butter the inside of the top section and set it on top of the bottom section. Cut a length of cheesecloth long enough to go around the rim of the bottom section with a slight overlap. Dampen the cheesecloth with water, squeeze dry, and sprinkle lightly with the flour. Fold the cheesecloth into a 2-inch-wide band, and wrap

the band around the rim between the top and bottom sections to seal the seam so no steam escapes. Turn the heat to medium and bring to a gentle boil. When the steam begins to rise through the perforations, add about half of the couscous in a layer. Then spoon the remaining couscous on top, piling it into a pyramid. Steam, uncovered, for 20 minutes. If you don't have a *couscoussière* use an 8-quart Dutch oven fitted with a large colander with small perforations. The colander should fit tightly in the pot without touching the bottom. Fill the pan one-fourth full with water and bring to a boil over medium heat. Place the colander on top of the pot and add the dampened couscous (see step 1) and steam as you would in a *couscoussière*.

4. Turn off the heat. Remove the upper section and turn the couscous out onto a platter, spreading it out with a wooden spoon. In a small bowl, stir together the water and salt. When the couscous is cool enough to touch, sprinkle it with the salt water and rake it with your fingertips to separate any clumps. Let the couscous rest for 10 minutes.

5. Meanwhile, in a small skillet, melt the butter over low heat. Add the almonds and cook, stirring, for 3 to 4 minutes, or until golden. Remove from the heat and set aside.

6. Turn the heat under the *couscoussière* back on to medium. When the steam begins to rise through the perforations, add about half of the couscous in a layer. Then spoon the remaining couscous on top, piling it into a pyramid. Steam, uncovered, for 15 minutes, or until light and fluffy. Spoon the cooked couscous onto a large serving platter.

7. Top the hot couscous with the almonds and melted butter and fluff with the tines of a fork. Serve at once.

COUSCOUS with FISH and VEGETABLE KEBABS and CHARMOULA SAUCE

PREP 45 | COOK TIME (couscous) 45 min | COOK TIME (kebabs) 15 min | SERVES 4–6

Charmoula is a spicy mixture used as a marinade and a sauce. Here, it is used to coat fish and vegetables both before and after grilling, and to flavor the couscous. Serve the kebabs and couscous with *harissa,* Morocco's fiery hot sauce.

Implements *Couscoussière,* Small Skillet, Mortar and Pestle, Blender, 3-Quart Saucepan, Strainer

Ingredients

1½ cups couscous, cooked (see Classic Couscous with Butter and Fried Almonds, page 317, omitting the butter and almonds)

CHARMOULA SAUCE

1 tablespoon cumin seeds

1 teaspoon ground ginger

1 teaspoon sweet paprika

1 teaspoon coarse salt

⅛ teaspoon cayenne

½ cup coarsely chopped lightly packed fresh Italian parsley

½ cup coarsely chopped lightly packed fresh cilantro

2 cloves garlic

¾ cup extra-virgin olive oil

⅓ cup freshly squeezed lemon juice, or more as needed

1½ pounds skinless firm white fish fillets (such as halibut, swordfish, or escolar)

1 teaspoon coarse salt

1 (1-pound) head cauliflower, cut into 1-inch florets

2 large red bell peppers, halved, seeded, and cut into 1-inch squares

12 ounces small zucchini, trimmed and cut into 1-inch-long rounds

2 tablespoons extra-virgin olive oil

Harissa, for serving

1. Prepare the Classic Couscous recipe as directed through step 4. Cover with a damp towel and let stand until about 20 minutes before serving time.

2. **MAKE THE SAUCE:** Place the cumin seeds in a small, dry skillet over medium heat and heat, stirring constantly, for 2 to 3 minutes, or until a shade darker and fragrant. Cool. Transfer to a mortar or an electric spice grinder and grind finely. In a small bowl, stir together the ground cumin, ginger, paprika, salt, and cayenne.

3. In a blender, combine the parsley, cilantro, and garlic and process to a paste. Alternatively, pound the ingredients to a paste in a mortar. Gradually add the spices and process or pound until blended. With the motor running, slowly add the olive oil, or work in the oil slowly with the pestle, until blended. Transfer to a bowl and stir in the lemon juice until blended. Taste and adjust the seasoning with salt and/or cayenne and lemon juice, if needed. Set aside.

4. Cut the fish into 1½-inch pieces and arrange in a single layer on a platter. Brush the fish on both sides with about 3 tablespoons of the sauce. Cover with plastic wrap and refrigerate until ready to cook.

5. Half fill a 3-quart saucepan with water and bring to a boil. Add the cauliflower and salt and boil, uncovered, for 3 minutes, or until the cauliflower is crisp-tender. Drain in a strainer and rinse with cold water. Spread on a folded kitchen towel to remove excess water.

6. In a large bowl or a large resealable plastic bag, combine the cauliflower, bell peppers, and zucchini. Add about 3 tablespoons of the *charmoula* sauce and shake the bag to coat the vegetables evenly. Refrigerate with the fish.

7. Complete step 6 of the Classic Couscous recipe, skipping steps 5 and 7.

8. Thread the fish and vegetables onto six 12-inch metal skewers, alternating the ingredients and dividing them evenly among the skewers. Lightly brush with some of the *charmoula* sauce.

9. Position an oven rack in the top of the oven so that the top of the broiler pan will be about 4 inches from the heat source, and preheat the broiler. Or, heat a charcoal or gas grill to medium high.

10. When ready to serve, broil or grill the kebabs, turning as needed, for 8 to 10 minutes, until the vegetables are browned and the fish is opaque at the center when tested with the tip of a knife.

11. Drizzle the olive oil on the hot couscous and fluff with the tines of a fork, then place the skewers on top of the couscous. Pass the reserved *charmoula* sauce and the *harissa* in small bowls at the table for diners to stir into their couscous to taste.

tip NO-SPIN KEBABS

To prevent food from spinning on the skewers when you turn them, use two skewers per kebab. Place a skewer at each end so they are parallel to each other. When the skewers are turned, the food stays in place and all sides get cooked evenly.

Making Bisteeya

Bisteeya—sometimes spelled *b'stilla, besteeya, bastila,* and myriad other ways—is an elaborate dish of pigeon (or chicken), spices, herbs, eggs, sugar, and almonds wrapped in thin pastry sheets. It is served at weddings, on holidays, and for other special occasions, and is traditionally made in a shallow, round copper pan called a *tobsil dial bestila,* which is not readily available in the United States. The following recipe uses a 10-inch springform pan, but other pans of similar size will work as well. (See page 21.)

The pan is lined with buttered leaves of ultrathin pastry known as *ouarka* (sometimes spelled *warka* or *warqa*), which is traditionally made by pressing small pieces of soft, spongy dough against a smooth, convex steel pan set over a charcoal brazier. The dough forms thin rounds that overlap slightly on the pan, and eventually form a single paper-thin sheet. This delicate sheet is then peeled from the hot pan and another sheet of *ouarka* is prepared the same way. Simply put, making *ouarka* is a true culinary art. In Morocco, home cooks can buy freshly made *ouarka,* but it is rarely found elsewhere. Fortunately, widely available commercial phyllo dough is an excellent substitute.

Tips for Making Bisteeya

If using a pan with a removable bottom, make sure the rim and the bottom fit snugly, and wrap the outside bottom of the pan in a sheet of aluminum foil to guard against leakage.

Read over the lengthy recipe and organize all the ingredients and equipment before getting started.

You can assemble the *bisteeya* several hours in advance and refrigerate it until baking.

Spread the preparations of the many ingredients over a couple of days. You can cook the chicken up to 2 days in advance, refrigerate it with a little of the broth to keep it moist, and then reheat gently before using. You can also toast the almonds and grind them with the sugar up to

2 days in advance; store in an airtight container.

If the phyllo is frozen, move it to the refrigerator to thaw 24 hours before assembling the *bisteeya*.

recipe   **Classic Chicken *Bisteeya***

CLASSIC CHICKEN BISTEEYA

PREP 1 hr | COOK TIME (chicken) 45 min | COOK TIME (almonds) 8 to 10 min | COOK TIME (*bisteeya*) 25 to 30 min | STAND TIME 20 min | SERVES 8–10

Combining sweet and savory flavors in one dish is prevalent throughout Morocco and this recipe for *bisteeya* is a classic example. In this elaborate dish cooked shredded chicken is combined with ground toasted almonds, confectioner's sugar, and eggs and layered between paper-thin sheets of buttered phyllo. Although the recipe appears lengthy the preparation can be spread out over a few days. Once assembled and baked it makes a splendid, easy-to-serve party dish.

Implements
10-inch Springform Pan, 8-quart Dutch Oven, Strainer, 2-Quart Saucepan, Fat Separator, Food Processor, Silicone Brush, Kitchen Scissors

Ingredients

2 tablespoons unsalted butter

1 medium yellow onion, chopped

12 bone-in chicken thighs, (about 3 pounds) fat and excess skin trimmed

Coarse salt

2 cups water

1 leafy sprig cilantro, plus 2 tablespoons finely chopped

1 leafy sprig Italian parsley, plus 2 tablespoons finely chopped

1 teaspoon crushed saffron threads

1 cinnamon stick

½ teaspoon freshly ground black pepper

½ teaspoon ground ginger

¼ teaspoon ground turmeric

4 large eggs

¼ cup plus 1 tablespoon confectioners' sugar

2 tablespoons freshly squeezed lemon juice

½ cup (1 stick) unsalted butter

ALMOND MIXTURE

2 cups whole blanched almonds

¼ cup confectioners' sugar

1 teaspoon ground cinnamon

1 box (1 pound) phyllo dough, thawed overnight in the refrigerator if frozen (12 x 17 inches)

1. In an 8-quart Dutch oven, melt the butter over low heat. Add the onion and cook over medium heat, stirring, for 5 minutes, or until softened. Add the chicken and sprinkle evenly with 2 teaspoons of salt. Add the water, cilantro and parsley sprigs, saffron, cinnamon, pepper, ginger, and turmeric. Cover and cook over medium heat for 15 minutes. Turn the chicken in the juices and cook for 15 minutes more, or until the chicken is cooked through. Remove the pan from the heat and let the chicken cool in the broth.

2. Set a large strainer over a 3- or 4-quart saucepan and strain the chicken from the broth. Discard the seasonings. Tear or cut the chicken into ½-inch pieces and place in a bowl. (If cooking the chicken in advance, dampen it with a little of the broth, cover, and refrigerate.) Bring the chicken broth to a gentle boil.

3. In a medium bowl, whisk the eggs until frothy. Adjust the heat under the broth to low and slowly stir the eggs into the simmering broth. Cook, stirring, for 1 to 2 minutes, or until the eggs are set in small curds. Set a strainer over a bowl and drain the eggs. Discard the broth. Add the cooked eggs, chopped parsley and cilantro, ¼ cup of the confectioners' sugar, the lemon juice, 1 teaspoon of salt, and a generous grinding of pepper to the chicken pieces. Stir gently to combine.

4. To clarify the butter see the technique box on page 323. Keep the clarified butter warm, not hot.

5. **MAKE THE ALMOND MIXTURE:** Preheat the oven to 350°F. Spread the almonds in a cake pan or other shallow pan and toast for 6 to 8 minutes, until toasted. Pour onto a plate and let cool. Turn the oven temperature to 400°F.

6. In a food processor, combine the cooled almonds, the confectioners' sugar, and the cinnamon, and grind the almonds finely. Set aside.

7. Use a silicone brush to coat the sides and bottom of a 10-inch springform pan with some of the clarified butter. Lay the phyllo sheets flat on a work surface, count out 16 sheets, and place in a separate stack. Using a 12-inch lid or dish as a template, cut through the 16 sheets with kitchen scissors or a pizza cutter to make 12-inch circles. Cover the circles with a sheet of plastic wrap. Dampen a kitchen towel, squeeze it dry, and lay it over the plastic wrap. Wrap any remaining phyllo sheets and return to the refrigerator for another use.

8. Lift 4 round sheets of phyllo, one at a time, from the stack and lightly brush each sheet with the clarified butter. Transfer the stack of 4 buttered sheets to the buttered pan, pressing along the bottom and partially up the sides of the pan. Spread half of the almond mixture on top of the buttered phyllo sheets. Lift 4 more sheets of phyllo, one at a time, from the stack and lightly brush each sheet with butter. Transfer this stack to the pan covering the almond layer and press the edges up the sides of the pan. Arrange all of the chicken mixture evenly on top. Lift 4 more sheets of phyllo, one at a time, from the stack and lightly brush each sheet with butter. Transfer the stack to the pan covering the chicken mixture and press the edges up the sides of the pan. Spread with the remaining almond mixture. One at a time, butter the final 4 sheets of phyllo and stack. Transfer to the pan covering the almond mixture. With the rounded end of a table knife or small spatula, push the excess phyllo from around the edges down along the sides of the pan.

9. Wrap the bottom of the pan with a large sheet of aluminum foil to prevent leakage, then place in the oven. Bake for 35 to 40 minutes, or until the phyllo is a dark golden brown.

10. Remove from the oven and let cool in the pan for 20 minutes. Set the pan on a kitchen towel or a triple layer of paper towels, run a thin knife or spatula down along the edges of the pan to loosen the pastry, release the catch, and lift off the sides. Blot any excess butter from the bottom of the pan and transfer to a round platter.

11. Put 1 tablespoon of confectioners' sugar in a small strainer, and dust the top of the *bisteeya* with the sugar. Cut into thin wedges and serve.

Clarified Butter

To make clarified butter, put cold butter (the amount doesn't matter, but it works best in ¼-cup increments) in a small, heavy saucepan and place over medium-low heat. As the butter slowly melts, the milk solids, or white residue, will slowly sink to the bottom of the pan and a bit of foam will rise to the top. Use a spoon to skim the foam from the surface. When the butter is completely melted, set a fine-mesh strainer or skimmer over a storage jar or other container, and slowly pour the clear yellow liquid through the strainer, leaving the milky residue in the pan. Any milky residue that escapes will stay in the strainer.

Let the butter cool, then cover with a tight-fitting lid and refrigerate until needed. French chefs use clarified butter because it has a higher smoke point than regular butter, which means it can be used for high-temperature sautéing without browning or burning. Indian cooks make and use clarified butter called ghee for the same reason, and also because once the milk solids have been removed, the butter can be stored without refrigeration and won't turn rancid. Some Indian cooks heat the clarified butter until the milk solids are toasted, giving the ghee a mildly nutty taste. Clarified butter will keep in a tightly closed container in the refrigerator for 3 months or longer.

A cloud of fragrant steam engulfed me as the waiter lifted the heavy conical lid from an earthenware platter containing a savory, mouthwatering tagine of chicken with preserved lemons, and olives. Its exquisite flavor was perfectly counterbalanced by a tagine of lamb, prunes, and sesame seeds in an unctuous sauce of honey, ginger, and cinnamon.

Kitty Morse, AUTHOR, *COOKING AT THE KASBAH*

Lamb Tagine with Artichoke Hearts,
Dried Apricots, and Preserved Lemon

Tagine

The glazed terra-cotta *tagine* is an eye-catching piece of cookware: a round, shallow base is topped by a tepee-shaped conical lid. As the food cooks and steam rises, condensation collects along the slanted walls of the lid and drips back down onto the stew—also called a *tagine*—always keeping it moist.

Traditional *tagine* recipes seldom call for browning meat, chicken, or fish before stewing, because the terra-cotta base cannot be used over high heat. But modern pots have either stainless steel–clad or cast-iron bases that can tolerate direct high heat, making browning possible.

Tips for Using

Traditional *tagines* are slowly cooked on top of the stove. However, the lid and pot can be used in the oven up to 450°F. Consult manufacturer's instructions.

If you have purchased a partially glazed terra-cotta *tagine,* soak the base in cold water for several hours before using it for the first time.

You can use this unique piece of cookware for any favorite stew recipe.

Because of the porous nature of terra-cotta, stew cooked in a *tagine* with a terra-cotta base will be less brothy than stew cooked in a *tagine* with a metal base. To reduce excess broth, remove the meat and/or vegetables to a side dish with a slotted spoon and boil the broth for 5 minutes or until reduced. Then return the meat and/or vegetables and reheat before serving.

A *tagine* with a stainless-steel clad or cast-iron base can double—without the conical lid—as a shallow baking dish or roasting pan.

Some highly decorative glazed all terra-cotta *tagines* can be used only for serving. Consult manufacturer's instructions.

Care in Using

Wash in warm, soapy water, using a soft brush.

Tagines are typically not dishwasher safe. Consult manufacturer's instructions.

Alternatives

A Dutch oven or braiser is good substitute for a *tagine*.

recipes
**Chicken Tagine with Prunes and Tomatoes |
Lamb Tagine with Artichoke Hearts, Dried Apricots, and Preserved Lemon |
Preserved Lemons**

CHICKEN TAGINE with PRUNES and TOMATOES

PREP 20 min | COOK TIME 1 hr | SERVES 4–6

Here, chicken thighs are simmered in a sauce in which the acidic character of tomatoes is balanced by the deep winelike sweetness of prunes. Garnish the *tagine* with toasted sesame seeds, which are available at Asian grocers. Alternatively, you can purchase untoasted sesame seeds and toast them yourself (see page 85.) Serve with a cooked salad of braised greens, such as escarole, tossed with olive oil, salt, and finely chopped preserved lemon. Like the lamb *tagine* (page 327), this recipe calls for browning meat, which you can do in a *tagine* if it is has a stainless steel–clad or cast-iron base. If your *tagine* is all earthenware, simply toss the chicken with the ingredients and simmer in the *tagine* over low heat. Alternatively, brown the chicken in a skillet and transfer it to the *tagine* for simmering, or prepare the entire dish in a Dutch oven or braiser.

Implements
Tagine, Small Skillet, Mortar and Pestle, Rubber Spatula, Tongs, Wooden Spatula, Slotted Spoon

Ingredients

8 bone-in chicken thighs, excess fat and skin trimmed
Coarse salt and freshly ground black pepper
1 teaspoon cumin seeds
1 teaspoon ground turmeric
2 tablespoons extra-virgin olive oil
1 large onion, cut into ⅛-inch wedges
½ cup low-sodium chicken broth
1 (28-ounce) can Italian plum tomatoes, drained
½ cup (about 4 ounces) packed pitted prunes
2 tablespoons honey
1 cinnamon stick
1 teaspoon toasted sesame seeds

1. In a large bowl, combine the chicken, 1 teaspoon salt, and a generous grinding of pepper. Place the cumin seeds in a small, dry skillet over medium heat and heat, stirring constantly, for 2 to 3 minutes, or until a shade darker and fragrant. Transfer to a mortar or an electric spice grinder and grind finely. Add the cumin and turmeric to the chicken and turn to coat with the spices.

2. Heat a stainless steel–clad or cast-iron base of a *tagine* (see headnote for alternatives) over medium-low heat and add the olive oil. When the oil is hot enough to sizzle a piece of chicken, add the chicken, skin side down. Use a rubber spatula to clean all the seasoning from the sides of the bowl and add it to the chicken. Increase the heat to medium and cook the chicken for 5 minutes, or until lightly browned on the first side. Use a spatula or tongs to turn the chicken pieces brown side up. Spread the onion wedges on top of the chicken and cook, occasionally stirring the onion and turning the chicken, for 10 minutes, or until the onion is wilted and golden.

3. Add the chicken broth, tomatoes, prunes, honey, and cinnamon, breaking up the tomatoes with the side of a wooden spatula. Cover and cook over medium-low heat for 35 to 45 minutes, until the chicken falls from the bone.

4. Uncover the *tagine* and use a slotted spoon to transfer the chicken and prunes to a plate. Cover with aluminum foil and keep warm in an oven set at 200°F. If there is an excess of broth, boil the liquid, uncovered, over medium heat for 5 minutes, or until reduced slightly. Taste and adjust the seasoning with salt and pepper. Return the chicken and prunes to the *tagine*.

5. Sprinkle the sesame seeds over the top. Re-cover the *tagine* and carry it to the table. Uncover and serve.

LAMB TAGINE with ARTICHOKE HEARTS, DRIED APRICOTS, and PRESERVED LEMON

PREP 30 min | COOK TIME 2 hr | SERVES 6

Lamb, artichokes, and dried fruit are a classic combination for a Moroccan *tagine,* but it is the bouquet of spices—saffron, cumin, ginger, coriander, cinnamon—that make this dish memorable. To savor the wonderful flavors in the sauce, spoon the *tagine* onto mounds of fluffy couscous (page 317). This recipe calls for browning the lamb, which you can do in a *tagine* if it is has a stainless steel–clad or cast-iron base. If your *tagine* is all earthenware, simply toss the meat with the ingredients and simmer in the *tagine* over low heat. Alternatively, brown the meat in a skillet and transfer it to the *tagine* for simmering, or prepare the entire dish in a Dutch oven or braiser.

Implements *Tagine,* Cutting Board, Chef's Knife, Paring Knife

Ingredients

2 to 2½ pounds trimmed, boneless lamb shoulder or lamb shank, cut into 1-inch chunks

2 teaspoons coarse salt

½ teaspoon freshly ground black pepper

3 tablespoons extra-virgin olive oil

2 cups ¼-inch-thick yellow onion wedges

10 saffron threads

1½ teaspoons ground cumin

1 teaspoon ground ginger

½ teaspoon ground coriander

1 cup peeled, sliced (¼ inch) carrot

1 cinnamon stick

1 cup low-sodium chicken broth or water, plus more as needed

1 cup drained canned Italian plum tomatoes, cut into 1-inch chunks

2 stems Italian parsley, plus 1 tablespoon finely chopped

2 stems cilantro, plus 1 tablespoon finely chopped

4 artichokes, preferably with stems, or 1 (10-ounce box) frozen artichoke hearts

1 lemon, halved

4 ounces (about 1 cup) dried apricot halves

2 tablespoons chopped preserved lemon rind (page 328)

1 tablespoon finely chopped fresh mint

1. Place the lamb in a large bowl, sprinkle with the salt and pepper, and toss to coat evenly. Set aside.

2. Heat a stainless steel–clad or cast-iron base of a *tagine* (see headnote for alternatives) over medium-low heat and add the olive oil. When the oil is hot enough to sizzle a piece of onion, increase the heat to medium, add the onion wedges, and cook, stirring, for 10 minutes, or until they wilt and begin to turn color. Meanwhile, in a small bowl, stir together the saffron, cumin, ginger and coriander.

3. Add the meat, carrot, and cinnamon to the onion, increase the heat to medium-high, and cook, stirring constantly, for 5 minutes, or until the meat begins to brown. Add the chicken broth, tomatoes, parsley and cilantro stems, and the saffron mixture and bring to a boil.

4. Place the lid on the *tagine,* decrease the heat to low, and cook, without disturbing the cover, for 1½ hours, adjusting the heat to keep the stew at a gentle simmer.

5. Meanwhile, if using fresh artichoke hearts, fill a medium bowl half full with water; squeeze the juice from a lemon half into the water, and add the spent lemon half to the water. Working with 1 artichoke at a time, pull the leaves back and tear them off where they meet at the base (bottom), until you reach the pale green inner leaves. (Reserve the leaves for another use.) Turn the artichoke on its side on a cutting board and, with a chef's knife, cut the attached leaves off just where they meet the base. Cut the stem off the base and reserve. With a paring knife, trim the dark green outer layer from the base. With the tip of a spoon, scoop the fuzzy portion from the center and discard. Rub the trimmed artichoke bottom with the

remaining lemon half. Cut the bottom into quarters and add to the lemon water. Peel the fibrous outer layer from the stem and cut crosswise into ½-inch lengths. Add to the lemon water. Repeat with the remaining artichokes.

6. After 1½ hours, test the meat for tenderness. It should be fork-tender. If it isn't, simmer it a little longer and test again.

7. When the meat is tender, drain the fresh artichokes and add them, or add the frozen artichoke hearts, and the apricots. Re-cover and cook for 30 minutes, or until the fresh artichokes are tender, or only 10 minutes if using frozen artichoke hearts. Stir in the preserved lemon.

8. If the stew is swimming in liquid, use a slotted spoon to transfer the solids to a bowl, cover with aluminum foil, and place in an oven set at 200°F. Boil the liquid, uncovered, for 10 minutes, or until reduced slightly. Return the solids to the *tagine.*

9. Sprinkle the finely chopped parsley, cilantro, and mint over the top. Re-cover the *tagine* and carry it to the table. Uncover and serve.

PRESERVED LEMONS

PREP 15 min | STAND TIME 4 to 6 weeks | MAKES 1 pint

For this recipe, the lemons must mature for several weeks before you can use them. If possible, use thin-skinned Meyer lemons, although any small lemons will work. In traditional Moroccan cooking, the rinds are diced and sprinkled on top of *tagines,* and the soft flesh is stirred into the broth or sauce. Add the rinds and flesh to salads and cooked vegetables, or as a flavorful topping for fish or chicken. Add them about 15 minutes before cooking, so they can begin flavoring the fish or chicken, and then roast in a hot oven. The pulp can be used in salad dressings, or mixed with mayonnaise or sour cream and served as a dip.

Implements Cutting Board, Chef's Knife
Ingredients

3 or 4 small lemons, preferably Meyer
About ¼ cup coarse salt
About 1 cup freshly squeezed lemon juice, preferably Meyer

1. Rinse and scrub the lemons with a stiff vegetable brush. Dry with a clean kitchen towel. Wash a pint canning jar with warm, soapy water, rinse well, and dry. Have ready a new lid and screw band.

2. Cut a thin slice from the stem end of 3 of the lemons. Place 1 lemon, cut side down, on a cutting board and, with a chef's knife, cut the lemon partially into quarters, stopping short of the base so the wedges hold together. Spread the wedges gently apart, and then partially cut each wedge lengthwise in half, still keeping the wedges attached to one another at the bottom. Repeat with the remaining 2 lemons. Spread the wedges apart and sprinkle the flesh of each lemon with about 1 tablespoon of the salt. Close the wedges of each lemon and pack the lemons into the clean pint jar. If the lemons don't fill the jar, cut and salt the remaining lemon and place it in the jar, pressing to compact the lemons.

3. Add any leftover salt to the jar. Then pour in enough lemon juice to cover the lemons by about ½ inch. Top the jar with the lid, twist on the screw band, and tighten securely. Let the jar stand in a dark corner on the kitchen counter, so you will remember to turn it over every day for the first 2 weeks. Let the lemons mature for 4 weeks before using.

4. Once the jar is opened, refrigerate it. To use the lemons, remove a lemon, cut off the desired amount, and return the unused part to the jar. The lemons will keep, refrigerated, for up to 6 months.

How to Trim Artichokes

Half fill a large bowl with water and add the juice of 1 lemon. Working with 1 artichoke at a time, cut off the stem flush with the bottom. Pull away and discard any blemished outer leaves. Lay the artichoke on its side and, with a large knife, cut about ½ inch off the top, to remove the prickly tips. Use kitchen scissors to snip off the prickly tips from the remaining leaves. Rinse the artichoke under running cold water and place in the bowl of lemon water. Repeat with the remaining artichokes. The artichokes are now ready to steam or boil until tender.

To remove the choke, invert cooked artichokes on a folded kitchen towel to drain and cool. Then stand the cooled artichokes stem side down. Use your fingers to gently spread open the leaves at the top to expose the prickly-tipped center leaves. Grasp the leaves with your fingers and pull them out. Reach down into the artichoke with the tip of a spoon and scrape away the fuzzy choke. The artichokes are now ready to stuff and bake, or chill and serve cold with mayonnaise or a vinaigrette dressing.

Acknowledgments

Although this book was a great deal of fun, it was a daunting project. As I step back I can see it reflects the hard work, dedication, and creativity of many. Although it's impossible for me to name everyone who helped make it a reality, there are a handful of folks who worked most closely with me, whom I must acknowledge:

I'm grateful to Doralece Dullaghan, director of strategic partnerships at Sur La Table, for her enthusiasm and unwavering support; Janis Donnaud, the agent for Sur La Table, whose savvy vision helped me to write the original proposal; my agent, Judith Weber, and Kirsty Melville, executive vice president and publisher at Andrews McMeel Publishing, for their support; Jean Lucas, senior editor at Andrews McMeel, for her keen intellect, attention to detail, and—when the going got rough—for her kindness and common sense; Rebecca Burgess, Sur La Table marketing coordinator, for keeping on top of my requests; and Phillip Stevenson, district manager, and the knowledgeable staff at the Berkeley Sur La Table, for their assistance with cookware and equipment.

For information and expert advice, I thank the many colleagues and friends—most of them fellow cookbook authors—who were generous with their time and expertise as I searched for the answers. There are too many to list here, but you know who you are. And, finally, thank you Brooke Jackson, a recipe tester par excellence.

—MARIE SIMMONS

From the time that this project was conceived it has been a dynamic experience involving not only crystallizing the concept but identifying the right folks to create the desired experience for the reader. Our agent, Janis Donnaud, was instrumental in providing a framework to create the proposal and identifying the publisher who would have the best synergy with our brand and staff. We can't thank her enough for that—a true mitzvah! From the moment we spoke with Marie Simmons we knew that she was the best choice to write this book. With over eighteen books to her credit and years of magazine writing and teaching experience with our products, we knew she would be the best choice for bringing together this complex project. We know, when you taste these recipes, you will agree with us.

Sur La Table has a lovefest with Andrews McMeel. From the connection that Kirsty Melville provides to our West Coast roots and her ability to bring everyone together to Jean Lucas's ability to keep us on course and the support we receive from Hugh Andrews gives us a comfort level that makes this first book for us very exciting. We also appreciate the efforts of Chris Schillig, Tammie Barker, Kathy Hilliard, Rosalyn Fisher, and the rest of the team at Andrews McMeel for staying the course with us to the finish line.

The staff members at Sur La Table who have provided invaluable support deserve recognition: Jacob Maurer, for being the "answer man" with all our product questions; Sue Pippy, Rebecca Burgess, Kathryn Habenicht, Nathan Slusser, Cory Chandler, Debby Bullock, Deb Pankrat, Phillip Stevenson, Claudia Hollis, Lorie Williams, Jason King, Kate Dering, Felicia Chao, and Susan Callahan, for getting all the products we needed to the right places at the right time; Susanna Linse, media relations manager extraordinaire, for communicating with passion and finesse the Sur La Table experience; the merchants and allocators, for their product support; our culinary coordinators and Kimberley Davis, for interpreting through their culinary expertise this book to our customers; Robb Ginter and the Creative Department for their creative vision; and Liz Paquette, for making sure all the little coordination details and the many meetings and conversations got handled with good cheer. Additionally, we would like to thank Gayle Novacek, for her product knowledge, and Kim Yorio, Caitlin Friedman, and Aimee Bianca for sharing the excitement of this book with the world on our behalf. Finally, thank you to Alison Lew, our designer; Ben Fink, our photographer; Sharon Silva, our copy editor; Sharon Ryan, our prop stylist; and Jamie Kimm and Alison Attenborough, our food stylists, for bringing the book to life with their creative talent and interpreting our vision through their considerable skill.

So now that the mise en place has been done and the book has been served, bon appétit!

—SUR LA TABLE

Shopping Sources

General

ADRIANA'S CARAVAN
www.adrianascaravan.com
1-800-316-0820
Spices, oils, vinegars.

BOB'S RED MILL
www.bobsredmill.com
1-800-349-2173
Whole grains and flours.

DEAN & DELUCA
www.deandeluca.com
1-800-221-7714
Salts, oils, vinegars, cheeses, spices.

ETHNIC ONLINE GROCERY STORE
www.ethnicfoodsco.com
1-952-593-3000
Indian, Thai, Japanese, Chinese,
Middle Eastern, and Greek foods.

FORMAGGIO KITCHEN
www.formaggiokitchen.com
1-888-212-3224
Cheeses, oils, vinegars, spices.

IGOURMET
www.igourmet.com
1-877-446-8763
Cheeses, wines, oils, vinegars.

LOTUS FOODS
www.lotusfoods.com
1-510-525-3137
Imported and domestic rice.

MARKET HALL FOODS
www.markethallfoods.com
1-888-952-4005
Pastas, oils, vinegars, cheeses,
condiments.

MURRAY'S CHEESE
www.murrayscheese.com
1-888-692-4339 Ext. 28
Cheeses, oils, vinegars.

PENZEYS SPICES
www.penzeys.com
1-800-741-7787
Spices.

SUR LA TABLE
www.surlatable.com
1-800-243-0852

ZINGERMAN'S
www.zingermans.com
1-888-636-8162
Oils, vinegars, cheeses, rice and other
grains, condiments.

Asian Ingredients

ASIAN FOOD GROCER
www.AsianFoodGrocer.com
1-888-482-2742

IMPORT FOOD
www.ImportFood.com
1-888-618-8424

KATAGIRI
www.katagiri.com
1-212-755-3566
Japanese ingredients.

Mexican Ingredients

BUENO
www.buenofoods.com
1-800-952-4453

CHILE TODAY-HOT TAMALE
www.chiletoday.com
1-800-468-7377

MEXGROCER
www.MexGrocer.com
1-877-463-9476

French Ingredients

L'EPICERIE
www.lepicerie.com
1-866-350-7575

LE VILLAGE
www.levillage.com
1-888-873-7194

Indian Ingredients

INDIRA FOOD LTD
www.indirafood.com
1-800-317-1229

ISHOPINDIAN
www.ishopindian.com
1-877-786-8876

KALUSTYAN'S
www.kalustyans.com
1-800-352-3451

Italian Ingredients

A. G. FERRARI
www.agferrari.com
1-877-878-2783

DITALIA
www.ditalia.com
1-888-260-2192

GUSTIAMO
www.gustiamo.com
1-718-860-2949

Iberian Ingredients

LA TIENDA
www.latienda.com
1-800-710-4304

THE SPANISH TABLE
www.spanishtable.com
1-505-986-0243

Moroccan Ingredients

KALUSTYAN'S
www.kalustyans.com
1-800-352-3451
Middle Eastern and Indian
ingredients.

Index

A

achiote and anchiote paste, 172

adobo de achiote. See achiote and anchiote paste

Aidells, Bruce, 46, 124

almond oil, 295

almonds, 241, 292

aluminum cookware, 8

amêijoas na cataplana, 298

Ancini di Pepe pasta, 258

Andoh, Elizabeth, 156

arrabbiata sauce, 259

artichokes, how to trim, 329

Asian dumplings, 150

Asian kitchen pantry, 144–47

Asian kitchen recipes, 150–169

asparagus

    Asparagus and Chopped Egg with Meyer Lemon Olive Oil, 275

    Asparagus with Miso-Sesame Sauce, 158

    Roasted Asparagus and Tomatoes with Bubbling Mozzarella, 107

B

bacalao, 294

bagna cauda, 256

baking dish, 5, 36, 37–39

    alternatives/substitutes for, 37

baking dish recipes

    Roasted Potatoes with Mushrooms and Red Bell Peppers, 39

    Sausage-Stuffed Roasted Artichokes with Tomato Sauce, 36, 38–39

baking pan liner, nonstick type of, 28

bamboo steamer, 21, 148, 149–52

    alternatives/substitutes for, 149

bamboo steamer recipes

    Shrimp and Pork Dumplings with Spicy Dipping Sauce, 148, 150–51

    Steamed Sea Bass in a Ginger and Scallion "Net," 151–52

basil, 89

bay leaf, 89

beans

    Baby Back Ribs with Cannellini Beans, 299

    Cannellini Bean Salad with Red Wine Vinaigrette, 61

    Green Bean, Tomato, and Potato Salad with Almond and Basil Pesto, 128, 131

    Mussel and Lima Bean Paella with Smoked Paprika, 309

    Oven-Baked Cannellini Beans, 61

Beard, James, 36

Becker, Ethan, 90

Becker, Marion Rombauer, 90

beef

    Balsamic-Marinated Beef Tenderloin with Herb and Dried-Tomato Sauce, 77

    Beef and Shiitake Broth, 198–99

    Beef Braciole Stuffed with Sausage, Two Cheeses, and Dried Currants, 40, 42–43

    Beef Daube with Zinfandel and Dried-Porcini Sauce, 203–5

    Chuck Steak with Braised Onions and Pan-Browned Potatoes, 44

    Oven-Braised Short Ribs with Fennel, 58, 60–61

    Stilton-Stuffed Burgers with Caramelized Red Onions and Balsamic Vinegar, 49

beet tops, use of, 107

Behnke, Renée, vi

bento, 162

besan, 246

bisteeya pan, 21, 320

    alternatives/substitutes for, 21

bisteeya recipe, Classic Chicken *Bisteeya,* 321–22

black pepper, 238

black salt, Hawaiian, 67

blenders, types of, 17. *See also* immersion blender

boef à la bourguignonne, 203

boning knife, 25

Boulud, Daniel, 116

bowls, types of, 14

braiser, viii, 5, 40, 41–45

    alternatives/substitutes for, 41

braiser recipes

    Beef Braciole Stuffed with Sausage, Two Cheeses, and Dried Currants, 40, 42–43

    Chuck Steak with Braised Onions and Pan-Browned Potatoes, 44

bread

    knife, 9

    machine, 30

breads

    Bread Crumbs, Fresh and Dried toasted, 219

    Chapatis, 250, 253

    Corn Tortillas, 186, 188

    Double Corn Bread with Smoked Mozzarella and Sun-Dried Tomatoes, 46, 48

    Rosemary and Cheese Whole Wheat Breadsticks, 281

    Toasted Pita Chips, 118

bresaola, 232

Brown, Alton, 132, 136

brushes, types of, 10–11

Bucatini pasta, 258

bulb baster, 26

butter, clarifying, 323. *See also* ghee

butters, flavored

    Asiago Cheese and Parsley Butter, 94

    Chipotle Chile and Honey Butter, 94

C

Callen, Anna Teresa, 260

Campanelle pasta, 258

can openers, types of, 11

Cannelloni pasta, 259

Capelli d'Angelo pasta, 258

cardamom, 239

Carucci, Linda, 78

carving knife and fork, 25

Casas, Penelope, 128, 300

cast-iron cookware, 7, 47

cast-iron skillet, 46, 47–49

    alternatives/substitutes for, 47

cast-iron skillet recipes

    Double Corn Bread with Smoked Mozzarella and Sun-Dried Tomatoes, 46, 48

    Stilton-Stuffed Burgers with Caramelized Red Onions and Balsamic Vinegar, 49

cataplana, 21, 296, 297–99

    alternatives/substitutes for, 297, 298, 299

cataplana recipes

    Baby Back Ribs with Cannellini Beans, 299